Company Law

Company Law

A Real Entity Theory

EVA MICHELER

OXFORD
UNIVERSITY PRESS

OXFORD
UNIVERSITY PRESS

Great Clarendon Street, Oxford, OX2 6DP,
United Kingdom

Oxford University Press is a department of the University of Oxford.
It furthers the University's objective of excellence in research, scholarship,
and education by publishing worldwide. Oxford is a registered trade mark of
Oxford University Press in the UK and in certain other countries

First Edition published in 2021

Impression: 1

Published in the United States of America by Oxford University Press
198 Madison Avenue, New York, NY 10016, United States of America

British Library Cataloguing in Publication Data

Data available

Library of Congress Control Number: 2021940439

ISBN 978–0–19–885887–4

DOI: 10.1093/oso/9780198858874.001.0001

Printed and bound by
CPI Group (UK) Ltd, Croydon, CR0 4YY

This book would never have been written without the help of my family. I would like to thank Steven for his love and support, Aurelia and Theodore for their encouragement and understanding and Elisabeth for being a wonderful sister.

Foreword

This book is the product of over 20 years of company law teaching, both at graduate and at undergraduate level. During this time, I have found that the current approaches for analysing company law are useful for some purposes but fall short for others. I took a sabbatical in 2015 to investigate an alternative model, real entity theory, which dominated company law scholarship into the first half of the 20th century. Real entity theorists at that time based their work on intuition. The study of organizations and human behaviour in organizational contexts had just started with contributors such as Frederick Winslow Taylor writing about optimizing production processes. Unfortunately, real entity theory started to wane in legal circles at about the same time as the study of organizations began to emerge in other social sciences. Today, we benefit from a rich body of contributions analysing and explaining how social forces shape organizational action and individual actions within organizations. This book relies on these contributions to advance a modern version of a real entity theory of company law.

The nexus of contract model and agency theory have cast a long shadow over the analysis of company law. Historically, the nexus of contract model does a reasonable job of explaining the deed of settlement companies that preceded the Companies Act 1844. These companies did not have a statutory basis. They were created by contracts and used trust law in a way that is similar to modern unit trusts. Unsurprisingly, the characteristics of the predecessors of modern companies informed the rules adopted in the early Companies Acts. The reforms that have taken place since then, however, have caused the law to outgrow the nexus of contract model. Shareholders continue to have some freedom to adopt a bespoke constitution, but the extent to which modern company law can be explained by contract law can be overstated. The nexus of contract model understates the extent to which the modern Companies Act contains mandatory rules. It also ignores that case law routinely declines to apply contract law to the analysis of the corporate constitution and that the ability of shareholders to enforce the constitution is severely limited. It will be concluded in chapter six that the constitution, which is sometimes referred to as a statutory contract, is better conceptualized as a statutory instrument adopted by private action.

Agency theory, for its part, helps with the analysis of conflicts of interest. It conceptualizes directors as agents of the shareholders and brings the inability of human beings to over-ride their self-interest into sharp analytical focus. This perspective is worth having. It falls short, however, of providing us with an accurate picture of the rules governing directors. The law explicitly states that the directors owe their duties to the company. The Companies Act does not provide for a legal relationship between the directors and the shareholders or any other constituency.

Moreover, agency theory prevents us from fully appreciating the role of directors. The Companies Act imposes a number of duties on directors. These do not require directors to maximize return for the shareholders. The overall picture is more nuanced. Shareholder interests take priority, but it would be wrong to conclude that the company is a vehicle serving shareholder interests only.

The current approaches for analysing companies also fall short because they do not fit with our experience of companies. In everyday life, we do not conceive of companies as contracts. We refer to them and experience them as actors. We speak of the corner shop, the GP practice, the school, the university, the library or the supermarket as an actor affecting our lives in particular ways.

This fits with evidence that human beings act in distinctive ways in groups and organizations. Human action is shaped by social forces. Interactions between human beings bring about habits, routines, processes and procedures causing organizations to become autonomous actors in their own right. These take on a life of their own affecting the behaviour of the participants. Participants can themselves affect organizational behaviour and modify habits, routines, procedures and culture but this takes time and effort. Organizations do not have a unique physical manifestation. They are nevertheless real in their consequences.

Company law finds this phenomenon and evolves with a view to supporting autonomous action by organizations. It will be demonstrated in this book that an approach that conceives companies as autonomous actors shaping the actions of individual participants through social forces explains cardinal features of company law as it stands. It will also be suggested that when corporate behaviour needs to be modified this is best done by interventions that alter corporate decision-making procedures. This is more likely to achieve the desired result than, for example, the adoption of a corporate purpose.

Real entity theory is sometimes expressed through a metaphor that likens the company to a human body, with the directors as the 'brain', taking the decision to be implemented by the workforce. This metaphor is not helpful. Organizations as real entities are not usefully compared to physical, biological entities. Instead, organizations are real because they create social rules that affect the behaviour of their participants. Company law helps organizations to operate autonomously and the law's content shaped by their special characteristics.

It is important to me that the theory advanced in this book holds true irrespective of how much influence any particular jurisdiction allocates to shareholders over other constituencies. This book does not argue in favour or against a stakeholder-oriented model of the company. From the perspective of this book, the shareholder versus stakeholder debate is a distraction. The debate is the product of the practice, supported by agency theory, of analysing company law through the lens of agents and principals. While this perspective helps us to better understand conflicts of interests, we should not limit ourselves to a perspective that distracts us from understanding the essence of organizational action.

Eva Micheler
August 2021

Acknowledgements

I am very grateful for generous comments by Paul Davies, David Gindis, Daniel Gozman, Jeremy Horder, David Kershaw, Stephan Leixnering and Rolf von Lüdow. I have greatly benefitted from the comments and recommendations for literature offered by the participants of the LSE Law staff seminar. I am grateful to Sarah Worthington and Louise Gullifer for inviting me to speak at the Cambridge Law Faculty and would like to thank Brian Cheffins for his comments in advance of that seminar. Dinoysia Katelouzou invited me to speak at The Dickson Poon School of Law at King's College London and I would like to thank Brenda Hannigan and John Lowry for their comments and questions. Tom Wetzer invited me to speak at Oxford University and I am grateful to John Armour and Josh Getzler for the comments they made at that seminar. Florian Heindler organized a seminar at the Sigmund Freud University in Vienna and I am grateful for the comments made by Walter Doralt. Carsten Gerner-Beuerle invited me to speak at the UCL Law Faculty and also gave me very generous comments after my presentation. I am also indebted to Marc Moore and Iris Chiu for their comments and questions. Matteo Solinas gave me the opportunity to present my theory at the Victoria University of Wellington and I am very grateful for the questions and comments made by Deborah Sabalot Deane at and after that seminar.

At LSE Law, Jo Braithwaite, Jacco Bomhoff, Veerle Heyvaert, Elizabeth Howell, Jo Murkens, Philip Paech, Sarah Paterson, Edmund Schuster, Mary Stokes and Emmanuel Voyakis have been a continuous source of strength during the pandemic, when finishing this book seemed like an impossible task.

Contents

Table of Cases   xix
Table of Legislation   xxix

1. A Real Entity Theory of Company Law   1
   1.1 Introduction   1
   1.2 Contract theory   2
       1.2.1 Introduction   2
       1.2.2 Nexus of contract and agency theory   2
       1.2.3 Shareholders versus stakeholders   5
       1.2.4 Evaluation   6
   1.3 Concession theory   12
       1.3.1 Introduction   12
       1.3.2 Modern concession theory   13
             Case law   14
             Academic contributions   15
             Evaluation   17
   1.4 Real entity theory   18
       1.4.1 Introduction   18
       1.4.2 Shareholders versus stakeholders   19
       1.4.3 Foundations of real entity theory   20
             About facts   20
             Natural, group, and organizational action   21
             Institutional theory   23
             Institutional theory in economics   26
             Conclusions   28
       1.4.4 Applying real entity theory to company law   29
       1.4.5 Structure of the book   32
       1.4.6 Shareholders versus stakeholders   36

2. Corporate Personality   37
   2.1 Introduction   37
   2.2 Legal personality for all lawful purposes   39
   2.3 One-person companies   41
   2.4 Corporate groups   42
   2.5 Beginning and ending companies   44
   2.6 Theoretical observations   46

3. Corporate Capacity   48
   3.1 Introduction   48
   3.2 Contract as explanation for the *ultra vires* doctrine   48
   3.3 The collapse of the *ultra vires* doctrine   51
   3.4 Corporate purpose   53
   3.5 Theoretical observations   54

4. Limited Liability   56
    4.1 Introduction   56
    4.2 Veil piercing   58
         4.2.1 Sham and facade   58
         4.2.2 Evasion   59
         4.2.3 Concealment   61
         4.2.4 Theoretical observations   62
    4.3 Personal liability for shareholders and directors   63
         4.3.1 Fraud   63
         4.3.2 Fraudulent trading   65
         4.3.3 Wrongful trading   65
         4.3.4 Phoenix companies   66
         4.3.5 Disqualification of directors   67
         4.3.6 Liability in tort   68
         4.3.7 Theoretical observations   69
    4.4 Applying statutes to companies   70
         4.4.1 Statutes generally   70
         4.4.2 Groups   71
         4.4.3 Theoretical observations   73
    4.5 Theoretical observations   74

5. Corporate Actions   77
    5.1 Contract   77
    5.2 Tort   80
    5.3 Crime   83
         5.3.1 Introduction   83
         5.3.2 Identification doctrine   84
                Introduction   84
                Statutory offences   86
                Common law crimes   88
         5.3.3 Critique of the identification doctrine   89
         5.3.4 Vicarious liability   90
         5.3.5 Strict liability offences with due diligence defences   91
         5.3.6 Organizational failure to prevent a crime   93
         5.3.7 Deferred prosecution agreements and rehabilitation   97
         5.3.8 Theoretical observations   97
    5.4 Conclusions   102

6. The Organizational Framework   103
    6.1 Introduction   103
    6.2 The role of the statute   103
         6.2.1 Introduction   103
         6.2.2 Constitutional matters   104
         6.2.3 Managing the company   105
         6.2.4 Record-keeping and reporting   106
         6.2.5 Procedures for shareholder decisions   108
         6.2.6 *Duomatic*   109
         6.2.7 Procedures for decisions of the directors   109
         6.2.8 Conclusions   111

6.3 The role and nature of the constitution   112
    6.3.1 Introduction   112
    6.3.2 Misrepresentation, duress, and undue influence   114
    6.3.3 Rectification   114
    6.3.4 Mutual understanding of quasi-partners   115
    6.3.5 Enforcement   116
        Membership rights only   116
        No 'mere internal irregularities'   118
        Theoretical observations   121
    6.3.6 Conclusions   122
6.4 Conclusions   123

7. The Role of the Directors   125
7.1 Introduction   125
7.2 Duties are owed to the company   128
7.3 Duty to act in accordance with the company's constitution and for a proper
    purpose   128
7.4 Duty to promote the success of the company   131
    7.4.1 Introduction   131
    7.4.2 Companies Act 2006, section 172   131
    7.4.3 Conclusions   135
    7.4.4 Theoretical observations   135
7.5 Duty to exercise independent judgement   137
7.6 Duty to exercise reasonable skill and care   138
    7.6.1 Introduction   138
    7.6.2 The early common law   139
    7.6.3 The later common law and statutory intervention   139
    7.6.4 Disqualification   142
    7.6.5 UK Corporate Governance Code 2018   146
    7.6.6 Conclusions   148
    7.6.7 Theoretical observations   149
7.7 Duty to avoid a conflict of interest   150
    7.7.1 Introduction   150
    7.7.2 Companies Act 2006, section 175   151
    7.7.3 Contrast with partnership law   153
    7.7.4 Approval of interested transactions   155
    7.7.5 Theoretical observations   157
7.8 Self-dealing   159
    7.8.1 Introduction   159
    7.8.2 Duty to declare an interest in proposed transactions or arrangements 160
    7.8.3 Approval of self-dealing   160
    7.8.4 Limits to shareholder approval   161
    7.8.5 Conclusions   162
7.9 Remuneration   162
    7.9.1 Introduction   162
    7.9.2 Equity and the statutory regime   162
    7.9.3 The role of shareholders   164
    7.9.4 Conclusions   166
    7.9.5 Theoretical observations   166

7.10 Duty to record and report   169
    7.10.1 Introduction   169
    7.10.2 Duty to keep accounting records   170
    7.10.3 Duty to prepare annual accounts   172
    7.10.4 Duty to prepare narrative reports   175
       Introduction   175
       Directors' report   176
       Strategic report   177
       Separate corporate governance statement   178
       Remuneration report   178
       Conclusions and theoretical observations   179
    7.10.5 Duty to have the accounts and reports verified   180
    7.10.6 Duty to publicize accounts and reports   183
    7.10.7 Reports on specific social and environmental matters   185
    7.10.8 Sanctions   186
    7.10.9 Conclusions and theoretical observations   187
7.11 Duty to abide by the statutory distribution rules   190
    7.11.1 Introduction   190
    7.11.2 No shareholder approval   191
    7.11.3 Liability of the directors   192
    7.11.4 Liability of the shareholders   193
7.12 Theoretical observations   193

8. The Role of the Shareholders   195
8.1 Introduction   195
8.2 Constitutional matters   197
    8.2.1 Forming and ending the company   197
    8.2.2 Power to amend the constitution   198
    8.2.3 Power to appoint and remove directors   200
    8.2.4 Directors are not agents of the shareholders   201
    8.2.5 Power to appoint and remove auditors   205
8.3 Managing the company   205
    8.3.1 Issuing shares   205
       Introduction   205
       Pre-emption rights   206
       Valuations of contributions in kind   208
       Issues at a discount   209
       Conclusions   209
    8.3.2 Takeovers   210
    8.3.3 Approving transactions   212
       Unfair prejudice   213
       Disguised returns of capital   214
    8.3.4 Ratification of breaches of duty by the directors   219
8.4 Accounting records and annual accounts   221
8.5 Distributions   223
8.6 Stewardship   224
8.7 Reflective loss   226
    8.7.1 Introduction   226
    8.7.2 Double recovery   228
    8.7.3 Causation   229

8.7.4	Ease of settling claims	230
8.7.5	Protecting the autonomy of the company	232
8.7.6	Theoretical observations	233
8.8	Conclusions	234

9. Enforcement   237

  9.1 Introduction   237
  9.2 Private enforcement   237
    9.2.1 Introduction   237
    9.2.2 The supremacy of the corporate decision-making process—*Foss v Harbottle*   238
    9.2.3 Fraud and wrongdoer control   239
    9.2.4 *Ultra vires* and illegality   241
    9.2.5 Special resolutions   242
    9.2.6 The statutory regime   243
    9.2.7 Stage one   243
    9.2.8 Stage two—permission must be refused   244
      Authorization or ratification by the company   244
      Person acting in accordance with section 172   245
    9.2.9 Stage two—discretion of the court   247
      Whether the member is acting in good faith in seeking to continue the claim   247
      Likelihood of authorization/ratification   247
      Decision of the company to not to pursue the claim   248
      Cause of action of the member in his own right   248
      Views of members without a personal interest   249
    9.2.10 Stage two—no prescribed standard of proof   249
    9.2.11 Limited permission to continue   251
    9.2.12 Indemnity for cost   251
    9.2.13 Theoretical observations   251
  9.3 Public enforcement   256

10. Stakeholders   259

11. Conclusions   263

Index   267

Table of Cases

UNITED KINGDOM

A Company, ex p Gossop, Re [1988] BCLC 570 . . . . 213, 214
A Company (No 007683 of 1984), Re [1986] BCLC 362 207
AAA v Unilever [2018] EWCA (Civ) 1532, [2018] BCC 959 68–69
Aas v Benham [1891] 2 Ch 244 153–55
Aberdeen Railway v Blaikie Brothers [1843–1860] All ER Rep 249 151–52
Adams v Cape Industries Plc [1990] Ch 433 . . . . 43, 58
Airey v Cordell [2007] BCC 785 246
Al-Dowaisan v Al-Salam [2019] EWHC 301 (Ch), [2019] 2 BCLC 328 68
Allen v Gold Reefs of West Africa Ltd [1900] 1 Ch 656 199
Allied Business and Financial Consultants Ltd v Shanahan [2009] EWCA Civ 751, [2009]
      2 BCLC 666 . . . . 152, 153, 154–55
Allied Carpets Group Plc v Nethercott [2001] BCC 81 191–92
AMT Coffee Ltd [2019] EWHC 46 (Ch), [2020] 2 BCLC 50 . . . . 161, 213–14
Antonio Gramsci Shipping Corporation v Recoletos Ltd [2013] EWCA Civ 730, [2013]
      4 All ER 157 64
Armes v Nottinghamshire CC [2017] UKSC 60, [2017] 3 WLR 1000 81
AS (Nominees) Ltd v Nottingham Forest FC Plc 5 April 2001 204
Asegaai Consultants Ltd, Re [2012] EWHC 1899, [2012] Bus LR 1607 143
Ashbury Railway v Riche (1874–75) LR 7 HL 653 . . . . 15, 49–50, 51
Astec (BSR) plc, Re [1998] 2 BCLC 556 254–55
Attorney General of Belize v Belize Telecom Ltd [2009] UKPC 10 114
Auden MacKenzie v Patel [2019] EWCA Civ 2291, [2020] BCC 316 192
Automatic Self Cleansing v Cuninghame [1906] 2 Ch 24 . . . . 202, 203, 204
Aveling Barford Ltd v Perion Ltd [1989] BCLC 626 216–17
Bairstow v Queen's Moat House [2001] EWCA Civ 712, [2001] BCLC 531 192
Baker v Secretary of State for Trade and Industry [2000] 1 BCLC 523 143–44
Bank of Credit and Commerce International SA, Morris v Bank of India [2005]
      EWCA Civ 693, [2005] 2 BCLC 328 (No 15), Re 65
Bank of Tokyo Ltd v Karoon (Note) [1987] AC 45 . . . . 10, 15
Barings Plc (No 5), Re [1999] 1 BCLC 433 145
Barrett v Duckett [1995] BCC 362 249
Beattie v Beattie [1938] Ch 708 116
Bednash v Hearsey [2001] 2 WLUK 426 163
Bell Houses Ltd v City Hall Properties Ltd [1966] 2 QB 656 (CA) 51
Bhullar v Bhullar [2003] EWCA Civ 424, [2003] 2 BCLC 241 . . . . 151–52, 156
Bhullar v Bhullar [2015] EWHC 1943 (Ch), [2016] 1 BCLC 106 . . . . 239–40, 246
Bilta v Nazir [2013] EWCA Civ 968, [2014] 1 BCLC 302 220
Bilta v Nazir [2015] UKSC 23, [2016] 1 AC 1 . . . . 15, 17–18, 41–42, 134–35
Bisgood v Henderson's Transvaal Estates Ltd [1908] 1 Ch 743 (CA) 117
Bishopsgate Investment Management Ltd v Maxwell (No 2) [1994] 1 All ER 261 141–42
Blackspur Group plc, Re [1998] 1 WLR 422 (CA) 143
Blue Arrow plc, Re [1997] BCLC 585 . . . . 213, 254–55
Blue Index Ltd, Re [2014] EWHC 2680 214
BM Electrical Solutions Ltd (In Liquidation), Re [2020] EWHC 2749 (Ch),
      14 Oct 2020 (unreported) 161

Boardman v Phipps [1966] 3 All ER 721, [1967] 2 AC 46 . . . . 151, 152, 154
Bolton v Graham [1957] 1 QB 159 . . . . .86–87, 98
Boston Trust Co Ltd v Szerelmey Ltd [2020] EWHC 1352 (Ch). 117
Bowe Watts Clargo Ltd (In Liquidation), Re aka Mander v Watts [2017] EWHC 7879 (Ch) . . . 134–35
Brady v Brady [1988] BCLC 20 131–32
Brannigan v Style [2016] EWHC 512 (Ch) 244, 246
Bratton Seymore Service Co Ltd v Oxborough [1992] BCC 471 .113, 114–15
Bray v Ford [1896] AC 44. . . . . .151–52, 157
Brazilian Rubber Plantations and Estates Ltd, Re [1911] 1 Ch 425. 139
Bridge v Daley [2015] EWHC 2121 (HC), 2015 WL 4744908. . . . . 246, 247, 248, 249, 256
British Thompson-Houston v Federated European Bank [1932] 2 KB 76. 77–78
Broadcasting Investment Group Ltd v Smith [2020] EWHC 2501 (Ch) 227
Brooklands Trustees Ltd [2020] EWHC 3519. 143–44
Brumder v Motornet Service and Repairs Ltd [2013] EWCA Civ 195, [2013] 1 WLR 2783, [2013]
    PIQR P13, Court of Appeal (Civil Division) 14 March 2013 . . . . 68, 141
BSB Holdings Ltd, Re (No 2) [1996] 1 BCLC 155 131–37
BTI 2014 LLC v Sequana SA [2019] EWCA Civ 112, [2019] BCC 631, [2019]
    1 BCLC 347 . . . . 15, 134–35, 192–93
Burnden Holdings (UK), Hunt v Fielding, Re [2019] EWHC 1566 (Ch), [2019]
    Bus LR 2878. 191–93
BW Estates Ltd, Re [2017] EWCA Civ 1201, [2017] BCC 406 109
Byng v London Life Association Ltd [1990] Ch 170 (CA). 120–21
Cane v Jones [1981] 1 All ER 533 198–99
Caparo Industries Ltd v Dickman [1990] 2 AC 605 . . . . 221, 222
Cardiff Savings Bank, Re [1892] 2 Ch 100 . . . . .139, 144–45
Carlen v Drury (1812) 1 Ves and B 149; 35 ER 61. . . . . 141, 254
Carruth v Imperial Chemical Industries Ltd [1937] AC 707. 119–20
CAS (Nominees) Ltd v Nottingham Forest FC Plc [2002] 1 BCLC 613 . . . . 105, 129
CF Booth Ltd, Re; Booth v Booth [2017] EWHC 457 (Ch). 163, 213–14, 224
Chalcot Training Ltd v Ralph [2020] EWHC 1054 (Ch) 217–18
Chandler v Cape plc [2012] EWCA Civ 525 68
Charles Forte Investments v Amanda [1964] Ch 240 (CA). 134
Charterbridge v Lloyds Bank [1970] Ch 62 134
Charterhouse Capital Ltd [2015] EWCA Civ 536, [2015] BCC 574. 199–200
Cherry Tree Investments Ltd v Landmain Ltd [2012] EWCA Civ 736, [2013] Ch 305 114
Chez Nico (Restaurants) Ltd, Re [1992] BCLC 192 128
Choudhury v Bhattar [2009] EWHC 314 (Ch), [2009] 2 BCLC 108 119
Ciban Management Corp v Citco (BVI) Ltd [2020] UKPC 21, [2020] BCC 964 109
Citco Banking Corporation NV v Pusser's Ltd [2007] UKPC 13 199–200
City Equitable Fire Insurance, Re [1925] Ch 407 139–40
Citybranch Group Ltd, Gross v Rackind, Re [2004] 4 All ER 735. 70
CJC Media Ltd v Clark [2020] SAC (Civ) 110 243–44
Clearwell International Ltd v MSL Group Holdings Ltd [2012] EWCA Civ 1440 215–16
Clegg v Pache (Deceased) Court of Appeal (Civil Division) 11 May 2017, [2017]
    EWCA Civ 256 61–62
Clemens v Clemens [1976] 2 All ER 268 (ChD) 207
CMS Dolphin Ltd v Simonet [2001] EWHC 415 [2001] 2 BCLC 704 151
Cohen v Selby [2001] 1 BCLC 176 140
Compound Photonics Group Ltd, Re [2021] EWHC 787 (Ch) 115
Cook v Deeks [1916] 1 AC 554 . . . . 128, 157, 159
Coroin Ltd, Re [2011] EWHC 3466 (Ch). 114–15, 151
Cosmetic Warriors Ltd v Gerrie [2017] EWCA Civ 324, [2017] 2 BCLC 456. 114
Cotman v Brougham [1918] AC 514 (HL) 51
Cotter v National Union of Seamen [1929] 2 Ch 58 . . . . .119–20, 242

Credit Suisse International v Stichting Vestia Groep [2014] EWHC 3103 (COMM) [2015]
    Bus LR D5 78
Criterion Properties Plc v Stratford UK Properties LLC [2002] EWHC 496 (Ch), [2003] 1 WLR
    2108, [2002] EWCA Civ 1783 [2003], 1 WLR 2108 129
Cullen v Brown [2015] EWHC 473, [2016] 1 BCLC 491 .... 244, 245, 246–47, 249–50, 251
D'Jan of London, Re [1994] 1 BCLC 561 ....106, 139–40, 141, 219
Dafen Tinplate Co Ltd v Llanelly Steel Co (1907) Ltd [1920] 2 Ch 124 199
Daimler v Continental Tyre and Rubber Co [1916] 1 AC 307. 70
Daniels v Anderson (1995) 16 ACSR 607 139–40
Darby, Re [1911] 1 KB 95. 63
Davies v Ford [2020] EWHC 686 (Ch) 152
DHN Food Distributors Ltd v Tower Hamlets LBC [1976] 1 WLR 852; [1976]
    3 All ER 462 (CA). 71
Director General of Fair Trading v Pioneer Concrete UK Ltd [1995] 1 AC 456 90–91
Director of Public Prosecutions v Kent and Sussex Contractors Ltd [1944] KB 146 .... 80, 86, 97
Director of the Serious Fraud Office v Airbus SE [2020] 1 WLUK 435 72
Dixon v Blindley Health Investments Ltd [2015] EWCA Civ 1023, [2016]
    4 All ER 490. ....109, 198–99
Dovey v Corey [1901] AC 477. 192–93
Dubai Aluminum v Salaam [2002] UKHL 48, [2003] AC 366 81
Duomatic Ltd, Re [1969] 2 Ch 365 ....106, 109, 111, 114–15, 123–24,
                                                                    161, 198–99, 214, 219, 220–21
East Asia Company Ltd v Pt Saria Tirtatama Energindo [2019] UKPC 30, [2020] 1 All ER 294 77
Ebbvale Ltd v Hosking [2013] UKPC 1, [2013] 2 BCLC 204. 60
Ebrahimi v Westbourne Galleries Ltd [1972] 2 All ER 492 115
Eclairs Group Ltd v JKX Oil and Gas plc [2015] UKSC 71, [2016] BCLC 1 ....114, 130, 212, 225
Edwardian Group Ltd, Re [2018] EWHC 1715 (Ch), [2019] 1 BCLC 171. ....115, 214
Edwards v Halliwell [1950] 1 All ER 1064 ....118–19, 120, 241, 242
Eley v Positive Government Security Life Assurance Ltd (1875) 1 ExD 20 aff'd (1876)
    1 ExD 88 (CA). 116
Elgindata Ltd, Re [1991] BCLC 959 141
Equitable Life Assurance Society v Bowley [2003] EWHC 2263, [2004] 1 BCLC 180. 141
Equity and Provident Ltd, Re [2002] EWHC 186 (Ch), [2002] 2 BCLC 78 ....46, 143–44
Ernest v Nicholls 419 ER 1358. 49–50
Ernest v Nicolls [1857] 6 HL Cas 401, ### ER ### 77, 78–79
Estmanco v Greater London Council [1982] 1 WLR 2 239
Euro Accessories Ltd, Re [2021] EWHC 47. 114
Evans v Chapman 86 LT 381 114–15
Exchange Banking Co, Flintcroft's case, Re (1882) 21 Ch 519 (CA). 191–92
Extrasure Travel Insurance Ltd v Scattergood [2003] 1 BCLC 598. 133
Fairford Water Ski Club Ltd v Cohoon [2021] EWCA Civ 143 (CA). 160
Famatina Development Corporation, Re [1914] 2 Ch 271 (CA) 116
FG Films Ltd, Re [1953] 1 WLR 483, [1953] 1 All ER 615 (ChD). 70
Flanagan v Liontrust Investment Partners LLP [2015] Bus LR 1172 114
Focus 15 Trading Ltd (In Liquidation), Re, Official Receiver v Duckett [2020] EWHC 3016 (Ch)
    [2020] 11 WLUK 143. ....67, 144–45
Forster Bryant Surveying Ltd v Bryant [2007] EWCA Civ 200, [2007] 2 BCLC 239 153
Foss v Harbottle (1843) 2 Hare 461, 67 ER 189 .... 122, 226–27, 237, 238–39, 240–41, 251, 256
Franbar Holdings Ltd v Patel [2008] EWHC 1534 (Ch), [2009] 1 BCLC 1 ....245, 246
Freelands v McClue [2014] 12 WLUK 28, 2015 GWD 4-78 42–43
Freeman & Lockyer v Buckhurst [1964] QB 480 77
Fullham Football Club Ltd v Cabra Estates plc [1994] 1 BCLC 363 (CA) 137–38
Gaiman v National Association for Mental Health [1971] Ch 317. 131–32
Gardener v Parker [2004] 2 BCLC 554. 227

Gencor ACP Ltd v Dalby [2000] 2 BCLC 734 62
GHLM Trading Ltd v Maroo [2012] EWHC 61 . . . . 132, 133, 134
Giles v Rhind [2002] EWCA Civ 1428, [2003] Ch 618. 227
Gilford Motors v Horne [1933] Ch 935 59–60
Glastnos Shipping Ltd and Continental Chartering & Brokerage Ltd Hong Kong
    Branch v Panasian Shipping Corpn and Withers (a firm), The Glastnos [1991]
    1 Lloyd's Rep 482 . . . . 43, 57, 60
Global Corporate v Hale [2018] EWCA Civ 2618, [2019] BCC 431. 109
Goldtrail Travel v Aydin [2014] EWHC 1587, [2015] 1 BCLC 89. . . . . .155–56, 220–21
Goldtrail Travel v Aydin [2016] EWCA Civ 371, [2016] BCLC 635. 155–56
Goodwin v Cook, Chancery Division 21 June 2018 HC-2017-000742 . . . . 246, 248
Gramophone and Typewriter Co Ltd v Stanley [1908] 2 KB 89 42–43
Granada UK v The Pension Regulator [2019] EWCA Civ 1032, [2020] ICR 747 71
Grayan Building Services Ltd, Re [1995] Ch 241 (CA) 143
Greenhalgh v Arderne Cinemas [1951] Ch 286 (CA) 207, 225
Guinness v Saunders [1990] 2 AC 663 163
Gunewardene v Conran Holdings [2016] EWHC 2983 (Ch), [2017] BCC 135 114–15
Halt Garage, Re [1982] All ER 1016 . . . . 163, 218
Hamblin v World First Ltd [2020] EWHC 2383 (Comm), [2020] 6 WLUK 314 17–18
Harris v Microfusion 2003-2 LLP [2016] EWCA Civ 1212, [2017] 1 BCLC 305 239
Hayes [2015] EWCA Crim 1944, [2016] 1 Cr App R(S) 63 89–90
Hely-Hutchinson v Brayhead [1968] 1 QB 549. 77
Hemsley v Graham [2013] EWHC 2232 (Ch), [2013] 7 WLUK 1048 63
Heron International v Lord Grade [1983] BCLC 244. 117
Hickman v Kent or Romney Marsh Sheep-Breeders' Association [1915] 1 Ch 881 . . . . 116, 118
HLC Environmental Projects Ltd, Re [2013] EWHC 2876 (Ch) 134–35
Hogg v Cramphorn [1967] Ch 254. . . . . 129, 130
Home Treat Ltd, Re [1991] BCLC 705 198–99
Hong Kong and China Gas Company v Glen [1914] 1 Ch 527 208–9
Hook v Sumner [2015] EWHC 3820, [2016] BCC 220 . . . . .244, 245, 246, 247, 249, 250, 251, 255
Houldsworth Village Management Co Ltd v Barton [2020] EWCA Civ 980 117
Howard Smith v Ampol [1974] AC 821 (PC) 129, 204
HRMC v Development Securities Plc [2020] EWCA Civ 1705, [2021] BTC 1 42–43
Hutton v West Cork Rly (1883) 23 ChD 654 133
Hydrodam (Corby) Ltd, Re [1994] 2 BCLC 180 66
Iesini v Westrip Holdings Ltd [2009] EWHC 2526 (Ch), [2011] 1 BCLC 498. . . . . . 243, 244, 245, 246,
                                                                                      248, 250, 251, 253–54
Ilse of White Railway Company v Tahourdin (1884) LR 25 ChD 320 202
In London Sack and Bag Co Ltd v Dixon and Lugton Ltd [1943] 2 All ER 763 (CA) 116
In Plus Group Ltd v Pyke [2002] EWCA Civ 370, [2002] 2 BCLC 201. . . . . 153, 155
Industrial Developments Consultants Ltd v Cooley [1972] 1 WLR 443 151
Interactive Technology Corp Ltd v Ferster [2018] EWCA Civ 1594, [2018] 2 P&CR DG 22 163
Introductions, Re [1969] 1 All ER 887 51
Irvine v Irvine [2006] EWHC 206 (Ch), [2007] 1 BCLC 349 213–14
IT Protect Ltd (In Liquidation), Re [2020] EWHC 2473 (Ch), 24 Sep 2020 (unreported) 141
It's a Wrap (UK) Ltd v Gula [2006] EWCA Civ 544, [2006] 2 BCLC 634. 193
Item Software (UK) Ltd v Fassihi [2004] EWCA Civ 1244, [2005] 2 BCLC 994 . . . . . .135–36, 158, 231
Jan Beaufort, Re [1953] Ch 131. 51
Johnson v Gore Wood [2000] UKHL 65, [2002] 2 AC 1 .227–28, 231, 233
Jones v Lipman [1962] 1 WLR 832 59–60
Julien v Evolving TecKnologies and Enterprise Development Co Ltd [2018] UKPC 2, [2018]
    BCC 376. 109
Kaye v Oxford House (Wimbledon) Management Co [2019] EWHC 2181 (Ch), [2020]
    BCC 117. 120

Kinsela v Russel Kinsela Pty Ltd (1986) 10 ACLR 395 (New South Wales
    Court of Appeal)..134–35
Kleanthous v Paphitis [2011] EWHC 2287, [2012] BCC 676 ....249, 250
Komercni Banka AS v Stone & Rolls Ltd [2002] EWHC 2263 (Comm), [2003]
    1 Lloyd's Rep 383 63
Komercni Banka AS v Stone & Rolls Ltd [2003] EWCA Civ 311, [2003] CP Rep 58 63
Kosar v Bank of Scotland plc (trading as Halifax) [2011] EWHC 1050 (Admin), [2011]
    BCC 500, [2011] All ER (D) 08 (May) QBD 83
Koza Ltd v Koza Altin Isletmeleri AS [2020] EWCA Civ 1018, [2020] 7 WLUK 469............. 70
Kuwait Asia Bank EC v National Mutual Life Nominee Ltd [1991] 1 AC 187................137–38
Lagunas Nitrate Company v Lagunas Syndicate [1899] 2 Ch 392 (CA)....................... 139
Lakatamia Shipping Co Ltd v Su [2014] EWCA Civ 636, [2014] CP Rep 37.................. 59, 70
Landhurst Leasing plc, Re [1999] 1 BCLC 286 145
Latin American Investments Ltd v Maroil Tranding Inc [2017] EWHC 1254 (Comm),
    [2017] 2 CLC 45 227
Lee Panavision v Lee Lighting [1992] BCLC 22 ....129, 132
Leeds United Holdings plc, Re [1997] BCC 131 254–55
Lehtimaki v Children's Investment Foundation Fund (UK) [2018] EWCA Civ 1605, [2019]
    Ch 139 113
Lehtimaki v Cooper [2020] UKSC 33, [2020] 3 WLR 461...........................113, 225
Lennard's Carrying Company v Asiatic Petroleum Company [1915]
    AC 705, HL 83–84, 86–87, 98, 99
Lexi Holdings Plc v Luqman & Ors [2009] EWCA Civ 117, [2009] 1 BCLC 1 140
Liberty Investing Ltd v Sydow [2015] EWHC 608 (Comm) [2015] 2 WLUK 497 43
Lonrho Ltd v Shell Petroleum Co Ltd (No 1) [1980] 1 WLR 627 70–71
Looe Fish, Re [1993] BCLC 1160 144
M v M [2013] EWHC 2534 (Fam) 61
MacDougall v Gardiner (1975) 1 ChD 13 119
MacPherson v European Strategic Bureau Ltd [2000] 2 BCLC 683 197–98
Macquarie International Investments v Glencor UK Ltd [2010] EWCA Civ 697..............107–8
MAD Atelier International BV v Manès [2020] EWHC 1014 (Ch), [2020] 3 WLR 631 42–43
Madoff Securities International v Raven [2013] EWHC 3147 (Comm) 140
Mahoney v East Holyford Mining Co [1875] LR 7 HL 869 77–78
Marex Financial Ltd v Sevilleja [2020] UKSC 31, [2021] AC 29.... 226–27, 228–29, 230, 231–32, 233
Marini, Re [2003] EWHC 334 (Ch), [2004] BCC 172 192
Mcmillan v Le Roi Mining Company Ltd [1906] 1 Ch 331 120
Mea Corporation Ltd, Re [2007] 1 BCLC 618.. 66
Mercia Enterprises Ltd v Mistry [2020] EWHC 1597 (QB)............................... 62
Meridian Global Funds Management Asia Ltd v Securities Commission [1995]
    2 AC 500 (PC), [1995] UKPC 5; M/F/R 641 ....14, 86, 87–88, 98, 99, 101
Miller v Bain [2002] 1 BCLC 266 131–32
Mission Capital plc v Sinclair [2008] EWHC 1339 (C), [2010] 1 BCLC 304.................. 248
Mohamed v Egyptian Association of Great Britain Ltd [2018] EWCA Civ 879 70–71
Montgold Capital LLP v Ilska [2018] EWHC 2982 (Ch), [2019] BCC 309 ......245, 246, 248, 249–51
Moore v I Bresler Ltd [1944] 2 All ER 515 86
Mumbray v Lapper [2005] EWHC 1152, [2005] BCC 990 249
Musselwhite v Musselwhite [1962] 2 Ch 964... 120
Mutual Life Insurance Co of New York v Rank Organisation Ltd [1985] BCLC 11 131–37
Naibu Global International Co Plc v Daniel Stewart and Co Plc [2020]
    EWHC 2719 (Ch), [2021] PNLR 4.. 227
NBH Lt v Hoare [2006] EWHC 73 (Ch), [2006] 2 BCLC 649............................. 161
Newton-Sealy v ArmorGroup Services Ltd [2008] EWHC 233 (QB) 68
Noble Vintners Ltd, Re [2019] EWHC 2806 (Ch), [2020] BCC 198....................... 67, 145
Norman v Theodore Goddard [1991] BCLC 1028 139–40

Nortel GmbH (in administration) and other companies, Re; Lehman Brothers International
    (Europe) (in administration) and other companies (Nos 1 and 2), Re [2013] UKSC 52,
    [2013] 2 BCLC 135 71
Northampton Regional Livestock Centre Co Ltd v Cowling [2015] EWCA Civ 651, [2015]
    4 Costs LR 477; [2016] 1 BCLC 431 81
Northern Counties Securities Ltd v Jackson & Steeple Ltd [1974] 1 WLR 1133 225
O'Neill v Phillips [1999] 1 WLR 1092 115
O'Rorke v Revenue and Customs Commissioners, Upper Tribunal (Tax and Chancery)
    04 October 2013, [2013] UKUT 499 (TCC), [2014] STC 279 71
Official Receiver v Jupe [2011] 1 BCLC 191 144
Okpabi v Royal Dutch Shell plc [2021] UKSC 3, [2021] 1 WLR 1294 68
Ooregum Gold Mining v Roper [1892] AC 125 208–9
Ortakligi v Schlegel Automotive Europe Ltd, QBD 12 Oct 2012, unreported. 42–43
PAG Asset Preservation Ltd, Re [2020] EWCA Civ 1017, [2020] BCC 979. 46
PAG Management Services Ltd, Re [2015] EWHC 2404 (Ch), (2015) BCC 720 46
Pavlides v Jensen [1956] Ch 565 239
Paycheck Services No 3, RCC v Holland, Re [2010] UKSC 51, [2011] 1 All ER 430. 66
Pender v Lushington (1877) 6 Ch D 70 120
Percival v Wright [1902] 2 Ch 421 128
Persad v Singh [2017] UKPC 32, [2017] BCC 779 59
Peskin v Anderson [2001] BCC 874 (CA) 128
Pickering v Stephenson, (1872) LR 14 Eq 322. 78
Pipia v BGEO Group Ltd [2020] EWHC 402 (Comm), [2020] 1 WLR 2582 70–71
Polly Peck International plc, Re [1996] 2 All ER 433 43
Poulton v The London and South Western Railway Company (1866–67) LRQB 534 80
Precision Dippings Ltd v Precision Dippings Marketing Ltd [1986] Ch 447. . . . . 191–92, 193
Prest v Petrodel [2012] EWCA Civ 1395, [2013] UKSC 34, [2013] 2 AC 415 . . . . 10, 15, 33, 40, 58–60,
                                                                         61, 63, 70, 74
Progress Property v Moore [2010] UKSC 55, [2011] 1 WLR 1 215–17
Prudential Assurance v Newman Industries [1982] 1 Ch 204 (CA) 118–19, 227–28, 229, 230, 239,
                                                         240–41, 243–44, 256
Punt v Symons & Co Ltd [1903] 2 Ch 506 . . . . 129, 198
R v A Ltd [2017] 1 Cr App R 1 88
R v Boyle Transport (Northern Ireland) Ltd [2016] EWCA Crim 19; [2016]
    4 WLR 63 (CA) (Crim Div). 59, 70
R v Cory Bros [1927] 1 KB 810 83
R v ICR Haulage Ltd [1944] KB 551 . . . . 83, 86, 88
R v Powell (Jacqueline) [2016] EWCA Crim 1043, [2016] Env LR 11 . . . . 59, 70
R v Scottish and Southern Energy Plc; Surrey Trading Standards v Scottish and
    Southern Energy Plc [2012] EWCA Crim 539 70
R v Seager (Mornington Stafford) [2009] EWCA Crim 1303, [2010] 1 WLR 815 70
R v St Regis Paper Company [2011] EWCA Crim 2524, [2012] 1 Cr App R 14 . . . . . . 84, 87–88, 92, 99
Raithatha v Baig [2017] EWHC 2059 (Ch) 141
Regal (Hastings) Ltd v Gulliver [1967] 2 AC 134 (HL) 128, 152–53, 156, 157, 158
Regentcrest plc v Cohen [2001] BCC 494 133
Revenue and Customs Commissioners v Holland [2010] UKSC 51, [2010] 1 WLR 2793. 192
Riche v The Ashbury Railway Carriage and Iron Company Ltd (1873–74) LR 9 Ex 224. 49
Richmond Pharmacology Ltd v Chester Overseas Ltd [2014] EWHC 2692, [2014]
    Bus LR 1110. 152
RJH Stanhope Ltd v Harris, Re [2020] EWHC 2808 (Ch) 134
Rolfe v Rolfe [2010] EWHC 244 (Ch) 106, 219
Rolled Steel v British Steel [1986] Ch 246 215
Rossendale Borough Council v Hurstwood Properties Ltd [2019] EWCA Civ 364, [2019]
    1 WLR 4567. 60

Routledge v Skerritt [2019] EWHC 573 (Ch), [2019] BCC 812 213–14
Royal British Bank v Turquand (1856) 6 E & B 327 77–78
Ruscoe Ltd, Re (2012) ChD (Companies Court) 07 August 2012 (unreported)............141, 192
Russel v Northern Bank Development Corporation Ltd [1992] 1 WLR 588.....................198
Saatchi v Gajjar [2019] EWHC 2472 (Ch)...249–50
Salmon v Quin & Axtens Ltd [1901] 1 Ch 311 ....117, 203
Salomon v Salomon [1896] UKHL 1, [1897] AC 22..............................14, 39, 74, 100
Samuel Sherman Plc, Re [1991] 1 WLR 1070 144–45
Saul D Harrison & Sons Plc, Re [1994] BCC 475 224
Scott v Frank F Scott (London) Ltd [1940] Ch 794 (CA)....................................114–15
Scottish Co-operative Wholesale Society Ltd v Meyer [1959] AC 324..............70, 132, 137–38
Secretary of State for Business, Innovation and Skills v Khan [2017] EWHC 288 (Ch)...........143
Secretary of State for Business, Innovation and Skills v Drummond [2015] CSOH 45,
    2015 GWD 14–241..143
Secretary of State for Business, Innovation and Skills v Millar [2014] CSOH 127,
    2014 GWD 28–556..143
Secretary of State for Business, Innovation and Skills v Reza [2013] CSOH 86,
    2013 GWD 19–380..144–45
Secretary of State for Business, Innovation and Skills v Whyte [2014] CSOH 148,
    2014 GWD 32–624..143–45, 161–62
Secretary of State for Trade and Industry v Amiss [2003] 2 BCLC 206 143–44
Secretary of State for Trade and Industry v Carr [2006] EWHC 2110 (Ch), [2007]
    2 BCLC 495..144–45
Secretary of State for Trade and Industry v Swan [2005] EWHC 603 (Ch).....................143
Secretary of State for Trade and Industry v Van Hengel [1995] 1 BCLC 545....................163
Senator Hanseatische Verwaltungsgesellschaft mbH, Re [1997] 1 WLR 515 (CA) 46
Serious Fraud Offce v Rolls Royce Plc [2017] Lloyd's Rep FC 18 72
Serious Fraud Office v Standard Bank Plc [2016] Lloyds' Rep FC 102...........................72
Sevenoaks Stationers, Re [1991] Ch 164 143
Sevilleja v Marex Financial Ltd [2018] EWCA Civ 1468, [2019] QB 173.......................227
SFO v Barclays Plc [2018] EWHC 3055 (QB), [2020] 1 Cr App R 28....................88, 89–90
Shaw v Shaw [1935] 2 KB 113 204
Shepherds Investments Ltd v Walters [2006] EWHC 836 [2007] 2 BCLC 202 151
Sherlock Holmes International Society Ltd, Re [2016] EWHC 1076 (Ch), [2017]
    2 BCLC 14...198–99
Shuttleworth v Cox Brothers and Co (Maidenhead) Ltd [1927] 2 KB 9.....................199–200
Singularis Holdings Ltd v Daiwa Capital Markets Europe Ltd [2019] UKSC 50, [2019]
    3 WLR 997...17–18, 41–42
Smith and Fawcett Ltd, Re [1942] Ch 204 (CA) 131, 134
Smith v Croft (No 2) [1988] 1 Ch 114............................... 118–19, 240–43, 249, 252
Smith v Henniker-Major & Co 51
Smith, Stone and Knight Ltd v City of Birmingham [1939] 4 All ER 116 71
Snook v London and West Riding Investments Ltd [1967] 2 QB 78..............................60
SSTI v Bairstow [2004] EWHC 1730 (Ch), [2005] 1 BCLC 136 144–45
Stainer v Lee [2010] EWHC 1539, [2011] BCC 134..........................244, 246, 249, 251
Standard Chartered Bank v Pakistan National Shipping Corporation [2003] 1 AC 959.........64, 82
Staray Capital Ltd v Yang (aka Stanley) [2017] UKPC 43 199–200
Stevens v Midland Counties Railway Company and Lander (1854) 10 Exchequer Reports
    (Welsby, Hurlstone, and Gordon) 352; 156 ER 480 80
Stobart Group Ltd v Tinkler [2019] EWHC 258 (Comm), [2019] 2 WLUK 235 .... 129, 132, 133,
                                                                              137–38, 201
Stone & Rolls v Moore Stephens [2009] UKHL 39, [2009] 1 AC 1391.................17–18, 41–42
Strahan v Wilcock [2006] EWCA Civ 12, [2006] 2 BCLC 555 115
Sunrise Radio [2010] 1 BCLC 367 207

Tavarone Mining Co, Pritchard's Case, Re (1873) 8 Ch App 956 116
Taylor v Rhino Overseas Inc [2020] EWCA Civ 353, [2020] Bus LR 1486 42–43
Taylor v Van Dutch Marine Holding Ltd [2016] EWHC 2201 (Ch), [2016] 9 WLUK 31 70
TCB Ltd v Gray [1986] Ch 621 51
Tesco Supermarkets Ltd v Nattrass [1972] AC 153 . . . . 86–87, 88, 99
Thakkar v Thakkar Family Court 10 February 2017, [2017] EWFC 13 61
Tintin Exploration Syndicate v Sandys [1947] 177 LT 412 208–9
Toone v Ross [2019] EWHC 2855 (Ch) 216
Toshiba Carrier UK Ltd v KME Yorkshire Ltd [2012] EWCA Civ 1190 72
Towers v Premier Waste Management Ltd [2011] EWCA (Civ) 923, [2012]
    1 BCLC 67 . . . . .152, 156, 158–59
Trustor AB v Smallbone (No 2) [2001] 1 WLR 177 . . . . 58, 61–62
TXU Europe Group Plc, Re [2011] EWHC 2072 (Ch), [2012] BCC 363 219
UCP Plc v Nectrus Ltd Damages [2019] EWHC 3274, [2020] PNLR 9 . . . . 227, 228
Ultraframe v Fielding [2004] RPC 479 220–21
Universal Project Management Services v Fort Gilkicker [2013] EWHC 348 (Ch),
    [2013] Ch 551 119
Various Claimants v Institute of the Brothers of the Christian Schools [2012] UKSC 56,
    [2013] 2 AC 1 81
VB Football Assets v Blackpool Football Club (Properties) Ltd [2017] EWHC 2767 (Ch) 115
Vedanta Resources Plc v Lungowe [2019] UKSC 20, [2020] AC 1045 68
Vehicle Operator Service Agency v FM Conway Ltd [2012] EWHC 2930 (Admin),
    [2013] RTR 17 . . . . 88, 99
Vivendi SA v Richards [2013] EWHC 3006 (Ch) 220
VTB Capital Plc v Nutritek International Corp [2012] EWCA Civ 808, [2012] 2 BCLC 437 60–61
VTB Capital plc v Nutritek International Corp and others [2013] UKSC 5, [2013] 2 AC 337 64
Walker v London Tramways Co (1879) 12 Ch D 705 198
Weavering Capital (UK) Ltd v Peterson [2012] EWHC 1480 aff'd [2013] EWCA Civ 71 140
Welfab Engineers Ltd, Re [1990] BCLC 833 133
West Mercia Safetywear v Dodd [1988] BCLC 250 134–35
Westlowe Storage and Distribution Ltd [2000] 2 BCLC 590 141
Westmid Packing Services Ltd, Re, SSTI v Griffiths [1998] 2 BCLC 646 144–45
White Star Line Ltd, Re [1938] Ch 458 208–9
Wilkinson v West Coast Capital [2005] EWHC 3009, [2007] BCC 717 156
Williams v Natural Life Health Foods Ltd [1998] 1 WLR 830 (HL) 68
Winkworth v Edward Baron Development Co Ltd [1986] 1 WLR 1512 (HL) 134
Wood v Odessa Waterworks Co (1889) 42 ChD 636 . . . . 117, 224
Woolfson v Strathclyde Regional Council (1978) SC (HL) 90 (HL) 71
Wragg, Re [1897] 1 Ch 796 208–9
Wright v Atlas Wright (Europe) Ltd [1999] 2 BCLC 301 109
Yukong Line Ltd of Korea v Rendsburg Investments Corporation of Liberia (No 2) [1998]
    1 WLR 294 134–35
Yusuf v Yusuf [2019] EWHC 90 (Ch) 162
Zavahir v Shankleman [2016] EWHC 2772, [2017] BCC 500 246

AUSTRALIA

ASIC v Cassimatis [2016] FCA 1023, 336 ALR 209 143–44
Gambotto v WPC Ltd (1995) 182 CLR 432 (High Court of Australia) 199–200
Mills v Mills (1938) 60 CLR 150 (High Court of Australia) 129, 132
Peso Silver Mines Ltd v Cropper [1966] SCR 673, (1966) 58 DLR (2d) 1 156
Peters' American Delicacy Co Ltd v Heath (1939) 61 CLR 457 (High Court of Australia) 199
Pilmer v Duke Group Ltd [2001] HCA 31, (2001) 207 CLR 165 208

CANADA

Bazley v Curry (1999) 174 DLR (4th) 45 (Sup Ct (Can)) 81
Canadian Aero Services Ltd v O'Malley (1973) 40 DLR (3d) 371 151

HONGKONG

Akai Holdings Ltd (in Liq) v Kasikornbank PCL [2011] 1 HKC 357 78–79

Table of Legislation

TABLE OF STATUTES

Bribery Act 2010 .... 75–76, 91, 93, 94–95, 97, 102
  s 7 94–95
  s 7(1) 72
  s 7(2) 72, 94–95
  s 8 72
Companies Act 1844 (7&8 Vict c 100) 13,
               37–38, 39, 49–50, 112
  s VII 112
  s VIII 112
Companies Act 1862 .... 38, 39, 40, 49
  s 1 49
  s 6 49
  s 7 49
  s 8 49
  s 10 49
  s 11 49
  s 12 49
  s 14 49
  s 50 49
Companies Act 1929 (19 & 20) Geo.
    5c 23 139–40
Companies Act 1948 .... 104–5, 201
Companies Act 1980 .... 105, 206
Companies Act 1985
  s 309(1) 133
  s 309(2) 133
Companies Act 2006 .... 9, 29–30,
    33–34, 97, 103–4, 105, 108, 112–13,
  125, 128, 129, 130, 133, 134, 137, 139–40,
  146, 155, 162, 163, 169–70, 181, 187,
      193, 200, 206, 213, 214, 219
  s 3(1) 57
  s 4 220
  s 7 112
  s 7(1) 41
  s 7(2) 40, 63
  s 8 112
  s 9 44–45
  s 12A 44–45
  s 14–15 44–45
  s 16 44–45
  s 16(2) 38
  s 16(3) 38
  s 17 112

  s 18 .... 112, 128, 198
  s 18(1) 122
  s 19 .... 112, 198
  s 20 .... 112, 198
  s 21 198
  s 21(1) 104
  s 22 104
  s 23 125
  ss 26–27 106–7
  s 30 125
  s 33 .... 112–14, 122
  s 33(1) 112
  s 39 .... 52, 53, 54
  s 40 .... 78, 79, 154
  s 40(2)(b)(iii) 78–79
  s 40(3) 78
  ss 53–65 44–45
  s 77 104
  s 78 104
  s 90 104
  s 97 104
  s 102 104
  s 105 104
  s 109 104
  s 112 .... 112, 208–9
  s 113 107
  s 116 117
  s 125 117
  s 154 200
  s 154(1) 103–4
  s 154(2) 103–4
  s 155 .... 42–43, 103–4
  s 160 200
  s 162 45
  ss 162–67 106–7
  s 162(5) 117
  s 167 45
  s 168 .... 8–9, 104–5, 139, 201, 234
  s 168(1) 201
  s 168(2)–(5) 104–5
  s 168(5)(b) 201
  s 169 .... 104–5, 201
  s 170 128
  ss 170–81 .... 127, 169–70
  s 170(2)(a) 151
  s 170(3) 125

s 170(4). 125
s 171 . . . . . . .78, 125–26, 128, 130, 217, 218
ss 171–177 128
s 171(a). 125, 128, 129
s 171(b) 125, 129
s 172 .5–6, 35, 125,
                      126, 131–35, 135–37, 163,
                      178, 179–80, 208–9, 217,
                      218, 245–47, 253–54, 259–60
s 172(1). 132–33
s 172(1)(a)–(f). 133
s 172(3). 134, 244–45
s 173 125–26
s 174 . . . . . . .125–26, 138, 140, 142, 144–45
s 174(1). 140
s 174(2). 140
s 175 . . . . .125–26, 151–53, 157, 231
ss 175–77 125
s 175(2). 151
s 175(3). 151
s 175(4). 153
s 175(5)(a) 155
s 175(5)(b) 155
s 175(6). 155
s 176 125
s 177 . . . . 125, 151, 160, 163
s 177(1). 160
s 177(4). 160
s 177(5). 160
s 177(6)(a) 160
s 177(6)(c) 163
s 180 161
s 180(1)(b) 160–61
s 180(1) last sentence 160–61
s 180(4). 106, 155–56, 213
s 182(4). 160
s 183 160
s 184 139
s 188(5). 164
s 186(1). 160
s 188 . . . . 106, 164, 213
ss 188–89 126
s 189 164
s 190 . . . . 161, 213
ss 190–96 126
s 190(1). 161
s 191 161
s 197 . . . . 106, 161, 213
ss 197–214 126
s 198 . . . . 106, 213
s 201 . . . . 106, 213
s 203 . . . . 106, 213
ss 215–22 126
s 217 . . . . 106, 213

s 218 . . . . 106, 213
s 219 . . . . 106, 213
s 212 161
s 215 164
s 217 164
s 218 164
s 222 164
s 226A(1) 164–65
s 226B. 106, 164–65, 213
s 226C. 106, 164–65, 213
s 226E(2) 164–65
s 229 117
s 231 160
s 231(3). 160
s 231(6). 160
s 232 219–20
s 234 219–20
ss 237–38 117
s 238 117
s 239 . . . . 106, 196, 219, 220
s 239(2). 253
s 239(3). 220
s 247 . . . . 105, 213
s 251(1). 66
s 251(3). 42–43
s 260(3). 243
s 260(5)(a) 243
s 260(5)(b) 243
s 261(4)(c) 248, 254
s 263(2). 244, 249
s 263(2)(a) 245, 250
s 263(2)(b) 244, 250
s 263(2)(c) 244
s 263(3). 244, 247, 249
s 263(3)(b) 245
s 263(3)(e) 106, 219
s 263(4). 249
s 270 103–4
s 271 103–4
s 273 103–4
ss 275–78 106–7
s 281 161
ss 281–354 108
s 281(3). 161
s 281(3)(a) 106, 155–56, 213
s 282 161
s 283 104
s 288 161
s 302 . . . . 108, 125
s 303 108
s 306 108
s 307 108
s 307A. 108
ss 308–9 108

s 311 108
s 311A............................. 108
s 314 108
s 319A............................. 108
s 336 .... 105, 213
s 355 107
s 358 117
s 366 176
s 385(2)......................... 164–65
s 386 .... 107, 125, 170
s 386(2)............................ 170
s 386(3)............................ 170
s 386(4)............................ 170
s 387 .... 107, 171, 187
s 387(2)............................ 171
s 389 187
s 393(1)......................... 107–8
s 394 .... 107, 125, 172
s 394A............................. 175
s 395 .... 107–8, 174
s 396(1)............................ 172
s 396(3)......................... 172–73
ss 399–402 44
ss 399–413 172
s 409 172
s 410A............................. 172
s 411 172
s 412 172
s 413 172
s 414(1)....................... 107, 174
s 414(2)....................... 107, 174
s 414(4)............... 174, 188, 256–57
s 414(5)............... 174, 188, 256–57
s 414A............................. 177
s 414B............................. 177
s 414C(1) 178, 179–80
s 414C(2) 177
s 414C(3) 177
s 414C(7) 177
s 414C(8) 177
s 414CA 177–78
s 414CB(1)...................... 177–78
s 414CB(2)(d) 177–78
s 414D(2).................. 188, 256–57
s 414D(3).................. 188, 256–57
s 415 176
s 419(1)............................ 177
s 419(3)............. 177, 178, 188, 256–57
s 419(4)............. 177, 178, 188, 256–57
s 419A............................. 178
s 420 178
s 421(3)............................ 178
s 421(4)............................ 178
s 422 179

s 422(2)....................... 179, 188
s 422(3)....................... 179, 188
s 423 221
s 423(1)............................ 183
s 425 .... 183, 187
s 430 184
s 430(6)....................... 184, 188
s 430(7)....................... 184, 188
s 431 .... 117, 183, 187, 221
s 431(3)............................ 183
s 431(4)............................ 183
s 432 187
s 433 187
s 433(4)............................ 184
s 434 187
s 435 187
s 437 183
s 438 .... 183, 188
s 439 179
s 439A..................... 164–65, 179
s 441 184
s 451 188
s 451(1)............................ 184
s 451(2)............................ 184
s 452 184
s 453 184
s 455 .... 174, 180
s 456 .... 174, 180
s 458 .... 174, 180
s 459 .... 174, 180
s 463 180
s 463(6)............................ 180
s 475 .... 103–4, 180–81
ss 475–79 103–4
s 475(2)............................ 181
s 475(3)............................ 181
s 476 .... 117, 182, 222
s 485 205
s 485(3)............................ 181
s 485(4)............... 104–5, 181, 182
s 485A............................. 181
s 485B............................. 181
s 486 181
s 486(1)................ 181, 182, 221–22
s 486(3)............................ 181
s 486(4)............................ 181
s 486A............................. 181
s 486A(1) 181, 182, 221–22
s 486A(2) 181, 182, 221–22
s 486A(5) 181
s 486A(6) 181
s 488 .... 182, 222
s 489 205
s 489(3)............................ 181

s 489(4)................. 104–5, 181, 182
s 489A............................ 181
s 489B............................ 181
s 490 181
s 490(1)............... 181, 182, 221–22
s 490(3)........................... 181
s 490(4)........................... 181
s 490A............................ 181
s 490A(1) 181, 182, 221–22
s 490A(2) 181, 182, 221–22
s 490A(5) 181
s 490A(6) 181
s 492 .... 106, 182
s 495 .... 103–4, 180–81
s 498 180–81
s 499(1)(a) 181–82
s 499(1)(b) 181–82
s 500 181–82
s 501(2)....................... 181–82
s 501(3)....................... 181–82
s 510 .... 104–5, 182, 205
s 511 181
s 511A................... 182, 221–22
s 511A(5) 182, 222
s 519A............................ 181
s 520(2)........................... 181
s 520(7)........................... 181
s 520(8)........................... 181
s 523 181
s 523(4)–(6)....................... 181
s 527 .... 108, 182, 222
s 530(2).................... 182, 222
s 531 219–20
ss 532–38 .... 182, 221–22
s 534 .... 106, 182
ss 534–36 205
s 550(b) 205
s 551(3).......................... 105
s 551(3)(a) 105, 206
s 551(3)(b) 206, 207
s 551(4)(a) 206
s 551(4)(b) 206
s 560 206
s 561 206
ss 561–73 105
s 561(1).......................... 206
s 561(2).......................... 206
s 561(4).......................... 206
s 562(2).......................... 206
s 563 105
ss 564–66 206
s 567 206–7
s 568 206–7
s 568(4).......................... 105

s 570(3).......................... 207
s 571(1).......................... 207
s 571(6).......................... 207
s 571(7)(a) 207
s 571(7)(b) 207
s 572 207
s 572(2).......................... 207
s 580 209
s 593 208
s 601 208
s 601(1).......................... 208
s 602 208
s 618(1)(a) 104
s 618(1)(b) 104
s 622(1).......................... 104
s 641 106
s 641(1)...................... 223–24
s 641(1)(b) 223–24
s 641(2)...................... 223–24
s 647 224
s 693 106
s 744(1).......................... 117
s 811 117
s 830 .... 125, 190, 215, 220
s 830(2).......................... 190
s 830(4).......................... 190
s 831 190
s 836 191
s 845 217
s 845(2)(b) 217
s 847 193
ss 942–91 210
s 979 199
s 993 65
s 994 .... .70, 115, 123, 213,
                        214, 224, 248, 249
s 1112......................... 106–7
s 1121......................... 106–7
s 1157 .... 141, 192
Explanatory Notes
    para 639................... 107, 170
Companies Clauses Consolidation Act
    1845 202
s 90 202
Company Directors Disqualification Act
    1986 .... .34, 67, 75, 126, 138,
                139–40, 141–42, 143–44,
                145–46, 161–62, 170, 171
s 1 67
s 1(1)(a) 142
s 1(1)(b) 142
ss 2– 3........................... 67
ss 2–5 257
s 6 .... 67, 143

s 6(1)............................ 144
s 6(1)(b) 142
s 6(3C) 67
s 7 145
s 8 143
s 8(1)............................ 145
s 8(2)............................ 142
s 8(2A) 145
s 12C.......................... 143–44
s 15A.............................. 67
ss 15A–15B 145
Sch 1(1) 143–44
Corporate Manslaughter Act 1997 89–90
Corporate Manslaughter and Homicide
      Act 2007 (c 9) 91, 93, 94, 102
s 1(1)............................. 94
Crime and Courts Act 2013
s 45 97
Sch 17............................ 97
Criminal Finances Act 2017 .... 93, 102
Pt 3 95
Ch 22 95
s 44 95–96
s 45 95–96
s 45(2).......................... 95–96
s 46 95
s 47 96
Explanatory Notes
      para 43.......................... 95
      para 44.......................... 95
Equality Act 2006
s 20 186
Equality Act 2010 .... 176, 185
Film Act.......................... 70
Financial Services and Markets Act 2000
      (c 8) 97
Pt 6 164–65
Finance Act 2009 (C 10).............. 171
s 1 .... 103–4, 171
s 5 171
Sch 46
      para 2(2) 171
      para 4.......................... 71
      para 93.................... 103–4, 171
Finance Act 2016 .... 176, 185
Sch 19............................ 186
Food Safety Act 1990
s 21(1)............................ 92
Insolvency Act 1986 141–42
s 74(2)(d)......................... 57
s 122(1)(a) 45, 197–98
s 122(2)(f) 197–98
s 124A............................ 46
s 213 65

s 214 .... 66, 139–40
s 214(4)..................... 66, 139–40
s 214(7)........................... 66
s 215 66–67
s 216 66–67
s 122(1)(a) 104
s 251 66
s 423 193
Joint Stock Companies Act 1844, s II
      (C 110, 70 & 80 Vic)
s 25 38
Joint Stock Companies Act 1856 (19&20
      Vict c 47) 48, 49–50, 112
s III 112
s IX.............................. 112
Limited Liability Act 1855 (18 &
      19 Vict c 133)......... 8–9, 37, 49–50,
                              56–57, 112
s I 112
s II.............................. 112
Merchant Shipping Act 1894
s 502 .... 84, 85
Modern Slavery Act 2015.............72–73,
                          75–76, 176, 185
s 54 72–73
s 54(4)........................... 185
s 54(11).......................... 186
Partnership Act 1890 (c 39)
s 5 78–79
s 29 153
s 32(c)........................ 197–98
Pensions Act 2004
ss 43–51 71
Political Parties, Elections and
      Referendums Act 2000
ss 139–40 176
Protection from Harassment
      Act 1997......................... 83
Small Business, Enterprise and
      Employment Act 2015 185–86
s 3 185–86
South Sea Bubble Act 1720, 6 Geo I,
      c 18...................... 13, 37–38
Trade Description Act 1968
s 11 86–87

TABLE OF STATUTORY INSTRUMENTS

Civil Procedure Rules 1998 (SI 1998/
      3132) (CPR) 70–71
r 19.9A(10) 243–44
r 31.8........................ 70–71
r 40.9........................ 70–71

Companies (Interest Rate for
    Unauthorised Political Donations or
    Expenditure) Regulations 2007 (SI
    2007/2242) 176
Companies (Miscellaneous Reporting)
    Regulations 2018 (SI 2018/860) 165
    reg 26(1)–(2) 111
Companies (Model Articles) Regulations
    2008 (SI 2008/3229) 244
    Sch 1 Model Articles for Private
    Companies Limited by Shares
        para 3. 78
        para 5. 78
        para 14. 163
        para 14(1) 160–61
        para 17. 200
        para 19(3) 162, 163
        para 30. 223
        para 30(6) 223
    Sch 3 Model Articles for Public Companies
        para 3. 78
        para 5. 78
        para 16(1) 160–61
        para 20. 200
        para 21. . . . . 200, 201
        para 23. 163
        para 23(3) 163
        para 23(3) 162
        para 70. 223
        para 70(6) 223
Company, Limited Liability Partnership
    and Business (Names and Trading
    Disclosures) Regulations 2015
    (SI 2015/17). 45
Defence (General) Regulations 1939 86
Equality Act 2010 (Gender Pay Gap
    Information) Regulations 2017
    (SI 2017/172). 165, 185
    reg 2 185
    reg 14 185
    reg 15 185
    reg 15(2). 185
    Explanatory Memorandum, para 7.12 . 186
Large and Medium-sized Companies
    and Groups (Accounts and Reports)
    Regulation 2008 (SI 2008/410)
    Sch 1
        para 17. 173
        para 18. 173
        para 45. 107–8
        part 1, section b, para 1 172–73
    Sch 7. 176
        para 3. 176
        para 4. 176
        para 7. 176

    para 10. 176–77
    para 11. 176–77
    para 6. 176
    para 8. 176
    para 9. 176
    para 11B 176–77
    para 13. 177
    para 15. 177
Pollution Prevention and Control
    (England and Wales) Regulation
    2000 (SI 2000/1973)
    reg 16(1). 91
    reg 28(2). 92
    reg 32(1)(b)–(d) 91
    reg 32(1)(e) 92
    reg 32(1)(g) 87–88
Reporting on Payment Practices and
    Performance Regulations 2017
    (SI 2017/395)
    reg 3 185–86
    reg 8 186
Small Companies and Groups (Accounts
    and Directors' Report) Regulations
    2008 (SI 2008/409)
    Sch 1
        Pt 1, para 1A–1C 183
        section b, para 1 172–73
        section c, para 1 173
        para 16. 173
        para 18. 173
    Sch 5. 176
        para 2. 176
        para 3. 176
        para 5. 176–77
Unfair Trading Regulations 2008
    reg 9 70

TABLE OF UK CODES

Cadbury Code 1992 . . . . 146, 149, 225
City Code on Takeovers and
    Mergers 105–6, 193, 210, 211, 212
    r 21 . . . . 105–6, 210
    r 21.1. 211
    r 21.1(a) 105–6, 210–12
    principle 1 210
    principle 2 210
    principle 3 210
UK Corporate Governance
    Code 2018 . . . . . 34, 54, 110, 111–12, 123
            138, 146, 148, 149, 162, 163–64,
            165–66, 167, 168, 175, 189, 197,
            200, 201, 235
    Principle A. 53
    Principle G. 110, 146

Principle K. 110, 146
Principle P 163–64, 167, 260–61
Principle Q 165–66
Principle R. 165–66
Provision 5. . . . . 54, 110, 200
Provision 9. . . . . 110, 146
Provision 17. . . . . 110, 146
Provision 18. 201
Provision 24. . . . . 110, 146
Provision 32. . . . . 110, 146, 165–66
Provision 33. 165–66
Provision 33. 165–66
UK Stewardship Code 2020. . . . . . .197, 225,
226–27, 236

EU LEGISLATION

Directives

Directive 68/151/EEC First Company
Law Directive of 9 March 1968 OJL
65/8 14.3 1968. 53
Art 9 82
Directive 2009/101/EC of 16 September
2009 OJL 258/11 of 1 Oct 2009
Art 10 53
Art 10(2) 78–79
Directive 2013/34/EU of 26 June 2013
Accounting Directive of 26 June 201
OJ L 182/19 of 29 June 2013. . . . . 176, 185
Preamble (44)–(53) 185
Arts 41–48 185

Second Company Law Directive
(CLR) 209

Regulations

EU Transparency Regulation 2004/109/
EC of 15 December 2004, Preamble
(14), OJ L390/38 of 31 December 2004
Preamble (14) 185
EU Transparency Regulation 2007. 176
Market Abuse Regulation 185

OTHER DOCUMENTS

Financial Conduct Authority (FCA)
Handbook, Listing Rules (LR) 161,
165, 196
ch10 105
LR 9.3.11R. 105
LR 9.4.1 . . . . 106, 165
LR 9.4.4 . . . . 106, 165
LR 9.4.4(2). 165
LR 10 213
LR 11.1.5–6 . . . . 106, 161
LR 11 Annex 1. . . . . 106, 161
LR 13.6.1(5). 161
Financial Conduct Authority (FCA)
Handbook, Disclosure and
Transparency Rules (DTR)
DTR 4.3A. 185
DTR 7.2 110
DTR 7.2.2. 178

1

A Real Entity Theory of Company Law

1.1 Introduction

This book advances a real entity theory of company law. In this theory the company is a legal entity allowing an organization to act autonomously in law and company law establishes procedures facilitating autonomous organizational decision-making.

The theory builds on the insight that organizations or firms are a social phenomenon outside of the law and that these are autonomous actors in their own right. They are more than the sum of the contributions of their participants. They also act independently of the views and interests of their participants. This occurs because human beings change their behaviour when they act as members of a group or an organization. In a group we tend to develop and conform to a shared standard. When we act in organizations habits, routines, processes, and procedures form and a culture emerges. These take on a life of their own affecting the behaviour of the participants. Participants can themselves affect organizational behaviour and modify habits, routines, procedures, and culture but this takes time and effort. Company law finds this phenomenon and evolves with a view to supporting autonomous action by organizations.

It will be shown in this book that a theory that conceives companies as vehicles for autonomous real entities that are characterized by their routines, procedures, and culture explains company law as it stands at a positive level. The theory also helps to formulate normative recommendations guiding law reform and judicial decision-making.

A real entity theory is sometimes associated with a normative argument advocating for more influence for stakeholders, such as employees. This book does not take a position on the normative question of whether stakeholders should have more influence than they currently have. The theory developed in this book holds irrespective of how the law fine-tunes the influence over corporate decision-making.

There are three main theories of the company. The first theory explains the company as a contract. It forms the basis on which agency theory builds. The second theory conceives the company as a concession of the state. The third theory characterizes the company as a real entity. They will be examined in turn below. This will be followed by a statement of a modern version of real entity theory.

Company Law. Eva Micheler, Oxford University Press. © Eva Micheler 2021. DOI: 10.1093/oso/9780198858874.003.0001

1.2 Contract theory

1.2.1 Introduction

The term 'contract theory' appears to have been coined in American scholarship.[1] The theory nevertheless resonates ideas that were expressed in the nineteenth century under the label of 'fiction theory'.[2] There were a number of variations of the theory, but they had common characteristics that correspond to those associated with the nexus of contract theory we know today. Fiction theory referred to what we now know as the 'company' as 'an artificial individual'.[3] In this framework the company is a 'single nexus' ('einheitliche[r] Beziehungspunkt') under which rights and obligations are held together through contracts.[4] The characterization of the company as a contract can justify why the legislature, which had already provided freedom of contract, should make incorporation available freely rather than by individualized concession.[5]

There was also a time in English legal history when contract and trust law were used to create deed of settlement companies.[6] This made it possible to provide investors with limited liability. Those who acted as trustees, however, were fully liable for the debt they incurred for the benefit of the assets held on trust.

1.2.2 Nexus of contract and agency theory

Contemporary scholarship builds on contributions made by neoclassical economic theory. It does not connect to historic material.[7] It nevertheless embraces contractarian arguments. At a positive level the company is characterized as a 'nexus of contract'.[8]

---

[1] Henry Butler, 'The Contract Theory of the Corporation', (1989) 11 George Mason Law Review 99.

[2] David Gindis, 'From Fictions and Aggregates to Real Entities in the Theory of the Firm' (2009) 5(1) Journal of Institutional Economics 25, 32; Friedrich Carl von Savigny, *System des heutigen Roemischen Rechts, Band 2* (Veit and Comp Berlin 1840) § 85 and §§ 89–90; HLA Hart connects the theory to Hohfeld (HLA Hart, 'Definition and Theory in Jurisprudence' in *HLA Hart, Essays in Jurisprudence and Philosophy* (OUP 1983) 40–43); see also Martin Petrin, 'Reconceptualizing the Theory of the Firm—From Nature to Function' (2013) 118 Penn St L Rev 1, 5 and 8–10.

[3] Otto von Gierke, *Deutsches Privatrecht, Band 1: Allgemeiner Teil und Personenrecht* (Verlag von Duncker & Humbolt 1895) 464 ('künstliches Individuum') (available from http://dlib-pr.mpier.mpg.de/index.htm).

[4] ibid 465.

[5] John Lowry and Arad Reisberg, *Pettet's Company Law: Company Law and Corporate Finance* (4th edn, Pearson 2012) 58–59.

[6] Michael Lobban, 'Joint Stock Companies' in William Cornish and others, *The Oxford History of the Laws of England, Volume XII, 1820–1914 Private Law* (OUP 2010) 613; William Cornish and others, *Law and Society in England 1750–1950* (Hart 2019) 243–44; John Armour, 'Companies and Other Associations' in Andrew Burrows (ed), *English Private Law* (OUP 2013) [3.45]; Paul Davies, *Gower's Principles of Modern Company Law* (6th edn, Sweet & Maxwell 1997) 29–31; John Morley, 'The Common Law Corporation: The Power of the Trust in Anglo-American Business History' (2016) 116 Columbia L Rev 2145; Joshua Getzler and Mike Macnair, *The Firm as an Entity before the Companies Act, University of Oxford Faculty of Law Legal Studies Research Paper Series*, Working Paper No 47/2006 (November 2006); Joshua Getzler, 'Plural Ownership, Funds, and the Aggregation of Wills' (2009) 10 Theoretical Inquiries in Law 241; see also Paddy W Ireland, 'The Rise of the Limited Liability Company' (1984) 12 International Journal of Sociology of Law 239, 241.

[7] David Gindis, 'From Fictions and Aggregates to Real Entities in the Theory of the Firm' (2009) 5 Journal of Institutional Economics 25, 26.

[8] Michael C Jensen and William H Meckling, 'Theory of the Firm: Managerial Behavior, Agency Costs and Ownership Structure' (1976) 3 Journal of Financial Economics 305.

Scholars in the nineteenth century viewed the company as a contract between the shareholders.[9] Company law was conceived of as a branch of partnership law.[10] Neither the directors nor any other participant in the company were part of the contract.

Modern contract theorists take a different approach. They rely on transaction cost economics and thus assume that all participants in a company are rational actors who each take decisions with a view to maximizing their return in monetary terms. Transaction cost economics builds on Ronald Coase's seminal article 'The Theory of the Firm', which was published in 1937 but only made an impact thanks to Oliver Williamson in the 1970s.[11] According to this approach many exchanges occur on the market. People buy and sell goods or services. Using the market for transactions involves cost. Examples for transaction costs are the time and money spent to travel to the market, the time and money spent to identify a buyer or seller on that market, the fee payable to an agent or the cost involved in paying a lawyer to draft a contract. The firm is a mechanism that helps to reduce these transaction costs. Rather than using the market repeatedly to buy a particular service people can establish long-term commercial relationships through the firm. A worker can agree to deliver services under the direction of a manager. From then on neither party needs to go to the market every day. The manager just instructs the worker to perform tasks as required for the firm. The firm is thus a nexus through which exchanges operate at transaction costs that are lower than the transactions costs for market exchanges. The firm is another form of a marketplace.[12] It aggregates the economic contributions of individual actors.[13] The firm is the sum of the contributions of its participants.

In addition to the nexus of contract theory modern scholars use agency theory to analyse the relationships around this contractual nexus. Agency theory was first articulated by Michael C Jensen, William H Meckling, and Eugene F Fama.[14] Agency theorists identify two participants between whom an agency relationship exists. Such a

[9] FW Maitland, *Otto Gierke, Political Theory of the Middle Age, reprint of the 1900 edition* (Thoemmes Press 1996) xxiv–xxv and xxii–xxiii; Nathaniel Lindley, *A Treatise of the Law of Partnerships, Including its Application on Joint-stock and other Companies* (T and JW Johnson 1980).

[10] Nathaniel Lindley, *A Treatise of the Law of Partnerships, Including its Application to Joint Stock and other Companies* (T & JW Johnson 1860).

[11] Ronald H Coase, 'The Theory of the Firm' (1937) 4 Economica 385; Oliver E Williamson, *Markets and Hierarchies: Analysis and Antitrust Implications* (Free Press, New York 1975); Oliver E Williamson, *The Economic Institutions of Capitalism* (Free Press, New York 1985).

[12] Oliver Williamson, 'Transaction-Cost Economics: The Governance of Contractual Relations' (1979) 22 Journal of Law and Economics 233 at 239.

[13] Grant M Hayden and Matthew T Bodie, 'The Uncorporation and the Unraveling of the "Nexus of Contract Theory"' (2010–2011) 109 Mich L Rev 1127 at 1129; William W Bratton Jr, 'The Nexus of Contract Corporation: A Critical Appraisal' (1989) 74 Cornell L Rev 407, 415; David Gindis, 'From Fictions and Aggregates to Real Entities in the Theory of the Firm' (2009) 5 Journal of Institutional Economics 25, 26, 28–31, and 36; see also David Wishart, 'A Reconfiguration of Company and/or Corporate Law Theory' (2010) 10(1) Journal of Corporate Law Studies 151, 159; James G March and Johan P Olsen, 'The New Institutionalism: Organizational Factors in Political Life' (1984) 78 The American Political Science Review 734, 736.

[14] Eugene F Fama, 'Agency Problems and the Theory of the Firm' (1980) 88 Journal of Political Economy 288; Eugene F Fama and Michael C Jensen, 'Agency Problems and Residual Claims' (1983) 26 Journal of Law and Economics 327; see also Michael C Jensen and William H Mecking, 'The Theory of the Firm: Managerial Behaviour, Agency Costs and Ownership Structure' (1976) 3 Journal of Financial Economics 305; John W Pratt and Richard J Zeckhauser, *Principals and Agents: The Structure of Business* (Harvard Business School Press 1985).

relationship arises in a situation where the actions of one individual (the agent) affects the welfare of another individual (the principal). The nexus established through the company is conceived of as facilitating a number of agency relationships between two particular participants.[15]

Agency theory does not put much if any weight on that fact that companies have separate legal personality. It observes that the welfare of shareholders depends on the actions of the directors and then characterizes the directors as the agents of the shareholders. This is because how well the shareholders do depends on the decisions of the directors. Likewise majority shareholders are the agents of minority shareholders because the welfare of the minority depends on the decisions of the majority. The analysis identifies bilateral relationships between two groups of participants. It focuses on the incentives of these respective two groups and on how these are in conflict with each other.

Renier Kraakman et al distinguish three agency conflicts. The first agency conflict arises between shareholders and directors. The second agency conflict arises between majority and minority shareholders. The third conflict arises 'between the firm itself—including particularly its owners—and the other parties with whom the firm contracts, such as creditors, employees and customers'.[16]

Interestingly the third conflict is expressed differently from the first two conflicts. It refers to the 'firm itself' and this acknowledges the separate legal personality of the company. This is of interest because there is in principle no difference between how directors, shareholders, creditors, employees, customers, and other constituencies interact with the company. They all have a legal relationship with the company which has separate legal personality and is thus the formal nexus. In a theory that characterizes the firm as a nexus which has no substance other than operating as a focus point for the mediation of bilateral relationships the third agency conflict should be articulated like the first two. It should be articulated as a conflict between, for example, creditors versus directors or creditors versus shareholders. The reason for the difference in characterizing creditor relationships is not explained in the book. It is possible to speculate that the authors believe that the relationships of directors and shareholders are different from the relationships of other participants.

In any event, agency theory focuses on the ability of agents to act in the interest of the principals. It assumes rational actors who aim to increase their own respective economic welfare. Agents thus act opportunistically. Adam Smith famously wrote, 'The directors of such companies [joint stock companies] . . . being the managers rather of other people's money than of their own, it cannot well be expected, that they should watch over it with the same anxious vigilance with which the partners in a private copartnery frequently watch over their own.'[17] Opportunistic action creates a cost for

---

[15] See eg Jeffrey N Gordon and Wolf-Georg Ringe, *The Oxford Handbook of Corporate Governance* (OUP 2018) or Reinier Kraakman and others, *The Anatomy of Corporate Law* (3rd edn, OUP 2017).

[16] Reinier Kraakman and others, *The Anatomy of Corporate Law* (3rd edn, OUP 2017) 30.

[17] Adam Smith, *The Wealth of Nations* (1778, Intelex Corporation, reprint 2000) 699.

the principal.[18] Examples of such agency costs are fraud or embezzlement, but also shirking or empire building. The role of the law is to reduce agency cost by ensuring that agents act in the interests of principals rather than in their own personal interest. Law does this by providing for the enforcement of contracts, facilitating contracting through disclosure and by reducing the cost of contracting through the provision of default rules. The law also has a role in setting up legal personality, allowing the assets of the company to become independent from those of the shareholders.[19] Otherwise, mandatory law should only be used in circumstances where the market has failed to address a particular aspect of an agency conflict.[20]

1.2.3 Shareholders versus stakeholders

On their own the nexus of contract and agency theories do not and cannot explain the allocation of power between shareholders and other participants or support a recommendation as to how power should be allocated.[21] A conception of the company as a nexus of agency relationships characterizes the nature of the relationship between the nexus and each participant as contractual but tells us nothing about the allocation of influence between participants.

It is impossible to do justice to the wide variety of theoretical contributions advanced around the nexus of contract theory. Nevertheless, it is fair to observe that most theorists in this field offer an explanation why shareholders have more influence than other participants at a positive level. They also recommend that company law enhance the interests of shareholders in priority over the interests of other participants at a normative level.[22] This is not because shareholders are conceptualized as owners or economic owners of the company. Shareholders take priority at a positive level and should take priority at a normative level because they are 'residual claimants'. They receive return only after the creditors have been paid. In a winding up this is established by the order in which participants are paid. While the company is a going concern this is enforced through the distribution rules. Being last in line will incentivize shareholders to exercise their influence in a way that is good for all.

The residual claimant argument can be persuasive in its own right. We will see below that the UK version of the company cannot be characterized as contractual in

---

[18] Reinier Kraakman and others, *The Anatomy of Corporate Law* (3rd edn, OUP 2017) 29.

[19] H Hansmann and R Kraakman, 'The Essential Role of Organizational Law' (2000) 110 Yale Law Journal 387 and John Armour and MJ Whincop, 'The Proprietary Foundations of Corporate Law' (2007) 27 Oxford Journal of Legal Studies 429.

[20] Brian Cheffins, *Company Law* (OUP 1997) 134–58; Brian Cheffins, 'Corporations' in Mark Tushnet and Peter Cane (eds), *The Oxford Handbook of Legal Studies* (OUP 2005) 485, 491.

[21] See also Olivier Weinstein, 'Understanding the Roots of Shareholder Primacy: the Meaning of Agency Theory, and the Conditions for its Contagion' in Thomas Clarke and others (eds), *The Oxford Handbook of the Corporation* (OUP 2019) 139, 149 and 161.

[22] Thomas Clark and Justin O'Brien, 'The Evolving Corporation: Economy, Law and Society' in Thomas Clarke and others (eds), *The Oxford Handbook of the Corporation* (OUP 2019) 1, 4.

nature.[23] But the residual claimant argument has nevertheless informed the drafting of Companies Act 2006, section 172, which as we shall see below states that the directors are to promote the success of the company 'for the benefit of its members as a whole' and in doing so 'have regard . . . to' amongst other things employees, suppliers, customers, and others. This assumes that there is overlap between the interests of the 'shareholders as a whole' and the other interest groups and that looking after other interest groups has benefits for the shareholders. We will see, however, that it would be wrong to use the provision as evidence for an exclusive shareholder focus of company law.[24]

There are scholars who follow agency theory and characterize the company as a nexus for rational action but do not operate a shareholder-centred model. Margaret M Blair and Lynn A Stout, for example, have developed a team production theory that builds on the nexus of contract model and agency analysis, but stresses that the company is a vehicle through which teams of shareholders, creditors, managers, employees, and other stakeholders give up control over firm-specific resources to a board of directors. The board co-ordinates team activity, allocates outputs, and mediates in disputes between members. This allows for the efficient collaboration of the team members, who are rational actors. They recognize the company as a separate legal entity but do not conceive of it as an autonomous actor. The purpose of separate legal personality is to isolate assets from the reach of the members of the production team.[25]

1.2.4   Evaluation

Agency theory and the nexus of contract explanation of company law are a dominant modern framework.[26] It is right to observe that the 'intellectual impact of agency theory is hard to overstate'.[27] There are a number of reasons for this.

---

[23] Section 6.3 of this book.
[24] Sections 7.4 and 7.12 of this book.
[25] Margaret M Blair and Lynn A Stout, 'A Team Production Theory of the Corporation' (1999) 85(2) Virginia L Rev 247; Margaret M Blair and Lynn A Stout, 'Specific Investment: Explaining Anomalies in Corporate Law' (2006) 31 Journal of Corporate Law 719 at 725; most recently, Margaret M Blair, 'Corporate Law as a Solution to Team Production Problems' in Thomas Clarke and others (eds), *The Oxford Handbook of the Corporation* (OUP 2019) 197 at 201–202; and Lynn Stout, 'Corporations as Sempiternal Legal Persons' in Thomas Clarke and others (eds), *The Oxford Handbook of the Corporation* (OUP 2019); Guiseppe Dari-Mattiacci and others, 'The Emergence of the Corporate Form' (2017) 33(2) The Journal of Law, Economics and Organization 193; see also Martin Petrin, 'Reconceptualizing the Theory of the Firm—From Nature to Function' (2013) 118 Penn State L Rev 1 at 35; see also John Armour and Michael J Whincop, 'The Proprietary Foundations of Corporate Law' (2007) 27 Oxford Journal of Legal Studies 429; Ronald Daniels, 'Stakeholders and Takeovers, Can Contractarianism be Compassionate?' 43 (1993) University of Toronto Law Journal 351; see also Brian Cheffins and Richard Williams, *Team Production Theory Across the Waves*, University of Cambridge Legal Studies Research Paper Series 2/2021.
[26] Ronald J Gilson, 'From Corporate Law to Corporate Governance' in Jeffrey Gordon and Wolf-Georg Ringe (eds), *The Oxford Handbook of Corporate Law and Governance* 4 (OUP 2018); Marc Moore and Martin Petrin, *Corporate Governance: Law, Regulation and Theory* (Macmillan 2017) 45–48.
[27] Ronald J Gilson, 'From Corporate Law to Corporate Governance' in Jeffrey N Gordon and Wolf-Georg Ringe (eds), *Corporate Law and Governance* (OUP 2018) 4; see also Marc T Moore and Martin Petrin, Corporate Governance, Law, Regulation and Theory (Macmillan 2017) at 45–46.

Agency theory relies on work originating from neoclassical economics.[28] Economics is a broad church and there are contributors who are critical of the neoclassical approach and of agency theory.[29] Neoclassical analysis nevertheless currently dominates economic scholarship and economics is, in the eyes of many, the leading discipline in the social sciences.[30]

A school of thought that is associated with economics is also intuitively well suited for a functional analysis of company law. After all, the company is a vehicle for economic activity. Economic considerations can usefully inform the analysis of company law.[31] This, however, does not mean that we should limit ourselves to the insights generated by the nexus of contract model or by agency theory. It will be shown below that there exist other approaches in economics and in the wider social sciences that are better suited to explaining the law as it stands and to formulate normative recommendations.[32]

Agency theory became a dominant theory in a specific societal environment. It fit well with the political and intellectual climate that prevailed when the theory became widely accepted.[33] Once a theoretical framework has taken hold it tends to be persistent.[34] As a society, we continue to believe in a market-based economy, but we have adopted a more critical attitude towards the laissez faire approach that was prevalent at that time.[35] When the nexus of contract and agency theory started to take hold, the assumption was that the maximization of value from the perspective of each of the participants will, through the invisible hand of the market, also enhance social welfare. We are now more sceptical about the ability of the market to deliver sustainable and resilient economic activity for the benefit of wider society. A theory which assumes efficient markets has therefore lost some of its appeal. It is time to consider a new paradigm for the analysis of corporate law.

---

[28] Brian Cheffins, 'Corporations' in Mark Tushnet and Peter Cane (eds), *The Oxford Handbook of Legal Studies* (OUP 2005) 485, 491, 493–94.

[29] See eg William Lazonick, *Business Organization and the Myth of the Market Economy* (CUP 1992); P Collier, *The Future of Capitalism* (Penguin 2018); see also cited in W Richard Scott, *Institutions and Organizations* (4th edn, Sage 2014) 33 as Geoffrey M Hodgson, 'The Return of Institutional Economics' in Neil J Smelser and Richard Swedberg (eds), *The Handbook of Economic Sociology* (Princeton University Press 1994) p 70 who write that the transaction cost-based theory of the firm has been criticized as being constructed in 'atomistic individualistic terms'. Its building block is the given 'opportunistic' individual. Proponents of the theory do not consider the possibility that the preferences of an individual may be shaped by the structure and culture of the firm or that this phenomenon may be significant in analysing and understanding firms.

[30] Marion Fourcade, Etienne Ollion, and Yann Algan, 'The Superiority of Economists' (2015) 29(1) Journal of Economic Perspectives 89.

[31] Stephen Copp, 'Company Law Reform and Economic Analysis: Establishing Boundaries' (2000) 1 Journal of Corporate Law Studies 1.

[32] Section 1.4.3 in this chapter.

[33] Brian Cheffins, 'Corporations' in Mark Tushnet and Peter Cane (eds), *The Oxford Handbook of Legal Studies* (OUP 2005) 485, 494; for the social and political benefits a shareholder-centred analysis can have see generally Jonathan Macey, 'The Central Role of Myth in Corporate Law' (ECGI Working Paper 519/2020).

[34] Brian R Cheffins, 'The Trajectory of (Corporate Law) Scholarship' (2004) 63 CLJ 456.

[35] Annie Pye, 'Boards and Governance: 25 Years of Qualitative Research with Directors of FTSE Companies' in Mike Wright and others (eds), *The Oxford Handbook of Corporate Governance* (OUP 2013) at 135 provides a succinct summary of the regulatory and theoretical changes that have occurred in relation to corporate governance since the mid 1980s; see also John Armour and Jeffrey N Gordon, 'Systemic Harms and Shareholder Value' (2014) 6 The Journal of Legal Analysis <https://papers.ssrn.com/sol3/papers.cfm?abstract_id=2307959#>.

Agency theory and the nexus of contract model have been praised for their 'intellectual elegance'.[36] This elegance is achieved by their simplicity. The theory invites proponents to identify two participants. It identifies the problems that arise between them. It then filters the legal rules that address this particular binary conflict and develops a view on their efficiency. This is useful. Conflicts of interest and incentives are important. They affect organizational decision-making. It is important to be aware of how incentives affect behaviour. Agency theory is an excellent tool to develop a granular understanding of situations in which a conflict of interest arises. It would be wrong to outright dismiss the contributions made by agency scholarship.

While agency theory allows us to define an important problem company law needs to solve, it does not provide guidance for a granular analysis of the law at a positive level. The residual claimant argument, for example, is elegant. It explains why at a positive level shareholders have more influence than other participants without having to (inaccurately) characterize them as 'owners'.

The residual claimant argument is also right at the highest level of abstraction. Ultimately the shareholders benefit from the surplus generated by the company. Shareholders receive that surplus in the form of dividends or increases in the share price. Dividends can only be paid if there is a distributable profit and the profit distribution rules ensure that there are sufficient assets in the company to meet creditor claims.[37] So at this level of analysis it is right to observe that the shareholders' welfare depends on the surplus generated by the company under the direction of the board.

It is also right to observe at a positive level that the current law gives shareholders the vast majority of governance rights in the company. But the residual claimant argument does not do more than explain that shareholders have comparatively more corporate rights than other participants. The argument can be used to explain the British, German, American, and any other country's model of the company. In all jurisdictions this author knows of shareholders have more rights than other participants. The level of shareholder influence differs nevertheless significantly in these different jurisdictions. The residual claimant argument cannot explain these differences. The residual claimant argument only explains or recommends that shareholders have or should have more rights than others. It does not help with understanding or determining the degree of influence that shareholders have or should have.

Agency theory is also sometimes right at a very granular level. Companies Act 2006, section 168 allows the shareholders to remove directors by a simple majority without reason. Analysed in isolation the rule supports the conclusion that directors are to favour shareholders in their decision-making. But it would be wrong to conclude on this

---

[36] Brian Cheffins, 'Corporations' in Mark Tushnet and Peter Cane (eds), *The Oxford Handbook of Legal Studies* (OUP 2005) 485.
[37] We will see below that this argument holds irrespective of which test is applied to determine the amount for distributable profit.

basis that company law serves the interests of shareholders only. Shareholders may have been the primary focus of company law when companies were incorporated through deeds of settlement and for some time after incorporation with limited liability became freely available.[38] But the statutory interventions that have followed since then, alongside with the evolving common law, have turned company law into a framework that cannot be characterized as displaying an exclusive shareholder focus. Shareholders have more rights than other constituencies and ultimately receive the profit generated by the company. The role of shareholders is, however, substantially limited by statute and by the common law. These limitations integrate the interests of other constituencies and so cannot be overridden by the articles.

Agency theory tempts its users to overstate the influence of shareholders.[39] This overstatement is the consequence of agency theory rather than of the law. The requirement to identify bilaterally opposing actors steers us towards filtering out rules that relate to the two respective participants. To explore the agency conflict between shareholders and directors we select the rules that affect the relationship between them and conclude that the shareholders have significant powers over the directors. If we stop the analysis at this point we overlook that directors owe a wide range of duties. Some of them concern shareholders. Others require directors to take actions that enhance the interests of creditors.[40] Directors need to observe both. A failure to comply with creditor-oriented duties can lead to disqualification and trigger criminal liability. We also overlook that shareholders are subject to constraints established at common law and in the Companies Act which further the interests of creditors.[41] It would therefore be wrong to conclude that directors are to run the company with a view to maximizing the wealth of shareholders. This has no basis in the Companies Act or in the case law.[42] Company law does not require the maximization of the wealth of any one participant.[43] It is also not oriented exclusively towards the interests of shareholders.[44]

It will be shown in this book that the law is not built around binary conflicts. It addresses the interests of various constituencies, at the same time establishing procedures through which these interests are considered and weighed against each other. Company law consists of rules that integrate the interests of various constituencies. Shareholders have more influence than others but they are not the exclusive focus of company law.[45]

---

[38] Limited Liability Act 1855 (18 & 19 Vict c 133).

[39] See also Jonathan R Macey, 'The Central Role of Myth in Corporate Law' (ECGI Law Working Paper No 519/2020) 22–32, available from <https://ecgi.global/working-paper/central-role-myth-corporate-law?mc_cid=c2b21cd551&mc_eid=4d7098df5d>; Lynn Stout and others, 'The Modern Corporation Statement on Company Law' (6 October 2016) available from <https://papers.ssrn.com/sol3/papers.cfm?abstract_id=2848833>; Simon Deakin, 'The Coming Transformation of Shareholder Value' (2005) 13(1) Corporate Governance 11.

[40] Chapter 7 in this book.

[41] Chapter 8 in this book.

[42] Chapters 8 and 7 in this book.

[43] Section 7.4 in this book.

[44] Chapter 8 in this book.

[45] Chapter 8 in this book.

Agency theory understates the importance of separate legal personality.[46] This is not a minor defect. Lord Sumption, for example, observed in *Prest v Petrodel*, 'The separate personality and property of a company is sometimes described as a fiction, and in a sense it is. But the fiction is the whole foundation of English company and insolvency law.'[47] An approach that ignores separate legal personality is not only legally inaccurate but also has been criticized as flying 'in the face of a blizzard of perspectives from other disciplines [in the wider social sciences] . . . which reveal and explain the social reality of firms'.[48]

In addition to legal personality there are a substantial number of other mandatory rules that agency theory has been shown unable to explain.[49] In particular, agency theorists advance the argument that mandatory law can be explained as market mimicking. This assumes that the legislature and the courts adopt rules with a view to imitating what parties would have wanted. They adopt rules that parties would have adopted in efficiently functioning markets.[50] Marc Moore has rightly pointed out that mandatory law by its nature is designed to replace an outcome that parties would have achieved if they had been allowed to bargain. In reality the legislature replaces market-based outcomes with outcomes that suit a particular economic or social regulatory preference.[51]

The simplicity of the nexus of contract and of the agency model not only prevents us from appreciating the nuances of the law at a positive level.[52] The theory is also unable to deliver granular guidance for the normative development of specific legal rules.[53]

Moreover, many of the factual assumptions made by the nexus of contract and the agency model have not held up in empirical testing. A recent survey of the literature

---

[46] David Gindis, 'Legal Personhood and the Firm: Avoiding Anthromorphism and Equivocation' (2015) Journal of Institutional Economics 1, 3–5; Eric W Orts, *Business Persons: A Legal Theory of the Firm* (OUP 2013) 66–67; Sarah Worthington, 'Shares and Shareholders: Property, Power and Entitlement: Part I' (2001) 22 Company Lawyer 258; Susan Watson, 'The Corporate Legal Person' (2019) 19 Journal of Corporate Law 137, 138; see also CW Maugham and Kevin McGuiness, 'Towards an Economic Theory of the Corporation' (2001) Journal of Corporate Law Studies 141.

[47] *Bank of Tokyo Ltd v Karoon* (Note) [1987] AC 45, 64.

[48] Eric W Orts, *Business Persons, A Legal Theory of the Firm* (OUP 2013) at 27.

[49] See most recently Marc T Moore, 'Private Ordering and Public Policy: The Paradoxical Foundations of Corporate Contractarianism' (2014) 34(4) Oxford Journal of Legal Studies 693; see also Simon Deakin, 'The Corporation as Commons: 'Rethinking Property Rights, Governance and Sustainability in the Business Enterprise' (2012) 37(2) Queen's Law Journal 367; David Gibbs-Kneller, David Gindis, and Derek Whayman, 'Not by Contract Alone: The Contractarian Theory of the Corporation and the Paradox of Implied Terms' [2021] EBOR (forthcoming); Grant M Hayden and Matthew T Bodie, 'The Uncorporation and the Unraveling of the "Nexus of Contract Theory"' (2010–2011) 109 Mich L Rev 1127 at 1135; Michael Klausner, 'The "Corporate Contract" today' in Jeffrey N Gordon and others (eds), *The Oxford Handbook of Corporate Law and Governance* (OUP 2018) 84; see also William M Bratton, 'The "Nexus of Contract" Corporation: A Critical Appraisal' (1989) 74 Cornell L Rev 407 and D M Daily, CR Dalton, and AA Canella, 'Corporate Governance: Decades of Dialogue and Data' (2003) 28(3) Academy of Management Review 371.

[50] Brian Cheffins, *Company Law* (OUP 1997) 227–49 and 264–307.

[51] Marc Moore, 'Private Ordering and Public Policy: The Paradoxical Foundations of Corporate Contracterianism' (2014) 34 Oxford Journal of Legal Studies 693, 711–14; Marc Moore, *Corporate Governance in the Shadow of the State* (Hart 2013) 227.

[52] See also Eric W Orts, *Business Persons: A Legal Theory of the Firm* (OUP 2013) 14.

[53] Stephen Copp, 'Company Law Reform and Economic Analysis: Establishing Boundaries' (2001) 1 Journal of Corporate Law Studies 1; Iain MacNeil, 'Company Law Rules: An Assessment from the Perspective of Incomplete Contract Theory' (2001) 1 Journal of Corporate Law Studies 107.

concluded that empirical scholars have 'left little if anything of the theory standing'.[54] For example, the assumption that stock market forces provide accountability for directors has been undermined by the empirical finding that share prices reflect a much broader range of information than the economic prospects of the company.[55]

The normative approach adopted by agency theory has been held responsible for causing harm. A recent project hosted by the British Academy and led by Colin Mayer concluded that the misconception and preoccupation with the shareholders as the one single party to the firm has been the cause of mounting environmental concerns, social tensions, and political backlash.[56] It has also been observed that a focus on firm performance can inspire illegal conduct.[57]

The theory's recommendation to use performance-related remuneration as a method of oversight by the shareholders has not withstood the test of time. Performance-related pay was originally characterized as a cure to an agency problem. The idea was that an alignment of executive pay with shareholder return can cause the board to advance the interests of the shareholders.[58] Now we understand executive pay as an example of an agency problem rather than a cure. The modern literature focuses on designing governance mechanisms that ensure that executive remuneration does not encourage excessive risk-taking.[59] It has yet to be shown that it is possible to design performance targets that steer directors towards long-term sustainable behaviours.[60]

The nexus of contract and agency theories help to better understand conflicts of interest, but narrow the analysis. They do not do justice to the framework as a whole. They assume an incomplete model of human action.[61] They conceive human beings as rational actors maximizing economic return. This approach does not help to analyse corporate problems that arise out of emotional, socially, culturally, and historically

---

[54] Michael Klausner, 'Fact and Fiction in Corporate Law and Governance' (2013) 65 Stanford L Rev 1325 at 1331; see also Catherine M Daily, Dan R Dalton, and Albert A Canella, 'Corporate Governance: Decades of Dialogue and Data' (2003) 28 The Academy of Management Review 371, 374–75.

[55] Andrei Shleifer and Lawrence H. Summers, 'The Noise Trader Approach to Finance' (1990) 4(2) Journal of Economic Perspectives 19; Robert J Shiller, 'From Efficient Markets Theory to Behavioral Finance' (2003) 17(1) Journal of Economic Perspectives; Ronald J Gilson and Reinier Kraakman, 'The Mechanisms of Market Efficiency Twenty Years Later: The Hindsight Bias' (2003) 28 Journal of Corporation Law 715.

[56] Colin Mayer et al, 'Reforming Business for the 21st Century, A Framework for the Future of the Corporation, The British Academy, Future of the Corporation' (November 2018) 14–15 <https://www.thebritishacademy.ac.uk/sites/default/files/Reforming-Business-for-21st-Century-British-Academy.pdf>; see also William Lazonick and others, 'The Modern Corporation Statement on Economics' (November 4, 2016), available at SSRN: <https://ssrn.com/abstract=2864246 or http://dx.doi.org/10.2139/ssrn.2864246>.

[57] Yuri Mishina and others, 'Why "Good" Firms Do Bad Things: The Effects of High Aspirations, High Expectations, and Prominence on the Incidence of Corporate Illegality' (2010) 53 Academy of Management Journal 701.

[58] In the 1980s performance related rewards came to be perceived to be a key ingredient of effective management (Noel M Tichy, 'Managing Change Strategically: The Technical, Political and Cultural Keys' (1982) 11(2) Organizational Dynamics 59, 65); see also Section 7.9 in this book.

[59] For an excellent overview see Guido Ferrarini and Maria Christina Ungureaunu, 'Executive Remuneration' in Jeffrey Gordon and Wolf-Georg Ringe (eds), The Oxford Handbook of Corporate Law and Governance (OUP 2018) at 334; see also Emilios Avgouleas, Governance of Global Financial Markets: The Law, the Economics, the Politics (CUP 2012) 125–26 and 289–94.

[60] See Section 7.9 in this book.

[61] Eric W Orts, Business Persons: A Legal Theory of the Firm (OUP 2013) 13–16.

determined human action.[62] It does not help us understand problems that arise at an organizational level. Sometimes organizations have problems because their procedures are outdated or their culture is toxic. Agency theory and the nexus of contract model cannot help with either analysing these or making recommendations for improving them. It has been rightly observed that while 'a narrow conception is easier to mathematize . . . if the guts of the causal process of institutional influence are left out of the model, then we successfully mathematize abstract empiricism, an empiricism without the complexity of real life.'[63]

1.3 Concession theory

1.3.1 Introduction

Concession theory puts the state in the driving seat. It posits that companies are creatures of the law. They exist because and only so far as the legislature gives them life. Historically, this is sometimes said to explain the way organizations were created in the Middle Ages in the form of guilds and administrative units such as the City of London Corporation which acts under the name 'Mayor and Communality and Citizens of the City of London'.[64] Other surviving examples include the Inns of Court and university colleges. At the time, society was organized hierarchically from the top downwards. The Crown awarded the privilege to carry out certain activity in a relatively self-governing manner.[65] This was done for a particular purpose, with the intention to endow that purpose with an existence independent of and a lifespan beyond its constituent members.[66]

From the seventeenth century onwards companies were also used to support the aims of mercantilism.[67] Britain began to acquire an empire and companies were used to assist

---

[62] Jean-François Chanlat, 'Corporations, Organization, and Human Action: An Anthropological Critique of Agency Theory' in Thomas Clarke and others (eds), *The Oxford Handbook of Corporations* (OUP 2019) 387, 393–406.

[63] Arthur L Stinchcombe, 'On the Virtues of Old Institutionalism' (1997) 23 Annual Reviews 1, 6; see also Mary Stokes, 'Company Law and Legal Theory' in W Twining (ed), *Legal Theory and Common Law* (Blackwell 1986) 155, 164 who observes that the idea of a nexus of contract is artificial in the case of large companies with dispersed shareholders. In such companies shareholders are hardly involved. Any notion that the internal division of power within a company is the result of a consensual arrangement between shareholders seems purely fictional.

[64] <www.cityoflondon.gov.uk/footer/legal-notices>.

[65] Paul Davies, Gower's Principles of Modern Company Law (6th edn, Sweet & Maxwell 1997) 18–19; JE Parkinson, *Corporate Power and Responsibility* (Clarendon Press 1993) 25–30; but see Antony Black (*Guild and State* (Routledge 2017)) who argues that guilds, towns, and universities petitioned to the Crown for corporate status. This suggests that they had existence prior to being granted a charter, which in turn supports a real entity approach (I am grateful to David Gindis for alerting me to this contribution).

[66] Leonardo Dvoudi, Christopher McKenna, and Rowena Olegario, 'The Historical Role of the Corporation in Society' (2018) 6(1) Journal of the British Academy 17. The connection between limited liability and public policy preferences for certain investments has also emerged in the modern discussion on stewardship and socially responsible investment (see eg Law Commission, Pension Funds and Social Investment, LawComNo 374 (2017)). Legal personality is also used to protect objects of natural and cultural significance such as the Whanganui River in New Zealand (<www.nationalgeographic.com/culture/2019/04/maori-river-in-new-zealand-is-a-legal-person/>, last visited 2 October 2020) or the Ganges River in India (<www.theguardian.com/world/2017/mar/21/ganges-and-yamuna-rivers-granted-same-legal-rights-as-human-beings>), last visited 2 October 2020.

[67] See also Leonardo Dvoudi, Christopher McKenna, and Rowena Olegario, 'The historical role of the corporation in society' (2018) 6(1) Journal of the British Academy 17.

in its administration. Companies were created by Royal Charter or by a Private Act of Parliament. Their names were derived from geographical regions: the Hudson Bay, East India, the South Sea. The Hudson Bay Company, for example, was incorporated 1670 with the name 'The Governor and Company of Adventurers of England trading into the Hudson's Bay'.[68] Its original purpose was to facilitate trade in the Hudson Bay. This included the collection of tax as well as judicial functions. It also included, however, the monopoly of carrying out certain economic activity in the area. Like the members of medieval guilds the members of the company originally traded on separate accounts.[69] Historically, the concession system subjected incorporation to ad hoc individual approval by a constitutionally appointed state body.

Over time companies emerged that traded on joint stock.[70] At that point the modern idea of a joint stock company was born. It was used until the South Sea Bubble Act to collect funds for a common purpose. Incorporation occurred on an ad hoc basis for certain approved purposes.

Between 1720 and 1844 the South Sea Bubble Act made incorporation very difficult.[71] It was next to impossible to obtain charters during that time. In the UK this led to the emergence of deed of settlement companies.[72] It has already been mentioned that these companies were established and operated on the basis of contract and trust law.[73]

1.3.2 Modern concession theory

Since the Companies Act of 1844 it has been possible to incorporate companies in the UK by registration rather than by individual concession. Since 1855 incorporation with limited liability has been available by registration.

There, nevertheless, exists a modern version of the concession theory. The theory advocates an understanding of the company solely on the basis of statutory provisions and case law.[74] Although not all proponents link their contributions to legal theory it is possible to establish a connection between concession theory and legal positivism, which posits that law is to be understood on its own terms rather than by reference to factors

---

[68] William Schooling, *The Governor and Company of Adventurers of England Trading Into Hudson's Bay During Two Hundred and Fifty Years, 1670–1920* (Hudson's Bay Company 1920); for an account of how this model can go wrong see William Dalrymple, *The Anarchy, The Relentless Rise of the East India Company* (Bloomsbury 2019).

[69] Paul Davies, *Gower's Principles of Modern Company Law* (6th edn, Sweet & Maxwell 1997) 20.

[70] Leonardo Dvoudi, Christopher McKenna, and Rowena Olegario, 'The Historical Role of the Corporation in Society' (2018) 6(1) Journal of the British Academy 17, 30; Giuseppe Dari-Mattiacci, Oscar Gelderblom, Joost Jonker, and Enrico C Perotti, 'The Emergence of the Corporate Form' (2017) 33(2) Journal of Law, Economics and Organizations 193.

[71] The South Sea Bubble Act 1720, 6 Geo I, c 18.

[72] Nathaniel Lindley and Samuel Dickinson, *A Treatise on the Law of Partnership Including its Application to Companies* (4th edn, Westminster Hall 1878) 7.

[73] Section 1.2.1 in this chapter.

[74] See also Katsuhito Iwai, 'Persons, Things and Corporations: The Corporate Personality Controversy and Comparative Corporate Governance' (1997) 47 American Journal of Corporation Law 583, 603.

such as efficiency or morality.[75] We will see in the next section that UK judges are most comfortable with this approach to company law.

Case law

Salomon v Salomon is an example of judges focusing on the meaning of the words used in the Companies Act and resisting the temptation to define the nature of companies outside the explicit legal requirements. They read the statute and interpret what they find. Lord Halsbury wrote in *Salomon v Salomon*, 'I am simply here dealing with the provisions of the statute, and it seems to me to be essential to the artificial creation that the law should recognize only this artificial existence'.[76] Lord Herschell said:

> I know of no means of ascertaining what is the intent and meaning of the Companies Act except by examining its provisions and finding what regulations it has imposed as a condition of trading with limited liability. . . The Legislature . . . clearly sanctions a scheme by which all the shares except six are owned by a single individual, and these six are of a value little more than nominal'.[77] . . .The statute . . . certainly contains no enactment that each of the seven persons subscribing the memorandum must be beneficially entitled to the share or shares for which he subscribes'.[78]

He conceded that a company constituted like Salomon Ltd may not have been 'in the contemplation of the Legislature at the time when the Act authorizing limited liability was passed'.[79] But he then continued, 'we have to interpret the law, not to make it.'[80]

Another example can be found in Lord Hoffman's speech in *Meridian Global Funds Management Asia Ltd v Securities Commission*,[81] where he wrote:

> It is worth pausing at this stage to make what may seem an obvious point. Any statement about what a company has or has not done, or can or cannot do, is necessarily a reference to the rules of attribution (primary and general) as they apply to that company. Judges sometimes say that a company 'as such' cannot do anything; it must act by servants or agents. This may seem an unexceptionable, even banal remark. And of course the meaning is usually perfectly clear. But a reference to a company 'as such' might suggest that there is something out there called the company of which one can meaningfully say that it can or cannot do something. *There is in fact no such thing as the company as such, no ding an sich, only the applicable rules.* To say that a company cannot do something means only that there is no one whose doing of that act would, under the applicable rules of attribution, count as an act of the company.[82]

---

[75] HLA Hart, *The Concept of Law* (3rd edn, OUP 2012).
[76] *Salomon v Salomon* [1896] AC 22, 30.
[77] ibid 45.
[78] ibid 45–46.
[79] ibid 46.
[80] ibid 46.
[81] *Meridian Global Funds Management Asia Ltd v Securities Commission* [1995] 2 AC 500 (PC), 506–07.
[82] Author's italics.

Lord Neuberger endorsed this observation in *Bilta v Nazir* when he wrote that 'the company is an artificial construct and can only act through natural persons. It has no actual mind, despite the law's persistent anthropomorphism—as to which see the references by Lord Hoffmann . . . to the absence of any "ding an sich" '.

Judges are not impressed by economy theory. In *Prest v Petrodel* Lord Sumption endorsed a dictum by Robert Goff LJ who observed that in this domain 'we are concerned not with economics but with law. The distinction between the two is, in law, fundamental'.[83] Lord Sumption continued:

> He could justly have added that it is not just legally but economically fundamental, since limited companies have been the principal unit of commercial life for more than a century. Their separate personality and property are the basis on which third parties are entitled to deal with them and commonly do deal with them.[84]

In addition to limiting their analysis to the law as they find it, the judges have also endorsed the idea that incorporation is a privilege granted by the legislature on certain terms. Lord Chelmsford, for example, pointed out in *Ashbury Railway v Riche* that the company is 'entirely a creation of the statute'.[85] It is necessary for the protection of those who enter into contracts with them that the 'privilege' of creating them should only be obtained upon certain conditions which should be made known to the public.[86]

A concession-style argument can also be found in more recent cases law. David Richards LJ rejected the proposition that limited liability is a privilege as 'mistaken' but went on to observe that limited liability 'is a right conferred by statute in unqualified terms, and it is a right that Parliament created over 170 years ago in the public interest and for the purpose of advancing the economic well-being of the country'.[87] While characterizing limited liability as a right rather than a privilege, the statement nevertheless endorses the idea that Parliament grants that right to incorporate a company in the public interest for certain policy objectives.

Academic contributions

Concession theory also has modern academic followers. Susan Watson characterizes the modern company as a creature of the state with corporate personality derived from the state through the process of incorporation.[88] Marc Moore stresses that companies are the product of public rather than private acting. They operate on the basis of a social licence to exercise power. Company law needs to be justified by public policy such as a

---

[83] *Bank of Tokyo Ltd v Karoon* (Note) [1987] AC 45, 64.

[84] *Prest v Petrodel* [2012] EWCA Civ 1395, [2013] UKSC 34, [2013] 2 AC 415, [476].

[85] *Ashbury Railway v Riche* (1874–75) LR 7 HL 653, 678; see also Lord Crains (670): 'the ambit and extent of vitality and power which by law are given to the corporation', Lord O'Hagan (690): The 'Act gave certain privileges and imposed certain conditions' and Lord Selborne (693): 'a statutory corporation, created by Act of Parliament for a particular purposed'.

[86] ibid 678; see also 684 (Lord Hatherely), 667 (Lord Chancellor Crains), 677–79 (Lord Chelmsford), 684 and 687 (Lord Hatherley), 690–92 (Lord O'Hagan), and 693–94 (Lord Selborn).

[87] *BTI 2014 LLC v Sequana SA* [2019] EWCA Civ 112, [2019] 1 BCLC 347, [151] (David Richards LJ).

[88] Susan Watson, 'The Corporate Legal Person' (2019) 19(1) Journal of Corporate Law Studies 137.

desire to balance 'economic-organizational power disparities' or to achieve 'manifestly public regarding objectives' (the public good), for example 'to ensure the legitimacy of corporate power' through accountability.[89] Corporate governance is 'ultimately an artificial and regulatorily founded phenomenon (albeit with a significant endogenous evolutionary dynamic)'.[90] Martin Petrin writes that a legal entity should be viewed simply as a tool by which the legislature has chosen to enable individuals to pursue certain goals in a more effective and convenient manner.[91] These are concession-style arguments. The state grants the corporate form and is entitled to set its terms reflecting the government's policy choices. The authors, however, do not endorse legal positivism.[92]

HLA Hart uses legal positivism to argue that theory obstructs the understanding of the law.[93] He writes that the question 'what is a corporation?' does not help with but rather confuses the proper analysis of legal rules. The better question is to ask, 'Under what types of conditions does the law ascribe liabilities to corporations?' In answering that question judges are steered towards determining if rules that were written for natural persons apply to corporations by analogy. This rephrasing of the question also reveals that if an analogy is accepted there will follow a 'shift' in 'meaning' which is necessary to adapt the rule concerned to the law underlying corporations.[94] This analysis can be connected to concession theory. The state makes available company law, which is to be understood on the terms set by the state.

Concession-style arguments can also be found in the non-legal literature. Eric Orts writes for an audience of law and economics scholars that a greater focus on the statute and case law that governs firms would assist a better understanding of the firm.[95] Grant Hayden and Matthew Bodie characterize the corporation as 'governmentally created organizational body that imposes specific constraints on participants'.[96] Neither of them connect the concession point with legal positivism.

From the perspective of concession theory company law serves the priorities of the government. It is the product of policy decisions made through the parliamentary process.

---

[89] Marc T Moore, *Corporate Governance in the Shadow of the State* (Hart Publishing 2013) 280–81; Marc T Moore, 'Private Ordering and Public Policy: The Paradoxical Foundations of Corporate Contracterianism' (2014) 34(4) Oxford Journal of Legal Studies 693.

[90] Marc T Moore, *Corporate Governance in the Shadow of the State* (Hart Publishing 2013) 280; Marc T Moore, 'Private Ordering and Public Policy: The Paradoxical Foundations of Corporate Contractarianism' (2014) 34(4) Oxford Journal of Legal Studies 693.

[91] Martin Petrin, 'Reconceptualizing the Theory of the Firm—From Nature to Function' 118 (2013) Penn State L Rev 1, 43

[92] Martin Petrin adopts a legal realist model when he recommends that the question of which rights and duties a firm has should be determined by reference to the underlying economic and social problems that the law is trying to solve ('Reconceptualizing the Theory of the Firm—From Nature to Function' 118 (2013) Penn State L Rev 1, 43, 48–49).

[93] HLA Hart, 'Definition and Theory in Jurisprudence' in HLA Hart, Essays in Jurisprudence and Philosophy (OUP 2012), 21 at 43–47; see also Martin Petrin, 'Reconceptualizing the Theory of the Firm—From Nature to Function' (2013) 118 Penn State L Rev 1 at 32.

[94] Martin Petrin, 'Reconceptualizing the Theory of the Firm—From Nature to Function' (2013) 118 Penn State L Rev 1 at 46.

[95] See eg Eric W Orts, *Business Persons: The Legal Nature of the Firm* (OUP 2013).

[96] Grant M Hayden and Matthew T Bodie, 'The Uncorporation and the Unraveling of the "Nexus of Contract Theory"' (2010–2011) 109 Mich L Rev 1127, 1141.

There are no normative recommendations on which interest group should be central focus of company law.

The theory can nevertheless operate as a springboard for scholars advocating greater involvement of stakeholders. It can be used to support an argument in favour of mandatory rules of corporate social responsibility.[97] The argument is that if the state makes available the possibility of incorporation it is entitled to ask for something in return.

Evaluation

Given that judges limit their analysis to the law as they see it and show no interest in incorporating theory, are we better off with legal positivism? Is it worth our while to engage in a theoretical debate?

It will be argued in this book that theoretical analysis is useful. An understanding of the phenomenon that legal rules grapple with illuminates the rules that the legislature has put in place and that in turn may help our understanding of these rules at a positive level. Theory can also help to make recommendations for improvements to the existing framework.

Moreover, legal positivism sometimes struggles to accommodate borderline phenomena. One classic example of such phenomena are one-person companies. Most recently this difficulty has been illustrated by the Supreme Court decision in *Stone & Rolls v Moore Stephens*.[98] It was held in that case that Stone & Rolls Ltd could not claim from its auditors who had negligently overlooked the fraud committed by the company's sole shareholder and director. The House of Lords held that the company was unable to claim as it was itself responsible for the fraud. It could not base a claim on its own wrongdoing. The case arguably overlooks the company's separate legal personality.[99] The company is independent of all of its participants.[100] Even if the company has only one shareholder, who is its only director, it is still an independent subject of the law and can be victim of a deceit by that shareholder director.

The common law, of course, sets itself right and swiftly too. Only six years after *Stone & Rolls* was decided, Lord Neuberger suggested in *Bilta v Nazir* that it should be put 'on one side', 'not to be looked at again'.[101] A few years after the decision in *Bilta* Lady Hale agreed with the first instance judge in *Singularis Holdings v Daiwa* that there is 'no principle of law that in any proceedings where the company is suing a third party for breach of duty owed to it by that third party, the fraudulent conduct of a director is to be attributed to the company if it is a one-man company'. The answer to any question 'whether

---

[97] Stefan J Padfield, 'Corporate Social Responsibility and Concession Theory' (2015) 6 Wm. & Mary Bus L Rev 1.

[98] *Stone & Rolls v Moore Stephens* [2009] UKHL 39, [2009] 1 AC 1391.

[99] Sarah Worthington, 'Corporate Attribution and Agency: Back to Basics' [2017] LQR 118 at 122; see also *Singularis Holdings Ltd v Daiwa Capital Markets Europe Ltd* [2019] UKSC 50, [2019] 3 WLR 997, [27], [31] and [34].

[100] *Singularis Holdings Ltd v Daiwa Capital Markets Europe Ltd* [2019] UKSC 50, [2019] 3 WLR 997, [27].

[101] *Bilta v Nazir* [2015] UKSC 23, [2016] 1 AC 1, [30].

to attribute the knowledge of a fraudulent director to the company is always to be found in consideration of the context and purpose for which the attribution is relevant'. Lady Hale agreed with this guiding principle and concluded that 'Stone & Rolls can finally be laid to rest'.[102]

Stone & Rolls nevertheless serves as an example that an understanding of the real-life phenomena the law is designed to solve can help to apply the rules. The separate legal personality of the company is not just a legal formality. It is necessary to permit company law to operate as a framework for the operation of an organization. Company law serves primarily shareholders but also creditors. A company can thus suffer harm through the actions of its sole shareholder director. It can also claim against a bank which carried out fraudulent instructions by the director in breach of the duty of care it owed to the company.[103]

1.4 Real entity theory

1.4.1 Introduction

The proposition that the company is a real entity is sometimes attributed to the writings of the German jurist Otto von Gierke and the social theorist Walter von Rathenau.[104] Otto von Gierke characterized the company as a 'living organism' and 'a real person, with body and members and a will of its own'.[105] Walter von Rathenau's work inspired the term of the 'enterprise as such' ('Unternehmen an sich').[106] Another eminent proponent of real entity theory is Frederic Maitland.[107]

---

[102] *Singularis Holdings Ltd v Daiwa Capital Markets Europe Ltd* [2019] UKSC 50, [2019] 3 WLR 997, [34]; *Hamblin v World First Ltd* [2020] EWHC 2383 (Comm), [2020] 6 WLUK 314.

[103] *Singularis Holdings Ltd v Daiwa Capital Markets Europe Ltd* [2019] UKSC 50, [2019] 3 WLR 997.

[104] Ron Harris, 'The Transplantation of the Legal Discourse on Corporate Personality Theories: From German Codification to British Political Pluralism and American Big Business' (2006) 63(4) Washington and Lee L Rev 1421, 1427, who traces the theory's earlier origins; see generally Joshua Getzler, 'Law, History and the Social Sciences: Intellectual Traditions of Late Nineteenth- and Early Twentieth-Century Europe' in Andrew Lewis and Michael Lobban (eds), *Law and History: Current Legal Issues, Volume 6* (OUP 2004) 215.

[105] FW Maitland, Introduction to Otto Gierke, (trans FW Maitland) *Political Theory of the Middle Age* (CUP 1900, reprinted Thoemmes Press in 1996) xxvi; Joshua S Getzler, 'Frederic William Maitland—Trust and Corporation' (2016) 35 University of Queensland Law Journal 171.

[106] Martin Gelter, 'Taming or Protecting the Modern Corporation? Shareholder-Stakeholder Debates in a Comparative Light' (2010–2011) 7 NYU JL&Bus 641 at 678–94; Stephan Leixnering, Renate E Meyer, and Peter Doralt, 'The Past as Prologue: Purpose Dynamics in the History of the Aktiengesellschaft' in Renate E Meyer, Stephan Leixnering, and Jeroen Veldman, *The Corporation: Rethinking the Iconic Form of Business Organization*, Research in the Sociology of Organizations volume 78 (Emerald Publishing Limited 2022) (forthcoming) ; see also Ewan McGaughey, 'The Co-determination Bargains: The History of German Corporate and Labor Law' (2016–17) 23(1) Columbia Journal of European law 135 at 138–45; Walter Rathenau, *Vom Aktienwesen; Eine geschaeftliche Betrachtung* (Fischer Verlag Berlin 1917); Walter Rathenau, *Von den kommenden Dingen* (Fischer Verlag Berlin 1918).

[107] FW Maitland and Otto Gierke, *Political Theory of the Middle Age* (CUP 1900, reprinted in 1996, Thoemmes Press); see also Frederick Hallis, *Corporate Personality A Study in Jurisprudence* (OUP 1930); see also Adolf Berle, 'The Theory of Enterprise Entity' (1947) 47 Columbia L Rev 343. Rathenau's work is cited in the seminal book Adolf Berle and Gardiner Means, *The Modern Corporation and Private Property* (Legal Classics Library 1993) at 352 (see Martin Gelter, 'Taming or Protecting the Modern Corporation? Shareholder-Stakeholder Debates in a Comparative Light' (2010–2011) 7 NYU JL&Bus 641, 644); see also Ernst Freund, *The Legal Nature of Corporations* (University of Chicago Press 1897).

In the very early days of company law the argument that the company is 'real' could have helped to justify a request to the legislature to make incorporation available freely rather than by concession. If companies really exist the legislature's role is to recognize this and to supply corporate personality.[108] In the early twentieth century real entity theory was arguably the preferred approach.[109] It appears to have been used in the United States to argue against state regulation of the corporation.[110] It also helped to support the proposition that companies rather than (or in addition to) their shareholders or directors are liable for crimes and enjoy human rights.[111]

1.4.2 Shareholders versus stakeholders

Real entity theory has a connection with scholars who propose an increase of influence on corporate decisions making for stakeholders. Marc Moore and Martin Petrin, for example, argue that entity theory cannot explain that shareholders have greater influence than other stakeholders.[112] They write that giving the firm autonomous status 'dictates' that a holder of organizational power should not be free to exercise it in their own interest, but rather '*in the interest of those affected by it*'.[113]

Along similar lines, Simon Deakin conceives companies as 'commons'.[114] A commons is a 'common-pool resource', which is collectively held and managed for the benefit of multiple interests. Examples are a collectively managed irrigation, fishery, or forest systems.[115] David Wishart conceives the company as 'a community of members' or a 'political institution with self-governing capacity' and observes that this enables us to move away from 'the sole focus of law being human beings'.[116] Ewan McGaughey characterizes the company as a 'social institution'.[117] All three authors adopt their respective

---

[108] John Lowry and Arad Reisberg, *Pettet's Company Law: Company Law and Corporate Finance* (4th edn, Pearson 2012) at 58.

[109] Daniel Lipton, 'Corporate Capacity for Crime and Politics: Defining Corporate Personhood at the Turn of the Twentieth Century' (2010) 96 Virginia L Rev 1911 citing scholars around Berle and Means; David Gindis, 'From Fictions and Aggregates to Real Entities in the Theory of the Firm' (2009) 5 Journal of Institutional Economics 25 at 34; see also Ewan McGaughey, 'Ideals of the Corporation and the Nexus of Contract' (2015) 76(6) MLR 1057, 1061.

[110] Daniel Lipton, 'Corporate Capacity for Crime and Politics: Defining Corporate Personhood at the Turn of the Twentieth Century' (2010) 96 Va L Rev 1911 at 1915–16.

[111] Mark M Hager, 'Bodies Politic: The Progressive History of Organizational "Real Entity" Theory' (1989) 50 University of Pittsburgh L Rev 575; Michael J Phillips, 'Reappraising the Real Entity Theory of the Corporation' (1994) 21 Florida State University L Rev 1061; Martin Petrin, 'Reconceptualizing the Theory of the Firm—From Nature to Function' (2013) 118 Penn State L Rev 1 at 10–13.

[112] Marc Moore and Martin Petrin, *Corporate Governance: Law, Regulation and Theory* (Macmillan Education 2017) at 26–27.

[113] Marc Moore and Martin Petrin, *Corporate Governance: Law, Regulation and Theory* (Macmillan Education 2017) at 27 (italics in the original).

[114] Simon Deakin, 'The Corporation as Commons: 'Rethinking Property Rights, Governance and Sustainability in the Business Enterprise' (2012) 37(2) Queen's Law Journal 367, 373–76.

[115] ibid 368.

[116] David Wishart, 'A Reconfiguration of Company and/or Corporate Law Theory' (2010) 10(1) Journal of Corporate Law Studies 151, 176.

[117] Ewan McGaughey, 'Ideals of the Corporation and the Nexus of Contract' (2015) 76(6) MLR 1057 at 1063.

theoretical positions with a view to endorsing a stakeholder-focused model of the company.

In relation to the nexus of contract and agency theories we have already seen that they on their own also do not explain why shareholders have more influence than other constituencies. To explain the comparatively larger influence of shareholders, agency theory needs to introduce an additional point: the residual claimant argument.

A real entity view is also not logically connected with the extent to which the influence of shareholders is designed in any corporate legal system. Real entity theory was originally conceived of against the background of a system where shareholders had more influence than other constituencies. German law introduced its current dual board model, which gives the board a comparatively high level of independence from the shareholders, in the 1930s, well after von Gierke first wrote. Admittedly von Rathenau was a proponent of real entity theory and was also critical of the level of shareholder influence that existed before the 1930 reforms. But this does not logically associate real entity theory with any particular level of shareholder influence. Like the nexus of contract theory and concession theory real entity theory does not tell us anything about how power is allocated between constituencies at a positive level or should be allocated between them at a normative level.

Indeed, it is the theory of this book that the current model of UK company is best characterized as involving a real entity approach while giving shareholders comparatively more rights than other interest groups in corporate decision-making. Shareholders are neither owners of the company nor is company law exclusively oriented towards their well-being. Company law operates a decision-making process which allows organizations to take autonomous decisions. How much influence shareholders have as compared to other constituencies is a function of a number of factors that are independent of whether we liken companies to contracts or to organizations.

1.4.3 Foundations of real entity theory

The claim that organizations 'are' real entities lies outside of the law. When nineteenth and early twentieth century scholars formulated entity theory they did not support this claim with either theoretical analysis or empirical evidence. Their claim was based on intuition. Today there exists scholarship that supports a real entity approach.

About facts
Before we proceed with an analysis of theoretical contributions that support real entity theory it is useful to establish what we mean by the assertion that a firm or an organization is a real entity. It is necessary to determine in what sense a fact can be characterized as 'existing in reality'.

Emile Durkheim famously coined the term 'social facts'. He observed that social inter-action leads to the creation of modes of behaviour. These modes are external to individ-uals and constitute the object of study for the field of sociology.[118] Richard Adelstein, an institutional economist, builds on this when he uses the distinction between 'brute facts' (rocks, trees, dogs, people) and 'social facts'.[119] Brute facts exist independently of any intention of human beings. Social facts exist because there is a collective intention and understanding that they exist. Firms are similar to football teams. They have two characteristics. First, the members intend to act not as individuals but as part of the firm. Second, non-members take part in this collective intention because they too agree that the members of the firm are together and constitute a social fact. This consensus makes firms real.[120] The firm is something that, by consensus, is treated by 'everyone' as an 'active social unit'.[121]

It is also possible to identify the characteristics of a social unit such as a firm. The firm acts through the visible performance of characteristic routines by real people in real time.[122] The firm's working rules are the firm.[123] This comes close to reifying the firm as an 'supraindividual being that acquires knowledge, makes decisions and acts in the market through the operation of routines'.[124] Interactions within firms create distinc-tive habits, routines, processes, and procedures and an organizational culture that are embodied at every moment in the changing roster of participants.[125] Routines are so-cial phenomena and firms are not 'living' organisms but nonetheless 'autonomous' even 'lifelike beings' existing apart from their temporal participants capable of intentionality and social action in their own right.[126]

This book accepts that organizations are real in a social sense. They are not tangible like brute facts but they affect human behaviour and so are real in their consequences. The next section will further discuss the point that social context affects human behaviour.

Natural, group, and organizational action

There exists a long-standing debate in the social sciences between positivism and interpretism.[127] Positivists connect to natural sciences and emphasize the necessity to measure and quantify. Interpretists, on the other hand, believe that the social world is predominantly subject to human interpretation. They do not believe that measurement or quantification helps to analyse social phenomena.

---

[118] Steven Lukes, *Durkheim: and Selected Texts on Sociology and its Method* (Macmillan Education 2013) 49–71.
[119] Richard Adelstein, 'Firms as Social Actors' (2010) 6(3) Journal of Institutional Economics 329 at 344–45; relying on John R Searle, *The Construction of Social Reality* (Free Press, New York 1995) at 2–26.
[120] Richard Adelstein, 'Firms as Social Actors' (2010) 6 Journal of Institutional Economics 329, 345.
[121] ibid 346.
[122] ibid 347.
[123] ibid 340.
[124] ibid 341–42.
[125] ibid 342.
[126] ibid 333.
[127] Michael Crotty, *The Foundations of Social Research: Meaning and Perspective in the Research Process* (Sage 2003).

This book does not endorse either view. It rather observes that the effect of groups and organizations on human action, which an interpretist would need no empirical proof to accept, is measurable and quantifiable and so also satisfies the methodological requirements
of positivist analysis.

Human beings act differently depending on social context. The author of this book adjusts
her behaviour depending on whether she acts in her private capacity or as an academic. In
her academic capacity her behaviour varies depending on whether she speaks to students,
to academic colleagues, or to individuals outside of the sector. Her behaviour also varies
depending on which particular university or department she is acting for. Her professional
conduct is informed by the processes, procedures, and policies adopted by that university
or department. It is also shaped by the informal understanding she has become aware of in
the course of interacting with other individuals working in the same social environment.

It has been empirically shown that human beings are capable of rational action but
that they do not always base their actions on rational decision-making. Rational action requires mental energy and takes time and so occurs infrequently.[128] Much of
human decision-making and behaviour is automated. Human beings adopt habits and
routines.[129]

It has also been shown that human behaviour is socially determined. The interaction with other people shapes how humans act. 'Group think' can cause individuals
to disengage their own judgement. 'Group loyalty' can lead members to continue
with practices that have proven to be ineffective. Organizations have a way of overriding individual judgement and attitudes.[130] Lynn Zucker, for example, has demonstrated in an experiment that individuals act differently when they perceive
themselves to be part of an organization. The perceived presence of an organizational context causes individuals to adjust their cognitive perception of real world
'brute' facts. Organizations bring about human behaviour that would otherwise
not exist.[131] Diane Vaughan has shown that the Space Shuttle Challenger disaster
was the result of an organizational environment that was characterized by a culture of high-risk technology and so normalized deviance from evidence that something was wrong. There was no single individual at fault. The cause of the disaster
was the 'banality of organizational life' rather than a breach of any particular safety

---

[128] Daniel Kahneman, *Thinking, Fast and Slow* (Penguin 2011) 21–38.

[129] See also Roger C Shank and Robert P Abelson, *Script, Plans, Goals and Understanding: An Inquiry into Human Knowledge Structures* (Hillsdale 1997) who argue that human action operates on the basis of pattern recognition. When new situations display similarities with previous experience they trigger pre-existing scripts and led
to sequences of action borrowed from a well-known situation.

[130] See further Christian List and Philipp Pettit, *Group Agency: The Possibility, Design, and Status of Corporate Agents* (OUP 2011); Susanna K Ripken, 'Corporations are People Too: A Multi-Dimensional Approach to the
Corporate Personhood Puzzle' (2009) 15 Fordham Journal of Corporate and Financial Law 98, 131–33 and also
Christian Witting, *Liability of Corporate Groups and Networks* (CUP 2018) 49.

[131] Lynne G Zucker, 'The Role of Institutionalization in Cultural Persistence' (1977) 42 American Sociological
Review 726.

rules.[132] Michel Ehrenhard and Timo Fiorito examined the behaviour of employees of twenty-five banks involved in corporate scandals. They found that the majority of these were attributable to systemic problems, of which multiple segments of the bank, often including the board, were knowledgeable.[133] The cause of the scandal was a particular culture rather than rogue individuals. Moreover, this was irrespective of the fact that these banks had adopted corporate values such as integrity, professionalism, and fairness.[134]

Institutional theory

So far, we have concluded that organizations are real in their consequences. They shape how human beings act. In this section theoretical contributions to the study of organizations will be analysed. These contributions use their own respective terminology. Economists tend to prefer the term 'firm'. Other social scientists tend to prefer the term 'organization'. We will not further dwell on this difference. The aim of the following analysis is to show there exists established scholarship which conceives firms and organizations respectively as autonomous actors characterized by their processes rather than as nexus points for agency relationships.

Institutional theory assumes that human action is shaped by social forces. When individuals interact they create laws, custom, and culture.[135] These forces shape human behaviour. The forces are referred to as 'institutions' and human and organizational behaviour is referred to as 'institutionalized'. Theorists in this field analyse the impact of these forces on individuals and also on organizations. They contribute to the disciplines of sociology, political science, and economics.[136]

The debate exists at two levels. There is a macro level debate where scholars discuss the extent to which organizational action is the product of external forces rather than of organizational agency. Paul DiMaggio and Walter Powell, for example, put much weight on macro social forces shaping organizational action.[137]

---

[132] Dianne Vaughan, *The Challenger Launch Decision* (University of Chicago Press 1996); see also David Welsh and others, 'The Slippery Slope: How Small Ethical Transgressions Pave the Way for Larger Future Transgressions' (2015) 100 Journal of Applied Psychology 114.

[133] Michel Ehrenhard and Timo Fiorito, 'Corporate Values of the 25 Largest European Banks: Exploring the Ambiguous Link with Corporate Scandals' (2018) 18 Journal of Public Affairs 1, 4 and 7; see also Henrich Greve, Donald Palmer, and Jo-Ellen Pozner, ' Organizations Gone Wild: The Causes, Processes, and Consequences of Organizational Misconduct' (2010) 4(1) The Academy of Management Annals 53.

[134] Michel Ehrenhard and Timo Fiorito, 'Corporate Values of the 25 Largest European Banks: Exploring the Ambiguous Link with Corporate Scandals' (2018) 18 Journal of Public Affairs 1, 7–8.

[135] For a foundational contribution to this school of thought see Peter L Berger and Thomas Luckmann, *The Social Construction of Reality: A Treatise in the Sociology of Knowledge* (Open Road Media 1967); see also Philip Selznick, 'Foundations of the Theory of Organization' (1948) 13(1) American Sociological Review 25; Philip Selznick, TVA and the Grass Roots: A Study in the Sociology of Formal Organization (Berkeley University of California Press 1949).

[136] W Richard Scott, *Institutions and Organizations* (4th edn, Sage 2014).

[137] Paul J DiMaggio and Walter W Powell, 'The Iron Cage Revisited: Institutional Isomorphism and Collective Rationality in Organizational Fields' (1983) 48 American Sociological Review 147, using a metaphor famously articulated by Max Weber.

Institutional theorists with a focus on organizational agency perceive this viewpoint as overly deterministic and argue that organizations experience discretion in responding to external pressures. Both camps, however, are sceptical of 'atomistic accounts of social processes, such as those provided by neoclassical economists.'[138]

At a micro-level the debate about structure versus human agency also appears. Again, there is agreement that structure and culture constrain human action. The discussion is over the extent to which human actors are determined by the processes, procedures, and culture that organizations impose on them. More recent scholarship tends to favour a mediating position that acknowledges human agency as well as organizational structure as determinants of organizational action.[139]

An example of a more structuralist view can be found in the work of Michael Hannan and John Freeman. They identify organizational structure as the 'central place' for understanding organizations.[140] To succeed organizations need to adapt to changes in their environment. Organizational structures are processes. These generate structural inertia limiting the ability of organizations to adapt.[141] Examples of internal structural arrangements that limit the agility of organizations are plants, equipment, and specialized personnel. The endemic inability of organizations to supply decision-makers with full information is another example. The most important example, however, is internal political constraints. Changes re-allocate power between organizational sub-units which will resist change. Finally, organizations are also constrained by their history. Once standards and procedures on the allocation of tasks and authority have become subject to normative agreement the cost of change is greatly increased.[142] While organizational structure limits the agility of organizations it is nevertheless a key ingredient of their survival. It allows organizations to reliably reproduce and store knowledge and information. In addition, structural inertia notwithstanding, there is room for change allowing organizations to adapt to changes in the environment surrounding them.[143]

W Richard Scott puts more weight on individual agency.[144] He characterizes organizations as 'figures' which are penetrated and constituted by the environments in which

---

[138] Pursey PMAR Heugens and Michel W Lander, 'Structure! Agency! (And Other Quarrels): A Meta-analysis of the Institutional Theories of Organisation' (2009) 52 Academy of Management Journal 61, 61.

[139] See eg Patricia H Thornton, William Ocasio, and Michael Lounsbury, *The Institutional Logics Perspective: A New Approach to Culture, Structure and Process* (2012 OUP); Thomas B Lawrence, Roy Suddaby, and Bernard Leca (eds), *Institutional Work* (CUP 2009); see also Pursey PMAR Heugens and Michel W Lander, 'Structure! Agency! (And Other Quarrels): A Meta-analysis of the Institutional Theories of Organisation' (2009) 52 Academy of Management Journal 61 92–95.

[140] Michael T Hannan and John Freeman, 'The Population Ecology of Organizations' (1977) 82(5) American Journal of Sociology 929; Michael T Hannan and John Freeman, 'Structural Inertia and Organizational Change' (1984) 49(2) American Sociological Review 149.

[141] Michael T Hannan and John Freeman, 'The Population Ecology of Organizations' (1977) 82(5) American Journal of Sociology 929, 930.

[142] Michael T Hannan and John Freeman, 'The Population Ecology of Organizations' (1977) 82(5) American Journal of Sociology 929, 931.

[143] Michael T Hannan and John Freeman, 'Structural Inertia and Organizational Change' (1984) 49(2) American Sociological Review 149.

[144] See also Julie Battilana and Thomas D'Aunno, 'Institutional work and the paradox of embedded agency' in Thomas B Lawrence, Roy Suddaby, and Bernard Leca, *Institutional Work* (CUP 2009) at 31

they operate.[145] With a nod to structuralism he points out that all (even innovative) action is affected by existing contexts and must adjust to it.[146] But he also stresses that the conception of organizations as characterized by their processes which affect human action should not be misunderstood as endorsement of a reactionary normative agenda. Processes also operate as channels through which change occurs. They are a double-edged sword.[147]

There is empirical evidence confirming organizational inertia. It has been shown, for example, that the strategy adopted by the founder of an organization continues to shape the strategy of firms throughout their lifecycle. Warren Boecker looked at a sample of fifty-three semiconductor firms and found that firms that were founded in the earlier era of the industry were more likely to continue to pursue a first-mover strategy while firms that were founded during the most recent period studied were more likely to develop and continue a niche strategy.[148] 'Decisions made at founding stage imprint organizational characteristics that help determine the organization's future direction.'[149] Warren Boeker also points out that imprinting forces are sometimes overlooked because of a tendency of researchers to explain current characteristics in terms of current phenomena.[150]

Likewise, Arthur Stinchcombe examined the characteristics of the new universities founded in the US during the period from 1870 to 1900. During that time universities were established 'in bursts'. They adopted different forms depending on the time when they were first established. These forms persisted over long periods of time. Organizations are thus 'imprinted' with the characteristics present at the time when they were first established.[151] As more organizations of the same time (or rather type) are created their legitimacy increases so that their structural templates are reinforced.[152]

Scholars who study corporate culture add another aspect to the analysis of the characteristics of organizations.[153] Culture is widely believed to matter for the success of an organization.[154] Culture is also believed to

---

[145] W Richard Scott, *Institutions and Organizations* (4th edn, Sage 2014) 262.

[146] See also V Lynn Meek, 'Organizational Culture: Origins and Weaknesses' (1988) 9(4) Organizations Studies 453 at 462–65.

[147] W Richard Scott, *Institutions and Organizations* (4th edn, Sage 2014) 272–73; see also Anthony Giddens, *The Constitution of Society* (Berkeley University of California Press 1984) 25–28 and 327 who observes that individuals are simultaneously constrained and empowered social structures; Joanne Martin and Caren Siehl, 'Organizational Culture and Counterculture: An Uneasy Symbiosis' (1983) 12(2) Organizational Dynamics 52.

[148] Warren P Boeker, 'The Development and Institutionalization of Subunit Power in Organizations' (1989) 34(3) Administrative Science Quarterly 388

[149] ibid at 408.

[150] ibid at 408.

[151] W Richard Scott, *Institutions and Organizations* (4th edn, Sage 2014) 194; Arthur L Stinchcombe, 'Social Structure and Organizations' in James G March (ed), *Handbook of Organizations* (Rand McNally 1965) 142.

[152] W Richard Scott, *Institutions and Organizations* (4th edn, Sage 2014) 194.

[153] V Lynn Meek, 'Organizational Culture: Origins and Weaknesses' (1988) 9(4) Organizations Studies 453.

[154] See eg Financial Reporting Council, Corporate Culture and the Role of Boards, July 2016, 2–3 (available from <www.frc.org.uk/getattachment/3851b9c5-92d3-4695-aeb2-87c9052dc8c1/Corporate-Culture-and-the-Role-of-Boards-Report-of-Observations.pdf>); Boris Groysberg and others, 'The Leader's Guide to Corporate Culture' (2018) Harvard Business Review <https://hbr.org/2018/01/the-culture-factor>; Julie Goran, Laura LaBerge, and

be a key ingredient affecting compliance by organizations with regulatory requirements.[155]

Organizational culture can be characterized as a 'multi-layered, scalar, social phenomenon concerned with values and related to actions.'[156] Examples of attributes of corporate culture are rituals, symbols, ideologies, and myths.[157] In relation to culture organizations are also conceived of as imprinted by their past.[158] Facebook and Apple are well-known examples of organizations with particularly distinct cultures shaped by the visions and personalities of their founders. Corporate culture is collectively held by the participants in organizations, affects them, but can also be changed by them. Here too, the debate about the extent of individual human agency versus cultural determinism exists. The discussion is about how much force culture exerts with contributors agreeing that change requires time and effort by individual actors.[159]

Institutional theory in economics

There are early institutional economists who emphasize that human behaviour is shaped by social interaction. Thorstein Veblen wrote at the beginning of the twentieth century that the individual's conduct is 'edged about and directed by his habitual relations to his fellows in the group' and that these relations are 'of an institutional character' and 'vary as the institutional scene varies.'[160]

The importance of routines, processes, and procedures shaping human action and organizational behaviour is also stressed in the work of Herbert Simon, Nobel Laureate in Economics.[161] His analysis focuses on organizational decision-making rather than on

Ramesh Srinivasan, 'Culture for a Digital Age'(July 2017) McKinsey Quarterly <https://www.mckinsey.com/business-functions/mckinsey-digital/our-insights/culture-for-a-digital-age#> .

[155] Financial Conduct Authority, Transforming Culture in Financial Services, DP 18/2 (March 2018) 9 <www.fca.org.uk/publication/discussion/dp18-02.pdf; Anthony Salz, Salz Review and Independent Review of Barclay's Business Practices (April 2013) 177–95, available from <https://online.wsj.com/public/resources/documents/SalzReview04032013.pdf>; Jitendra Aswani and Franco Fiordelisi, 'Tournament Culture and Corporate Misconduct: Evidence Using Machine Learning' <https://papers.ssrn.com/sol3/papers.cfm?abstract_id=3708313>.

[156] Nien-he Hiseh, Benjamin Lange, David Rodin, and MLA Wolf-Bauwens, 'Getting Clear on Corporate Culture: Conceptualisation, Measurement and Operationalisation' (2018) 6 Journal of the British Academy 155, 156.

[157] Andrew M Pettigrew, 'On Studying Organizational Cultures' (1979) (24)3 Administrative Science Quarterly 570; see also John W Meyer and Brian Rowan, 'Institutionalized Organizations: Formal Structure as Myth and Ceremony' (1977) 83 American Journal of Sociology 340.

[158] Andrew M Pettigrew, 'On Studying Organizational Cultures' (1979) (24) 3 Administrative Science Quarterly 570.

[159] See eg Mats Alvesson and Stefan Sveningsson, Changing Organizational Culture: Cultural Change Work in Progress (Routledge 2008); Kim S Cameron and Robert E Quinn, Diagnosing and Changing Organizational Culture: Based on a Competing Values Framework (3rd edn, Jossey-Bass 2011); W Brook Tunstall, 'Cultural Transition at AT&T' (1983) 25(1) Sloan Management Review 15; Noel M Tichy, 'Managing Change Strategically: The Technical, Political and Cultural Keys' (1982) 11(2) Organizational Dynamics 59;

[160] Thorstein Veblen, 'The Limitations of Marginal Utility' (1909) 17 Journal of Political Economy 235, 245; see also Andrew Van de Ven, 'The Institutional Theory of John R Commons: A Review and Commentary' (1993) 18 Academy of Management Review 129.

[161] Herbert Simon, Administrative Behavior: A Study of Decision-making Processes in Administrative Organizations (4th edn, The Free Press 1997).

individual incentives.[162] In his framework human actors are capable of acting rationally but also display non-rational forms of behaviour. Organizations help individuals to act rationally by establishing processes.[163] Routines are the essence of organizational acting. They supply performance programmes that guide human action.

To be sure, Herbert Simon's contribution stresses the influence of organizations on individual action. He does not suggest that there is a social dimension to humans acting together that makes organizational acting independent of the contributions and intentions of the contributors. His work is nevertheless of interest here because it conceives organizations as processes rather than as aggregators of individual contributions.

Richard R Nelson and Sidney G Winter use evolutionary theory to explain patterns of economic change. For them too, routines play a pivotal role. Firms are historical entities. To succeed in competitive markets they adopt routines. These routines are the result of an endogenous, experience-based learning process.[164] They consist of conscious and tacit knowledge. This knowledge is 'socially held'.[165] It is stored in the form of routines. These shape organizational behaviour.[166] In Nelson and Winter's work there is very little attention to the level of individual agents. Their theory therefore has been characterized as working with 'aggregate entities, notably routines and organizational capabilities, that are not explicitly reduced to individual behavior'.[167] It is not consistent with the 'methodological individualism' that forms the basis of neoclassical economics.[168] In their framework organizational behaviour goes beyond the idea of bounded rationality as developed by Herbert Simon. It has been characterized as introducing a concept of 'organic rationality'.[169] It has been criticized for not sufficiently explaining the connection between individual action and tacit knowledge/organizational behaviour.[170] It is nevertheless worth observing that there exists an established school of thought in the economics literature that conceives firms as entities capable of their own distinct organizational behaviour.

Tacit knowledge and routines also play a key role in the field of resource-based economics.[171] The field takes inspiration from the work of Edith Penrose who stressed that

---

[162] Michael Mintrom, 'Herbert A Simon, Administrative Behavior: A Study of Decision-Making Processes in Administrative Organizations' in Martin Lodge and others (eds), *The Oxford Handbook of Classics in Public Policy and Administration* (OUP 2015) 16–17.

[163] Michael Mintrom, 'Herbert A Simon, Administrative Behavior: A Study of Decision-Making Processes in Administrative Organizations' in Martin Lodge and others (eds), *The Oxford Handbook of Classics in Public Policy and Administration* (OUP 2015) 12.

[164] W Richard Scott, *Institutions and Organizations* (4th edn, Sage 2014) 36.

[165] Nicolai J Foss, 'Bounded Rationality and Tacit Knowledge in the Organizational Capabilities Approach: An Assessment and a Re-evaluation' (2003) 12(2) Industrial and Corporate Change 185 at 186.

[166] ibid 190.

[167] ibid 186.

[168] ibid 186 and 198.

[169] Ibid 191.

[170] Ibid 198.

[171] The importance of tacit knowledge is also emphasized in recent legal contributions: see eg Brian Cheffins, 'Corporations' in Mark Tushnet and Peter Cane (eds), *The Oxford Handbook of Legal Studies* (OUP 2005) 485, 497; Edward B Rock and Michael L Wachter, 'Islands of Conscious Power: Law, Norms, and the Self-Governing Corporation' (2001) 149 U Pa L Rev 1619.

the most important asset of the firm is its specialized use of resources (including the skill of workers) and founded a sub-field referred to as resource-based economics.[172] Unlike neoclassical economics, this discipline insists that some resources are not readily available in the market even if the price is right.[173] They develop over time and are difficult to reproduce because they are based on tacit knowledge. This knowledge enables the firm to produce complex constellations of other variables. In this model the firm is conceived of as the holder of knowledge which allows the firm to put to use specific resources rather than as nexus aggregating contributions from individuals with particular incentives.

Most recently David Gindis, who contributes to the field of institutional economics, presented a theory of the firm that explicitly connects to the real entity approach advanced in early twentieth century legal scholarship. He distinguishes 'aggregates' or 'heaps' from social entities that are 'identifiable' and have a 'characteristic constitutive structure'.[174] Social entities have the 'power to affect other things and to be affected by them'.[175] He refers to social entities as 'wholes'. Those arise from a constitution and are 'qualitatively different from their parts taken separately or collectively'.[176] It is no longer possible to hold that these wholes are 'nothing but' the parts composing them, or 'nothing over and above' these parts.[177] He stresses that the constitution is 'the essential basis of an organization' and that 'procedural rules underlie organized action . . . and constitute organizations as corporate actors'.[178] The firm is economically and legally persistent 'through time, based on its constitutive structure that allows the replication of behavioural patterns and collective routines'. '[A]ny particular firm continues to exist even if all its present human members are progressively replaced. Such independence qualifies the firm as a real entity'.[179]

Conclusions

From our perspective it is important to note that human action is characterized by habits and that social interaction brings about routines, process, procedures, and culture. Together these can be referred to as social structure. Organizations are the social structure which comes about when human beings work together. Social structure is persistent. New participants join, learn the behaviour, adopt it, and teach it to those who join after them. Because social structure shapes human behaviour we can conclude that organizations are real. They are real not in a tangible way but rather in their consequences.

---

[172] Edith Penrose, *The Theory of Growth of the Firm* (4th edn, OUP 1995); W Richard Scott, *Institutions and Organizations* (4th edn, Sage 2014) 37–38.
[173] W Richard Scott, *Institutions and Organizations* (4th edn, Sage 2014) 37.
[174] David Gindis, 'From Fictions and Aggregates to Real Entities in the Theory of the Firm' (2009) 5 Journal of Institutional Economics 25, 37.
[175] ibid 37.
[176] ibid 38.
[177] ibid 38.
[178] ibid 39.
[179] ibid 39.

There nevertheless exists human agency, which is capable of deviating from social structure. Human agency also modifies social structure over time.

This book assumes that organizations are real social actors that both shape human action and are shaped by human action. The interaction between routines, process, procedures and culture on the one hand and human agency on the other is complex. It is useful to analyse the consequences of individual incentives and of conflicts of interest. But company law cannot be collapsed into straightforward bilateral relationships or into an aggregation of individually identifiable contributions. A theory that characterizes organizations as autonomous actors comes closer than a nexus of contract model to capturing the empirical phenomenon that company law is designed to support.

1.4.4 Applying real entity theory to company law

So far, we have established that firms or organizations are autonomous actors. They are more than the aggregation of the contributions from their participants. To be sure, this does not characterize them as human beings and so is not an anthropomorphic exercise. Anthropomorphism is wrong because the metaphor only fits with an extreme structural model where there is no human agency. Organizations are characterized by the habits, routines, processes, procedures, tacit knowledge, and culture that human social interaction brings about. These are not biological but social phenomena which can be and are researched and understood by the methods available to the social sciences. In addition to the social structure shaping human action and thereby creating organizational action, there exists human agency, which is capable of deviating from social structure.

What then is the role of law in this? Historically the provision of a legal form for organizations coincided with the period following the Enlightenment. From this time onwards individuals, organizations and the nation state became the primary categories of actors. The recognition of separate legal personality through law is not the cause for the rise of organizations but an 'indicator of the growing independence of these new corporate forms as they become recognized as legal persons in the eyes of the law'.[180]

Law finds organizations as a social phenomenon and makes the following contributions. It makes available separate legal personality allowing organizations to function as subjects in the eyes of the law.[181] The Companies Act also sets out a procedural framework for the operation of the company.[182] It defines roles for participants and assigns

---

[180] W Richard Scott, *Institutions and Organizations* (4th edn, Sage 2014) 89.

[181] See also David Gindis, 'From Fictions and Aggregates to Real Entities in the Theory of the Firm' (2009) 5 Journal of Institutional Economics 25 at 39 and 41; Legal personality also shields the assets of organizations from the reach of the shareholders and their creditors (H Hansmann and R Kraakman, 'The Essential Role of Organizational Law' (2000) 110 Yale Law Journal 387); see also David Gindis, 'Ernst Freund as the Precursor of the Rational Study of Corporate Law' (2020) 16(5) Journal of Institutional Economics 597.

[182] See also Edward B Rock and Michael L Wachter, 'Islands of Conscious Power: Law, Norms and the Self-Governing Corporation' (2001) 149 University of Pennsylvania L Rev 1619; see also Ronald J Gilson, 'From

powers to these roles thus facilitating organizational decision making which then leads to organizational action. The Companies Act appoints the corporate constitution further formalize the procedures for the taking corporate decisions. In large companies routines are then further defined through policies and procedures. The Companies Act requires listed companies, for example, to develop a policy for executive remuneration. This policy is to be drawn up by the board and adopted by the shareholders.

Company law also deals with situations where the formalized structures are disconnected from informal arrangements. This problem is, for example, addressed by the rules governing unfair prejudice claims which spring into action when the constitution does not reflect the understanding of the company's members. The *Duomatic* principle gives legal force to informal but unanimous shareholder decisions.

Ronald Gilson writes that corporate law makes it possible for a corporation to become a 'real boy'.[183] I suggest that the opposite is true. Corporate law makes it possible for real entities to become formal subjects of the law. It allows a social reality to become formally integrated into the legal system.

To be sure not all organizations are companies. Organizations sometimes operate on an unincorporated basis and the legislature makes a number of organizational forms available. In the UK the variety of corporate forms is not as broad as in other jurisdictions. The corporate form made available by the Companies Act 2006 is used to operate the vast majority of commercial organizations. But all corporate forms are designed to serve organizations.

Companies are also used more widely than for the operation of commercial organizations. They operate charities, for example, or administer blocks of flats. They are also used as special purpose vehicles to structure loans and other financing arrangements. There is no organizational component to this particular use of the corporate form. Company law permits this use. But this does not undermine the observation that the company is built to facilitate organizational action.

Company law legislation is the product of an evolutionary process. The legislature shapes the Companies Act and related legislation integrating the policy preferences of the day. These interventions are designed with a view to being effective in a real life rather than a theoretical environment. At common law the integration of the characteristics of organizations emerges organically through the case law which treats each case on its respective organizationally determined facts. The common law moulds itself around the social reality of firms or organizations.

Corporate Law to Corporate Governance' in Jeffrey N Gordon and Wolf-Georg Ringe (eds), The Oxford Handbook of *Corporate Law and Governance* (OUP 2018) 3 at 7–8.

[183] Ronald Gilson, 'From Corporate Law to Corporate Governance' in Jeffrey N Gordon and Wolf-Georg Ringe (eds), *The Oxford Handbook of Corporate Law and Governance* (OUP 2015) 7.

Admittedly size matters. Social structure is more developed and more persistent in large companies than in small companies. But habits and routines form also in small organizations. Moreover, company law is built to serve companies of all sizes. The insight that organizational action is shaped around routines and procedures and influenced by culture and that these are persistent characteristics of organizational life that are outside of the immediate influence of the participants provides us with a granular understanding of organizations. The understanding of the underlying phenomenon helps to explain statutory as well as case law.

The theory advanced in this book is that company law can be better understood if we conceive companies as autonomous actors with processes that shape and are shaped by natural actors. This perspective helps to understand the law as it stands and allows us to make recommendations at a normative level.

Individual agency plays a role in company law. The law addresses the problem that conflicts of interest affect the ability of directors to abide by their duties. Agency theory helps with a granular analysis of conflict of interest situations. The conflict of interest, however, does not arise between the directors and the shareholders but between the directors and the company.

At a normative level it is useful to be aware of conflicts of interest, but it is also important to be aware that this does not capture the full range of problems that company law needs to address. Agency theory can illuminate a conflict between the company and directors. Sometimes, however, the problem is not located in any one person. Sometimes the social structure is toxic. Decision-making structures and procedures can lead to undesirable outcomes. At a normative level those designing legal intervention need to be aware of both human agency and also the potential toxicity of social structure.

At a positive level company law does not engineer alignment of incentives between the directors and the shareholders of the company. It rather acknowledges conflict of interest situations and addresses these through procedure. Moreover, interventions that manipulate the incentives of directors are difficult to design. We will see below that the Greenbury Report recommended the alignment of directors' remuneration with shareholder return. This has caused remuneration to increase but has failed to ensure that directors are rewarded for success rather than failure.

More generally, the book will conclude that any further integration of stakeholder interests into company law, if this was desired, is unlikely going to be achieved through a statement of corporate purpose, a redesign of remuneration packages, or an amendment of Companies Act 2006, s 172. Such an integration is more likely to occur through the creation of roles that represent these interests in the corporate decisions-making process.

1.4.5 Structure of the book

The book is structured as follows. We will see in chapter 2 that separate legal personality can be explained as a solution developed by company law to address the problem that organizations are social rather than brute facts.

Brute facts have a unique physical manifestation and the law can connect to that manifestation. We do not need to register ourselves as human beings for the law to recognize us as subjects.

Social facts have an impact on the physical world through the consequences of human action. But while we can identify physical objects which are affected by an organization, there is not one physical object that can be permanently identified as the organization. Separate legal personality addresses this characteristic feature of organizations. It will be shown in section 2.5 that for a company to come into existence certain documents need to be registered. These contain information that facilitates the interaction between the company and third parties. Registration as a company gives an organization a public legal manifestation.

Moreover, normally the parties to a contract can end it by agreement. This is not possible for companies, which need to be wound up and then removed from the register for their separate legal personality to end. Along the same lines a contract that is affected by illegality or fraud is normally considered null and void. This does not apply to companies. They continue to exist until they are wound up, vitiating factors notwithstanding.

We will see in sections 2.2–2.4 that the Companies Act does not limit the corporate form to organizational action. The corporate form can therefore be used for other purposes and organizational boundaries do not align with legal personality. But this does not undermine the observation that company law is designed for the operation of organizations.

We will see in chapter 3 that the capacity of companies used to be limited by the objects stated in its memorandum. This was at the time explained by a concession-style argument and the legal doctrine producing this effect came to be known as the *ultra vires* doctrine. The effect of limited capacity can also be explained through contract law. If an arrangement is set up through a contract the rights arising from that contract are necessarily limited by its terms. The *ultra vires* doctrine was abolished because it turned out to be unsuitable for the operation of commercial organizations. These need flexibility and the law adapted to the requirements of organizational action, and now mandates that all non-charitable companies have unlimited capacity.

We will see in chapter 4 that the rules normally referred to as providing for 'veil piercing' impose liability on those using companies for fraudulent or sham purposes but do not undermine the separate legal personality of the company. Companies used for fraudulent or sham purposes continue to have separate legal personality, their defects notwithstanding. This special legal treatment of the company as a legal form gives an organization run through a company an anchor on which third parties can rely. There is no doubt as to the legal existence of a registered company. No matter what the company has been up to, it exists and can only come to an end through an orderly winding up process during which the interests of all its participants are taken into account.

Organizational reality is nevertheless integrated into legal analysis. The common law developed a narrow rule permitting what is referred to as veil piercing. Before *Petrodel v Prest* it was held that veil piercing was permitted when the company was a 'sham'. Since that case veil piercing is considered possible only when a company is used to evade an existing obligation. In addition, the courts will, if companies are used to conceal facts, ignore the smoke screens and establish the facts as they see them. We will see in section 4.2.2 that the courts consider instances of evasion to be rare. We will also see that the metaphor of veil piercing, which seems to suggest that the company's legal personality is compromised, is misleading. The effect of veil piercing is rather that limited liability is removed with the result that the company becomes liable for a debt of a shareholder or vice versa. Moreover, limited liability is taken away when shareholders step out of their role and come to act as shadow directors.[184] In addition there are a number of statutory rules that impose personal liability on both shareholders and directors in circumstances that can be characterized as abuses of the corporate form. We will also see that the courts have used the law of negligence to address cases where parent companies have stepped outside of their role as shareholders and have involved themselves directly in the operation of a subsidiary. Finally in recent years a number of statutes have emerged that regulate corporate groups in specific contexts.

We will see in section 5.1 that company law facilitates organizational action by endowing the directors with authority to bind the company in contract and authorize others to do so. This authority cannot be limited by the constitution of the company and so the company can act through its directors independently from its shareholders. Section 5.2 will show that the company is itself liable in tort. This tells us that the law recognizes companies as autonomous actors. Companies are also autonomously liable criminally and recently attribution rules have been developed that connect to organizational fault (section 5.3).

Chapters 6, 7, and 8 discuss the organizational framework made available by company law. In chapter 6 we will see that the Companies Act establishes that framework by defining the roles of the directors, the shareholders, the auditors, and the company secretary. The statute appoints the shareholders to decide constitutional matters and to participate in certain management decisions. It delegates the maintenance of financial records and the production of financial reports to the directors and carves out a role for the company secretary and the auditors. The Act also imposes mandatory procedures for shareholder meetings. The common law permits these to be overridden by an

---

[184] Section 4.3.5 in this book.

informal unanimous decision (*Duomatic*) and in this way allows for organizational reality to override the formal legal process. The UK Corporate Governance Code contains
generally accepted recommendations structuring decision-making by the directors.

The constitution is adopted by those setting up a company. It is the product of private
action but derives its force from the statute. Chapter 6.3 will show that standard contract law does not apply to the constitution. Instead the unfair prejudice remedy and
the rules on just and equitable winding up serve as a mechanism for resolving situations where the mutual understanding of a quasi-partnership is not reflected in the
constitution. Chapter 6 will concluded that the constitution is best characterized as the
foundational document for the operation of an organization and that it has more in
common with secondary legislation adopted by private action on a statutory basis than
with a contract.

In chapter 7 the role of the directors will be analysed. The duties of the directors are
owed to the company and while the shareholders are the primary indirect beneficiaries
of those duties the law integrates the interests of creditors and also of wider society. We
will see that the law is primarily focused on ensuring compliance with the Companies
Act and the constitution rather than with the enhancement of economic interests (section 7.3). The law does not instruct the directors to maximize return however defined.
The directors are responsible for defining in their subjective judgement what is best
for the success of the company (section 7.4). The objective standard of skill and care
was introduced with the public interest in mind (section 7.6). It is interpreted by reference to the organizational role performed by each individual director. Directors are
encouraged to operate a process giving them adequate financial information, ensuring
supervision of delegated activity, and compliance with the law. The Company Directors
Disqualification Act 1986 serves as a mechanism through which the public interest is
integrated into company law. The enforcement of this Act is funded by the public purse
rather than by the company or its shareholders. The UK Corporate Governance Code
adds a further procedural dimension to the operation of the board of directors.

We will see that agency theory is useful to illuminate the problems arising in conflict of
interest situations but that the law governing such transactions goes beyond protecting
the economic interests of the company (section 7.7). It requires all conflicted transactions to be approved by the company through the relevant procedures. A director
who failed to seek such approval is liable even if the company benefitted economically
from the transaction. It will be argued in section 7.9 that the problem associated with
directors remuneration are evidence that incentive based interventions are difficult to
design and that it may be time to abandon the attempt of remunerating directors in a
way that aligns their interests with those of either the company or its shareholders. We
will see that in section 7.10 that the directors have exclusive responsibility to record
financial information and to create financial and narrative reports. The content of the
records and the reports is set out in the respective accounting regulations and cannot be
modified by the shareholders. Directors are also bound by the distribution rules which

prioritize the interests of creditors over those of the shareholders (section 7.11). We will conclude by observing that the characterization of the directors as agents of the shareholders is not only formally wrong. It also does not adequately reflect the depth and breadth of their overall responsibilities.

In chapter 8 we will see that the shareholders have substantial governance rights but that they should not be characterized as principals of either the directors or of the company. This is because the law has put in place restrictions for the benefit of minority shareholders and creditors that limit their ability to exercise their rights freely. It is also because they are bound by the distribution rules and so cannot determine the amount of return to be paid to them.

In chapter 9 we will examine the enforcement of the duties of the directors. It will be concluded that the courts and the statute defer to the corporate decision-making process. Derivative claims are only successful if that process cannot be made to work independently of the wrong-doing directors. The law is deliberately designed with a view to preventing shareholders from undermining the organizational decision-making process. We will also see that for duties that are aimed at protecting third parties interacting with the company the law has supplied enforcement mechanism that are publicly funded and so arguably these duties receive a higher level of protection than shareholder-oriented duties.

The book will conclude by observing that company law at a positive level is best explained by a real entity theory that conceives companies as vehicles for autonomous organizational action.

This insight is also useful for the design of normative intervention. For example, we will observe in section 3.4 that the idea of encouraging companies to adopt a purpose on its own is unlikely to cause them to contributing to the public good. Along similar lines it will be argued in section 7.4.2 that a modification of the duty in Companies Act 2006, section 172 in a way that puts stakeholders on the same plane as shareholders will also be largely cosmetic. We will further observe in section 7.9.5 that designing the remuneration of directors to align with the interests of either shareholders or stakeholders is unlikely to produce an outcome that serves the interests of those constituencies. These interventions are unlikely to succeed because they are too removed from the way companies take decisions. For an integration of wider interests to be effective these need to be institutionalized. This can happen through the creation of specific roles, such as the designation of directors, who have the responsibility of representing these interests in the corporate decision-making process.

At a normative level the book will further observe that the reluctance of the courts to interfere with corporate litigation decisions by permitting individual shareholders to claim derivatively could be overcome by taking inspiration from the unfair prejudice remedy. The courts have rightly not hesitated to intervene in circumstances where they were given access to a remedy that allowed them to order shareholders to be bought out by the wrongdoers. This way of intervening does not interfere with organizational decision-making but nevertheless delivers accountability. If there was a desire to increase the accountability of directors, it would be possible to design a remedy that permits substantial minority shareholders to request that wrong-doing directors purchase their shares on terms set by the discretion of the courts.[185]

1.4.6 Shareholders versus stakeholders

It has already been mentioned that the characterization of the company as a vehicle for the operation of an autonomous real entity does not tell us anything about how decision-making power is allocated between the participants in the company. The adoption of an entity model also does not tie our hands with regards to where the balance between shareholders and stakeholders should be struck. It has also been mentioned that the residual claimant argument can be used independently of the nexus of contract framework to explain positively why shareholders have more influence than other participants and to argue normatively that shareholders should have more influence than other participants. The book does not take a position as to how the balance between shareholders and other participants should be struck.[186] It is possible to adopt the real entity approach advanced in this book while at the same time committing to an economic normative argument in favour of a shareholder-centred model of the company. It is also possible to accept real entity theory as stated in this book while relying on arguments that justify a stakeholder-oriented model.

This author believes that that question of how much stakeholder influence there should be is to be resolved by reference to economic and political considerations which are outside the scope of this book. Historical factors and culture also play a role in explaining the how the law currently strikes this balance and can help to predict how the law is likely to evolve going forward.

---

[185] Section 9.2.13 in this book.

[186] For a recent and high-profile academic statement in favour of a greater integration of stakeholder concerns into company law see Andrew Johnston and others, 'Corporate Governance for Sustainability' 11 December 2020 <https://papers.ssrn.com/sol3/papers.cfm?abstract_id=3502101>; see also Abraham A Singer, *The Form of the Firm* (OUP 2019), and Ewan McGaughey, *Principles of Enterprise Law* (CUP forthcoming).

2

Corporate Personality

We need to distinguish between separate legal personality and limited liability. It is tempting to assume that the primary advantage of the corporate form was the provision of limited liability. This is, however, not the case. Historically the primary objective of the corporate form was to make available separate legal personality.[1] Limited liability did not become available until the Limited Liability Act 1855.[2]

The distinction is also useful for the analysis of modern law. Separate legal personality is robust. It begins on registration and ends with removal of the company from the register. Separate legal personality can be used for all legal purposes. A company can have commercial as well as charitable purposes, and while company law is designed for the operation of an organization, the corporate form can also be used for purposes that do not involve organizational action. If the corporate form is used to operate an organization it is not necessary for legal boundaries to align with organizational boundaries. A company can thus be used for a one-person business as well as for the operation of corporate groups.

2.1 Introduction

Through the provision of separate legal personality the law acknowledges a social reality and responds to it by providing a formal framework. Initially legal personality was only available ad hoc on the basis of a Royal Charter or a Private Act of Parliament. That route became blocked by the South Sea Bubble Act, which made it difficult to incorporate companies in this way.[3] Contract law was used to work around this effect of the Act. Companies were set up by a contract which created a trust. They were referred to as 'deed of settlement companies'. They were similar to modern-day unit trusts. The investors transferred assets to trustees. Directors were appointed to manage the business. The investors received shares, with such rights to terminate their interest and to transfer the shares as the deed of settlement provided.[4] The principles of the law of partnerships, slightly modified, were thought to be applicable to

---

[1] Paul Davies, *Gower's Principles of Modern Company Law* (6th edn, Sweet & Maxwell 1997) 21, 30 and 31.
[2] Limited Liability Act 1855 (18 & 19 Vict c 133).
[3] 6 Geo 1 c 18.
[4] Michael Lobban, 'Joint Stock Companies' in William Cornish and others, *The Oxford History of the Laws of England, Volume XII, 1820–1914 Private Law* (OUP 2010) 613; William Cornish and others, *Law and Society in England 1750–1950* (Hart 2019) 243–44; John Armour, 'Companies and other Associations' in Andrew Burrows (ed), *English Private Law* (OUP 2013) [3.45]; Andreas Televantos, *Capitalism Before Corporations: The Morality of Business Associations and the Roots of Commercial Equity and Law* (OUP 2020).

Company Law. Eva Micheler, Oxford University Press. © Eva Micheler 2021. DOI: 10.1093/oso/9780198858874.003.0002

these companies.[5] Deed of settlement companies were, however, very cumbersome to operate. The Companies Act 1844 was therefore adopted to make available a more suitable legal vehicle for the businesses of that time.

Separate legal personality has administrative advantages that facilitate organizational action. It makes it possible for the company to exist in perpetuity and independently of the identity of its members and its shareholders. It also makes it possible to formally distinguish between contracts made by the members in their personal capacity and contracts made by the business in which other members participate. This was initially achieved by allowing companies to possess a common seal.[6] Without separate legal personality it is also very difficult for businesses to participate in litigation. Actions originally had to be brought against all the partners which caused great difficulty when there were changes in membership.[7] Because of separate legal personality documents in relation to ownership of land can be issued in the name of the company and do not require modification as participants change.

The provision of the separate legal personality of the company coincided with the rise of the modern economy.[8] Up to the middle of the nineteenth century an incorporated company was its members, albeit those members 'united so as to be but one person in law'.[9] There was no complete separation of the company and its members.[10] Companies Act 2006, section 16(2) shows traces from these roots of company law. It states that upon registration the subscribers to the memorandum 'are' (rather than 'form') a 'body corporate' by the name stated in the certificate of incorporation. The Companies Act 1862 then adopted wording indicating that the company had an existence external to the members.[11] Today Companies Act 2006, section 16(3) gives the company legal independence from its members. It states that the company as a body corporate 'is capable of exercising all the functions of an incorporated company'.

---

[5] P Ireland, 'Company Law and the Myth of Shareholder Ownership' (1999) 62 MLR 32, 39.

[6] Paul Davies, *Gower's Principles of Modern Company Law* (6th edn, Sweet & Maxwell 1997) 21.

[7] Michael Lobban, 'Joint Stock Companies' in William Cornish and others, *The Oxford History of the Laws of England, Volume XII, 1820–1914 Private Law* (OUP 2010) 613; William Cornish and others, *Law and Society in England 1750–1950* (Hart 2019) 243-44.

[8] Paddy Ireland, Ian Grigg-Spall, and Dave Kelly, 'The Conceptual Foundations of Modern Company Law' (1987) 14 Journal of Law and Society 149, 151.

[9] ibid 150; The Joint Stock Companies Act 1844 (c 110) stated in s 25 that 'on the complete registration being certified by the Registrar of Joint Stock Companies such company and the then shareholders therein, and all the succeeding shareholders, whilst shareholders, shall be and are hereby incorporated as from the date of such certificate by name of the company as set forth in the deed of settlement.'

[10] LS Sealy, 'Directors' Wider Responsibilities—Problems Conceptual, Practical and Procedural' (1987) 13 Monash U L Rev 164, 165.

[11] Paddy Ireland, Ian Grigg-Spall, and Dave Kelly, 'The Conceptual Foundations of Modern Company Law' (1987) 14 Journal of Law and Society 149, 150; The Joint Stock Companies Act 1856, s 13 read, 'The subscribers of the memorandum of association, together with such other persons as may from time to time become shareholders of the company, shall thereupon [upon registration] be a *body corporate* by the name prescribed in the memorandum of association' (author's italics).

2.2 Legal personality for all lawful purposes

When incorporation required either a Royal Charter or a Private Act of Parliament the Crown or the Government determined which ventures were deserving of incorporation. In the early nineteenth century the idea that the state should be involved in screening which types of businesses should benefit from incorporation was abandoned. The Companies Act 1844 did thus not restrict the corporate form to any particular venture. There was, nevertheless, a concern about illegitimate use. The First Report of the Parliamentary Select Committee leading to the adoption of the Companies Act 1844 lamented the phenomenon of 'bubble companies', which were set up to defraud investors. The conclusion was, however, that a public censor of incorporation can also fall victim to deception and is in no better position than anyone else to identify legitimate businesses. The Act then was designed with a view to preventing such 'bubble companies'.[12]

There was a requirement that the corporate form be connected to a significant number of members. The Companies Act 1844 required that a company be set up by at least twenty-five members.[13] That requirement was later reduced to seven. On the basis of this requirement it would be possible to conclude that a small business cannot avail itself of the corporate form. A policy justification could be found in the fact that the corporate form should be limited to projects that are administratively difficult to operate as partnerships.

This was, however, not how the law was drafted. *Salomon v Salomon* confirmed that the requirement for a certain number of members was a formal one. The Court of Appeal observed that Aaron Salomon had set up the company in a 'mere scheme to enable him to carry on business in the name of the company with limited liability contrary to the true intent and meaning of the Companies Act 1862'.[14] Lindley LJ held that six of the seven members 'were members simply in order to enable the seventh himself to carry on business with limited liability. The object of the whole arrangement is to do the very thing which the Legislature intended not to be done'.[15]

At first instance the company was held to be an agent of Mr Salomon. At the Court of Appeal the conclusion was that it was his trustee. The House of Lords, however, unanimously concluded that the company had been validly incorporated and was neither. The fact that a certain number of individuals need to participate in the formation process did not mean that they have to make any other contribution. In particular it did not matter that six of the seven could be characterized as 'dummies' of the dominant shareholder. The company was set up by 'seven actual living persons'.[16] All other formalities had been duly complied with. There was no evidence of fraud, agency, or express trust.

[12] Parliamentary Papers (1844) Vol 7, iii–vii.
[13] Companies Act 1844, s II (C 110, 7° & 8° Vic).
[14] *Salomon v Salomon* [1896] AC 22, 37, 43, 44.
[15] ibid 31.
[16] ibid 26 (Lord Halsbury).

No rule of equity was cited by counsel that supported the conclusion of a constructive trust.[17]

The decision was reached by the judges consulting the Companies Act 1862 and concluding that it did not attach any substantive requirements to the number of shareholders. Lord Halsbury observed, 'I am simply here dealing with the provisions of the statute and it seems to me to be essential to the artificial creation that the law should recognise only that artificial existence—quite apart from the motives or conduct of individual corporators.'[18] Lord Herschell said:

> I know of no means of ascertaining what is the intent and meaning of the Companies Act except by examining its provisions and finding what regulations it has imposed as a condition of trading with limited liability. . . . The Legislature . . . clearly sanctions a scheme by which all the shares except six are owned by a single individual, and these six are of a value little more than nominal[19] . . . The statute . . . certainly contains no enactment that each of the seven persons subscribing the memorandum must be beneficially entitled to the share or shares for which he subscribes.[20]

Since a company can be used for all legal purposes it can operate a for-profit commercial venture as well as a charitable organization.[21] It may not be formed for an unlawful purpose.[22] There are no other restrictions in the Companies Act on what the corporate form can be used for. In *Prest v Petrodel* Lord Neuberger endorsed the dictum by Lord Halsbury LC where he said that a 'legally incorporated' company must be treated 'like any other independent person with its rights and liabilities appropriated to itself . . . whatever may have been the ideas or schemes of those who brought it into existence'.[23]

From a theoretical perspective the approach adopted by the courts is best characterized as endorsing legal positivism and thus fits well with a concession model of the company.[24] The company is a creation of the Act and it may be that a company like Mr Salomon's was not in the contemplation of the legislature at the time when the Act was passed and that the legislature would have imposed stricter requirements if this had been foreseen, but this is irrelevant because judges 'have to interpret the law and not make it'.[25] We will see in the next section, however, that using purely formal legal analysis without an understanding of the phenomenon the law is trying to address can cause problems.

---

[17] ibid 55 (Lord Davey).

[18] ibid 30.

[19] ibid 45.

[20] ibid 45–46.

[21] See, however, Michael Galanis, who argues that the corporate form is unsuitable for anything other than the promotion of economic growth (Michael Galanis, 'Growth and the Lost Legitimacy of Business Organisations: Time to Abandon Corporate Law Reform' [2020] JCLS 291).

[22] Companies Act 2006, s 7(2).

[23] *Prest v Petrodel* [2013] UKSC 34, [2013] 2 AC 415 [66].

[24] See also Martin Petrin, 'Reconceptualizing the Theory of the Firm—From Nature to Function' (2013) 118 Penn State L Rev 1, 43 who recommends that a legal entity should be viewed simply as a 'tool' through which the legislature has chosen to enable individuals to pursue goals in an effective and convenient manner.

[25] *Salomon v Salomon & Co Ltd* [1897] AC 22, 46.

2.3 One-person companies

The corporate form can be used for purposes that do not involve organizational action and the boundaries of organizations do not have to align with the boundaries of the corporate form. This is because the law does not restrict the use of the corporate form in this way. This has two consequences. The first one will be discussed in this subsection.

A company can be incorporated by a single person.[26] It is also possible for that single individual to act as the company's only director. It is also possible for this individual to act as the sole employee as well as the sole lender of that company. In such circumstances the company does not operate an organization but provides a vehicle for a business controlled by one person. That is fine as far as the Companies Act is concerned.[27] Once the company is registered it is considered a person separate from this single individual.

That is not to say that the courts find it easy to come to terms with one-person companies. Most recently the difficulties associated with the analysis of such companies have been illustrated by the Supreme Court decision in *Stone & Rolls v Moore Stephens*.[28] It was held in that case that Stone & Rolls Ltd could not claim damages from its auditors who had negligently overlooked the fraud committed by the company's sole shareholder and director. The House of Lords held that the company was unable to claim as it was itself responsible for the fraud. It could not base a claim on its own wrongdoing. The case arguably does not have due regard to the company's separate legal personality.[29] The company is independent of all of its participants.[30] Even if the company has only one shareholder who is its only director it is still an independent subject of the law and can be the victim of a deceit by that shareholder director.

The common law, of course, sets itself right and swiftly too.[31] Only six years after *Stone & Rolls* was decided, Lord Neuberger suggested in *Bilta v Nazir* that it should be put 'on one side', 'not to be looked at again'.[32] A few years after the decision in *Bilta* Lady Hale agreed with the first instance judge in *Singularis Holdings v Daiwa* that there is 'no principle of law that in any proceedings where the company is suing a third party for breach

---

[26] Companies Act 2006, s 7(1).

[27] There is nevertheless an increasing concern about the use of companies for criminal purposes. The latest reform proposals relating to 'Corporate transparency and register reform: powers of the registrar' can be found here: https://www.gov.uk/government/consultations/corporate-transparency-and-register-reform-powers-of-the-registrar.

[28] *Stone & Rolls v Moore Stephens* [2009] UKHL 39, [2009] 1 AC 1391.

[29] *Singularis Holdings Ltd v Daiwa Capital Markets Europe Ltd* [2019] UKSC 50, [2019] 3 WLR 997 at [27], [31], and [34]; see also Sarah Worthington, 'Corporate Attribution and Agency: Back to Basics' [2017] LQR 118, 122 and Ivan Sin, 'Corporate Attribution and the Fallacy of the "One-man Company": Finale of an Unfortunate Saga' [2020] JBL 542.

[30] *Singularis Holdings Ltd v Daiwa Capital Markets Europe Ltd* [2019] UKSC 50, [2019] 3 WLR 997 at [27].

[31] Veltrice Tan, 'The Invisible Piercing of the Corporate Veil' (2020) 41 Comp Law 263 discusses the Singapore Court of Appeal ruling in *Red Star Marine Consultants Pte Ltd v Personal Representatives of Satwant Kaur d/o Sardara Singh* on whether an individual who was in effect the sole shareholder and director of a company was the sole beneficiary of claims the company might make against another party. That individual was party to a fraud penetrated by an employee of the company and so the company could not claim against the estate of that employee. Distinguishes *Singularis Holdings* and *Bilta*.

[32] *Bilta v Nazir* [2015] UKSC 23, [2016] 1 AC 1 at [30].

of duty owed to it by that third party, the fraudulent conduct of a director is to be attributed to the company if it is a one-man company'. Lady Hale agreed with this guiding principle and concluded that '*Stone & Rolls* can finally be laid to rest'.[33]

From a theoretical perspective, *Stone & Rolls* serves as an example that an understanding of the real-life phenomena the law is designed to solve can help in applying the rules. The separate legal personality of the company is not just a legal formality and the company is not just a front for its shareholder(s). The company is designed to allow organizations to operate autonomously. The Companies Act contains rules that serve shareholders as well as creditors.[34] A company can thus suffer harm through the actions of its sole shareholder director. It can also claim against a bank which carried out fraudulent instructions by the director in breach of the duty of care it owed to the company.[35]

There are also policy reasons supporting the availability of the corporate form for a one-person business. Company law can operate as an incubator facilitating a healthy population of micro-enterprises which, taken together, are an important ingredient of a successful economy. Moreover, not much harm can be done by any individual small-scale business. In addition, we will see below that rules have developed over time that remove limited liability for controllers of companies who step outside of their statutory roles as shareholders or directors but these do not affect the separate legal personality of the company.[36]

2.4 Corporate groups

The second consequence of the unrestricted availability of the corporate form is that companies can be used to form corporate groups. A company can be a shareholder in another company.[37] Provided that a company has at least one natural person acting as a director, a company can also act as a director of another company.[38] A corporate director is not to be regarded as a shadow director of any of its subsidiary companies for the purposes of directors' general duties, transactions requiring members' approval, or the contract with a sole member who is also a director.[39] A large organization that operates as a single economic unit can consist of a number of legally independent companies. A subsidiary is also not considered the agent of a parent company purely

---

[33] *Singularis Holdings Ltd v Daiwa Capital Markets Europe Ltd* [2019] UKSC 50, [2019] 3 WLR 997 at [34].

[34] See in particular chapters 7, 8, and 9.

[35] *Singularis Holdings Ltd v Daiwa Capital Markets Europe Ltd* [2019] UKSC 50, [2019] 3 WLR 997.

[36] Chapter 4.

[37] There was a time when the holding of shares in other companies was considered to be *ultra vires* but the law changed in the mid-nineteenth century (Christian A Witting, *Liability of Corporate Groups and Networks* (CUP 2018) 65–66).

[38] Companies Act 2006, s 155; The UK Government is however currently consulting on putting into force rules prohibiting corporate directors (BEIS, Corporate Transparency and Register Reform Consultation on implementing the ban on corporate directors 9 December 2020 available from <https://assets.publishing.service.gov.uk/government/uploads/system/uploads/attachment_data/file/942194/Corporate_Directors_Consultation.pdf>).

[39] Companies Act 2006, s 251(3).

because the parent holds all of the shares of the subsidiary.[40] Such an agency relationship only exists when the parent has given either express or ostensible authority to the subsidiary.[41] A judgment obtained against a subsidiary does not give rise to an issue estoppel against the controller of that subsidiary.[42]

In *Adams v Cape*, Cape Industries Plc was the parent company of a number of subsidiaries which formed a single economic unit engaging in the mining, processing, and distribution of asbestos and asbestos-related products. Slade J pointed out that

> [t]here is no general principle that all companies in a group of companies are to be regarded as one. On the contrary, the fundamental principle is that 'each company in a group of companies (a relatively modern concept) is a separate legal entity possessed of separate legal rights and liabilities'.[43]

Like the asbestos industry, the shipping trade is organized on the basis of group structures. In the latter case, groups frequently consist of one-ship companies which are ultimately controlled by one individual or family.[44] Likewise in the pharmaceutical industry, businesses are incorporated through separate individual companies.[45] In all of these examples the organizational boundaries of the group are wider than the legal boundaries of the companies that form part of the group.

A separate company can also be used as a special purpose vehicle where its role is reduced to issuing a bond, receiving funds from bond investors, and lending these funds onwards to the parent of the same group. In *Re Polly Peck International plc*, Robert Walker J (as he then was) upheld the separate legal personality of the special purpose vehicle. He permitted that vehicle to claim as a creditor in the administration of the parent company. The investors, who claimed against the parent under a guarantee, had tried to stop this claim on the basis that the special purpose vehicle was a 'sham'.[46] A special purpose vehicle does not operate an organization but rather helps with the administration of the performance of a contract.

Separate legal personality for sub-units that form part of an overreaching economic unit makes it easier for them to be run relatively autonomously from the centre and

---

[40] *Gramophone and Typewriter Co Ltd v Stanley* [1908] 2 KB 89; but see *HRMC v Development Securities Plc* [2020] EWCA Civ 1705, [2021] BTC 1.

[41] *Taylor v Rhino Overseas Inc* [2020] EWCA Civ 353, [2020] Bus LR 1486; *Ortakligi v Schlegel Automotive Europe Ltd*, QBD 12 Oct 2012, unreported; see also *Freelands v McClue* [2014] 12 WLUK 28, 2015 GWD 4-78 where it was held that a director who has ostensible authority to bind the company in the ordinary course of business does not automatically have authority to cause the other director to incur personal liability to a contractual partner; see also Colin Mackie, 'Corporate Groups, Common Officers and the Relevance of "Capacity" in Questions of Knowledge Attribution' [2020] Journal of Corporate Law Studies 1.

[42] *MAD Atelier International BV v Manès* [2020] EWHC 1014 (Ch), [2020] 3 WLR 631.

[43] *Adams v Cape Industries Plc* [1990] AC 433 at 532; see also Steyn J (as he then was) in *The Glasnos* [1991] 1 Lloyd's Rep 482 at 491 and *Liberty Investing Ltd v Sydow* [2015] EWHC 608 (Comm) [2015] 2 WLUK 497.

[44] *The Glasnos* [1991] 1 Lloyd's Rep 482 at 491 (Steyn J).

[45] Christian A Witting, Liability of Corporate Groups and Networks (CUP 2018) 6 and 40–41.

[46] *Re Polly Peck International plc* [1996] 2 All ER 433, 447 (Robert Walker J); see also *The Glasnos* [1991] 1 Lloyd's Rep 482 at 491: 'A great many shipping groups, structured in one ship companies, are ultimately controlled by one individual or family' (Steyn J).

from other units. It makes it possible to replace a command-and-control structure with a more flexible model where the parent company does not normally provide daily oversight of operations but focuses on setting a group strategy and assessing the financial performance of subsidiaries.[47]

Separate legal personality also assists sub-units to source independent external debt and equity finance.[48] In the context of financial regulation separate legal entities are used with a view to protecting retail customers of banks from risks elsewhere in a banking group.[49] For international groups separate legal personality facilitates compliance with the regulatory rules in different jurisdictions.[50] There is, of course, also a dark side to the use of separate legal personality with groups setting up foreign subsidiaries to avoid taxes or particular aspects of regulatory regimes.[51]

The law, which recognizes the separate legal personality of individual companies within a group, nevertheless acknowledges the social phenomenon underpinning corporate groups. The Companies Act contains special reporting requirements for companies that form part of an economic entity.[52] The UK Government has recently announced that it will take further steps to enhance stewardship of the largest companies, through stronger mandates and greater transparency over group structures and dividend policies. The Government will pursue options to require groups to provide explanations of their corporate and subsidiary structures such as the provision of an organogram and an explanation of how corporate governance is maintained through the group.[53]

We will discuss instances where the law introduces liability of parent or subsidiary companies.[54] It suffices to note here that none of these instances ignore the separate personality of the company. There is no case or statute where a company's separate legal personality has been disregarded such that a court held that the company did not exist.

2.5 Beginning and ending companies

Contracts cannot create separate legal persons. For that a statute is required. Contracts begin when parties agree for them to start and can also be ended by agreement. Under the statutory regime a company is set up by private action of one of more individuals but that is not enough for the company to come into existence. For a company to come into existence a number of documents need to be produced. These show that companies

---

[47] Christian A Witting, *Liability of Corporate Groups and Networks* (CUP 2018) 37.
[48] ibid 47–48.
[49] Thom Wetzer, 'In Two Minds: The Governance of Ring-Fenced Banks' [2019] JCLS 197.
[50] Christian A Witting, *Liability of Corporate Groups and Networks* (CUP 2018) 47–48.
[51] ibid 52–60.
[52] Companies Act 2006, ss 399–402.
[53] <https://assets.publishing.service.gov.uk/government/uploads/system/uploads/attachment_data/file/736163/ICG_-_Government_response_doc_-_24_Aug_clean_version__with_Minister_s_photo_and_signature__AC.pdf> [1.10–1.11].
[54] Section 4.3 of this book.

are designed as vehicles for organizations. The registration documents, for example, need to state the company's name, which must be distinct from the name of companies that have already been registered and otherwise comply with the requirements set out in Companies Act 2006, sections 53–65, its type (private or public, with or without a share capital), its registered office, and its first officers.[55] There is also a requirement to disclose any persons with significant control.[56] Companies House verifies if the documents required are present and complete and then registers the company and issues a certificate of incorporation.[57] The separate legal personality of a company begins only once it has been registered.[58] The certificate of incorporation evidences that the company has been duly registered and states the name of the company, its registration number, its date of incorporation, its type, and the jurisdiction of its registered office.[59]

In addition to supplying the company with proof of its legal existence, Companies House makes available information on all registered companies to the public for inspection.[60] In addition a company must disclose the following on its websites: its registered name, the part of the UK in which it is registered, its registered number, and its registered office address.[61] Each company must keep available for inspection at its registered office a register of its directors.[62] It must also notify the registrar within fourteen days from a person becoming or ceasing to be a director.[63] This allows members of the public to overcome the problem that legal persons do not have a physical existence.

The rules governing the formation of companies support the conclusion that companies are designed as vehicles for organizational action. Registration on a publicly available register ensures that those setting up a company establish facts that make it possible for that company to act independently of its members and also that third parties have an independent source to verify the existence and other key facts relating to that company.

Along similar lines the members of a company can decide to bring the company to an end.[64] But for its separate personality to come to an end it needs to be removed from the register. Moreover, this removal can only happen after the company has either undergone reorganization proceedings or been wound up. Both procedures take into account the interests of creditors. One-person companies are no exception to this. Companies that operate as special purpose vehicles are in reality no different from contracts but can also not be terminated by agreement and need to be wound up.

---

[55] Companies Act 2006, s 9.
[56] ibid s 12A.
[57] ibid ss 14–15.
[58] ibid s 16.
[59] ibid s 15.
[60] < https://beta.companieshouse.gov.uk/company/00070527/filing-history>.
[61] Company, Limited Liability Partnership and Business (Names and Trading Disclosures) Regulations 2015/17.
[62] Companies Act 2006, s 162.
[63] ibid s 167.
[64] Insolvency Act 1986, s 122(1)(a).

We will see below that fraud 'unravels everything'.[65] This is true also in company law, but while an illegal contract is declared null and void, a company pursuing illegal activity has legal personality from registration to the point in time when it is dissolved and removed from the register. The Secretary of State can ask the court to wind up a company if this is expedient in the public interest and the court will make a winding-up order if it is just and equitable for the company to be wound up.[66] The winding up of a company, which operated an illegal lottery, has, for example, been held to be in the public interest.[67] Another example is a company that has been set up to operate a tax minimization scheme that subverts the purpose of insolvency law.[68]

2.6 Theoretical observations

From a theoretical perspective it is worth observing that separate legal personality does not arise through private ordering alone. It is thus not possible to explain its existence through a nexus of contract or agency framework.

In the first instance, separate legal personality serves administrative purposes. It creates a formal legal unit which can operate independently from its members and directors. The requirement for registration and the public availability of the register enable third parties to verify the existence of a company independently. This makes it possible for an organization to use a company to act autonomously in law. As with the formation of a company, its termination requires the completion of a special process that ensures that the interests of third parties are considered. This gives the company a level of stability that goes beyond contract law.

The fact that legal personality is determined independently from organizational boundaries also provides for certainty. An organization is a social phenomenon that acts through and interacts with human beings who participate with different levels of intensity. The level of intensity of these connections also varies between organizations. It is difficult to draw generally applicable boundaries on who is outside and who is inside an organization. Legal personality overcomes this problem. While the boundaries of legal personality do not always coincide with social reality, they are certain and it is easy to determine who is inside and who is outside of the company. The phenomenon of corporate groups nevertheless requires regulatory attention and we will see below that there are a growing number of statutory rules that define and regulate corporate groups for the purposes of particular regulatory aims.

---

[65] Section 4.3.1 of this book.
[66] Insolvency Act 1986, s 124A.
[67] *In Re Senator Hanseatische Verwaltungsgesellschaft mbH* [1997] 1 WLR 515 (CA); see also *Re Equity and Provident Ltd* [2002] EWHC 186 (Ch), [2002] 2 BCLC 78 where the company was compulsorily wound up because it sold worthless motor warranty plans.
[68] *Re PAG Management Services Ltd* [2015] EWHC 2404 (Ch), (2015) BCC 720; but see *Re PAG Asset Preservation Ltd* [2020] EWCA Civ 1017, [2020] BCC 979.

The Companies Act does not limit the use of the corporate form to any particular purpose and so companies can be used to generate profit but also to promote charitable aims. They can but do not have to be used to operate an organization. A single controller can run a microbusiness through a separate entity and groups can break up a single economic unit into separate legal entities.

The law could, of course, limit the availability of the corporate form not only to lawful activity but also tie it more closely to organizational purposes and boundaries. It could, for example, require for there to be a certain number of fully engaged members. It could prohibit the use of special purpose vehicles or of shell companies or require economic entities to incorporate as one legal unit rather than as a web of separate legal entities. None of this is wise, however. We have seen that there are good reasons for permitting one-person companies as well as single entities within groups.

The fact that it is possible to use a company for more than organizational action, however, does not deflect from the observation that company law is built to serve organizational action. The Companies Act has designed company law with organizations in mind. It balances the interests of shareholders and creditors and so it is not possible to characterize the company as identical with its owner. All companies including special purpose vehicles need to go through a process of being wound up before they can end. Likewise companies serving illegal purposes are not nullified by the courts. They too have to go through a process of winding up where their activity is ended in an orderly manner and their creditors are paid. This supports the theory of this book that company law is designed to operate organizations, which are real entities acting autonomously through a decision-making process that is established and protected by legislation and by the common law.

3

Corporate Capacity

3.1 Introduction

In this chapter we will examine the *ultra vires* doctrine, under which the capacity of companies used to be limited by their objects. We will see that the doctrine could be justified through a concession-style argument as well as through contractual analysis. The doctrine, however, proved unsuitable. It will be argued that this is evidence that contract law is not adequate basis for the operation of an organization. We will also analyse the recent recommendation for companies to set themselves a purpose discouraging them from making the generation of financial return their primary objective. It will be argued that the programmatic statement of a corporate purpose is likely to bring about only cosmetic changes. If there is a desire for wider aims to be integrated into corporate decisions these would have to be institutionalized. This can be achieved, for example, by identifying a board member to represent these interests on the board.

3.2 Contract as explanation for the *ultra vires* doctrine

The fact that companies take their origins from contract and trust law explains what was to become the *ultra vires* doctrine. If the basis of a company is a contract or a trust, the boundaries of the company are determined by that contract or trust. The company cannot exist outside that foundational arrangement. The parties to the contract and the trustees of a trust only have the rights given to them by the contract or deed. Third parties who act on the basis of someone else's contract or trust are naturally also affected by this. The *ultra vires* doctrine can thus be explained as giving proper effect to the contractual arrangement between the shareholders.[1]

The genesis of the doctrine illustrates this point. The Companies Act 1856 was silent about the capacity of companies. There was no provision limiting the capacity of companies. There were also no provisions providing for unlimited capacity.

When the courts had to decide whether companies had limited capacity there were two options available to the judges. The first option would have been to conclude that, as there was no express limit in the Act capacity was unlimited. The second option was

---

[1] Armour and Whincop in John Armour and Michael J Whincop, 'The proprietary Foundations of Corporate Law' (2007) 27(3) Oxford Journal of Legal Studies 429, 443–4 and 448 refer to this effect as 'multital' or 'loosely' proprietary, but labelling the effect in those terms does not explain why the shareholders' ability to shape the capacity of the company has been removed.

to say that because there is no express provision in favour of full capacity, capacity was limited.

Mr Gifford, QC and Mr Benjamin, QC argued in favour of the first option in *Ashbury Railway v Riche*.[2] The argument persuaded Blackburn J, who held at first instance that a corporation at common law has the same rights as a natural person and, as nothing in the Companies Act 1862 'by express provision, or by necessary implication' excludes this for companies, these too have unlimited capacity.[3]

Blackburn J, was, of course, overruled. The House of Lords concluded that the capacity of companies was limited by its objects. Their Lordships examined Companies Act 1862, sections 1, 6, 7, 8, 10, 11, 12, 14, and 50, none of which explicitly limited the capacity of the company. Their Lordships nevertheless focused on the fact that the Act did 'not speak of that incorporation as the creation of a corporation with inherent common law rights'.[4] This distinguished companies from corporations established by charter.

LCB Gower in the first edition of Principles of Modern Company Law makes a constitutional point in support of the decision of the House of Lords. He observes that, unlike the Crown, Parliament had the *vires* to 'limit the potential activities of its creatures in any way it liked'.[5] He also observed that for statutory (as opposed to chartered) corporations the *ultra vires* doctrine was 'being slowly evolved' at the time and so the courts rightly chose to 'equate' registered companies with statutory corporations.[6]

It is submitted here that the *ultra vires* doctrine also chimes with the contractual pedigree that underpinned the deed of settlement companies from which modern companies evolved. The Companies Act 1844, while making separate legal personality generally available, clearly displayed the legacy of the deed of settlement framework.[7] Evidence for this can be found in the terminology used in the Act. Sections VII and VIII contained the terms 'deed of settlement' and 'supplementary deed of settlement' to refer to the company's constitution. The Limited Liability Act 1855 also used the term 'deed of settlement' (sections I and II).[8] Lord Wensleydale used the term 'copartnership deed' in *Ernest v Nicholls*.[9] He also said that 'the company exists only in the directors and officers acting by and according to the deed'.[10] This suggests that the contract-based framework that operated before 1844 was still present in the analysis of early companies. The Joint Stock Companies Act 1856 replaced the terminology and introduced the terms 'memorandum' (section III) and 'articles of association' (section IX).[11]

---

[2] *Ashbury Railway v Riche* (1874–75) LR 7 HL 653, 661.
[3] *Riche v The Ashbury Railway Carriage and Iron Company Ltd* (1873–74) LR 9 Ex 224 (264–66); this, at the time, appears to have been the view of 'many' (JCB Gower, *The Principles of Modern Company Law* (Stevens & Sons 1954) 81).
[4] *Ashbury Railway v Riche* (1874–75) LR 7 HL 653 at 668 (Lord Crains).
[5] JCB Gower, *The Principles of Modern Company Law* (Stevens & Sons 1954) 81.
[6] ibid 83.
[7] Companies Act 1844, 7&8 Vict c 100.
[8] Limited Liability Act 1855, 18&19 Vict c 133.
[9] *Ernest v Nicholls* (1857) VI HLC 401, 419; 10 ER 1357, 1358.
[10] *Ernest v Nicholls* (1857) VI HLC 401, 423; 10 ER 1357, 1360.
[11] Joint Stock Companies Act 1856, 19&20 Vict c 47.

Notwithstanding this change in statutory wording, no change in approach to the nature of these documents appears to have occurred. In *Ashbury Railway v Riche*, Lord Crains, as the Lord Chancellor, said about the memorandum and the articles that they formed the 'title deeds of companies'.[12]

In presenting the bill to the House of Commons, Mr Lowe, the Vice President of the Board of Trade at the time, stressed that incorporation is not a privilege, but a right. He said, 'The principle is freedom of contract, and the right of unlimited association— the right of people to make what contracts they please on behalf of themselves'.[13] Mr Lowe then elaborated that he was in favour of 'human liberty—that people may be permitted to deal how and with whom they choose without the officious interference of the State . . .'.[14] The effect of throwing 'obstacles in the way of limited companies being formed' would be 'to arrest ninety-nine good schemes in order that the bad hundredth might be prevented'.[15] The court should be armed 'with sufficient power to check extravagances or roguery'.[16] The legislature should otherwise only interfere to 'give the greatest publicity to the affairs of such companies, that everyone may know on what grounds he is dealing'.[17] This reads like a modern textbook summary of the nexus of contract theory both as a positive and as a normative statement.

Notwithstanding the view expressed by the Vice-President of the Board of Trade, Mr Lowe, to the House of Commons, the judges themselves would not have characterized their reasoning as capable of being explained by a contractual theory. Their approach fits most closely with the concession theory of incorporation: The company is created by the Act and the Act shapes its existence. Lord Chelmsford, for example, pointed out that the company is 'entirely a creation of the statute'.[18] It is necessary for the protection of those who enter into contracts with them that the 'privilege' of creating them should only be obtained upon certain conditions which should be made known to the public.[19]

Their decision is also motivated by the fact that the Act makes it possible to incorporate companies with limited liability. This was previously 'wholly unknown in the general conduct of mercantile affairs in this country'.[20] Every person entering into a partnership subjects the whole of his property to the demands of his creditors. When an Act departs from the principle upon certain conditions to be expressed in the Act of Parliament it is impossible not to feel that creditors and shareholders should be protected.[21]

---

[12] *Ashbury Railway v Riche* (1874–75) LR 7 HL 653 at 667.
[13] Commons Sitting Friday, 1 February 1856, Hansard 3rd Series, Volume 140 Year 19 pp 129–30.
[14] ibid 131.
[15] ibid.
[16] ibid.
[17] ibid.
[18] *Ashbury Railway v Riche* (1874–75) LR 7 HL 653, 678, 670 ('the ambit and extent of vitality and power which *by law* are given to the corporation' (Lord Crains)), 690 (The 'Act gave certain privileges and imposed certain conditions' (Lord O'Hagan)), and 693 ('a statutory corporation, created by Act of Parliament for a particular purposed' (Lord Selborne)).
[19] ibid 678; see also 684 (Lord Hatherly).
[20] ibid 684 (Lord Hatherly).
[21] ibid 684 (Lord Hatherly).

It is nevertheless the case that when they turn their minds to giving meaning to the words used in the statute, their reasoning fits with the deed of settlement framework that preceded modern companies. That framework operated on the basis of contract law. At a positive level, the *ultra vires* doctrine fits well with an analysis that equates the constitutional documents with a contract.

3.3 The collapse of the *ultra vires* doctrine

It is well known that the approach of determining the capacity of companies through the company's foundational documents did not work. This was notwithstanding the fact that the contract forming the basis of the company was publicly available. Contract law was unable to provide a stable constitutional basis upon which companies could operate.

Those setting up companies tried to avoid the doctrine by adopting all-encompassing object clauses.[22] Brian Cheffins comments on this phenomenon by pointing out that the judges did not like this attempt to undermine the *ultra vires* doctrine and tried to rein in these tendencies to widen the scope of the capacity of companies.[23] He does not show, however, that the judges did anything more than what they normally do when construing terms of contracts. Rather than showing the inability of judges to deliver commercially sound results this development shows that contract is ultimately not a basis upon which companies are best built.

The contractual analysis that was the historic starting point for company law over time proved to be unsuitable for corporate life. Its effect has been described as imposing 'artificial limitations' on the acts which a company was regarded, in law, as capable of doing.[24] The doctrine was said to lead to 'commercial inconvenience' and 'frequent injustice'.[25] It was also criticized as leading to random results and as lacking clarity.[26] These comments, however, overlook that the task of the judges was to construe individual contractual terms.[27] They had no instructions to produce results that would be reconcilable across the spectrum of all or even most companies.

The doctrine operated as a trap for the 'unwary' and became a hazard to the very people it was supposed to protect.[28] It represented an obstacle to enterprise and worked so

---

[22] *Cotman v Brougham* [1918] AC 514 (HL); *Bell Houses Ltd v City Hall Properties Ltd* [1966] 2 QB 656 (CA); Sarah Worthington, *Sealy and Worthington's Texts and Materials on Company Law* (11th edn, OUP 2016) 88; Report of the Committee on Company Law Amendment (Cohen Report) 1945 Cmd 6659, 1945 para 12.
[23] Brian Cheffins, *Company Law* (OUP 1997) 296.
[24] Sarah Worthington, *Sealy and Worthington's Texts and Materials on Company Law* (11th edn, OUP 2016) 87.
[25] Browne-Wilkinson VC in *TCB Ltd v Gray* [1986] Ch 621, 635; This was cited with approval by Robert Walker LJ (as he then was) in *Smith v Henniker-Major & Co* [2002] EWCA Civ 762, [2003] Ch 182 [25].
[26] Sarah Worthington, *Sealy and Worthington's Texts and Materials on Company Law* (11th edn, OUP 2016) 89; *Re Introductions* [1969] 1 All ER 887; *Re Jan Beaufort* [1953] Ch 131.
[27] See eg the analysis adopted by Lord Crains in *Ashbury Railway Carriages v Riche* (1874–75) LR 7 HL 653, 664–67.
[28] Daniel D Prentice, Reform of the Ultra Vires Rule, A Consultative Document (Department of Trade and Industry 1986) 18.

capriciously that it was doubtful whether it offered any real protection to anyone.[29] It was criticized as a pitfall for third parties dealing with companies, as serving 'no positive purpose' but causing unnecessary 'prolixity and vexation'.[30] The legislature intervened and, after several attempts, eliminated the external effect of the doctrine. The directors, however, continue to be bound by the object clause contained in the constitution.[31]

The move from contractually limited capacity to unlimited capacity was not an easy one. In particular there was concern that the unlimited powers of the company would be 'exercisable in their entirety by the directors'.[32] The Jenkins Committee noted that 'present complaints' of company law are often to the effect that shareholders should be given greater and more effective control over the activities of directors.[33] An 'omnibus delegation' to the directors of all powers of a natural person conferred on the company seemed to them a 'retrograde step'.[34]

The Jenkins Committee further observed that the injustice wrought to third parties has to a great extent been eliminated by the use of wide-form object clauses and that instances of injustice have in fact, as of late years, seemed rare.[35] They recommended not to repeal the doctrine, but to provide protection to third parties dealing with the company in good faith thereby eliminating instances of unfairness.[36] The Jenkins Committee also recommended that the Companies Act contain a 'common form of an-cillary powers' which are incidental to the carrying on of a company's main business to avoid doubt and to help reduce the length of the object clauses.[37]

This was not implemented. Instead, the UK decided to fully close the door to the external effect of the company's object clause. Companies now have unlimited capacity. Companies no longer have to state an object. If they do not state an object, the objects are unrestricted. In addition, the memorandum has ceased to have constitutional significance.

Companies Act 2006, section 39 is entitled 'A company's capacity' and reads:

> The validity of an act done by a company shall not be called into question on the ground of lack of capacity by reason of anything in the company's constitution.

This is a move that does not fit with contract law. It prevents those setting up a company to determine the capacity of that company in their agreement. Third parties are given

---

[29] Daniel D Prentice, Reform of the Ultra Vires Rule, A Consultative Document (Department of Trade and Industry 1986) 1.

[30] Report of the Committee on Company Law Amendment (Cmd 6659, 1945) (Cohen Report) para 12.

[31] Section 7.3 in this chapter.

[32] Report of the Company Law Committee (Jenkins Committee) Cmnd 1749, 1962 para 39 (iv).

[33] ibid para 39 (v).

[34] ibid para 39 (v); This point also appears in Marc T Moore, Corporate Governance in the Shadow of the State (Hart 2013) 152–53. He writes that this increased 'managerial power'. It is worth pointing out that directors over-step the corporate objects at their own peril. Transactions may be valid, but the directors can be held liable for breach of duty. When they act outside the constitution directors do not benefit from limited liability.

[35] Report of the Company Law Committee (Jenkins Committee) Cmnd 1749, 1962 para 40.

[36] ibid para 42.

[37] ibid para 43.

rights arising out of transactions that have not been contemplated by the document agreed upon by the founders of the company. This helps companies to operate as organizations that are autonomous of their members.

Companies Act 2006, section 39 goes beyond what was required by the First Company Law Directive. That Directive requires Member States of the European Community to implement legislation whereby acts done by the organs of the company are binding upon it even if those acts are not within the objects of the company unless such acts exceed the powers that the law confers or allows to be conferred on those organs.[38] It would seem that a solution, similar to that proposed by the Jenkins Committee whereby the Act provides for a 'common form of [] powers', would have been compliant with the Directive. It would have been possible, for example, to limit the power of the directors to the 'ordinary course of business'. Moreover, Member States are free to provide that the company shall not be bound by acts outside its object if the third party knew that the acts were outside the objects of could have been aware of it.[39] The UK took neither option when adopting its law to the Directive.

3.4 Corporate purpose

Following the Brexit referendum a debate has started about corporate purpose. The idea is to ensure that the economy works for everyone and the hope is that this can be facilitated by asking companies to set themselves a purpose in addition to the realization of return. The expectation is that companies will solve the problems of the planet and its people in a profitable manner rather than just aim to make a profit.[40] This debate is not intended to revive the *ultra vires* doctrine. It is rather intended to steer corporate decision-makers away from the 'greed is good' motto that was associated with the societal climate that prevailed when agency theory started to emerge. Doubts have been raised as to whether a statement of corporate purpose can achieve the desired outcomes.[41] From the perspective of this book we can observe that the theory advanced here holds true irrespective of the purpose those setting up and managing companies have set for themselves.

---

[38] Article 9 of the First Company Law Directive of 9 March 1968 (68/151/EEC) OJL 65/8 14.3 1968, now recast in article 10 Directive 2009/101/EC of 16 September 2009 OJL 258/11 of 1 Oct 2009.

[39] ibid.

[40] <https://www.thebritishacademy.ac.uk/programmes/future-of-the-corporation/>;   UK   Corporate Governance Code, principle A; Colin Mayer, 'The Future of the Corporate and the Economics of Purpose, European Corporate Governance Institute—Finance Working Paper No 710/2020' [2021] Journal of Management Studies (forthcoming)

[41] David Kershaw and Edmund Schuster, 'The Purposive Transformation of Company Law' The American Journal of Comparative Law (forthcoming); Amir N Licht, 'Varieties of Shareholderism: Three Views of the Corporate Purpose Cathedral' European Corporate Governance Institute—Law Working Paper No 547/2020; Barnali Choudhury and Martin Petrin, 'Corporate Governance that 'Works for Everyone': Promoting Public Policies through Corporate Governance Mechanism' [2018] JCLS 381; Lucian A Bebchuk and Roberto Tallarita, 'The Illusory Purpose of Stakeholder Governance' [2020] 106 Cornell L Rev 91.

At a normative level it is nevertheless worth observing that a statement of the purpose which a company intends to serve is, on its own, unlikely to affect those taking decisions for the company. This book builds on the insight that organizations are characterized by routines, process, and procedures. These operate independently of any mission a company adopts. From this perspective the integration of wider aims is better achieved through a modification of the company's social structure. An example of how this can be done can be found in the UK Corporate Governance Code 2018. It recommends that the concerns of the work force of listed companies are represented on the board through either a director appointed from the workforce, a formal workforce advisory panel, or a designated non-executive director.[42] It would be possible to integrate other interests through the designation of a role that represents these interests in the corporate decision-making process.[43] The influence of such a role can be fine-tuned to suit the respective policy aims of those implementing any reform. There is, of course, a risk that a company develops habits and a culture that erode the influence of such a role. There is also a risk that the personification of a particular interest through a designated role gives other members of an organization a license to ignore this particular aspect of the business of the company. But overall, the institutionalization of wider aims is likely to affect corporate decision-making to a greater degree than the adoption of a corporate purpose statement.

3.5 Theoretical observations

It is important to note that the change from contractually limited to unlimited capacity was not optional. Companies Act 2006, section 39 is mandatory. Shareholders cannot establish a limited company for non-charitable purposes with limited capacity. A contractual theory cannot explain the capacity of modern companies at a positive level.[44]

A better explanation of the rules providing for unlimited capacity focuses on the nature of organizations. We have seen above that organizations are more than aggregates of bilateral relationships between human beings.[45] An organization is a social fact. By working together humans create formal and informal constraints that bind participants and thus create stability. The structure that holds organizations together is, however, also flexible. By interacting with its participants an organization changes. This adaptation is shaped by participants but cannot be controlled by any of them on their own.

---

[42] UK Corporate Governance Code 2018, provision 5.

[43] See for example Irene-Marie Esser and Iain MacNeil, Disclosure and Engagement: Stakeholder Participation Mechanisms' (2019) 30 European Business L Rev 201; Benedict Sheehy, 'Sustainability, Justice and Corporate Law: Redistributing Corporate Rights and Duties to Meet the Challenge of Sustainability' (April 19, 2021). Available at SSRN: <https://ssrn.com/abstract=3829319>.

[44] John Armour and Michael J Whincop, 'The proprietary Foundations of Corporate Law' (2007) 27(3) 429 at 452.

[45] Section 1.4 in this chapter.

The initial purpose of a company can over time lose significance. It is developed and changes as the organization and the world around it evolves. Limiting the capacity of the company by reference to its original objects goes against the very nature of the mechanism holding organizations together. It ossifies ideas that the organization may have left behind. This helps to explain why the *ultra vires* doctrine ultimately did not succeed and unlimited capacity was imposed by the legislature.

In relation to corporate purpose, this book is agnostic as to how the balance between shareholders and other stakeholder is to be struck. It was nevertheless observed that the integration of wider aims is best achieved by creating designated role that represents these in the corporate decision-making process.

4

Limited Liability

4.1 Introduction

Limited liability is a feature of company law that makes it possible for shareholders and directors to participate in corporate decisions without incurring personal liability. It also protects creditors of the company from claims of the personal creditors of the shareholders and director. While separate legal personality is unwaveringly robust, limited liability is sometimes removed, with the common law or statute providing for the liability of the company for obligations owed by a shareholder or director or for the liability of a shareholder or director for a debt owed by the company. This is sometimes referred to as 'piercing the veil'. It is important to note from the outset that this metaphor is misleading. It seems to suggest that the separate personality of the company is removed. That is not the case. We will see below that the veil piercing rules only concern instances where liability is shared between companies and their shareholders or directors.

Instances of what can be termed abuses of the corporate form are addressed through liability rules rather than through an ad hoc removal of separate legal personality. This fits with the theoretical stance that companies are designed as operators of organizations. If abuse occurs it is possible to impose personal liability. It has been mentioned above that illegal companies can also be forced into a winding up, which ensures that the organization run through the company is ended in an orderly way. For that, legal personality needs to persist until the winding up is completed, illegality or abuse notwithstanding. It would therefore not be advisable to have rules that disable the separate legal personality of the company on an ad hoc basis.

Eleven years after separate legal personality had become available the Limited Liability Act 1855 was passed and made limited liability generally possible.[1] Limited liability performs an important function. It would have been difficult to fund the large-scale ventures of the Industrial Revolution on the basis of debt finance. These projects required funds on a scale that the lenders of the time would have struggled to supply. They were also associated with a level of uncertainty that would have been difficult for a lender to assume. The provision of funding through transferable equity, which permits the company to retain the funds in perpetuity and does not impose a duty on the company to produce returns but permits the investor to transfer the investment when his preferences change, is ideally suited to the financing of large scale and high-risk

---

[1] Limited Liability Act 1855, 18 & 19 Vict c 133.

Company Law. Eva Micheler, Oxford University Press. © Eva Micheler 2021. DOI: 10.1093/oso/9780198858874.003.0004

projects. Investors can, as we know, be persuaded to make available a portion of their assets for the use in open-ended ventures but they are much less likely to expose their entire financial wealth to any single such venture. The use of limited liability for the large-scale infrastructure projects of the Industrial Revolution can be justified on social utility grounds. Indeed, in the context of the modern debate we can observe that the making available of assets accumulated by pension savers for infrastructure-related projects is something that we continue to consider desirable.[2]

The corporate form is designed to be used by shareholders to set up and fund a business without incurring personal liability.[3] The Companies Act grants limited liability to shareholders precisely because this makes it possible for them to invest in an entrepreneurial venture without having to put at risk all of their personal assets. Limited liability also benefits creditors of companies. It insulates the company from the claims of the personal creditors of shareholders and directors.[4]

Like separate legal personality, limited liability is available for one-person companies as well as for corporate groups. This use of limited liability by a one-person company can be justified as permitting small business to be launched without putting at risk all of the personal assets of their controller. Group structures can provide multiple layers of protection against the entrepreneurial liability.[5] This permits large organizations to engage in different ventures without jeopardizing their entire asset portfolio. Shipping groups, for example, use one ship companies for this purpose.[6]

Over time the law has nevertheless accepted that it is possible in certain exceptional circumstances to 'pierce the corporate veil'. The term is best used to describe circumstances when either shareholders or directors are held liable in relation to an obligation owed by the company or when the company is liable in connection with an obligation owed personally by a shareholder or a director.

The term veil piercing can also be used to refer to instances where the company is characterized in a certain way because of the identity of their shareholders and directors and also where a statute is applied to companies as well as their parent company or another company within the same group. In this context a particular company is analysed to determine how to apply the respective statute. It is suggested here that such cases are better conceptualized as involving questions relating to the scope of application of a particular statute rather than as examples of veil piercing. While it is useful and indeed necessary for company lawyers to know of and analyse the respective statutory rules,

---

[2] Law Commission, Pension Funds and Social Investment, Law Com No 374 (2017).
[3] Companies Act 2006 (CA 2006), s 3(1) and Insolvency Act 1986 (IA 1986), s 74(2)(d).
[4] Henry Hansmann and Richard Squire, 'External and Internal Asset Partitioning: Corporations and Their Subsidiaries' in Jeffrey N Gordon and Wolf-Georg Ringe (eds), *Corporate Law and Governance* (OUP 2018) 251; Henry Hansmann and Reinier Kraakman, 'The Essential Role of Organizational Law' (2000) 110 Yale Law Journal 387; Thom Wetzer, 'In Two Minds: The Governance of Ring-Fenced Banks' [2019] JCLS 197.
[5] Christian A Witting, *Liability of Corporate Groups and Networks* (CUP 2018) 72.
[6] *The Glasnos* [1991] 1 Lloyd's Rep 482, 490 (Steyn J).

the separate legal personality of the company and the limited liability of the share-holders and directors of that company is not removed in these instances.

In the following sections we will first analyse rules that remove limited liability for shareholders and directors as well as for companies. We will see that while separate legal personality is immovably robust, limited liability is a more nuanced concept. It is worth stressing from the outset that the Companies Act permits veil piercing only in extremely rare cases. These are now referred to as evasion cases. But the courts have used the tools of the common law, and the legislature has created separate tools that to-gether determine circumstances in which shareholders or directors as well as the com-panies they control share liability. Abuses of the corporate form are addressed through the modification of the limited liability principle, rather than through a rule removing the separate legal personality of the company on an ad hoc basis.

4.2 Veil piercing

4.2.1 Sham and facade

The courts have sometimes held that the corporate veil can be pierced if the company is used as a 'sham' or 'mere façade'. Such dicta can be found in relation to one-person com-panies as well as in the context of corporate groups.[7]

Instances of veil piercing on the ground of 'sham' or 'façade' are rare. More often than not, the dicta referring to 'sham' or 'façade' were made *obiter* with the court observing that if the company was a sham or mere façade it would pierce the corporate veil.[8] Moreover, as Lord Sumption observed in *Prest v Petrodel*, most cases where veil piercing on the grounds that a company was a sham was permitted can be explained on other grounds.[9]

In *Prest v Petrodel* Lord Sumption concluded that references to 'sham' and 'façade' were unhelpful as they beg too many questions and so do not provide a source for a satisfac-tory answer.[10] He observed that in these instances the courts grapple with what a civil lawyer would call an 'abuse of rights'.[11] That doctrine does not exist in English law.[12] He thus suggested distinguishing between evasion and concealment.[13] In both instances

---

[7] Robert Miles and Eleanor Holland, 'Piercing the Corporate Veil' in Edwin Simpson and Miranda Steward (eds), *Sham Transactions* (OUP 2013) 207; *Trustor v Smallbone (No 2)* [2001] 1 WLR 1177 [22]; *Adams v Cape Industries plc* [1990] Ch 433, 539 paras F–H and 540 para A.

[8] *Prest v Petrodel* [2013] UKSC 34, [2013] 2 AC 415 [27]; *Adams v. Cape Industries plc* [1990] Ch 433, 539 paras F–H and 540 para A.

[9] *Prest v Petrodel* [2013] UKSC 34, [2013] 2 AC 415, [29]–[30].

[10] ibid [28].

[11] ibid [17].

[12] ibid [18]

[13] ibid [18], see also [60] (Lord Neuberger) but note [103] (Lord Clarke).

liability is imposed on both companies and their shareholders or directors. They will be discussed in turn below.

4.2.2 Evasion

Lord Sumption held in *Prest v Petrodel* that a company can be liable for an obligation of a shareholder when that shareholder is its controller and uses the company to deliberately evade or frustrate the performance of an existing personal obligation. In such a case, the court can 'pierce the corporate veil' for the purpose only of depriving the company or its controller of the advantage that they have obtained by the use of the company.[14] For a claim to be successful there must be evidence that the controller had deliberately used the company to avoid a legal obligation which he or she personally owed.[15] There are two examples for this.

In *Jones v Lipman* the seller of land wanted to avoid an order for specific performance and transferred the land to a company under his control. The buyer succeeded in claiming the land from the company because it was 'a device and a sham, a mask which [Mr Lipman] holds before his face to avoid the recognition by the eyes of equity'.[16] In *Guildford Motor Co v Horne* Mr Horne had agreed not to compete with a former employer. He set up a company which carried on a competing business. The court issued an injunction against Mr Horne and also against the company, which was, of course, not bound by the agreement between Mr Horne and his former employer. This was because the company was a 'mere cloak or sham' or a 'mere channel' and the business was really carried out by Mr Horne.[17]

While these two cases are said to be a genuine example of veil piercing under the Companies Act it is worth observing that rules outside of company law could produce the same result. In *Jones v Lipman* the same outcome could have been achieved by characterizing the company as a constructive trustee.[18] In *Gilford Motors v Horne* the remedy sought was an injunction where courts provisionally issued instructions to preserve the current state of affairs. The grant of the injunction could have been justified on other grounds.[19]

Either way, the courts in *Gilford* and in *Jones* did not base their decision on more orthodox principles but on the basis of characterizing the company as a 'sham'. The

---

[14] ibid [29].

[15] *Persad v Singh* [2017] UKPC 32, [2017] BCC 779 paras 14–26; see also *R v Boyle Transport (Northern Ireland) Ltd* [2016] EWCA Crim 19; [2016] 4 WLR 63 (CA) (Crim Div) and *R v Powell (Jacqueline)* [2016] EWCA Crim 1043, [2017] Env LR 11.

[16] *Jones v Lipman* [1962] 1 WLR 832 at 836.

[17] *Guildford Motor Co Ltd v Horne* [1933] Ch 935 (961, 962, and 966).

[18] *Prest v Petrodel* [2013] UKSC 34 [2013] 2 AC 415, [73] (Lord Neuberger).

[19] ibid [71] (Lord Neuberger); Moreover, the courts frequently grant interim relief by instructing directors and shareholders of companies not to dispose of assets held by companies (see for example *Lakatamia Shipping Co Ltd v Su* [2014] EWCA Civ 636; [2014] CP Rep 37).

Supreme Court in *Prest v Petrodel* held that the two decisions should be taken at face value and more generally concluded that it would be wrong to fully shut the door to a stand-alone veil piercing remedy.[20] Not all judges agreed on this point. Lord Walker observed that veil piercing was simply a 'label' and Lord Neuberger was 'strongly' attracted by the argument that the doctrine, which was controversial and uncertain and which appears never to have been invoked successfully and appropriately in its eighty years of supposed existence should be given its 'quietus'.[21]

Lord Sumption re-characterized *Jones v Lipman* and *Gilford Motors v Horne* as 'evasion' cases observing that the companies were deliberately used in both cases to avoid the performance of an existing obligation. The Supreme Court also observed that other instances of veil piercing are conceivable but likely to be rare. The point that while in theory possible, veil piercing as a stand-alone category is rare, has been further emphasized by the Supreme Court in *Hurstwood Properties (A) Ltd v Rossendale Borough Council*.[22]

From a theoretical perspective it is worth observing that both in *Jones* and in *Guildford* the company was considered to be bound by an obligation of its controller. Its separate legal personality was not questioned. The term 'sham' therefore does not carry the same meaning in company law as it does in contract law. In contract law a sham is a transaction that is not intended by the parties themselves to be valid and effective as between them.[23]

An example of a sham can be found in *Singularis Holdings v Daiwa* where the judge at first instance concluded that an agreement between Singularis and a hospital to pay the expenses of the hospital was a sham and the payments made to the hospital were in reality a misappropriation of the company's money.[24] A sham transaction can also be said to have occurred where an individual purports to sell a valuable property to a close relative two days before he is adjudicated bankrupt.[25] In such circumstances it is possible to conclude that the parties never intended to enter into a binding agreement. They nevertheless pretended that such a contract existed. The courts then proceed on the basis that, since the parties never agreed to be bound, there was no contract.

In evasion cases the existence of the company is not disregarded. It is not possible therefore to speak of this company as being a sham.[26] It is, of course, possible that someone

---

[20] *Prest v Petrodel* [2013] UKSC 34, [2013] 2 AC 415, [29] (Lord Sumption), [79] (Lord Neuberger), [100] (Lord Mance), and 103 (Lord Clarke).

[21] ibid [79] (Lord Neuberger) and [106] (Lord Walker).

[22] *Hurstwood Properties (A) Ltd v Rossendale Borough Council* [2019] [2021] UKSC 16, [2021] 2 WLR 1125 [71]–[76].

[23] *Glastnos Shipping Ltd and Continental Chartering & Brokerage Ltd Hong Kong Branch v Panasian Shipping Corpn and Withers (a firm), The Glastnos* [1991] 1 Lloyd's Rep 482 at 486 applying a dictum by Lord Justice Diplock in *Snook v London and West Riding Investments Ltd* [1967] 2 QB 78.

[24] *Singularis Holdings Ltd v Daiwa Capital Markets Europe Ltd* [2019] UKSC 50, [2019] 3 WLR 997, [10].

[25] *Ebbvale Ltd v Hosking* [2013] UKPC 1, [2013] 2 BCLC 204.

[26] Robert Miles and Eleanor Holland, 'Piercing the Corporate Veil' in Edwin Simpson and Miranda Steward (eds), *Sham Transactions* (OUP 2013) 206; see also *VTB Capital Plc v Nutritek International Corp* [2012] EWCA Civ 808, [2012] 2 BCLC 437, [68].

pretends to have sold an asset to a company when in fact no such sale ever occurred. That pretend sales contract would then be characterized as a sham. But that does not call into question the existence of the company.

4.2.3 Concealment

When companies are used for the purposes of 'concealment' of salient facts the courts will, as they always do, ignore the smoke screens and establish for each case the respective factual merits. In such cases companies have sometimes been referred to 'shams' or 'façades' but that characterization on its own did not justify the outcome of the decision. The court justified that outcome on the basis of equitable rules and would have taken the same decision if the defendant had used his uncle instead of a company to conceal facts.[27]

An example of a mechanism through which companies can become liable for obligations owed by their controllers is trust law. It is possible for a company to be liable as a trustee or as a constructive trustee for assets it has received from a controller.

In *Prest v Petrodel*, for example, a number of companies owned certain London properties. The indirect controller of these companies was involved in divorce proceedings. The question was whether the properties formed part of the matrimonial estate to be divided up in the proceedings. The court concluded that they did but on the basis that the companies held the properties on trust for the benefit of the husband. This was because of the husband's intentions in relation to these properties.[28]

This outcome could be described as the court ignoring the separate legal existence of the company, as the husband was unable to disassociate himself from the companies he controlled and thus had to share his beneficial interest in the matrimonial proceedings. But the validity of the company was accepted as the court found that it was a trustee. The result would have been no different if the husband's uncle had held the companies on trust for him. The company is characterized as a trustee in the same way as a natural person would be considered to be a trustee in the same circumstances.[29]

Companies can also come to be characterized as constructive trustees. This happens when property has been misappropriated and transferred to a company in circumstances where the company knew about the misappropriation. Again, there is no specific company law problem here. If a recipient of property knows of a misappropriation he is considered to hold the asset on trust and needs to give the asset back or account for it. If the recipient is a company under control of the person who misappropriated

[27] *Prest v Petrodel* [2013] UKSC 34, [2013] 2 AC 415, [31].
[28] ibid; see also *M v M* [2013] EWHC 2534 (Fam) [248] and *Thakkar v Thakkar* Family Court 10 February 2017, [2017] EWFC 13.
[29] *Prest v Petrodel* [2013] UKSC 34, [2013] 2 AC 415 [31]; see also *M v M* [2013] EWHC 2534 (Fam) [248] and *Thakkar v Thakkar* Family Court 10 February 2017, [2017] EWFC 13.

the assets, the company will be considered to know of the misappropriation. This happened, for example, in *Clegg v Pache*.[30] The director of a company had breached his fiduciary duty by diverting funds and business opportunities to a second company in which he had a concealed beneficial interest. The second company was thus required to account to the first company for the profits it received through these breaches.[31]

When a company has received money misappropriated by its controller the company is liable to account as a trustee but that is not where liability ends. In addition to the company the controller is considered personally liable because through his control of the recipient of the misappropriated funds he is considered under ordinary equitable principles to be a recipient himself.[32]

4.2.4 Theoretical observations

It is misleading to speak of 'veil piercing' or 'sham companies'. Veil piercing is a metaphor that seems to suggest that the company's separate personality is not recognized. That is not the case. When the courts pierce the corporate veil they do not disregard the separate legal personality of the company. Veil piercing is rather best characterized as providing an exception to limited liability causing a company, the separate legal personality of which is upheld, to be liable for an obligation owed by its controller.

While in theory the courts have said that they are prepared to pierce the corporate veil on the grounds of evasion when the facts are right it is nevertheless fair to say that the remedy is 'rarely if ever seen in the wild'.[33] Cases of concealment are frequent but do not constitute an exception to company law. They are decided on normal equitable rules that apply to human actors as well as to companies. Companies are recognized as separate legal entities but can become characterized as trustees when they, for example, have knowingly received assets that have been misappropriated by their controller.

The term 'sham companies' is misleading because a sham is something the courts do not recognize as existing. A sham contract, for example, is not recognized as a contract by the courts because those pretending that the contract exists have not agreed to be bound by it. In both instances of evasion and concealment the company is recognized as a separate legal actor.

Evasion cases are most likely to occur in the context of one-person companies set up by an individual with the intention to avoid an existing obligation. It is, of course possible for a company within a corporate group to be set up for such a purpose.

---

[30] *Clegg v Pache (Deceased)* Court of Appeal (Civil Division) 11 May 2017, [2017] EWCA Civ 256.
[31] See also *Trustor AB v Smallbone* (No 2) [2001] 1 WLR 177.
[32] *Gencor ACP Ltd v Dalby* [2000] 2 BCLC 734; see also *Mercia Enterprises Ltd v Mistry* [2020] EWHC 1597 (QB).
[33] Robert Miles and Eleanor Holland, 'Piercing the Corporate Veil' in Edwin Simpson and Miranda Steward (eds), *Sham Transactions* (OUP 2013) 192, 206

The theory of this book is that company law at a positive level can be explained as providing a procedural framework for autonomous organizational action. Separate legal personality is an essential ingredient serving this purpose. It provides the organization which operates through a company with a legal anchor allowing it to interact with the world. Separate legal personality overcomes the problem that organizations are social rather than brute facts. They do not have a unique physical manifestation and so it is important that the legal anchor establishing their existence in law is robust.

4.3 Personal liability for shareholders and directors

In the following sections the rules that introduce personal limited liability for shareholders or directors will be analysed. We will see that taken together they provide for a balanced framework that manages instances of irresponsible use of the corporate form while retaining the separate legal personality of the company. The first and most obvious example is fraud.

4.3.1 Fraud

Fraud 'unravels everything'.[34] We have seen above that the Companies Act only permits the use of the corporate form for legal purposes.[35] We have also seen that if a company carries out illegal activity its separate legal personality is nevertheless recognized and only ends after it has been wound up and removed from the register.[36]

The fact that an illegal company needs to be wound up to be removed from the register for it to disappear does, however, not mean that it continues to operate as a shield supplying limited liability. For obvious reasons the law does not permit the use of a company to avoid the personal liability that is associated with fraudulent conduct. Individuals who operate companies for fraudulent purposes are personally liable for activity conducted formally by a company, limited liability notwithstanding.

In Re Darby two individuals, who had already acquired a notorious reputation, set up a company through which they promoted securities in another company. This made it possible for them to avoid having their identities appear in the sale of these securities. It later came to light that they had overstated the value of an asset that they had transferred to the second company. The court held them personally liable for this fraud.[37]

---

[34] *Prest v Petrodel* [2013] UKSC 34, [18] (Lord Sumption), [83] (Lord Neuberger).
[35] CA 2006, s 7(2).
[36] Section 2.5 in this book.
[37] In *Re Darby* [1911] 1 KB 95; see also *Komercni Banka AS v Stone & Rolls Ltd* [2002] EWHC 2263 (Comm), [2003] 1 Lloyd's Rep 383. An appeal against the first instance decision was allowed but only in relation to quantum (*Komercni Banka AS v Stone & Rolls Ltd* [2003] EWCA Civ 311, [2003] CP Rep 58) and *Hemsley v Graham* [2013] EWHC 2232 (Ch), [2013] 7 WLUK 1048.

In *Standard Chartered Bank v Pakistan National Shipping Corporation* the managing director of Standard Chartered Bank persuaded the Pakistan National Shipping Corporation to backdate a bill of lading causing Standard Chartered Bank to release funds to the company. The House of Lords held both the company and its managing director liable for fraud.[38] Lord Hoffmann pointed out that the managing director made a fraudulent misrepresentation intending Standard Chartered Bank to rely upon it and that Standard Chartered Bank did rely on it.[39] He also explained that in the context of negligent misrepresentation a director is personally liable if he has assumed personal responsibility. In relation to deceit, however, a director cannot escape liability for his fraud by saying, 'I wish to make it clear that I am committing this fraud on behalf of someone else and I am not to be personally liable.'[40]

In relation to fraud claims against directors or controlling shareholders of a company questions of jurisdiction can arise. Under the Brussels Regulation a person could be sued in the UK if they resided here or if they had agreed for the case to be heard by UK courts. Such an agreement could be made ad hoc but is sometimes contained in a contract that the parties have entered into at an earlier point in time. If a fraudster causes someone else to enter into a contract with a company he controls and that contract contains a jurisdiction clause pointing to the UK, the English courts have jurisdiction to hear a claim against the company. If the victim of the fraud prefers to sue the fraudster as well as the company in the UK and if the fraudster is not resident here, the question arises of whether the jurisdiction clause contained in the contract is a basis for UK jurisdiction. The obvious problem is that the fraudster is not a party to that contract. He has nevertheless orchestrated that contract to come about by way of fraud. This, however, does not amount to a submission to the jurisdiction of the English courts.[41] The courts rightly formally distinguish between the company and its controller. It is also worth noting that this is not a question of company law but a question of determining the meaning of submission under the respective jurisdiction rules. In particular it is possible for the fraudster to be subject to UK jurisdiction on other grounds, for example the fact that the damage has occurred in the UK.[42]

From a theoretical perspective it is worth observing that, if an individual uses a company for fraudulent purposes, he is liable not because he was a director or a shareholder of the company but because he committed a fraud. The separate legal personality of the company is not removed or undermined in this case. It is nevertheless possible to observe that fraud is a boundary for the use of limited liability as long as one keeps in

---

[38] *Standard Chartered Bank v Pakistan National Shipping Corporation* [2003] 1 AC 959.
[39] ibid [20].
[40] ibid [22].
[41] *VTB Capital plc v Nutritek International Corp and others* [2013] UKSC 5, [2013] 2 AC 337; see also *Antonio Gramsci Shipping Corporation v Recoletos Ltd* [2013] EWCA Civ 730, [2013] 4 All ER 157.
[42] Regulation (EC) 864/2007 of 11 July 2007 on the law applicable to non-contractual obligations (Rome II Regulation) [2007] OJ L199/40, art 4.

mind that the same outcome would be achieved where a fraudster used a friend or relative as a front to conduct illegal activity. In both cases the fraudster will be personally liable.

4.3.2 Fraudulent trading

The fraudulent trading rules apply if in the course of the winding up of a company it appears that any business of the company had been carried out with the intent to defraud creditors of the company. The court may declare that any persons who were knowingly parties to the carrying on of the business in a fraudulent manner are liable to make such contributions as the court thinks proper.[43] This dispenses with the requirement to prove strict causation between the acts of the participants of the fraud and any particular loss. Liability arises for directors, managers, shareholders, and anyone else who is knowingly a party to the fraud. In *Re BCCI (No 15)*, for example, the Bank of India, which took deposits from the Bank of Credit and Commerce International SA (BCCI), was liable for fraudulent trading conducted by employees. BCCI was liable because a senior manager, who had authority to represent the Bank of India in relation to BCCI, turned a blind eye on the fraud conducted by employees of BCCI.[44]

In addition, there is criminal liability attached to fraudulent trading. A person guilty of fraudulent trading is liable for on conviction on indictment to imprisonment for a term not exceeding ten years or a fine (or both).[45]

Like fraud, Insolvency Act 1986, section 213 does not disregard the separate legal personality of a company but removes the limited liability for individuals who use the corporate form for fraudulent purposes. In that sense they create a boundary for the use of the corporate form.

4.3.3 Wrongful trading

Another avenue which sets boundaries for the use of limited liability are the rules wrongful trading. These also leave the separate legal personality intact but instead introduce personal liability for controllers of companies who use limited liability irresponsibly.[46]

---

[43] IA 1986, s 213.

[44] *Re Bank of Credit and Commerce International SA, Morris v Bank of India* [2005] EWCA Civ 693, [2005] 2 BCLC 328.

[45] CA 2006, s 993; see, for example, <www.lawgazette.co.uk/news/sfo-charges-three-men-over-axiom-legal-financing-fund/5105394.article>.

[46] The Cork Committee observed that 'a director, who, when judged by current standards of commercial morality, is found to have abused the privilege of limited liability, will forfeit that privilege'. His position will be the same as if he had been trading 'on his own account and at his own risk' (Kenneth Cork, Insolvency Law and Practice, Report of the Review Committee, June 1982, Cmnd 8558 [1807]).

A director of a company is liable to make a personal contribution as the court thinks fit if they continued to trade beyond the point where they knew or ought to have concluded that the company was not going to avoid insolvent liquidation or administration.[47] They are not liable if they took every step with a view to minimizing the potential loss for creditors. For the purposes of determining the facts which a director ought to know, the conclusions he ought to have reached, and the steps he ought to have taken the director will be judged against an objective standard as well as against a subjective standard. They have to abide by the standard of a reasonably diligent person with the general knowledge, skill, and experience that may reasonably be expected of a person carrying out the same functions as are carried out by that director as well as by the general knowledge, skill, and experience that director has.[48]

The rules not only apply to those who have been appointed as directors but also to corporate controllers who are involved in the governance of a company in a way a director normally is. Insolvency Act 1986, section 214 also applies to de facto and shadow directors. De facto director 'assume to act as directors without having been appointed validly or at all'.[49] Shadow directors are defined as persons in accordance with whose instructions the directors are accustomed to act.[50] He or she 'lurks in the shadows, sheltering behind' the de jure or de facto director.[51] A parent company can find itself in the position of facing liability for wrongful trading if it acts as a shadow director.[52]

From a theoretical perspective it is worth observing that wrongful trading introduces personal liability for controllers of companies who take decisions that harm creditors. If a company is in a financial position where it cannot avoid insolvent liquidation or administration, a director or other controller needs to take every step with a view to minimizing the loss to creditors. Wrongful trading provides a boundary for the use of limited liability while leaving separate legal personality intact.

4.3.4 Phoenix companies

Personal liability also attaches to directors and shadow directors of companies which have gone into insolvent liquidation if they become involved with the management of a company with the same or a similar name as the insolvent company within five years from the beginning of the liquidation of the insolvent company.[53]

---

[47] IA 1985, s 214.

[48] ibid s 214(4).

[49] Re Hydrodam (Corby) Ltd [1994] 2 BCLC 180, 182 (Millet J).

[50] IA 1986, ss 214(7) and 251 as well as CA 2006, s 251(1).

[51] Re Hydrodam (Corby) Ltd [1994] 2 BCLC 180, 183 (Millet J); Re Mea Corporation Ltd [2007] 1 BCLC 618, [106] (Lewison J).

[52] Re Paycheck Services No 3, RCC v Holland [2010] UKSC 51, [2011] 1 All ER 430, [40] (Lord Hope DP); Re Hydrodam (Corby) Ltd [1994] 2 BCLC 180, 183 (Millet J); but see CA 2006, s 251(3) in relation to the liability of parent companies for breaches of the general duties of a director.

[53] IA 1986, ss 215 and 216.

This is designed to curb the 'phoenix phenomenon', where the same individuals incorporate one company after another, each under similar sounding names, each of which continues the business of their respective predecessor, and all of which in due course find themselves unable to pay their debts. By imposing personal liability on those who do not respect the prohibition it also sets a boundary for the use of limited liability without undermining the separate legal personality of each of these companies.

4.3.5 Disqualification of directors

The Company Directors Disqualification Act 1986 (CDDA 1986) instructs the court to make a disqualification orders against a person in any case where it is satisfied that he is or has been a director of a company which has at any time become insolvent and that his conduct as a director of one or more other companies makes him unfit to be concerned with the management of the company.[54] The rule applies if the company goes into liquidation at a time when its assets are insufficient for paying its debt and the winding-up expenses. It also applies when the company goes into administration or when an administrative receiver has been appointed. Unfitness will be discussed in the context of the duty of skill and care.[55] Here it suffices to mention that disqualification orders for unfitness can also be issued against de facto and shadow directors.[56]

Disqualification order can also be made following a conviction of an indictable offence in connection with the promotion, formation, management, liquidation, or striking off of a company or for persistent breaches of companies' legislation.[57] These include the rules requiring the filing of returns, accounts, or other documents to the registrar of companies.

Disqualification orders provide for a boundary for the use of limited liability because they ban individuals who have proven themselves to be irresponsible users of limited liability from being concerned with the management of limited liability companies for a certain period of time.[58] They also set a boundary because it is possible for the court to make an order requiring a disqualified person who has caused a loss to one or more creditors of an insolvent company to pay compensation.[59] Like the wrongful trading rules these orders re-introduce personal liability for individuals who have irresponsibly used limited liability.

---

[54] Company Directors Disqualification Act 1986 (CDDA 1986), s 6.
[55] Section 7.6.4 in this book.
[56] CDDA 1986, s 6(3C); *Re Focus 15 Trading Ltd* [2020] EWHC 3016 (Ch), [2020] 11 WLUK 143.
[57] CDDA 1986, ss 2–3.
[58] ibid s 1.
[59] ibid s 15A; *Re Noble Vintners Ltd* [2019] EWHC 2806 (Ch), [2020] BCC 198.

Disqualification is a prophylactic measure, quarantining individuals who have shown that they are unsuitable to be concerned with the management of a company from access to limited liability.

4.3.6 Liability in tort

In relation to corporate groups tort law has recently been used as a tool for imposing liability across legal boundaries. The starting point is that shareholders and directors are not liable in negligence if the company has acted negligently. The landmark case illustrating this is *Williams v Natural Life Health Foods Ltd*.[60] In that case the House of Lords held that the principal shareholder and director was not liable to customers of the company notwithstanding the fact that his persona was heavily relied on in advertisements of the company. This was because he had not assumed personal responsibility towards the clients of the company and so was not liable for negligent misstatement.[61]

It is however possible for a controller of a company to be a wrongdoer in its own right which then affects its ability to claim in tort from the company. In *Brumder v Motornet Service and Repairs Ltd*, for example, the sole director and shareholder of the company suffered a workplace injury operating a hydraulic pump. He was himself responsible in his capacity as the company's director to carry out statutory health and safety checks and had neglected to do this for many years. His contributory negligence thus fully eclipsed the claim he had against the company and as a consequence the company did not have a claim against its insurers.[62]

In recent years there has been a substantial amount of litigation by tort victims claiming against parent companies of subsidiaries. The more involved the parent company is in the management of the subsidiary's affairs the more likely it is for the parent to be characterized as a wrongdoer.[63]

Again, however, the basis of the liability is not rooted in company law. There is no doctrine that makes parent companies liable for torts committed by subsidiaries. There are certain cases where a parent might become liable on the basis of the scope it had to intervene in the affairs of the subsidiary. Such cases generally arise where either the parent is managing the relevant activity of the subsidiary solely or jointly with the subsidiary or where the parent had given specific advice to the subsidiary about the management of the risk in question.[64]

---

[60] *Williams v Natural Life Health Foods Ltd* [1998] 1 WLR 830 (HL).

[61] See also *Al-Dowaisan v Al-Salam* [2019] EWHC 301 (Ch), [2019] 2 BCLC 328 where the directors had not assumed the role of a fiduciary in relation to an investor.

[62] *Brumder v Motornet Service and Repairs Ltd* [2013] EWCA Civ 195, [2013] PIQR P13, Court of Appeal (Civil Division) 14 March 2013.

[63] *Chandler v Cape plc* [2012] EWCA Civ 525; *Newton-Sealy v ArmorGroup Services Ltd* [2008] EWHC 233 (QB); *Vedanta Resources Plc v Lungowe* [2019] UKSC 20, [2020] AC 1045; *Vedanta Resources Plc v Lungowe* [2019] UKSC 20, [2020] AC 1045; *Okpabi v Royal Dutch Shell plc* [2021] UKSC 3, [2021] 1 WLR 1294.

[64] *AAA v Unilever* [2018] EWCA (Civ) 1532, [2018] BCC 959.

The fact that an individual holds directorships in parent as well as in subsidiary companies does, however, not implicate the parent in the operation of the subsidiary. The individuals wear several hats one at a time and, however unrealistic this may seem, the roles are considered independent of each other.[65]

At a normative level it has been argued that there should be direct liability of shareholders towards tort victims who suffer loss as a result of the negligence or recklessness of companies. Explanations justifying liability in these circumstances range from economic reasoning to arguments based on moral considerations.[66] Given the current interest of the UK government in human rights issues in the context of multinational organizations and supply chains it is possible that these proposals will fall on fertile ground in the future.

Tort law is nevertheless a mechanism through which the organizational reality of a corporate group is recognized by the law. A parent company which steps outside of its role as a shareholder of a subsidiary and involves itself in the negligent operation of that subsidiary risks becoming a tortfeasor in its own right. Tort law polices the use of limited liability in the context of corporate groups. It is possible to argue that more needs to be done to protect vulnerable subsidiaries suffering injury at the hands of subsidiaries of multinational groups.[67] From a theoretical perspective we can predict that any new measures, while imposing liability on certain actors, will not affect the legal personality of the company.

4.3.7 Theoretical observations

Fraud, fraudulent and wrongful trading, phoenix and disqualification rules, as well as tort law together set up a framework imposing personal liability on controllers of companies who have acted irresponsibly or involved themselves in the negligent running of the affairs of a subsidiary. They do not undermine the separate legal personality of the company. This can be explained from the perspective of the theory advanced in this book. Because companies are designed to enable organizations to operate autonomously separate legal personality is best preserved until the company and the organization it runs have been wound up in an orderly manner and so it is better to address abuses of the corporate form through liability rules.

---

[65] Christian A Witting, *Liability of Corporate Groups and Networks* (CUP 2018) 184.

[66] ibid; Christian Witting, 'Modelling Organisational Vicarious Liability' (2019) 39 Legal Studies 694; Jonathan Crowe, 'Does Control Make a Difference? The Moral Foundations of Shareholder Liability for Corporate Wrongs' (2012) 75 MLR 159; Henry Hansmann and Reinier Kraakman, 'Towards Unlimited Shareholder Liability for Corporate Torts' (1991) 100 Yale Law Journal 1879; see also Thilo Kuntz, 'Asset Partitioning, Limited Liability and Veil Piercing: Review Essay on Bainbridge/Henderson, *Limited Liability*' (2018) 19 EBOR 439; see also Beate Sjåfjell, 'How Company Law Has Failed Human Rights—And What to Do about It' (2020) 5(2) Business and Human Rights Journal 179.

[67] See eg Christian Witting, *Liability of Corporate Groups and Networks* (CUP 2018).

4.4 Applying statutes to companies

4.4.1 Statutes generally

Cases where the court finds a parent company or a shareholder liable for a debt owed by the company need to be distinguished from instances where the courts interpret statutory rules.[68] When the courts determine the scope of application of a particular statute they may decide to take into account the nationality, residence, or other characteristics of the company's shareholders or directors. This can lead to the conclusion that a film company that is registered in the UK cannot be considered to have produced a British film for the purposes of the Film Act.[69] It can lead to the result that a UK registered company is characterized as German for the purposes of the Trading with the Enemy Act.[70]

A company can also come to be considered to be the recipient of the proceeds of a crime committed by its controllers.[71] Under Companies Act 2006, section 994 it is possible for unfair prejudice to occur through the way in which the affairs of a subsidiary company are run.[72] Injunctions can be issued against shareholders or directors prohibiting them from causing the company to make dispositions that are likely to reduce the value of the shares in the company.[73] It is also possible for shareholder directors to be liable in contempt of court for failing to ensure that the company complies with disclosure orders relating to corporate assets.[74] A holding company that had no employees but operated through subsidiaries which employed door-to-door sales staff nevertheless can be considered a 'trader' under the Unfair Trading Regulations 2008, regulation 9.[75]

There are also cases where the courts have declined to extend the scope of application to shareholders or directors. The Civil Procedure Rules (CPR) require defendants to give up certain documents provided that they are in their 'control'.[76] A party has control over a document if they either have physical possession, a right to possession of it, or a right to inspect or take copies of it. The House of Lords held in *Lonrho v Shell* that documents held by a wholly-owned subsidiary are not by virtue of that fact alone in the control of the parent company.[77] A parent company only has control where there is an existing arrangement providing it with a right of access to the documents, or where it

---

[68] See also *Prest v Petrodel* [2013] UKSC 34, [2013] 2 AC 415, [21] (Lord Sumption).

[69] *Re FG Films Ltd* [1953] 1 WLR 483, [1953] 1 All ER 615 (ChD).

[70] *Daimler v Continental Tyre and Rubber Co* [1916] 1 AC 307.

[71] *R v Seager (Mornington Stafford)* [2009] EWCA Crim 1303, [2010] 1 WLR 815; *R v Boyle* [2016] EWCA Crim 19, [2016] 4 WLR 63; *R v Powell (Jacqueline)* [2016] EWCA Crim 1043, [2016] Env LR 11; see also Karl Laird, 'Piercing the Corporate Veil in Confiscation Proceedings' (2017) 133 LQR 217.

[72] *Re Citybranch Group Ltd, Gross v Rackind* [2004] 4 All ER 735 and *Meyer v Scottish Cooperative Wholesale Society Ltd* [1959] AC 324.

[73] *Lakatamia Shipping Co Ltd v Su* [2014] EWCA Civ 636, [2014] CP Rep 37; see also *Koza Ltd v Koza Altin Isletmeleri AS* [2020] EWCA Civ 1018, [2020] 7 WLUK 469.

[74] *Taylor v Van Dutch Marine Holding Ltd* [2016] EWHC 2201 (Ch), [2016] 9 WLUK 31.

[75] *R v Scottish and Southern Energy Plc; Surrey Trading Standards v Scottish and Southern Energy Plc* [2012] EWCA Crim 539.

[76] CPR r 31.8.

[77] *Lonrho Ltd v Shell Petroleum Co Ltd (No 1)* [1980] 1 WLR 627.

has an enforceable legal right to obtain them.[78] In *Mohamed v Egyptian Association of Great Britain Ltd* it was held that an individual director is not a person directly affected by a default judgment and so cannot apply under CPR 1998, r 40.9 to set aside a default judgment.[79]

It also sometimes happens that similar statutory wording is construed in different ways. This has happened when courts determined the value of a property that has been expropriated.[80]

4.4.2 Groups

More generally it is worth observing that the legislature is gradually finding ways of regulating corporate groups in specific contexts. These are focusing on protecting creditors that are sometimes described as non-adjusting, such as the tax authorities and contract creditors who do not have bargaining power to manage their exposure to limited liability. They are also addressing public policy aims such as fair competition, the prevention of bribery, modern slavery, or human trafficking.

In the context of tax law, for example, there are statutory rules imposing personal liability on directors. If the failure of a company to pay national insurance contributions is attributable to the fraud or neglect of one or more of its officers each of these officers can be made personally liable for the contributions due from the company.[81] The test for 'neglect' has been held to be objective. The court determines if the officer fails to meet the standard of a 'reasonable and prudent man of business'.[82] Along similar lines senior accounting officers, who need to be appointed by certain large companies, are personally liable for a fine under the Finance Act 2009, Sch 46 para 4 if they do not ensure that the company establishes and maintains appropriate tax accounting arrangements.

The pension entitlements of employees are protected through the Pensions Act 2004, sections 43–51 whereby The Pensions Regulator has a power to require other companies in a group to provide reasonable financial support for an under-funded or insufficiently resourced occupational pension scheme managed by a service company within the group.[83]

---

[78] See eg most recently *Pipia v BGEO Group Ltd* [2020] EWHC 402 (Comm), [2020] 1 WLR 2582.

[79] *Mohamed v Egyptian Association of Great Britain Ltd* [2018] EWCA Civ 879.

[80] *DHN Food Distributors Ltd v Tower Hamlets LBC* [1976] 1 WLR 852; [1976] 3 All ER 462 (CA) to be contrasted with *Woolfson v Strathclyde Regional Council* (1978) SC (HL) 90 (HL); see also *Smith, Stone and Knight Ltd v City of Birmingham* [1939] 4 All ER 116.

[81] Social Security Administration Act 1992, s 121C.

[82] *O'Rorke v Revenue and Customs Commissioners*, Upper Tribunal (Tax and Chancery) 04 October 2013, [2013] UKUT 499 (TCC), [2014] STC 279, at [4].

[83] *Re Nortel GmbH (in administration) and other companies; Re Lehman Brothers International (Europe) (in administration) and other companies (Nos 1 and 2)* [2013] UKSC 52, [2013] 2 BCLC 135; see also *Granada UK v The Pension Regulator* [2019] EWCA Civ 1032, [2020] ICR 747; for other albeit rare instances of pooling of assets of group companies in insolvency and reorganization proceedings see Christian A Witting, *Liability of Corporate Groups and Networks* (CUP 2018) 220.

Consumers receive protection through product liability rules under which producers and importers can be liable to injured persons irrespective of whether they have a contractual relationship with either of them.[84]

Under EU cartel rules a company which has decisive influence over another company will be imputed with the knowledge, intent, or unlawful conduct of the other company. Under the Treaty on the Functioning of the European Union, Article 101 liability attaches to companies which form an economic unit irrespective of the boundaries established by company law. In EU jurisprudence, the (rebuttable) presumption is that a parent company exercises a decisive influence over the market conduct of a wholly owned subsidiary and that they therefore constitute a single undertaking within Article 101.[85]

Under the Bribery Act 2010, section 7(1) a commercial organization which fails to prevent the payment of bribes by another person associated with it intending to obtain or retain business for that commercial organization is guilty of an offence. These rules are designed with organizational action in mind. It is not necessary to prove fault on the part of the directors. Rather a commercial organization is liable unless it can prove that it had in place adequate procedures designed to prevent persons associated with it to undertake such conduct.[86] An associated person is defined as a person who performs services for or on behalf of a commercial organization. The capacity in which these services are performed does not matter. Accordingly the person may be an employee, an agent, or a subsidiary.[87] What matters is not who acts but whether there was a suitable system of prevention in place.[88]

Another area on which there has been a recent focus is modern slavery and human trafficking. The Modern Slavery Act 2015 also focuses on prevention procedures. It requires companies to publish a statement setting out if and how they ensure that modern slavery is not occurring in either its own organization or in its supply chain. For the time being measures are light touch. The requirement to report, for example, applies to commercial organizations which carry on a business or part of a business in the UK. The presence of a subsidiary company in the UK will not, in itself, mean that the parent company is carrying on business in the UK since the subsidiary 'may act completely independently of its parent or other group companies'.[89] It is therefore possible to avoid the reporting requirement by setting up an appropriately crafted group

---

[84] Christian A Witting, *Liability of Corporate Groups and Networks* (CUP 2018) 236–42.

[85] *Toshiba Carrier UK Ltd v KME Yorkshire Ltd* [2012] EWCA Civ 1190 at [38].

[86] Bribery Act 2010, s 7(2).

[87] ibid s 8; A commercial organization which hires a third party to win sales contracts in return for a commission can also incur criminal liability for bribes paid by that third party (*Director of the Serious Fraud Office v Airbus SE* [2020] 1 WLUK 435; see also *Serious Fraud Offce v Rolls Royce Plc* [2017] Lloyd's Rep FC 18.

[88] *Serious Fraud Office v Standard Bank Plc* [2016] Lloyds' Rep FC 102.

[89] HM Government, UK Government Modern Slavery Statement (26 March 2020) <www.gov.uk/government/publications/uk-government-modern-slavery-statement> [3.8]; see also Local Government Association, Modern Slavery in Local Government Supply Chains: Transparency Statement Guidance and Procedures (19 October 2020) <www.local.gov.uk/modern-slavery-local-government-supply-chains-transparency-statement-guidance-and-procedures>.

structure.[90] Moreover, while disclosure is required, a company is permitted to publish a statement setting out that it has taken no steps to prevent modern slavery and human trafficking. Enforcement is, for the time being, left to consumers, investors and non-governmental organizations (NGOs).[91]

The Government is, however, in the process of stepping up the pressure.[92] In relation to its own procurement it has adopted rules allowing the exclusion of bidders where they have violated certain environmental, social, and labour laws including human rights matters.[93] The Government has also published its own Modern Slavery Statement setting out its own procedures for the prevention of modern slavery in its supply chain.[94]

On 22 September 2020 the Government announced plans to require organizations to publish their statements on a new Government digital reporting service. The plan is also to enhance the quality of reporting by requiring organizations to report against specific topics, such as how they assess risk in the supply chains and the due diligence they have undertaken, and to state clearly if they have omitted a topic. There is also a plan for the civil penalties for non-compliance.[95]

4.4.3 Theoretical observations

From a theoretical perspective we can observe that the rules discussed in the section above are instances where particular statutory rules have been applied to companies. In such cases the courts sometimes draw the scope of application in a way that crosses formal legal boundaries. This could be characterized as an instance of veil piercing but is best understood as a matter for each individual statue.

The courts interpret the specific terms of legislation against the background of a specific policy objective. From a theoretical perspective we can observe that at the centre stage here is not company law but the respective statute and its aims. The courts take the

---

[90] Taskin Iqbal, 'The Efficacy of the Disclosure Requirements on s 54 of the Modern Slavery Act' (2018) 39 Comp Law 3, 7.

[91] The Home Secretary, Transparency in Supply Chains etc. A Practical Guide (29 October 2015) [2.8] <https://assets.publishing.service.gov.uk/government/uploads/system/uploads/attachment_data/file/649906/Transparency_in_Supply_Chains_A_Practical_Guide_2017.pdf>.

[92] There is an independent review of the Modern Slavery Act: <www.gov.uk/government/publications/independent-review-of-the-modern-slavery-act-final-report>; There is also an ongoing Parliamentary enquiry into the use of forced labour in UK value chains (18 September 2020) <https://committees.parliament.uk/work/593/forced-labour-in-uk-value-chains/publications/>; The UK Government is also currently consulting on putting in place prohibitions on corporate directors (BEIS, Corporate Transparency and Register Reform Consultation on implementing the ban on corporate directors 9 December 2020 available from <https://assets.publishing.service.gov.uk/government/uploads/system/uploads/attachment_data/file/942194/Corporate_Directors_Consultation.pdf>).

[93] UK Government Modern Slavery Statement (26 March 2020) <https://www.gov.uk/government/publications/uk-government-modern-slavery-statement>; see also Written Evidence from BEIS on behalf of HMG (FL0002) <https://committees.parliament.uk/writtenevidence/13063/html/>.

[94] HM Government, UK Government Modern Slavery Statement (26 March 2020) <www.gov.uk/government/publications/uk-government-modern-slavery-statement>.

[95] Written evidence from BEIS on behalf of HMG (FL0002) 3 November 2020 [6] available from <https://committees.parliament.uk/writtenevidence/13063/pdf/>.

organizational reality of the company into account with a view to doing justice to goals that lie outside of the scope of company law. These goals vary across legislative acts and so it not surprising that decisions can point in different directions. Either way separate legal personality is not called into question.

We can also observe that there is a trend for the legislature to increase its focus on corporate groups and supply chains. A number of recent initiatives have involved regimes putting the onus on UK-based companies to ensure that prohibited activity does not occur in either their organization or in their supply chains. This approach again acknowledges the separate legal personality of all of the units involved but nevertheless requires parent companies to become responsible for activity that occurs outside its formal legal boundaries. It does not rely on identifying individual culprits but focuses on ensuring that adequate prevention mechanisms are in place. These interventions could be described as piecemeal but it is also possible that a targeted design of legislation will ultimately best serve the respective protected interests.

4.5 Theoretical observations

The corporate form is robust. The *Salomon* case has been described as an unyielding rock on which company law is constructed.[96] Not even fraud nullifies companies. They need to be dissolved and removed from the register to disappear as a subject of the law. That is necessary because the company is designed to run an organization. It cannot be created and undone by simple agreement of its members. It is also not undoable through the rules that apply to shams. A process is required that ensures that there are directors acting on its behalf and, on termination, making sure that the company's activity is brought to an orderly conclusion. In this way the company is suitable to act as a stable and permanent vehicle for organizational action. There is no doubt whether a company exists. As long as it is registered a third party can be sure that they deal with a legally valid entity. There is also no doubt on the boundaries of the company. The robustness of separate legal personality provides for a stable connection point through which an organization can operate autonomously.

There are nevertheless a number of provisions in the Companies Act as well as in other legislation that set boundaries to the use of limited liability. These reflect the interests of creditors and show that the corporate form cannot be used with a view to undermining their interests. Evasion causes a company to be responsible for an obligation its controller was trying to avoid. Under the label of concealment the principles of trust law apply to render companies and their controllers liable as recipients of misappropriated assets.

---

[96] *Prest v Petrodel* [2013] UKSC 34 [66] (Lord Neuberger).

Limited liability disappears for shareholders and directors who act fraudulently, who engage in fraudulent or wrongful trading, or who are involved in the running of phoenix companies. The Company Directors Disqualification Act 1986 imposes a quarantine and liability on individuals who have shown that they are unfit to be concerned with the management of a company. These rules aim to encourage the responsible use of limited liability but refrain from undermining the separate legal personality of the company.

Tort liability arises for a parent company when it involves itself in the negligent operation of a subsidiary such that it becomes a tortfeasor in its own right. This constitutes an avenue through which situations where the legal boundaries of a company have become disconnected from the boundaries of an organization can be scrutinized by law.

Along similar lines it is possible for legislation to apply in a group context by reference to organizational criteria rather than formal legal boundaries. This is a matter for the respective statute, its wording, and the underlying policy aims, and cannot be fully answered by reference to the way in which company law supports the functioning of organizations. We can, however, observe that there has been recent and targeted legislative action attempting to deal with corporate groups. These attempts acknowledge that organizational boundaries do not line up with legal boundaries and that connections between organizations and their participants can be legally structured through a variety of arrangements. These arrangements include employment, supply contracts, a parent–subsidiary relationship, and also informal ways of cooperation. The failure-to-prevent model adopted in the Bribery Act 2010 is well suited to establishing liability along organizational lines.

There exists a normative discussion about the extent to which corporate groups should be liable for claims of tort victims. Tort victims of subsidiaries of multinational groups are frequently vulnerable individuals and so a case can be made for the introduction of special liability rules permitting such individuals to claim against parent companies or other group members. These arguments are supported by economic rationales as well as on moral grounds.[97]

We have seen above that legislation recognizes corporate groups for reporting purposes. The legislature has recently also put in place rules allowing The Pension Regulator to impose liability on companies within groups. The Bribery Act has introduced liability for the failure to prevent wrongdoing in supply chains. The Modern Slavery Act also

---

[97] Christian A Witting, *Liability of Corporate Groups and Networks* (CUP 2018); Jonathan Crowe, 'Does Control Make a Difference? The Moral Foundations of Shareholder Liability for Corporate Wrongs' (2012) 75 MLR 159; Henry Hansmann and Reinier Kraakman, 'Towards Unlimited Shareholder Liability for Corporate Torts' (1991) 100 Yale Law Journal 1879; see also Thilo Kuntz, 'Asset Partitioning, Limited Liability and Veil Piercing: Review Essay on Bainbridge/Henderson, *Limited Liability*' (2018) 19 EBOR 439; see also Martin Petrin and Barnali Choudhury, 'Group Company Liability' [2018] EBOR 771; Peter Hommelhoff, 'Protection of Minority Shareholders, Investors and Creditors in Corporate Groups: the Strengths and Weaknesses of German Corporate Group Law' [2001] EBOR 61; Thomas Thiede and Andrew J Bell, 'Picking the Piper, the Payment, and Tune—The Liability of European Textile Retailers for the tTorts of Suppliers Abroad' (2017) 33(1) Professional Negligence 25–40: this article analyses the position in German law in relation to claims by employees of subsidiaries located in low-pay jurisdictions.

applies to groups and is in the process of being upgraded. We may see legislative intervention for the benefit of tort claimants in the future. The rationale of such an intervention will be guided by economic, moral, as well as political considerations.

From the perspective of real entity theory having unimpeachable rules of separate legal personality with a more nuanced regime for limited liability is certainly the right approach. If the corporate form is to facilitate autonomous organizational action it needs to be permanent and removable only following an orderly process. The social phenomenon of organizational action is also too fluid, on its own, to supply clear boundaries.

As far as a normative intervention through the finetuning of limited liability is concerned the legislature should continue to be focused on procedure. That is better than a focus on the incentive of individual decision-makers. Organizations naturally adopt their own processes and corporate behaviour is best steered by focusing on them. We will see later in this book that while it is sometimes possible to attribute blame to individual actors it is also necessary to intervene when blame is spread across an organization. The models adopted by the Bribery Act and also by the Modern Slavery Act have been designed with a view to steering organizational behaviour in the right direction.[98]

---

[98] Section 5.3 in this book.

5

Corporate Actions

Companies have separate legal personality and require human beings to act for them. In this part we will discuss the rules that determine the attribution of human actors to companies. We will see that these contain elements that demonstrate that company law is designed for the operation of organizations and that therefore a real entity theory is best suited to explain the law as it stands and also to formulate normative recommendations.

5.1 Contract

According to standard agency principles the principal determines the scope of the authority of an agent. In the case of actual authority this is done when the agent is appointed either in writing or orally.[1] Actual authority can also be inferred from an appointment to a role which is normally associated with certain powers to enter into contracts with third parties.[2] The principal is also able to control ostensible authority which arises when a third party relies on a representation by the principal.[3] This can be done by communicating to third parties the scope of authority that has been granted to individuals employed by or engaged with the affairs of the principal.

For companies the position was historically in alignment with the standard agency framework. The shareholders determined the power of the company' agents. They adopted the articles of the company which set the scope of the power of directors and other agents. These articles were communicated to third parties through registration. Because the articles were a publicly available document third parties were presumed to know of their content. As in the case of capacity third parties dealing with the company were under constructive knowledge of the content of the articles.[4]

The scope of the constructive notice doctrine was clarified by *Royal British Bank v Turquand*.[5] Jervis CJ explained that a party dealing with a company was bound to read the deed of settlement. But he was not bound to do more. If the articles contained a permission to borrow money but only on certain conditions, a third party had 'a right to infer the fact of a resolution authorizing that which on the face of the document appeared to be legitimately done'.[6] He does not need to enquire as to whether a shareholder

---

[1] *Freeman & Lockyer v Buckhurst* [1964] QB 480 at 502.
[2] *Hely-Hutchinson v Brayhead* [1968] 1 QB 549.
[3] See recently *East Asia Company Ltd v Pt Saria Tirtatama Energindo* [2019] UKPC 30, [2020] 1 All ER 294.
[4] *Ernest v Nicolls* (1857) 6 HL Cas 401, 419; 10 ER 1351, 1358.
[5] *Royal British Bank v Turquand* (1856) 6 E & B 327; see also: *Mahoney v East Holyford Mining Co* [1875] LR 7 HL 869 and *British Thompson-Houston v Federated European Bank* [1932] 2 KB 76.
[6] *Royal British Bank v Turquand* (1856) 6 E & B 327, 332.

Company Law. Eva Micheler, Oxford University Press. © Eva Micheler 2021. DOI: 10.1093/oso/9780198858874.003.0005

resolution has been passed or if quorum requirements have been met. Third parties could assume that all internal procedures had been complied with.

As in the case of capacity, the standard agency approach in relation to the scope of authority of the directors of the company was abandoned. Questions of capacity and questions of agency are in fact closely connected.[7] There would have been little use in abolishing the external effect of the *ultra vires* doctrine but at the same time allowing the constitution to operate as a limitation on the scope of the directors' power to act as agents.[8] Companies Act 2006 (CA 2006), section 40 now regulates the power of directors to bind the company in contract.

Companies Act 2006, section 40 states that, in favour of a person dealing with a company in good faith, the power of the directors to bind the company, or authorize others to do so, is deemed to be free of any limitation under the company's constitution.[9] The power of the directors is also free of limitations arising from a resolution of the company or of any class of shareholders or from any agreement between the members of the company or of any class of shareholders.[10]

This deprives the shareholders of the ability to shape the scope of power of the directors by way of limiting their authority to bind the company in contracts with third parties through the constitution.[11] In line with this the Model Articles state that the directors are responsible for the management of the company's business, for which purpose they may exercise 'all the powers of the company'.[12] In addition directors can delegate any of their powers 'as they think fit'.[13]

Normally no principal is bound if the third party knew that the agent exceeded his authority or if the third party was put on enquiry.[14] This principle applies to partnerships,[15] but does not apply to companies.[16] In company law, a person dealing with the company can rely on the directors' statutory authority even if

---

[7] At common law, an agent does not have authority to act outside the capacity of principal: *Pickering v Stephenson*, (1872) LR 14 Eq 322, 340. This applies irrespective of how the power of the agent has been defined by the principal. It also applies to apparent authority: *Credit Suisse International v Stichting Vestia Groep* [2014] EWHC 3103 (COMM) [2015] Bus LR D5 [279].

[8] Report of the Company Law Committee (Jenkins Committee) (Cmnd 1749, 1962) para 38.

[9] This also includes limitations arising out of shareholder resolutions or shareholder agreements (Companies Act 2006 (CA 2006), s 40(1)).

[10] CA 2006, s 40(3).

[11] Note that the powers set by the constitution continue to shape the duties of directors (CA 2006, s 171). Directors incur liability to the company if they overstep constitutional limitations. The company, however, is nevertheless bound.

[12] Para 3 of both the Model Articles for public and for private companies (The Companies (Model Articles) Regulations 2008, SI 2008/3229, Sch 1 (Model Articles for Private Companies Limited by Shares) and Sch 3 (Model Articles for Public Companies)).

[13] Para 5 of both the Model Articles for public and for private companies.

[14] *East Asia Co ltd v PT Satria Tirtatama Energindo* [2019] UKPC 30, [2020] 2 All ER 294 [93]; Hugh Beale (ed), *Chitty on Contracts* (33rd edn, 2nd supplement, 2020) para 31-056.

[15] Partnership Act 1890, c 39, s 5; see also *Ernest v Nicolls* (1857) 6 HL Cas 401, 418–19; 10 ER 1351, 1358, where companies are distinguished from partnerships.

[16] This would have contradicted what is now article 10(2) of the First Company Law Directive (Directive 2009/101/EC of 16 September 2009 OJ L 258/11, 1 October 2009).

he knows that an act is beyond the powers of the directors under the company's constitution'.[17]

Like the rule establishing unlimited capacity, CA 2006, section 40 is mandatory. The company's articles are unable to override the provision. Providing a third party with notice also does not avoid its application. Starting out with a standard agency approach company law has moved the capacity of companies and the scope of the authority of directors outside of the realm of private ordering.

The inability of the shareholders to limit the power of the directors can be justified by reference to the fact that the company is an organization. By interacting with each other its participants generate habits, rules, and procedures that are not static but dynamic, and hence subject to change as participants leave and join and external actors, who are themselves sometimes embedded in an organization and subject to their own external pressures, interact with it.

Against this background the law facilitates external interaction of the organization by creating a mandatory rule. The directors are nominated as the holders of master authority that is outside the reach of directors and shareholders. External actors are thus liberated from making enquiries into the relational web the exists inside of the company and that is made up of formal as well as informal rules.

Giving the directors of companies unlimited authority has an important stabilizing effect. Whenever the directors act, the company is bound. In addition, and perhaps even more importantly, whoever the directors authorize can bind the company. This gives the organization run by a company a stable connection point. All delegations that derive from the directors provide office holders with authority in their interaction with third parties. It supplies the organization run by a company with a 'Grundnorm' that is outside the reach of the shareholders and from which the company enters into contracts.

The directors play a dual role. They are agents, but they also act as principals.[18] They act as top-level superior agents who hold master-authority, the scope of which the shareholders cannot modify. They act as 'quasi-principals'.[19]

This chimes with observations made in the Prentice report.[20] Dan Prentice writes, 'In determining the company's liability on transactions with third party allegedly entered into on its behalf by its directors, it was natural that the concepts of agency should be invoked. But in many ways the concepts of agency are not wholly appropriate and the courts have recognized that, at least in certain circumstances, the board is an independent organ of the company and is not just its agent. The board is clearly the principal

[17] CA 2006, s 40(2)(b)(iii).
[18] Eric W Orts, *Business Persons: The Legal Nature of the Firm* (OUP 2013) 59.
[19] ibid; see also Rachel Leow, *Corporate Attribution in Private Law*, (Hart Publishing forthcoming), ch 3.
[20] Department of Trade and Industry, Reform of the Ultra Vires Rule: A Consultative Document (Prentice Report) (HMSO 1986).

organ for conducting its business activities, something which is reflected in the fact that the board has almost invariably conferred upon it the widest jurisdiction possible to manage the company's affairs.'[21]

A theoretical approach that characterizes company law as designed for the operation of an organization is well suited to explaining the law as it stands.

5.2 Tort

Corporate liability in tort and crime have evolved in a way that supports the theory put forward in this book. It is possible to take the view that the company is not a human being and that therefore it cannot be liable in tort either directly or vicariously.[22] This would, of course, not affect the liability of the individuals who acted.

A position along these lines was adopted by Anderson, B in *Stevens v Midland Counties Railway Company and Lander*.[23] He held that no action for malicious prosecution lies against a corporation aggregate for 'it must be shewn that the defendant was actuated by a motive in his mind, and a corporation has no mind'.[24] But there already the two other judges based their decision on the ground that the corporation was not liable because it had not given 'directions' and that the person acting acted 'on his own account'.[25]

Another possibility would be to say that limitations in capacity affect liability in tort such that there is no liability in tort for *ultra vires* acts or for acts that have not been authorized.[26] This, however, is not what the modern law does.[27] Companies are liable in tort and irrespective of their capacity. In fact, limiting tortious liability through the capacity of companies has been referred to by contemporary observers as 'perverse'.[28] It would give the company an advantage (ie an escape from vicarious liability) which it would not have had it conducted the business in a lawful way.[29]

[21] Department of Trade and Industry, Reform of the Ultra Vires Rule: A Consultative Document (Prentice Report) (HMSO 1986) para [24].
[22] In *Director of Public Prosecutions v Kent and Sussex Contractors Ltd* [1944] KB 146 at 157 Mr Justice Hallett observes that 'at one point the existence, and later the extent and conditions of...[a body corporate's]...liability in tort was a matter of doubt...and it required a long series of decisions to clear up the position'.
[23] *Stevens v Midland Counties Railway Company and Lander* (1854) 10 Exchequer Reports (Welsby, Hurlstone, and Gordon) 352 at 356; 156 ER 480 at 482.
[24] ibid.
[25] ibid at 356 (482) (Platt, B) and at 357 (482) (Martin, B) respectively; see also Nathaniel Lindley, Samuel Dickinson, and Marshall D Ewell, *A Treatise on the Law of Partnerships, Including its Application to Companies* (4th edn, Callaghan & Company 1881, reprinted by BiblioLife, LLC) at 301.
[26] *Poulton v The London and South Western Railway Company* (1866–67) LRQB 534; Lindley and Dickinson 300.
[27] Lord Cook of Thorndon, *Turning Points of the Common Law*, The Hamlyn Lectures, Forty-Seventh Series, (Sweet & Maxwell 1997) 23.
[28] David Kershaw, *Company Law in Context* (2nd edn, OUP 2012) 134.
[29] Paul Davies, *Gower and Davies Principles of Modern Company Law* (8th edn, Sweet & Maxwell 2008) 179.

The liability of companies in tort is governed by the rules on vicarious liability. An employer (regardless of whether they are a human individual or a company) is liable for torts committed by those who they employ.[30]

Accepting, as the courts have, that companies are liable in tort, the next question is to determine how to identify which human acts the company is vicariously liable for. The test determines if there is a sufficiently close connection with the business of the company. This includes employees at all levels provided that their acts have the required close connection.

It also includes what is referred to as the 'directing mind and will' of the company and individuals who are identifiable by the 'primary rules of attribution'. We will see below that uncontroversial examples of the latter are the directors and the shareholders taking decisions through resolutions either in a meeting or unanimously under the *Duomatic* principle.[31] From the perspective of these high-ranking individuals a separate test is strictly speaking not required in the context of tort law. They are attributable to the company also under the general test.

There nevertheless exists a view that a company could also be 'directly' in addition to 'vicariously' liable in tort when it acts through resolutions of its board of directors or of its shareholders, who would be considered to personify the company.[32] The concept of direct liability could act as a tool overcoming the boundaries that tort law sets for vicarious liability. There was a time when the rules on vicarious liability were applied in a more limited way than they are now. This was because particularly challenging questions arise when torts are committed by employees or agents in breach of their instructions. The issue arises perhaps to the greatest possible extent when employees or agents commit torts with intent. Examples are fraud, intentional bodily harm, or sexual abuse.[33] It is easy to see why the courts would pause before they attribute liability to an employer who has issued instructions which the agent violated. On closer investigation, however, it seems that the employee or agent acts for the benefit of the employer, and so the risk of employing a rogue individual should rest on that employer provided that there is a sufficiently close connection.[34]

---

[30] For the debate amongst tort lawyers on whether the acts are attributed to the principal or whether the tort is attributed to him or her see most recently Warren Swain, 'A Historical Examination of Vicarious Liability: A "Veritable Ypas Tree?' (2019) 78 CLJ 640

[31] See section 6.2.6 in chapter 6.

[32] David Kershaw, *Company Law in Context* (2nd edn, OUP 2012) 133–34; Paul Davies and Sarah Worthington, *Gower & Davies: Principles of Modern Company Law* (10th edn, OUP 2016) paras 7–37.

[33] See now *Armes v Nottinghamshire CC* [2017] UKSC 60, [2017] 3 WLR 1000; *Bazley v Curry* (1999) 174 DLR (4th) 45 (Sup Ct (Can)); *Various Claimants v Institute of the Brothers of the Christian Schools* [2012] UKSC 56, [2013] 2 AC 1.

[34] *Dubai Aluminum v Salaam* [2002] UKHL 48, [2003] AC 366, [22]; see also *Northampton Regional Livestock Centre Co Ltd v Cowling* [2015] EWCA Civ 651, [2016] 1 BCLC 431: Both partners in a firm of property consultants were jointly and severally liable on account of a breach of fiduciary duty by one of them, where the partner in question was not acting on a frolic of his own but was at all times carrying out the partnership's business, albeit in a misguided fashion; Tomlinson LJ observed at [89] that the touchstone for partnership liability is not whether the partner was authorized but 'whether the connection was such that the wrongful conduct might fairly and properly be regarded as done by the partner while acting in the ordinary course of the business of the partnership.'

If tort law adopted a narrower approach and did not make available vicarious liability for intentional torts, the question of what to do about companies would be pushed into company law. On an identification approach the question would become one of determining which individuals 'are' the company. They would not be attributed to the company (tort law would stand in the way of that). But they would be considered to 'be' or to 'personify' the company. At that point the directing mind and will test would be used. This would create an avenue towards placing the risk of at least some rogue agents on the organizations they are acting for. The avenue would however be limited and tort law would soon experience the same problems that have been observed in relation to the directing mind and will test in the context of criminal law.[35] Happily we do not need to do this.

From a theoretical perspective it is worth keeping in mind that the company is liable in addition to the individual actors, who, having committed an intentional tort, are without doubt already personally liable.[36] The law recognizes companies as tortfeasors, who are independent of their participants. The rules on vicarious liability adequately accommodate companies.[37] Unlike in the context of criminal law where, as we shall see, attribution has been a problem, employers and agents operating at all levels are attributable to the company.

If companies were fictional entities which aggregate contributions we would not trouble with their liability in tort. We would be satisfied with the personal liability of the person acting. But we are not. It is suggested here that this is because the organizations operating in the form of companies are real and distinct from the contribution of their participants. This, rather than the fact that anthropomorphism is useful, is the reason why it has been so hard to eradicate.[38] Anthropomorphism is indeed unhelpful. It has already been mentioned that anthropomorphic metaphors wrongly suggest an extreme structural model where there is no room for agency.[39] But the fact that organizations, for which company law is designed, are real in a social sense cannot be ignored either. There is a way out, however. It is possible to accept that companies are entities with real social rather than biological properties without having to resort to metaphors involving parts of the human body.

It is also the case that tort law has developed in a direction that makes vicarious liability available for intentional torts. Given that the 'directing mind and will' of the company, its shareholders and directors, fall within what tort law characterizes as an agent or

---

[35] See section 5.3.2 in this chapter.

[36] *Standard Chartered Bank v Pakistan National Shipping Corp (No 2)* [2002] UKHL 43, [2003] 1 AC 959.

[37] For a normative argument in favour of organizational vicarious liability see: Christian Witting, 'Modelling Organisational Vicarious Liability' (2019) 39 Legal Studies 694.

[38] Eilis Ferran, 'Corporate Attribution and the Directing Mind and Will' (2011) 127 LQR 239, 259 observes that anthropomorphism has proven 'too handy to give up'. She also cites Lord Cooke: a kind of anthropomorphism is very hard to eradicate from criminal law. Jennifer Payne, 'Corporate Attribution and the Lessons of Meridian' in Paul S Davies and Justine Pila (eds), *The Jurisprudence of Lord Hoffmann* (Hart Publishing 2015) 357, 363 writes that anthropomorphism is hard to eradicate.

[39] See section 1.4.4 in this book.

employee, it would be better to banish the 'directing mind and will' metaphor from the realm of tort law.

5.3 Crime

5.3.1 Introduction

Similar to tort law, the analysis in criminal law started from the position that companies were not liable in crime. This had procedural reasons. For example, there was a time when the accused had to be physically present at trial and initially it was not possible for corporations to be present through a representative.[40] Also sanctions involving corporal punishment, banishment, or prison cannot be directly applied to companies, who after all have no body to harm, and cannot be removed to far-away lands or secure locations.[41]

In particular for common law crimes involving a *mens rea* element the position was initially that companies do not have a human mind and so cannot satisfy the *mens rea* requirement.[42] Along similar lines limitations in the capacity of companies were considered to be a barrier to criminal liability.[43] In the 1940s that attitude changed.[44] From then on the default position became that companies can be guilty of fault-based crimes.[45] The modern debate focuses on how corporate criminal liability is best designed.[46]

This then leads to the problem of whose acts to ascribe to the company for the purposes of criminal law. The courts adopted the identification doctrine. That doctrine attempts to identify the individuals who 'are' the company. It relies on anthropomorphic metaphors. The language conceptualizes companies as human bodies with a 'brain' or 'nerve centre' and 'hands' holding 'tools'.[47] The company is only liable if its 'brain' or 'directing mind and will' has caused the criminal conduct while displaying the required mental

---

[40] Law Commission, Legislating the Criminal Code, Involuntary Manslaughter, Item 11 of the Sixth Programme of Law Reform: Criminal Law, Law Com No 237 4 March 1996 para 6.5, footnote 5, available from <www.lawcom.gov.uk/project/criminal-law-involuntary-manslaughter/>.

[41] CMV Clarkson, 'Kicking Corporate Bodies and Damning Their Souls' (1996) 59 MLR 557; *R v ICR Haulage Ltd* [1944] KB 551, 554; Susanna K Ripken, 'Corporations are People Too: A Multi-Dimensional Approach to the Corporate Personhood Puzzle' (2009) 15 Fordham Journal of Corporate and Financial Law 98.

[42] *R v Cory Bros* [1927] 1 KB 810.

[43] RB Cooke, 'A Real Thing: Salomon v Salomon' in *Hamlyn Lectures, Turning Points of the Common Law* (Sweet & Maxwell 1997) 23.

[44] Law Commission, *Criminal Liability in Regulatory Contexts* (Law Com No 195, 2010) para 5.16.

[45] See eg *Kosar v Bank of Scotland plc (trading as Halifax)* [2011] EWHC 1050 (Admin), [2011] BCC 500, [2011] All ER (D) 08 (May) QBD: a company can commit an offence of harassment under the Protection from Harassment Act 1997; see also RB Cooke, 'A Real Thing: Salomon v Salomon' in *Hamlyn Lectures, Turning Points of the Common Law* (Sweet & Maxwell 1997) 23.

[46] See most recently the project on Corporate Criminal Liability launched by the Law Commission on 3rd November 2020 (<www.lawcom.gov.uk/project/corporate-criminal-liability/>); for an overview of the discussion on the philosophical underpinnings of corporate criminal liability see Nick Friedman, 'Corporations as Moral Agents: Trade-Offs in Criminal Liability and Human Rights for Corporations' (2020) 83 MLR 255, 260–67.

[47] *Bolton v Graham* [1957] 1 QB 159, 172–73 (Lord Denning).

element. Normally the board of directors or the shareholders in general meeting will be identified as the 'ego' and 'centre of the personality' of the company.[48]

It will be suggested in this chapter that the identification doctrine is both right and wrong. It is right in that it characterizes companies as autonomous entities with an 'ego' of their own. It is wrong in using a metaphor that does not capture the characteristics of company's 'ego'. Companies formalize organizations and so help them to act autonomously of any of their participants. Organizations do not have features that correspond to human bodies. Moreover, by inviting an analysis that identifies individuals with the company the very essence of organizational behaviour is overlooked.

It will be shown that criminal law has begun to develop techniques that are better suited than the identification doctrine to address the essence of corporate behaviour. These focus on procedures and processes within organizations rather than on the acts and mental state of individuals. At a positive level these new ways of attributing liability to companies can be explained by a real entity theory. At a normative level the real entity theory supports these new approaches and recommends them for further applications.

5.3.2 Identification doctrine

Introduction

Under the identification doctrine the court determines the individuals who for the purposes of criminal law 'are' the company. Their conduct is 'characterized' as the company's conduct. This has the same effect as attribution but is theoretically different. It involves a search for the individuals who 'personify' the company. The default approach is to identify the company with the individuals who act as its 'directing mind and will'.[49] The members of the board of directors or the shareholders in general meeting are undisputed examples of who qualifies as the company's directing mind and will. Sometimes courts have also identified lower-ranking individuals with the company.[50]

That test was established by *Lennard's Carrying Company v Asiatic Petroleum Company*.[51] The cargo of a ship owned by the Lennard's Carrying Company was destroyed by a fire. The case involved a claim for damages for loss of cargo by the cargo owners against the ship owners. It required the court to interpret section 502 of the Merchant Shipping Act 1894. The provision reads:

> The owner of a British sea-going ship . . . shall not be liable to make good . . . any loss or damage happening without his actual fault or privity in the following cases; namely,—
> (i.) Where any goods, merchandise, or other things whatsoever taken in or put on board his ship are lost or damaged by reason of fire on board the ship.

---

[48] *Lennard's Carrying Company v Asiatic Petroleum Company* [1915] AC 905, 713 (Viscount Haldane).
[49] *R v St Regis Paper Company* [2011] EWCA Crim 2527, [2012] 1 Cr App R 14.
[50] Law Commission, *Criminal Liability in Regulatory Contexts* (Law Com No 195, 2010) paras 5.48–5.68.
[51] *Lennard's Carrying Company v Asiatic Petroleum Company* [1915] AC 705, HL.

The question arose as to whether the loss of cargo was caused 'without the fault or privity' of Lennard's Carrying Company. The manager of the Lennard's Carrying Company was another company, John M Lennard & Sons, Limited, and the managing director of that company was John M Lennard. Mr Lennard was also a director (although apparently not a managing director) of the Lennard's Carrying Company. In addition, he was registered as the managing owner of the ship.[52]

Viscount Haldane observed:

> I think that it is impossible in the face of the findings of the learned judge, and of the evidence, to contend successfully that Mr. J. M. Lennard has shown that he did not know or can excuse himself for not having known of the defects which manifested themselves in the condition of the ship, amounting to unseaworthiness. Mr. Lennard is the person who is registered in the ship's register and is designated as the person to whom the management of the vessel was entrusted. He appears to have been the active spirit in the joint stock company which managed this ship for the appellants.[53]

Viscount Haldane then established the foundations for the directing mind a will test by reasoning further:

> Now, my Lords, did what happened take place without the actual fault or privity of the owners of the ship who were the appellants? My Lords, a corporation is an abstraction. It has no mind of its own any more than it has a body of its own; its active and directing will must consequently be sought in the person of somebody who for some purposes may be called an agent, but who is really the directing mind and will of the corporation, the very ego and centre of the personality of the corporation. That person may be under the direction of the shareholders in general meeting; that person may be the board of directors itself, or it may be, and in some companies it is so, that that person has an authority to co-ordinate with the board of directors given to him under the articles of association, and is appointed by the general meeting of the company, and can only be removed by the general meeting of the company. My Lords, whatever is not known about Mr. Lennard's position, this is known for certain, Mr. Lennard took the active part in the management of this ship on behalf of the owners, and Mr. Lennard, as I have said, was registered as the person designated for this purpose in the ship's register. Mr. Lennard therefore was the natural person to come on behalf of the owners and give full evidence not only about the events of which I have spoken, and which related to the seaworthiness of the ship, but about his own position and as to whether or not he was the life and soul of the company. For if Mr. Lennard was the directing mind of the company, then his action must, unless a corporation is not to be liable at all, have been an action which was the action of the company itself within the meaning of s. 502.[54]

---

[52] ibid 712.
[53] ibid 712.
[54] ibid 713.

This paragraph contains a number of anthropomorphic metaphors. The learned judge used the words 'active and directing will', 'directing mind and will', the 'very ego and centre of the personality' of the company and the 'life and soul' of the company. This language borrows from biology suggesting that companies consist of parts that correspond to parts of the human body. We will see later that this approach rightly conceives the company as independent actor, but that the method of determining whether the company has acted criminally has given rise to problems and has rightly been criticized.

The 'directing mind and will' test was developed to interpret a particular statutory provision. In addition to receiving criticism in other areas of the law that have later used the test, it has not lasted in the context for which it was originally formulated. Later cases dealing with the respective provision in the Admiralty Court have moved away from the directing mind and will criterion.[55]

Lennard's Carrying was not a criminal case. It had to do with statutory liability by ship owners. The test nevertheless moved into criminal law.[56] In *DPP v Kent and Sussex Contractors* it was held that a company can be liable for a statutory criminal offence involving the need to prove fault. The company was found to have formed the 'intent to deceive' under the Defence (General) Regulations, 1939. Its transport manager had signed incorrect statements that were submitted to the rationing authority. In *R v ICR Haulage* a company was held liable for a common law rather than statutory misdemeanour which involved a conspiracy to defraud. The acts of the managing director were held to be the acts of the company.[57] Neither case used the directing mind and will or any other test. They nevertheless used an identification approach. In *Kent and Sussex Contractors* Viscount Caldecote held that the directors and the managing director 'are' more than just agents, they 'are' the company.[58] In *ICR Haulage* the Court of Appeal accepted the decision of the jury and the presiding judge that the acts of the managing director were the acts of the company.[59]

Statutory offences

For statutory offences the default position is that a company is liable if its directing mind and will has caused the offence while displaying the required mental element. The landmark case establishing this rule is *Tesco Supermarkets Ltd v Nattrass*.[60] That case involved an alleged breach of the Trade Description Act 1968, section 11. Lord Reid set out a distinction between vicarious liability and identifying the person who does not act as an agent or servant, but who 'is' the company. That person 'is acting as the company and his mind which directs his acts is the mind of the company'.[61] He

[55] Hoffmann in *Meridian Global Funds Management Asia Ltd v Securities Commission* [1995] UKPC 5, 510; M/ F/R 641.
[56] Law Commission, *Criminal Liability in Regulatory Contexts* (Law Com No 195, 2010) para 5.16.
[57] *R v ICR Haulage* (1944) KB 551.
[58] *Director of Public Prosecutions v Kent and Sussex Contractors Ltd* [1944] KB 146 at 155.
[59] *ICR Haulage* (1944) KB 551 at 559; see also *Moore v I Bresler Ltd* [1944] 2 All ER 515 at 515–17.
[60] *Tesco Supermarkets Ltd v Nattrass* (1972) AC 153, 171.
[61] ibid 170 paras E–G.

referred to *Lennard's Carrying* and Lord Denning's speech in *Bolton v Graham* and, using both as authority, adopted the 'directing mind and will' test to conclude that neither the stock boy nor the branch manager were the company for the purposes of the offence concerned.[62] Lord Diplock did not use the phrase 'directing mind and will' but wrote that 'those natural persons who by the memorandum and articles of association or as a result of action taken by the directors, or by the company in general meeting pursuant to the articles, are entrusted with the exercise of the powers of the company' are to be treated as the company.[63] All judges agreed that the acts of neither the branch manager nor the stock boy were attributable to the company for the purposes the Trade Description Act 1968, s 11.

Tesco v Natrass is succeeded by a number of cases where the same test was applied but which have been more prepared to identify lower-ranking individuals with the company.[64] In *Meridian Global Funds Management Asia Ltd v Securities Commission*, Lord Hoffman was critical of anthropomorphic metaphors. He held that the question is not one of working out which individuals 'are' the company in some metaphorical sense. He used the concept of attribution. The question was one of statutory interpretation. There was not one test that serves for all of criminal law.[65] For statutory offences courts first needed to determine if the respective statute applies to companies. The next step was to work out whose acts for the purposes of that statute are to be attributed to the company. This recommends that the courts abandon an analysis based on anthropomorphic metaphors. It also suggests that the individuals whose acts are attributed to the company can be located at the highest level but can also be at any other level of the organization concerned. It does not suggest that there is a default preference for attributing only the highest-level individuals to the company.

The idea of abandoning metaphoric reasoning has, however, not taken root. Neither has the open-mindedness in relation to where individuals whose actions are attributed to the company are to be located in its hierarchical structure. In *R v St Regis Paper Company* the decision in *Meridian* was qualified by the Court of Appeal.[66] The case concerned a company which had five paper mills and 129 employees. The technical manager of the smallest of these mills was responsible for producing and delivering daily environmental reports in respect of material flowing out of the plant into the nearby river. He deliberately recorded false readings and returned these to the Environmental Agency. The company and the manager were charged under the Pollution Prevention and Control (England and Wales) Regulation 2000, section 32(1)g. At first instance the judge relied on *Meridian* and directed the jury that the company would be liable if their

[62] ibid 171 paras C–D, see also Lord Morris at 180 paras C and D, Viscount Dilhorne at 187–88 and Lord Pearson at 190.
[63] ibid at 200 para A.
[64] Law Commission, *Criminal Liability in Regulatory Contexts* (Law Com No 195, 2010) paras 5.53–5.68 and 5.90; Law Commission, *Involuntary Manslaughter* (Law Com No 237, 1996) paras 6.35–6.39.
[65] See also the cases referred to in Law Commission, *Criminal Liability in Regulatory Contexts* (Law Com No 195, 2010) paras 5.48–5.68.
[66] *R v St Regis Paper Company* [2011] EWCA Crim 2527, [2012] 1 Cr App R 14.

technical manager to whom management functions had been delegated, who had full discretion in performing these functions, and who was in actual control of the operations, had committed the offence. The jury concluded that these facts were present and that the company was thus liable.

The Court of Appeal overturned this and held that the company was not liable. The manager was not the 'directing mind and will' of the company. The directing mind and will are the board of directors, the managing director, and other superior officers of the company, who carry out the functions of management and speak and act as the company. The court reasoned that the directing mind and will test was reaffirmed by *Meridian*. It is the default method of identifying individuals whose acts cause a company to incur criminal liability.[67] An analysis of the regulatory provision concerned revealed that there was 'no warrant for imposing liability by virtue of the intentions of one who cannot be said to be the directing mind and will of the St Regis Paper Company'.[68] The Regulation contained offences involving strict liability of which the company was convicted. It also contained offences requiring the making of a statement knowing that it was false, 'intentionally' making a false record, or an 'intent to deceive'.

Moses LJ concluded: 'There is, in those circumstances, no basis for suggesting that the Regulations, designed as they are to protect the environment and prevent pollution, cannot function without imposing liability on the company in respect of one who is not the directing will and mind of the company.' It was not necessary therefore to relax the rule in *Tesco* to avoid emasculating the regulation. 'Parliament has chosen to protect the environment against pollution in circumstances to which the Regulations apply by imposing strict liability in some cases but requiring mens rea in others.'[69] The regulation recognizes the importance of protecting the environment 'in a carefully graduated way imposing both offences of strict liability and those which require proof of intention'.[70]

Common law crimes

For common law crimes the law developed along the same lines. At first the understanding was that companies could not be the subjects of criminal law. That approach was also abandoned in the 1940s.[71] It has already been mentioned that in *ICR Haulage* the acts of the managing director were considered to be the acts of the company and it was convicted for a common law misdemeanour involving a conspiracy to defraud.[72] As in the case of statutory crimes the courts use the identification doctrine to identify the company's directing mind and will whose acts and mental state 'are' the company for the purposes of common law crimes.

---

[67] See also *R v A Ltd* [2017] 1 Cr App R 1, at paras 27–28 and *Vehicle Operator Service Agency v FM Conway Ltd* [2012] EWHC 2930 (Admin), [2013] RTR 17; *SFO v Barclays Plc* [2018] EWHC 3055, (QB) [2020] 1 Cr App R 28.
[68] *R v St Regis Paper Company* [2011] EWCA Crim 2527, [2012] 1 Cr App R 14 [12].
[69] *R v St Regis Paper Company* [2011] EWCA Crim 2527, [2012] 1 Cr App R 14, para 14.
[70] ibid para 23.
[71] *R v ICR Haulage* [1944] KB 551, 556.
[72] ibid 551.

5.3.3 Critique of the identification doctrine

The identification doctrine has received significant criticism in criminal law circles. The courts have struggled to apply the test consistently. In particular, in the context of statutory offences some cases seem content with identifying lower-ranking employees to the companies while other cases insist on locating the company with its directors or similarly high-ranking individuals. This has created uncertainty.[73]

More prominently in the 1990s a landmark discussion took place in relation to manslaughter. The focus of the criticism was that the identification doctrine only leads to a criminal conviction of a company if its directing mind and will has caused a death while displaying the required mental element. The effect of this is that a small company, where the directors are involved at an operational level, was convicted of manslaughter.[74] Large companies on the other hand could not be convicted because their leaders were typically not involved to the required degree at the right level.[75] The prosecution service thus tended to act against small companies more readily than against large ones.[76]

The fact that large companies are outside the reach of criminal law is unappealing. Their potential impact on public life is significant. People can and have died in large scale factory or building site accidents which are and have been preventable. The London Underground, for example, did not guard against the unpredictability of a fire and no one person was in charge.[77] The Clapham rail crash revealed working practices that were positively dangerous.[78] At a more general level it was observed that an identification regime encourages shrewd and unscrupulous managers to delegate health and safety practices to the lowest and remotest possible level.[79]

The Law Commission's report preceding the Corporate Manslaughter Act 1997 further illustrated the problem.[80] Respondents to the consultation paper reported that, under a regime requiring the identification of the directing mind and will, junior employees were held personally responsible, but there was no responsibility on their employers, who are operating and profiting from the services they provide to the public. There was a widespread feeling that this was wrong.[81] Likewise following the LIBOR scandal

---

[73] Law Commission, *Criminal Liability in Regulatory Contexts* (Law Com No 195, 2010) paras 5.53–5.68 and 5.90; see also Law Commission, *Involuntary Manslaughter* (Law Com No 237, 1996) paras 6.35–6.39.

[74] *Kite and OLL Ltd*, Winchester Crown Court, 8 December 1994.

[75] Law Commission, *Criminal Liability in Regulatory Contexts* (Law Com No 195, 2010) para 174; see also Law Commission, *Corporate Criminal Liability* (3 November 2020) (https://www.lawcom.gov.uk/project/corporate-criminal-liability/).

[76] Law Commission, *Criminal Liability in Regulatory Contexts* (Law Com No 195, 2010) para 5.87.

[77] Law Commission, *Involuntary Manslaughter* (Law Com No 237, 1996) para 1.12.

[78] ibid para 1.14.

[79] ibid para 1.17.

[80] Law Commission, *Involuntary Manslaughter* (Law Com No 237, 1996); see also Law Commission, *Criminal Liability in Regulatory Contexts* (Law Com No 195, 2010) paras 1.63–1.67.

[81] Law Commission, *Involuntary Manslaughter* (Law Com No 237, 1996) para 1.10; see also Celia Wells, 'Corporate Criminal Liability: a Ten Year Review' [2014] Crim LR 849, 853.

Tom Hayes, an employee of UBS, was successfully prosecuted but the bank itself was not.[82]

The problem is not only one of being able to identify the company with the right person in the corporate hierarchy. The Health and Safety Executive advised the Law Commission in relation to corporate manslaughter that injury and death are generally the result of failure in systems for controlling risk. The carelessness of an individual or individuals is only a (more or less important) contributory factor.[83] The Sheen Report on the Herald of Free Enterprise accident described negligent corporate behaviour by observing that the company operating the ferry was 'from top to bottom' infected with 'the disease of sloppiness'.[84]

A doctrine that tries to identify companies with specific individuals does not address this. It fails to 'capture the complexity of the modern company'.[85] CMV Clarkson points out that the reality of modern corporate decision-making is often the product of 'corporate policies and procedures rather than individual decision making'.[86] It has been observed that there are 'limitations inherent in the controlling officer, directing mind, conception of liability' which does not capture the 'corporateness' of corporate conduct.[87]

5.3.4 Vicarious liability

One way of avoiding the limitations of the identification doctrine would be the use of vicarious liability as a tool for attribution not only for tort law but also for criminal law.[88] The company would be liable for anyone acting for it in the course of their agency or employment while displaying the required mental state. Vicarious liability has not been traditionally used in English criminal law but can be found in individual statutory offences.[89]

One example is the well-known decision of the House of Lords in *Director General of Fair Trading v Pioneer Concrete UK Ltd*.[90] The case concerned the offence of contempt

---

[82] *R v Hayes* [2015] EWCA Crim 1944, [2018] 1 Cr App R 10; *SFO v Barclays Plc* [2018] EWHC 3055 (QB), [2020] 1 Cr App R 28.

[83] Law Commission, *Involuntary Manslaughter* (Law Com No 237, 1996) para 7.13.

[84] Mr Justice Sheen, MV *Herald of Free Enterprise*: Report of the Court (No 8074), Department of Transport (1987) para 14.1; Law Commission, *Involuntary Manslaughter* (Law Com No 237, 1996) paras 6.55 and 8.45–8.50.

[85] J Gobert, 'Corporate Criminality: Four Models of Fault' (1994) 14 Legal Studies 393, 395 cited in Law Commission, *Criminal Liability in Regulatory Contexts* (Law Com No 195, 2010) para 5.85.

[86] CVM Clarkson, 'Kicking Corporate Bodies and Damning Their Souls' (1996) 59 MLR 557, 561; see also Jennifer Hill, 'Legal Personhood and Liability for Flawed Corporate Culture', ECGI Working Paper 431/2018 https://papers.ssrn.com/sol3/papers.cfm?abstract_id=3309697 .

[87] Cited in Law Commission, *Criminal Liability in Regulatory Contexts* (Law Com No 195, 2010) para 5.86.

[88] See most recently Mark Dsouza, 'The Corporate Agent in Criminal law–An Argument for Comprehensive Identification' (2020) 79 CLJ 119.

[89] Law Commission, *Involuntary Manslaughter* (Law Com No 237, 1996) paras 6.8–6.26 and 7.29.

[90] *Director General of Fair Trading v Pioneer Concrete UK Ltd* [1995] 1 AC 456; see Law Commission, *Involuntary Manslaughter* (Law Com No 237, 1996) paras 6.24–6.26.

of court. To comply with regulatory requirements the company had issued explicit instructions to its employees to avoid certain practices. It had also put in place a compliance system. Notwithstanding this, certain employees entered into agreements with competitors which fixed prices and allocated work. The company was found to be vicariously liable for the acts of these employees. The compliance system qualified as a mitigating factor but did not shield the company from liability.[91]

Vicarious liability can be harsh. It leads to liability even when a company operates exemplary compliance systems. In the context of tort law we do not mind this effect as much. Tort law is concerned with compensating innocent victims for loss. It seems fair that the company rather than the tort victim should be saddled with the risk of the rogue actor employed by the company.

Criminal law is also concerned with making good as far as possible the injury sustained by victims but also has additional aims. Criminal law aims to punish wrong-doers, deter them from offending (again), remove them from society, and/or rehabilitate them.

Both in the debate preceding the Corporate Manslaughter and Homicide Act 2007 and the Bribery Act 2010 the point was made that the identification doctrine should not be replaced with vicarious liability for the purposes of criminal law. The reason was that this would be too narrow a test, requiring liability to 'flow through an individual, however great the fault of the corporation', but also too wide a test, by 'blaming the corporation whenever the individual employee is at fault, even in the absence of corporate fault'.[92]

5.3.5 Strict liability offences with due diligence defences

Another solution to the problem of capturing corporate criminal conduct is the use of strict liability offences. These can be implemented by statute and provide that a company is liable if they have displayed a certain conduct and that that liability arises irrespective of any mental element.

Traffic offences frequently operate on a strict liability basis. Another example of a strict liability offence can be found in the Pollution Prevention and Control (England and Wales) Regulations 2000, reg 32(1)(b)–(d) which provide:

(1) It is an offence for a person –
    (b) to fail to comply with or to contravene a condition of a permit;
    (c) to fail to comply with regulation 16(1);

---

[91] *Director General of Fair Trading v Pioneer Concrete UK Ltd* [1995] 1 AC 456 at 475 para C.
[92] Celia Wells, 'Corporate Criminal Liability: a Ten Year Review' [2014] Crim LR 849 at 864–65; Law Commission, *Involuntary Manslaughter* (Law Com No 237, 1996) paras 7.29–7.31.

(d) to fail to comply with the requirements of an enforcement notice or a sus-
pension notice . . .

Liability arises in those circumstances irrespective of any mental element.[93] The company is liable if anyone whose actions are attributable to it has caused it to act in an unlawful manner and irrespective of whether that person has displayed fault.[94]

Strict liability is harsh. It can be problematic from a policy perspective. Criminal law
normally requires both physical and mental capacity for either doing what the law requires or for abstaining from what it forbids and a fair opportunity to exercise these
capacities. It is morally wrong to punish somebody who 'could not have helped it'.[95]
Strict liability offences are therefore suitable only in specific circumstances.

Offences that are too strict can also encourage judges to develop techniques to avoid
convicting actors, ultimately undermining the policy objectives of the statute.[96] The
harshness of strict liability has, for example, led to the development of a presumption of
fault. When a statute creating a criminal offence remains silent as to the fault element
required, the courts, in order to prevent criminal law from operating 'unfairly to the
prejudice of accused persons', presume a requirement for fault.[97] This has led to uncertainty while not preventing unfair outcomes.[98] It is, for example, not clear what type
of fault is required under the presumption. Courts decide this on a case-by-case basis
against the specific context.[99]

Professor Celia Wells points out that that the harshness of strict liability offences can be
mitigated through due-diligence defences.[100] These are common in the regulation of
business conduct.[101] An example of such a defence can be found in section 21(1) of the
Food Safety Act 1990 which provides a defence:

> for the person charged to provide that he took all reasonable precautions and exercised
> all due diligence to avoid the commission of the offence by himself or by a person
> under his control.

Along similar lines Pollution Prevention and Control (England and Wales) Regulations
2000, reg.32(1)(e) makes it an offence for a person:

> to fail, without reasonable excuse, to comply with any requirement imposed by a no-
> tice under regulation 28(2) . . .

---

[93] *R v St Regis Paper Company* [2011] EWCA Crim 2527, [2012] 1 Cr App R 14 at para 14 per Moses, LJ.
[94] ibid at paras 21–23 per Moses, LJ; Celia Wells, Corporate Criminal Liability: A Ten Year Review [2014] Crim
LR 849 at 852.
[95] Law Commission, *Involuntary Manslaughter* (Law Com No 237, 1996) para 4.16 and para 4.4.
[96] Law Commission, *Criminal Liability in Regulatory Contexts* (Law Com No 195, 2010).
[97] Law Commission, *Criminal Liability in Regulatory Contexts* (Law Com No 195, 2010) paras 6.2 and 6.9.
[98] ibid paras 6.2–6.3.
[99] ibid paras 6.9–6.15.
[100] ibid paras 6.64 and Appendix C.
[101] ibid para 6.24.

Instead of requiring fault they provide for affirmative defences which the defendant company must prove. The company avoids conviction provided that it can prove it has taken 'all reasonable precautions' and 'all due diligence' or that it has a 'reasonable excuse'. Liability is thus 'strict', but not 'absolute'. This helps to make these offences more acceptable to the business community.[102]

A combination of strict liability and a due diligence defence captures the essence of corporate conduct better than an identification approach requiring judge to determine if individuals at the helm of an organization were at fault. Asking if corporate leaders had caused an operational failure is the wrong question. It is better to ask if they had exercised 'due diligence in all the circumstances', as through the provision of adequate policies and compliance, to ensure that the offence was not committed by employees of the company.[103] The Law Commission has therefore recommended that the presumption of fault be replaced with a presumption of due diligence.[104]

A combination of strict liability with a due diligence defence does rely on a mental element. It operates differently from a standard fault requirement. Under a standard fault requirement the company is liable if it (its directing mind and will) has been causal for the particular event and at fault. Under a due diligence regime the company will avoid prosecution if it took the precautions required.[105] At that point the identification doctrine can resurface. The company avoids a criminal conviction if it can prove that it has an appropriate and functioning control system. If lower-level employees habitually fail in complying with the system criminal liability is only triggered if the ineffectiveness of that control system is attributable to the directing mind and will.

Strict liability offences combined with due diligence defences are more suitable for addressing corporate criminal conduct than identification rules. Their focus on adequate control systems better captures the determinants of corporate acts.

5.3.6 Organizational failure to prevent a crime

The idea of focusing on procedures and control systems rather than identifying individuals embodying the company is also becoming the standard method for addressing corporate criminal conduct outside the realm of statutory offences.[106]

Four examples will be analysed here: the Corporate Manslaughter and Homicide Act 2007, the Bribery Act 2010, the Criminal Finance Act 2017, and the Australian Criminal Code.

---

[102] Deborah Parry, 'Judicial Approaches to Due Diligence' [1995] Crim LR 695.
[103] Law Commission, *Criminal Liability in Regulatory Contexts* (Law Com No 195, 2010) paras 6.6 and 6.17–6.18.
[104] Law Commission, *Criminal Liability in Regulatory Contexts* (Law Com No 195, 2010) Part 6.
[105] Peter Cartwright, *Consumer Protection and Criminal Law* (Cambridge University Press 2001) 110 and Law Commission, *Criminal Liability in Regulatory Contexts* (Law Com No 195, 2010) Appendix B.
[106] Celia Wells, 'Corporate Failure to Prevent Economic Crime—A Proposal' [2017] Crim LR 427 at 428–29.

The first such attempt at this approach is contained in the Corporate Manslaughter and Homicide Act 2007. According to section 1(1) of that Act, a company is guilty of an offence if the way in which its activities are managed or organized causes a person's death, and amounts to a gross breach of a relevant duty of care owed by the organization to the deceased.[107]

The company is, however, only guilty of the offence if the way in which its activities are managed or organized by its 'senior management' is a substantial element in the breach. The Explanatory Notes set out that the breach must be 'the result of the way in which the activities of the organisation were managed or organised'. While the test is not linked to any particular level within the company and aims to consider how an activity was managed within the organization as a whole it nevertheless refers to 'senior' managers and the company as a 'whole'.[108]

Senior management are 'persons who play significant roles' 'in the making of decisions about how the whole or a substantial part of its activities are to be managed or organised', or in 'the actual managing or organising of the whole or a substantial part of those activities'.

It has been pointed out that this attempt at capturing organizational fault is flawed.[109] The test is too narrow.[110] The terms 'whole' and 'substantial part' can be interpreted as referring to a narrow range of individuals whose responsibility is again central to the company's decision-making. There have thus been few cases and all have involved small companies.[111]

The Bribery Act 2010 has been referred to as a role model for capturing corporate criminal conduct.[112] Section 7 of that Act stipulates criminal liability which is triggered by a failure of a company to prevent bribery. The model involves a two-stage approach. The company is liable if a person who is associated with it bribes another person to obtain or retain business for the company or to obtain or retain an advantage in the conduct of business for the company (stage one). This liability arises unless the company can show that it had in place 'adequate procedures designed to prevent persons associated with ... [the company] ... from undertaking such conduct' (stage two).[113] Celia Wells points out that the success of the model lies in the reversal of the

---

[107] Corporate Manslaughter and Homicide Act 2007 c 19; see the analysis of this in Law Commission, *Reforming Bribery* (Law Com No 313, 2008) paras 6.33–6.38 and Law Commission, *Criminal Liability in Regulatory Contexts* (Law Com No 195, 2010) paras 5.92–5.96.

[108] For a critical analysis of causation in this context see Celia Wells, 'Corporate Criminal Liability: a Ten Year Review' [2014] Crim LR 849 at 855–56.

[109] James Gobert, 'The Corporate Manslaughter and Corporate Homicide Act 2007–Thirteen Years in the Making but Was It Worth the Wait?' (2008) 71(3) MLR 413–63; Mohammed Saleem Tariq, 'A 2013 Look at the Corporate Killer' [2014] Company Lawyer 17.

[110] Celia Wells, 'Corporate Criminal Liability: a Ten Year Review' [2014] Crim LR 849at 856–57.

[111] ibid at 860–62.

[112] The Serious Fraud Office has recommended an extension of the bribery model to financial crimes in general: ibid footnote 84.

[113] Bribery Act 2010, s 7(2); Law Commission, *Criminal Liability in Regulatory Contexts* (Law Com No 195, 2010) para 5.97–5.102.

burden of proof.[114] While there is a requirement for fault at stage one, there is no such requirement at stage two. Criminal liability is triggered if adequate procedures are lacking and irrespective of whether the company's directing mind and will or any other individual working for the company display a mental element in relation to the lack of such procedures.[115]

The Ministry of Justice has issued guidelines on adequate procedures. These set out the following six principles: proportionate procedures, top level commitment, risk assessment, due diligence, communication and training, and monitoring and review.[116] It is possible to be critical of the scope of these offences.[117] From the perspective of this book they nevertheless serve as evidence of a move away from identifying the company with individuals and towards conceptualizing them as organizations with procedures that are independent from individual actions.

The failure to prevent model was also used in part 3 of the Criminal Finances Act 2017.[118] Sections 45 and 46 of that Act contain two criminal offences: failure to prevent facilitation of UK tax evasion offences and failure to prevent facilitation of foreign tax evasion offences. The Explanatory Notes to the Act point out that a person commits a criminal offence when he or she 'is knowingly concerned in, or takes steps with a view to, the fraudulent evasion of a tax owed by another'. It is also a crime to 'aid or abet another person to commit a tax evasion offence'.[119] When a banker, an accountant, or any other person facilitates a client to commit a tax evasion offence, the banker or accountant commits a crime.[120] When a banker or accountant criminally facilitates a customer to commit a tax evasion offence, the taxpayer and the banker or accountant committed a criminal offence. The company, which employed the banker or accountant, however, did not. The company remained safe beyond the reach of the criminal law even when it tacitly encouraged its staff to maximize the company's profit by assisting customers to evade tax. It was felt that this was wrong.[121]

Criminal Finances Act 2017, sections 44 and 45 aim to address the problem. Organizations including companies are accountable for the actions of their employees, agents, or service providers regardless of the level at which they operate.[122] If such a person helps someone else to commit a criminal tax evasion offence, the company for which the person acted is guilty of a criminal offence. Liability is strict, but the company can avoid criminal charges by proving that it 'had in place such prevention procedures as it was reasonable in all the circumstances to expect . . . [the company] . . . to

[114] Celia Wells, 'Corporate Failure to Prevent Economic Crime—A Proposal' [2017] Crim LR 427, 434.
[115] Andrew Ashworth, 'Positive Duties, Regulation and the Criminal Sanction' (2017) LQR 606, 627–28.
[116] Celia Wells, 'Corporate Criminal Liability: a Ten Year Review' [2014] Crim LR 849, 870–71.
[117] ibid 870–71.
[118] Criminal Finance Act 2017, ch 22.
[119] Criminal Finance Act 2017, Explanatory Notes para 43.
[120] ibid para 43.
[121] ibid para 44.
[122] Criminal Finances Act 2017, s 44.

have in place' or that 'it was not reasonable in all the circumstances to expect . . . [the company] . . . to have any prevention procedures in place.'[123]

HMRC has published guidance about the procedures that companies can put in place to prevent persons acting in the capacity of an associate person from committing UK or foreign tax evasion facilitation offences.[124] In those guidelines they explain that the previous law was unsatisfactory as it required prosecutors to 'show that the senior members of the relevant body were involved in and aware of the illegal activity, typically those at the board of directors level'.[125] That created a climate where large companies were more likely than small companies to avoid prosecution, where senior members of all companies were encouraged to turn a blind eye to criminal acts of their representatives, and where all the reporting of criminal activity to such senior members was discouraged. This meant that companies which 'refrained from implementing good corporate governance and strong reporting procedures were harder to prosecute.'[126]

Perhaps the most advanced example of an attempt to capture corporate criminal conduct has been identified by Professor Wells. She points to the Australian Criminal Code. Under that act, intention, knowledge, or recklessness will be attributed to a corporate body whenever it expressly, tacitly, or impliedly authorized or permitted the commission of an offence. Such authorization or permission may be established, for example, where the 'corporation's culture encourages situations leading to an offence'. Corporate culture is defined as 'an attitude, policy, rule, course of conduct, or practice existing within the body corporate generally or in the part of the body corporate in which the relevant activities take place'.[127]

All these examples acknowledge that procedures play an important role in corporate life and determine what human actors do within an organization. Procedures are at the heart of what organizations are. Those responsible for leading an organization can put in place adequate procedures and operate compliance systems, but they cannot fully control what the members of an organization do.[128]

---

[123] ibid s 45(2).

[124] ibid s 47; HMRC, 'Tackling tax evasion: Government guidance for the corporate offences of failure to prevent the criminal facilitation of tax evasion, Government Guidance 1 September 2017' available from <https://www.gov.uk/government/uploads/system/uploads/attachment_data/file/672231/Tackling-tax-evasion-corporate-offences.pdf>.

[125] Criminal Finances Act 2017, HMRC Guidance, 3.

[126] ibid.

[127] Celia Wells, 'Corporate Criminal Liability: a Ten Year Review' [2014] Crim LR 849, 865; There has never been a prosecution on this basis and so a recent review of corporate criminal liability has recommended more use of regulatory penalties (https://www.alrc.gov.au/inquiry/corporate-crime/); Jeremy Horder has pointed out that a failure to prevent model is best supplemented by a 'regulatory strategy' focused on the prevention and minimization of risk, the prohibition of unacceptably risky practices, the use of specialized context-specific criminal offences, and enforcement through an expert body (Jeremy Horder, 'Deterring Bribery: Law, Regulation and the Export Trade' in Jeremy Horder and Peter Alldridge (eds), *Modern Bribery Law: Comparative Perspectives* (CUP 2013) 196.

[128] See also Ian B Lee, Corporate Criminal Responsibility as Team Member Responsibility (2011) 31 OJLS 755, 772–74.

5.3.7 Deferred prosecution agreements and rehabilitation

The importance of corporate procedures is also reflected in the Crime and Courts Act 2013, s 45 and Schedule 17. These make deferred prosecution agreements possible in relation to crimes such as conspiracy to defraud or cheating the public revenue and statutory offences such as theft, false accounting, fraudulent tax evasion, forgery, and specified offences under the Companies Act 2006, the Financial Services and Markets Act, and the Bribery Act 2010.[129] A deferred prosecution agreement (DPA) is a contract entered into between the Crown Prosecution Service (CPS) and a company. The CPS agrees to drop charges. The company agrees to pay a fine and abide by certain other conditions. It requires the approval of the court. Interestingly from the perspective of this book one of the conditions that a DPA may include is the implementation of a compliance programme or the making of changes to an existing compliance programme, relating to policies, or to the training of employees, or both.[130] In terms of steering corporate conduct into the right direction a focus on their procedures for compliance is superior to a regime where those who lead the company are encouraged to remove themselves as far as possible from the company's routine operations.

5.3.8 Theoretical observations

From a theoretical perspective it is significant that the law has moved away from an approach where companies stood outside of the criminal law to an approach where they are firmly within the reach of criminal law. Mr Justice Hallett commented this development in *Director of Public Prosecutions v Kent & Sussex Contractors Ltd*:

> With regard to the liability of a body corporate for torts or crimes, a perusal of the cases shows . . . that there has been a development in the attitude of the courts arising from the large part played in modern times by limited liability companies. At one time the existence, and later the extent and conditions of such a body's liability in tort was a matter of doubt, due partly to the theoretical difficulty of imputing wrongful acts or omissions to a fictitious person, and it required a long series of decisions to clear up the position. Similarly, the liability of a body corporate for crimes was at one time a matter of doubt, partly owing to the theoretical difficulty of imputing a criminal intention to a fictitious person and partly to technical difficulties of procedure. Procedure has received attention from the legislature . . . and the theoretical difficulty of imputing criminal intention is no longer felt to the same extent.[131]

The fact that the law treats companies as independent subjects capable of their own criminal conduct cannot be explained through a nexus of contract model. If companies

---

[129] Celia Wells, 'Corporate Failure to Prevent Economic Crime—A Proposal' [2017] Crim LR 427, 429.
[130] ibid 430.
[131] *DPP v Kent & Sussex Contractors Ltd* [1944] KB 156, 157.

were fictitious entities aggregating contributions from participating individuals, it would not be necessary or helpful to attach criminal liability to that fictitious nexus.[132] It would be sufficient to prosecute individual human actors.

Under concession theory corporate criminal liability can be explained as a quid pro quo for the privilege of incorporation.[133] At a positive level this is the approach adopted by Lord Hoffmann in *Meridian*. He relies on legal positivism when he says that a 'company exits because there is a rule (usually in a statute) which says that a persona ficta shall be deemed to exist and to have certain of the powers, rights and duties of a natural person'.[134] In his analysis there are two questions: Does the statute apply to companies? If it does whose acts are attributable to the company for the purpose of the statute? This approach observes that corporate criminal liability is something that the legislature can, if they so choose, write into legislation. Judges determine the scope of the respective legislation. It does not explain when and how the legislature should intervene. It also does not help to identify rules of attribution for the purposes of criminal law.

In the context of corporate criminal liability, a theory that conceptualizes companies as real entities is helpful both at a positive and at a normative level. At a positive level it is close to what the majority of cases have been holding at common law. It also explains the most recent statutory developments.

In terms of the common law further analysis is required. The common law is rooted in a real entity approach but operates a test that suggests that companies work in the same way as human bodies. This has made it difficult for the common law to capture a significant factor determining corporate conduct. The root of the problem is however not the real entity theory, but rather its expression in anthropomorphic terms.

It has already been mentioned that anthropomorphic language was first used by Viscount Haldane in *Lennard's Carrying*.[135] Lord Denning built on this in his well-known remarks in *Bolton v Graham*. He wrote,[136]

> So the judge has found that this company, through its managers, intend to occupy the premises for their own purposes. [Counsel acting for the company] . . . contests this finding, and he has referred us to cases decided in the last century; but I must say that the law on this matter and the approach to it have developed very considerably since then. A company may in many ways be likened to a human body. It has a brain and nerve centre which controls what it does. It also has hands which hold the tools and act

---

[132] John Lowry and Arad Reisberg, *Pettet's Company Law: Company Law and Corporate Finance* (4th edn, Pearson 2012), 36, including footnote 35; Martin Petrin 'Reconceptualizing the Theory of the Firm—From Nature to Function' (2013) 118 Penn St L Rev 1, 26–31; Ian B Lee, 'Corporate Criminal Responsibility as Team Member Responsibility' (2011) 31 (4) OJLS 755.

[133] Ian B Lee, 'Corporate Criminal Responsibility as Team Member Responsibility' (2011) 31(4) OJLS 755 at 754 with references.

[134] *Meridian Global Funds Management Asia Ltd v Securities Commission* [1995] UKPC 5, [1995] 2 AC 500 at 506.

[135] *Lennard's Carrying Company v Asiatic Petroleum Company* [2015] AC 905.

[136] *Bolton v Graham* [1957] 1 QB 159, 172–73.

in accordance with directions from the centre. Some of the people in the company are mere servants and agents who are nothing more than hands to do the work and cannot be said to represent the mind or will. Others are directors and managers who represent the directing mind and will of the company, and control what it does. The state of mind of these managers is the state of mind of the company and is treated by the law as such. So you will find that in cases where the law requires personal fault as a condition of liability in tort, the fault of the manager will be the personal fault of the company.'[137]

Like Viscount Haldane in *Lennard's Carrying*, Lord Denning used anthropomorphic metaphors. He expressly stressed that 'a company may in many ways be likened to a human body'. He uses the words 'brain and nerve centre', 'hands', 'tools', 'mind or will' and 'directing mind and will'.

Lord Denning's reasoning including his metaphors was endorsed by House of Lords in *Tesco v Nattrass*.[138] Lord Reid cited Lord Denning's speech and pointed out that it would be wrong to attribute 'all servants of a company whose work is brain work to it'.[139] Lord Pearson used the term 'brains' as an alternative to 'directing mind and will' in his speech.[140] Lord Diplock and Lord Dilhorne also endorsed Denning's metaphors.[141]

Lord Denning's remarks have, as we have seen, since been qualified in the *Meridian* case by Lord Hoffmann, who did not think that theoretical analysis was helpful here. He observed that there is no 'ding an sich', just statutes that require interpretation.

Lord Hoffman's intervention, however, has not put an end to anthropomorphic analysis in the cases. *Meridien* has been qualified in *St Regis Paper Company*. Admittedly that qualification did not go back to endorse Lord Denning's approach. It did however, re-introduce the words 'directing mind and will' test, which Lord Hofmann carefully avoided.[142] In a recent High Court case a company was not convicted of an offence under the Goods Vehicles (Licensing of Operators) Act 1995 because H did not fall within the class of persons who could properly be held to be within C's 'brains' such that he could have committed an offence in C's name.[143] At common law we need to wait and see how the law will develop further. There is a good chance that the 'directing mind and will test' will re-establish itself and that its scope will continue to oscillate between the various ranks of company decision makers.[144]

From a theoretical perspective we need to observe that identification doctrine has received severe criticism. The criticism has been articulated as an objection to anthropomorphic analysis. In this the critics are right. Companies do not replicate biological

---

[137] ibid 173 (author's italics).
[138] *Tesco v Nattrass* [1972] AC 153.
[139] ibid 171.
[140] ibid 190.
[141] ibid 200 and 187 respectively.
[142] *R v St Regis Paper Company* [2011] EWCA Crim 2527, [2012] 1 Cr App R 14 [12].
[143] *Vehicle Operator Service Agency v FM Conway Ltd* [2012] EWHC 2930 (Admin); [2013] RTR 17 [30]
[144] See also Law Commission, *Reforming Bribery* (Law Com No 313, 2008) para 6.26 footnote 33.

processes.[145] They operate through habits, routines, processes and procedures that emerge through social interaction between human beings. These do not display the same rigid structure as scientific processes. Anthropomorphism is unhelpful and misleading because it wrongly suggests that human behaviour is fully determined by social structure.

But this does not mean that the real entity theory is wrong. Critics have assumed that anthropomorphism is a necessary ingredient of a real entity theory. Lord Wedderburn observed this assumption when he wrote that one objection against the real entity view is that it has been perceived to 'delight in analogies between the body corporate and the human body'.[146]

It is submitted here that the assumption that real entity theory is necessarily connected with anthropomorphism is wrong, and that it is possible to recognize companies as real entities without assuming that they are like human bodies. The statement that companies are real entities means that they are autonomous actors whose actions can be autonomous in the sense that they are not fully controllable by any one group of human actors. In his Clarendon lecture Lord Cook of Thorndon traces the insight that companies are real entities back to a paragraph from the judgment delivered by Lord Halsbury in *Salomon v Salomon*:[147]

> My Lords, the learned judges appear to me not to have been absolutely certain in their own minds whether to treat the company as a real thing or not. If it was a real thing; if it had a legal existence, and if consequently the law attributed to it certain rights and liabilities in its constitution as a company, it appears to me to follow as a consequence that it is impossible to deny the validity of the transactions into which it has entered.

He goes on to comment that:

> Lord Halsbury's simple words about a real thing have a ring of practical truth. To think of a company as a set of rules is helpful up to a point and does shed some light on the subject of company responsibility. Yet it also seems to miss something. The Common People whom the Hamlyn Lectures are supposed to serve might sense that there is more to many companies than that. The McDonald's Corporation has spent more than 300 days in the High Court in the Strand, in the longest trial in British history, demonstrating its own reality. . . . Perhaps it is not over-bold to predict that one day a company will be found guilty of murder and that on another day a company will be credited with performing a life-saving operation.[148]

---

[145] Eilis Ferran, 'Corporate Attribution and the Directing Mind and Will' (2011) 127 LQR 239; Jennifer Payne, 'Corporate Attribution and the Lessons from Meridian' in Paul S Davies and Justine Pila (eds), *The Jurisprudence of Lord Hoffman* (Hart 2015) 357, 361, and 363; KW Wedderburn, 'Corporate Personality and Social Policy—The Problem of the Quasi-Corporation' (1965) 28 MLR 62, 68.

[146] KW Wedderburn, 'Corporate Personality and Social Policy—The Problem of the Quasi-Corporation' (1965) 28 MLR 62, 58.

[147] *Salomon v Salomon* [1897] AC 22, 33.

[148] RB Cooke, 'A Real Thing: Salomon v Salomon' in Hamlyn Lectures, *Turning Points of the Common Law* (Sweet & Maxwell 1997) 11 and 27.

Recognizing that there is a 'practical truth' in the reality of companies and that there is 'more to many companies than' 'a set of rules' does not necessarily mean that they are like human bodies.

The directing mind and will metaphor is misleading. It encourages us to search for individuals and investigate their mental state. John Lowry and Arad Reisberg have observed this. They favour a real entity approach but articulate this approach in a way that circles back to the identification principle. They remark that in a jurisprudential sense the fictional entity theory is not a sufficient explanation for the phenomenon of corporate liability in tort and crime that, to some extent, the company soon has to be regarded in law as the people in it, thus lending support to the real entity theory of incorporation.[149] This seems to suggest that a real entity approach necessarily involves finding individuals who 'are' the company.

The problem with this analysis is not just that it only identifies the highest-ranking individuals within the company. The problem is that it does not capture the reality of companies as organizations. It acknowledges that they are real things, but then circles back to an aggregation approach, limiting itself to trying to identify the individuals who 'are' the company. That is not always possible. Companies are real but they are more than aggregates. By trying to locate their essence in any of particular individuals working for the company and irrespective of where they are in the hierarchy we only capture part of the phenomenon.

Lord Hoffman's analysis in *Meridian* helps to widen the circle of individuals who, for the purposes of criminal law, are attributable to the company, but does not address the problem that companies are not aggregates and that they can act criminally as organizations in circumstances where the blame is on the organization without being located in any one particular individual or group of individuals.

The problem is not only one of bringing in all levels of an organization. The problem is more fundamental. A real entity approach properly understood does not only search for individual people who 'are' or 'embody' the company. It looks at more than the acts of individuals. It also examines the procedures and habits that have formed within the organization and that determine how individuals act. This captures circumstances where decision-makers are not directly at fault but the organization runs nevertheless according to processes that lead to blameworthy conduct.

Anthropomorphism directs us away from seeing and analysing the factors that lead to corporate conduct. Criminal law has started to recognize that corporations are not comparable with private individuals although they operate and act through them. Corporate activity, both licit and illicit, utilizes complex corporate structures, agents, and intermediaries.[150]

---

[149] John Lowry and Arad Reisberg, *Pettet's Company Law: Company Law and Corporate Finance* (4th edn, Pearson 2012) 36, including footnote 35; see also Petrin (2013) pages 26–31.

[150] Celia Wells, 'Corporate Failure to Prevent Economic Crime—A Proposal' [2017] Crim LR 427 at 433.

Organizational cultures and structures of corporations create conditions in which criminal conduct is encouraged.[151] Criminal law has also developed solutions trying to conceptualize corporate fault. The Corporate Manslaughter Act 2007, the Bribery Act 2010, and the Criminal Finances Act 2017 focus on the procedures operated by companies to prevent wrongdoing. That addresses corporate reality much better than any attempt to identify companies with specific human individuals.

Unfortunately for the common law the directing mind and will test was formulated at a time that predates modern understanding of organizations. Changing the tracks of the common law is not straightforward. Judges need to apply precedent and do not have the constitutional powers to make policy decisions.[152] The government is constitutionally responsible for setting policy priorities but Parliamentary time is scarce. At a normative level reforms that focus on corporate culture in addition to high-level fault would nevertheless be welcome.[153]

5.4 Conclusions

Conceiving companies as real entities helps to explain the approach taken by the common law in relation to corporate criminal liability. Companies are actors whose acts are sometimes determined by their shareholders and directors. But these do not fully control what companies do. Companies act autonomously through habits and procedures that have formed between the individuals who act for and contribute to them. These procedures cause companies to become independent of their individual actors and can lead to blameworthy conduct. The autonomy of companies increases with their size. In larger companies, directors and shareholders are less able to affect what individual contributors are doing.

Companies are real entities. They are more than aggregates and can act autonomously. The human being contributing to the company interact through habits and procedures which can create results that were unintended by the company's directors and shareholders.

---

[151] Nicolas Lord, *Regulating Bribery in International Business: Anti-Corruption in the UK and Germany* (Ashgate 2014) 3.
[152] KW Wedderburn, 'Corporate Personality and Social Policy—The Problem of the Quasi-Corporation' (1965) 28 MLR 62 at 71 and Eilis Ferran, 'Corporate Attribution and the Directing Mind and Will' (2011) 127 LQR 239, 248.
[153] There is also a body of literature that recommends that a model that operates on deterrence should be replaced by a model that encourages a culture of compliance (see eg Christopher Hodges, 'Science-Based Regulation in Financial Services: From Deterrence to Culture', Oxford Legal Studies Research Paper No 19/2020 available from <https://papers.ssrn.com/sol3/papers.cfm?abstract_id=3590176>>; see also Mihailis Diamantis, 'Ditching Deterrence: Preventing Crime by Reforming Corporations Rather than Fining Them' (2018) <https://papers.ssrn.com/sol3/papers.cfm?abstract_id=3099156>).

6

The Organizational Framework

6.1 Introduction

The aim of this chapter is to demonstrate that the organizational framework of the company is set out in the first instance through mandatory law contained in the Companies Act. The articles of association, which are now referred to as the constitution of the company, are only able to add further detail to the statutory structure. The government also provides guidance on how the boards of certain companies should be organized which does not have formal legal force but with which the vast majority of companies comply. It will also be shown that the constitution of the company is adopted by private action but should not be characterized as a contract. It is best characterized as akin to secondary legislation, adopted on a statutory basis through private action and setting out procedures allowing an organization to act autonomously of its participants.

6.2 The role of the statute

6.2.1 Introduction

The Companies Act determines the structure of a company by establishing four distinct roles: directors, shareholders, company secretaries, and auditors.[1] A public company has to have at least two directors.[2] Private companies need to have at least one director.[3] Every company has to have at least one director who is a natural person.[4] The government is currently consulting on implementing legislation banning the use of corporate directors.[5] A public company needs to have a company secretary which needs to be qualified according to Companies Act 2006 (CA 2006), section 273 and is responsible for assisting the directors with the maintenance of the records and registers a company is required to keep. A public company and a large private company have to have an auditor.[6] An auditor is responsible for verifying the compliance of the annual accounts

---

[1] Additional roles are sometimes established by other legislation. Finance Act 2009, (c 10) s 1 and schedule 46 para 93 require large companies to identify a Senior Accounting Officer. The office holder has overall responsibility for the company's financial accounting arrangements. The role cannot be assumed by an agent or advisor (Senior Accounting Officer Guidance 16 March 2016 last updated on 28 January 2020 (<www.gov.uk/hmrc-internal-manuals/senior-accounting-officers-guidance/saog12200>)).

[2] Companies Act 2006 (CA 2006), ss 154(2) and 271.

[3] ibid ss 154(1) and 270.

[4] ibid s 155. This provision was introduced through the Companies Act 2006 and constitutes an additional move away from a contractual model.

[5] <www.gov.uk/government/consultations/corporate-transparency-and-register-reform-implementing-the-ban-on-corporate-directors>.

[6] CA 2006 ss 475–79.

Company Law. Eva Micheler, Oxford University Press. © Eva Micheler 2021. DOI: 10.1093/oso/9780198858874.003.0006

and sections of the annual reports with the statutory requirements.[7] We will examine the roles of directors and shareholders in detail below.[8] The analysis in this section is therefore limited to showing that the modern Companies Act determines to a substantial extent the allocation of responsibility between the shareholders and the directors.

6.2.2 Constitutional matters

The Companies Act not only requires companies to have a shareholder meeting it also gives that shareholder meeting exclusive powers to take decisions on constitutional matters. The shareholders are, for example, responsible for amending the constitution.[9] This is mandatory law. The constitution can adopt additional procedural requirements for amendments.[10] But it would not be possible for the constitution to delegate the amendment of the articles to the directors. The shareholders are also required to approve the registration of a private company becoming public,[11] the registration of a public company becoming private,[12] a private company becoming unlimited,[13] an unlimited company becoming limited,[14] and a public company becoming private and unlimited.[15] Shareholders must approve a subdivision of shares into a smaller nominal amount than its existing shares.[16] They must also approve a consolidation of shares into shares of a larger denominational amount than its existing shares.[17] The redenomination of the share capital of a company from one currency into another requires the approval of the shareholders.[18] They are also responsible for the decision to wind up a solvent company.[19]

The shareholders are responsible for controlling which individuals occupy the board of directors. The Act does not prescribe by whom the directors are to be appointed but gives the shareholders a mandatory right to remove them.[20] This mandatory right was introduced by the Companies Act 1948 following a recommendation by the Cohen Committee in 1945.[21] It can now be found in CA 2006, section 168. A director can be removed without reasons but special procedures apply giving the director concerned a

---

[7] ibid ss 475 and 495; The government is currently consulting on measures increasing the role of auditors (Department for Business, Energy and Industrial Strategy, Restoring Trust in Audit and Corporate Governance, CP 382, March 2021).
  [8] Chapter 7 (directors) and chapter 8 (shareholders) of this book.
  [9] CA 2006, ss 21(1) and 283; a qualified majority of the shareholders must also approve a change of the name of a company (CA 2006, ss 77 and 78).
  [10] ibid s 22.
  [11] ibid s 90.
  [12] ibid s 97.
  [13] ibid s 102.
  [14] ibid s 105.
  [15] ibid s 109.
  [16] ibid s 618(1)(a).
  [17] ibid s 618(1)(b).
  [18] ibid s 622(1).
  [19] Insolvency Act 1986, s 122(1)(a).
  [20] CA 2006, s 168.
  [21] Report of the Committee on Company Law Amendment (Cohen Report 1945) (Cmd 6659) [130].

right to be heard on the resolution at the meeting.[22] There is also a requirement for special notice for this meeting and the director concerned is entitled to receive a copy of the notice of the meeting.[23] Shareholders appoint auditors and have a power to remove them at any time by ordinary resolution subject to special notice requirements.[24]

6.2.3 Managing the company

The Companies Act also contains prescriptions determining decision-making in relation to the management of the company. These decisions are shared between the shareholders and the directors.

The Act appoints shareholders to decide on all political donations.[25] They also approve provisions that are made for employees on cessation of the company's business.[26] In relation to listed companies the shareholders need to approve significant transactions that the company enters into with third parties. These are transactions that have passed both certain quantitative thresholds and are outside of the company's ordinary course of business.[27]

The power to issue shares was once a matter which the shareholders could fully delegate to the directors.[28] This is no longer the case. The Companies Act 2006 now sets out mandatory rules limiting the ability of shareholders to give authority to the directors to issue shares.[29] We will see below that an authorization must state a maximum amount of shares that may be allotted and that it must be time-limited.[30] There are also rules requiring companies to issue shares on a pre-emptive basis.[31] These were introduced by the Companies Act 1980 and are fortified by a personal liability of every officer of the company.[32] They are supplemented by rules contained in the Financial Conduct Authority (FCA) Handbook Listing Rules for companies with a premium listing.[33]

In addition to the Companies Act, the City Code on Takeovers and Mergers ('Takeover Code') sets limits on the ability of shareholders to give the directors powers to defend takeover bids. In particular the board of the offeree company must not issue any shares or sell treasury shares, issue or grant options, issue securities convertible into shares, sell, dispose of, or acquire assets of a material amount or enter into contracts otherwise than in the ordinary course of business unless they have received shareholder

---

[22] CA 2006, ss 168 (2)–(5) and 169.
[23] ibid s 169.
[24] ibid ss 485(4), 489(4), and 510.
[25] ibid s 336.
[26] ibid s 247.
[27] Financial Conduct Authority (FCA) Handbook, Listing Rules (LR) ch 10 Significant transactions.
[28] *CAS (Nominees) Ltd v Nottingham Forest FC Plc* [2002] 1 BCLC 613 [40].
[29] CA 2006, s 551(3).
[30] ibid s 551(3)(a).
[31] ibid ss 561–73.
[32] ibid ss 563 and 568(4).
[33] FCA Handbook LR 9.3.11R.

approval.[34] The process requires shareholder approval at the time the bid is imminent and not at any point before.[35]

Shareholders also have exclusive responsibility for deciding transactions that are entered into between the shareholders and the directors. They approve contracts between the company and a third party in circumstances where all directors have a conflict of interest.[36] They approve substantial property transactions and loans, quasi-loans, and credit transactions between the company and a director.[37] The Listing Rules contain additional requirements for such transactions requiring shareholder approval for a slightly broader range of transactions.[38] The shareholders are responsible for the approval of long-term service contracts, the remuneration policy, and payments for loss of office.[39] The Listing Rules require shareholders to approve long-term incentive schemes of directors and senior employees.[40] Shareholders of listed companies also need to approve discounted option arrangements.[41]

The shareholders ratify breaches of duty by the directors and the views of the majority of the shareholders are taken into account when courts decide on whether to authorize a derivative action.[42]

Shareholders are also responsible for taking decisions on the contract that is entered into between the company and its auditor. They determine the auditor's remuneration and approve permitted limited liability agreements.[43] Shareholders also approve reductions of capital and permitted purchases of the company's own shares.[44]

6.2.4 Record-keeping and reporting

There are also mandatory statutory rules that allocate responsibility to the directors. The first of these ensure that third parties interacting with the company are supplied with accurate information about the company. Together with the company secretary the directors are considered to be the officers of the company.[45] These are exclusively responsible for ensuring that the information maintained and made publicly available by Companies House is accurate. They need to file constitutional amendments with Companies House.[46] They need to maintain a register of directors, which must contain

---

[34] City Code on Takeovers and Mergers ('Takeover Code'), rules 21.
[35] Takeover Code, rule 21.1(a).
[36] ibid ss 180(4) and 281(3)(a); see sections 7.7.4 and 8.3.3 in this book.
[37] ibid ss 197, 198, 201, and 203; see sections 7.8.3 and 8.3.3 in this book.
[38] FCA Handbook LR 11.1.5–6 with exceptions set out in LR 11 Annex 1.
[39] ibid s 188 (long-term service contracts), ss 226B and 226C (remuneration policy), ss 217, 218, and 219 (loss of office).
[40] FCA Handbook LR 9.4.1 (as of 1 September 2020).
[41] FCA Handbook LR 9.4.4 (as of 1 September 2020).
[42] CA 2006, s 239 (ratification), s 263(3)(e) (derivative actions); see further section 8.3.4.
[43] CA 2006, ss 492 and 534.
[44] FCA Handbook, ss 641 (reductions) and 693 (purchase of own shares).
[45] CA 2006, s 1121.
[46] ibid ss 26–27.

certain information, and notify Companies House of the beginning and end of the appointment of each individual director.[47] The Act also requires officers to maintain a register for and notify Companies House of particulars relating to company secretaries.[48] Failure to do any of this triggers a fine.[49]

The directors also play an important role in ensuring that the shareholders can exercise their membership rights. They are responsible for maintaining and making available for inspection a register of members.[50] Directors are also required to ensure that shareholder meetings are conducted in compliance with the extensive statutory requirements and that the company maintains records of resolutions and minutes of all proceedings at the shareholder meeting.[51]

Directors need to cause the company to record the assets the company owns and the liabilities it owes.[52] The format of these records differs depending on the nature and complexity of the company's business.[53] The requirements for record keeping are mandatory for all companies. They are fortified by criminal liability.[54]

Based on the company's accounting records the directors of every company must take stock of the company's financial position at the end of each financial year. They must prepare accounts for the company.[55] The responsibility for producing annual accounts cannot be delegated to the shareholders. The board of directors must approve the accounts. These must be signed on behalf of the board by a director of the company.[56] The signature and the name of the director who signed must be on the company's balance sheet.[57]

In addition, these accounts must be prepared either in accordance with the Companies Act or in accordance with International Accounting Standards.[58] International Accounting Standards are adopted by the International Financial Reporting Standards Foundation.[59] The Financial Reporting Council (Audit, Reporting and Governance

---

[47] ibid ss 162–67.

[48] ibid ss 275–78.

[49] See also ibid s 1112.

[50] ibid s 113.

[51] ibid s 355.

[52] ibid s 386.

[53] Explanatory Notes to the Companies Act 2006, para 639; see also ICAEW, Technical Release: TECH 01/11: Guidance for directors on accounting records under the Companies Act 2006 (<www.icaew.com/-/media/corporate/files/technical/technical-releases/legal-and-regulatory/tech-01-11-guidance-for-directors-on-accounting-records-under-the-companies-act-2006.ashx?la=en>).

[54] CA 2006, s 387.

[55] ibid s 394.

[56] ibid s 414(1).

[57] ibid s 414(2); the UK Government is currently consulting on new, more onerous, reporting and attestation requirements for directors (Department for Business, Energy & Industrial Strategy, Restoring Trust in Audit and Corporate Governance, CP 382, March 2021 <https://assets.publishing.service.gov.uk/government/uploads/system/uploads/attachment_data/file/970676/restoring-trust-in-audit-and-corporate-governance-command-paper.pdf>).

[58] CA 2006, s 395.

[59] <www.ifrs.org>; recently the principle of prudence has been re-introduced into chapter 2 of the Conceptual Framework for Financial Reporting (<www.iasplus.com/en/news/2018/03/cf>).

Authority) publish the UK Generally Accepted Accounting Principles (UK GAAP). UK GAAP is not mandatory in the same way as the Regulations made by the Secretary of State. Large companies are required, nevertheless, to state whether their accounts have been prepared 'in accordance with applicable accounting standards and particulars of any material departures from those standards and the reasons for it must be given'.[60] In addition the directors of companies of all sizes must be satisfied that the accounts give a true and fair view of the assets, liabilities, financial position and profit and loss of the company.[61] There is well established jurisprudence that compliance with UK GAAP is prima facie evidence that the accounts comply with the true and fair view requirement.[62] This gives UK GAAP a legal force that elevates them above the level of default rules.

6.2.5 Procedures for shareholder decisions

The Companies Act 2006 prescribes in great detail how decisions are taken by the shareholders either at a meeting or in writing.[63] These rules were introduced following a recommendation of the Cohen Committee with a view to making it more difficult for directors to secure the hurried passing of shareholder resolutions.[64] It is normally for the directors to call a meeting.[65] But members with at least 5 per cent of paid up capital can request a meeting to be called.[66] This right is enforceable by court order.[67] There are mandatory notice periods and mandatory rules about the manner in which notice is to be given.[68] The content of the notice for a meeting is also set out in statute.[69] Members with 5 per cent of paid-up share capital can require the circulation of a statement at a shareholder meeting.[70] Every shareholder of a traded public limited company (plc) is entitled to ask questions at the annual general meeting.[71] They can also request the publication of matters relating to audit or auditors.[72]

---

[60] Large and Medium-sized Companies and Groups (Accounts and Reports) Regulation 2008/410, Schedule 1, para 45.

[61] CA 2006, s 393 (1).

[62] *Macquarie International Investments v Glencor UK Ltd* [2010] EWCA Civ 697; Marc Moore, Opinion for the Financial Reporting Council, International Accounting Standards and the True and Fair View, 8 October 2018 available from <www.frc.org.uk/getattachment/5d0b34be-5742-41d8-a442-6ad22d2b878e/Martin-Moore-QC-Opinion-3-October-2013-sig.pdf>.

[63] CA 2006, ss 281–354.

[64] Report of the Committee on Company Law Amendment (Cohen Report 1945) (Cmd 6659) [124]–[129].

[65] CA 2006, s 302.

[66] ibid s 303.

[67] ibid s 306.

[68] ibid ss 307 and 307A, ss 308–09.

[69] ibid ss 311 and 311A.

[70] ibid s 314.

[71] ibid s 319A.

[72] ibid s 527.

6.2.6 *Duomatic*

The statutory procedural requirements for decision-making by shareholders are mandatory. It is nevertheless possible for shareholders to take decisions informally provided that all shareholders agree.[73] It is necessary for all shareholders to participate in the decision-making. If one of the shareholders is a company which has been dissolved the remaining shareholder is unable to rely on *Duomatic*.[74]

The *Duomatic* case concerned a situation where the directors drew funds according to their personal needs. No resolution by shareholders authorizing the directors to receive remuneration was ever passed. None of the directors had a service contract. At the end of each financial year the sums were totalled, grossed up for tax, and entered into the accounts as directors' salaries. The directors were nevertheless entitled to keep the remuneration paid to them. This was because all the shareholders who had a right to attend and vote at the general meeting assented to this practice this was held to binding on the company in the same way as a resolution of the general meeting.[75]

From a theoretical perspective we can observe that the *Duomatic* principle operates as a mechanism through which the law allows informal organizational decision making to override the formal decision-making process. It is worth observing, however, that the principle only heals formalities that would otherwise be required for the shareholders to take a decision. It does not expand the powers of the shareholders. In *Global Corporate v Hale* the Court of Appeal decided a case where a director paid himself interim dividends during the financial year.[76] If at the end of the financial year numbers did not add up to show a profit these were recharacterized as salary in the accounts. The director concerned had to return the payments made to him. They were unlawful distributions. The company had paid dividends in circumstances where there was no profit. The *Duomatic* principle does not enable shareholders to ratify actions that are *ultra vires* or dishonest.[77]

6.2.7 Procedures for decisions of the directors

The statute does not contain instructions on how directors are to take their decisions. In recent years this vacuum has been filled by codes of best practice which are not formal

---

[73] *Re Duomatic Ltd* [1969] 2 Ch 365.

[74] It is necessary for all shareholders to participate in the decision-making. If one of the shareholders is a company which has been dissolved the remaining shareholder is unable to rely on *Duomatic* (*Re BW Estates Ltd* [2017] EWCA Civ 1201, [2017] BCC 406); see also *Dixon v Blindley Health Investments Ltd* [2015] EWCA Civ 1023, [2016] 4 All ER 490, [108] where doubt was expressed as to whether the *Duomatic* principle can apply when some shareholders are represented by proxies held by other shareholders.

[75] *Re Duomatic* [1969] 2 Ch 365 (Buckley J); see also *Wright v Atlas Wright (Europe) Ltd* [1999] 2 BCLC 301.

[76] *Global Corporate v Hale* [2018] EWCA Civ 2618, [2019] BCC 431.

[77] See most recently *Ciban Management Corp v Citco (BVI) Ltd* [2020] UKPC 21, [2020] BCC 964 [40] and [43] (Lord Burrows); see also *Julien v Evolving TecKnologies and Enterprise Development Co Ltd* [2018] UKPC 2, [2018] BCC 376.

legislation but have nevertheless been developed at the instance and with the support of the government.

The UK Corporate Governance Code makes detailed and comprehensive recommendations for the structure of the board of directors. It recommends that board include an appropriate combination of executive and non-executive (and, in particular, independent non-executive) directors, such that no one individual or small group of individuals dominates the board's decision-making. There should be a clear division of responsibilities between the leadership of the board and the executive leadership of the company's business.[78] The board and its committees should have a combination of skills, experience, and knowledge.[79] The roles of the chair of the board and of the chief executive director should not be exercised by the same individual.[80] The Code also recommends that board sub-committees are set up for topics such as nomination, remuneration, and audit which are thus removed from the direct influence of executive directors.[81]

The Code applies to all premium-listed companies but contains guidance rather than formally binding law. It operates on a comply or explain basis. Companies can either adopt the recommendations or give reasons in their annual corporate governance statement as to why they have chosen to adopt an alternative arrangement.[82] There exists an ongoing debate about how to best ensure that companies avoid box-ticking and ensure that they comply with the spirit rather than the letter of the recommendations.[83]

The Code is nevertheless backed up by an understanding that the government will be prepared to intervene with formal legislation should companies decide not to engage with the recommendations of the Code. This connection between the Code and government policy can be illustrated by the events preceding the most recent update of the Code. When Theresa May campaigned to become prime minister she pledged to put employees on boards of companies in the UK.[84] That pledge was implemented through an amendment of the UK Corporate Governance Code which now contains recommendation for companies to adopt one of three options for employee representation.[85]

In addition, compliance levels are high and notwithstanding the ability of companies to deviate from the Code. The vast majority of companies comply with the vast majority of

---

[78] UK Corporate Governance Code, Principle G.

[79] ibid Principle K.

[80] ibid Provision 9.

[81] ibid Provision 17 (nomination); Provision 24 (audit); Provision 32 (remuneration); banks now also require a risk committee.

[82] FCA Handbook, DTR 7.2.

[83] See most recently Bobby V Reddy, 'Thinking Outside the Box—Eliminating the Perniciousness of Box-Ticking in the New Corporate Governance Code' (2019) 82 MLR 692.

[84] https://www.ft.com/content/3d70421e-4759-11e6-b387-64ab0a67014c

[85] https://www.ft.com/content/009ebf92-9550-11e6-a1dc-bdf38d484582; UK Corporate Governance Code 2018 provision 5.

the provisions of the Code.[86] The Code appears to have an effect that is likely to be similar to that of formal legislation.

The Government has also involved itself in the organization of boards of large private companies. These are now required to publish a statement setting out their corporate governance arrangements by reference to a corporate governance code.[87] To inform this disclosure the Financial Reporting Council has published the Wates Corporate Governance Principles for Large Private Companies.[88] Similar to the UK Corporate Governance Code these recommend the separation of roles of the chair and the chief executive officer and the formation of board committees for matters such as financial reporting, risk, succession, and remuneration.[89] It is possible and may well have been intended by the Government that the Wates Principles will over time achieve the same level of general acceptance as the UK Corporate Governance Code has.[90]

6.2.8 Conclusions

The statute contains significant rules that set up the organizational structure of the company and allocate decision-making between the directors and shareholders. It also allocates a role to auditors and to a company secretary. Shareholders are responsible for overseeing constitutional matters and transactions between the company and its directors. They control who is appointed as a director and as an auditor. They also have mandatory powers in relation to share issues and capital reductions. Directors have statutory responsibilities relating to record-keeping and reporting. There are also mandatory rules allocating management decisions between the shareholders and the directors.

The statute contains granular rules for shareholder meetings and written resolutions. These formalities can be overridden by an unanimous agreement of the shareholders under the rule in *Duomatic*. This rule recognizes an informal organizational act. The rule, however, only replaces procedural formalities of the constitution; it does not constitute a basis through which the competencies of the shareholders are extended.

The UK Corporate Governance Codes contain government-backed guidance for the organization of the board of directors of premium-listed companies and large private

[86] 95 per cent of companies comply either with all or all but one provision of the Code (Financial Reporting Council, Annual Review of the UK Corporate Governance Code, January 2020 (3)).

[87] The Companies (Miscellaneous Reporting) Regulations 2018, reg 26(1)–(2).

[88] Wates Corporate Governance Principles for Large Private Companies, December 2018 <www.frc.org.uk/getattachment/31dfb844-6d4b-4093-9bfe-19cee2c29cda/Wates-Corporate-Governance-Principles-for-LPC-Dec-2018.pdf>.

[89] ibid 13 (chair) and 18 (committees).

[90] James Wates CBE writes in the foreword to the Principles that it is his 'hope that a wide range of companies—and not just those included in the new legislative requirement to report on the corporate governance arrangements—will use the Wates Principles' (Wates Corporate Governance Principles for Large Private Companies, December 2018, 1 <www.frc.org.uk/getattachment/31dfb844-6d4b-4093-9bfe-19cee2c29cda/Wates-Corporate-Governance-Principles-for-LPC-Dec-2018.pdf>).

companies. The role of directors will be further examined in chapter 7; the role of share-holders will be analysed in chapter 8. At this stage it suffices to observe that the basis of the organizational structure of a company is established by the Companies Act rather than by the constitution.

6.3 The role and nature of the constitution

6.3.1 Introduction

In this section it will be argued that the constitution, while adopted through the private actions of the first shareholder(s), should not be characterized as a contract.

Historically the last time the foundational document was explicitly referred to as a formal contract was in the Companies Act 1844 and in the Limited Liability Act 1855, which both used the terms 'deed of settlement'.[91] The Companies Act 1856 introduced new terminology and required two constitutional documents: a 'memorandum' (section III) and 'articles of association' (section IX).[92] This terminology continued until the Companies Act 2006. The memorandum included information which was of interest to the outside world, while the articles dealt with the internal constitution of the company.[93] In the early days of company law the memorandum could not be altered. Until 2006 the requirements for amending the memorandum were more onerous than requirements for amending the articles. This made it possible to use the memorandum to entrench provisions.[94] The term 'constitution' was introduced by the Companies Act 2006.

The constitution of a company is adopted through private action. The initial share-holders of the company adopt the company's first articles, which together with any later amendments are now referred to as the constitution,[95] by agreement.[96] If there is only one shareholder setting up the company that person determines the content of the constitution. If the first shareholder(s) does(do) not adopt bespoke articles the Model Articles prescribed by the Secretary of State apply.[97] The fact that the constitution is adopted by individual private action does, however, not mean that it is a contract.

Companies Act 2006, section 33 provides: 'The provisions of a company's constitution bind the company and its members to the same extent as if there were covenants on the

---

[91] Companies Act 1844, ss VII and VII (7&8 Vict c 100) and Companies Act 1855, ss I and II (18&19 Vict c 133).

[92] Companies Act 1856, 19&20 Vict c 47. The Companies Act 1848 (7&8 Vict c 100), ss VII and VIII and the Limited Liability Act 1855 (18&19 Vict c 133), ss I and II were under the influence of the deed of settlement companies that prevailed at the time and used the terms 'deed of settlement'.

[93] The Company Law Steering Group, *Modern Company Law for a Competitive Economy, Company Formation and Capital Maintenance* (October 1999) [2.13].

[94] ibid [2.27].

[95] CA 2006, s 17.

[96] ibid ss 7, 8, and 18.

[97] ibid ss 19 and 20.

part of the company and of each member to observe those provisions.'[98] The term 'covenants' likens the constitution to a contractual arrangement. It could be said that this means that the basis on which the constitution applies is contractual. But that is not right. Companies Act 2006, section 33 does not say that the constitution is a contract; it just states that the company and its members are bound to the same extent 'as if they were' covenants. This suggests that the source of the binding force of the constitution is the statute rather than contract law.

This conclusion is supported by case law. Steyn LJ reasoned in *Bratton Seymore Service Co Ltd v Oxborough* that the 'articles of association become, upon registration, a contract between the company and its members. It is, however, a statutory contract of a special nature with its own distinctive features. It derives its binding force not from the bargain struck between parties but from the terms of the statute. It is binding only in so far as it affects the rights and obligations between the company and the members acting in their capacity as members.[99]

The point that the statute rather than a contract is the foundation for the binding effect of the constitution is also supported by the genesis of CA 2006, section 33. The section was added to the Companies Act when companies began to be established by registration. When companies are established by registration the problem arises that the company cannot join the constitution as a contractual party when it is set up. This is because the company does not exist before it is registered. There was thus a time when case law was divided as to whether the company itself is bound by the constitution.[100] CA 2006, section 33 was drafted to clarify the point. It does something that contract law could not achieve: bind the company to what is now the constitution.

Contract law is also a fickle tool to ensure that members who join after the company has been incorporated are bound by the constitution. They join the company by being admitted as members. Transfers occur by registering the name of the transferee on the register of members.[101] The joining member does not formally agree to become bound by the constitution. Companies Act 2006, section 33 ensures that all registered members are, without further ado, bound by the constitution.

Companies Act 2006, section 33 thus, rather than characterizing the constitution as a contract, overcomes the problem that contract law is not an adequate tool to establish a basis for an organizational framework binding both the company itself and members joining after incorporation. While the constitution is adopted by private action of the first shareholder(s) of the company statute is the formal foundation giving the

---

[98] ibid s 33(1).

[99] *Bratton Seymore v Oxborough* [1992] BCC 471 at 475; endorsed by *Lehtimaki v Children's Investment Foundation Fund (UK)* [2018] EWCA Civ 1605, [2019] Ch 139, [37] (Richards LJ, Newy LJ, and Dame Elizabeth Gloster) (The decision was overturned by the Supreme Court in *Lehtimaki v Cooper* [2020] UKSC 33, [2020] 3 WLR 461 but on different grounds).

[100] Sarah Worthington, *Sealy and Worthington's Texts and Materials on Company Law* (11th edn, OUP 2016) 262 and 265–68.

[101] CA 2006, s 112.

constitution the comprehensively binding effects it needs to function as the foundational document of the company.

6.3.2 Misrepresentation, duress, and undue influence

In addition, the standard rules causing contracts to be considered null and void have been held not to apply to the constitution of a company. The constitution of a company is not defeasible on the grounds of misrepresentation, duress, or undue influence.[102] The ordinary principles as to the termination of a contract for repudiatory breach also do not apply.[103] This is in line with the observation made earlier that fraud does not affect the separate legal personality of the company.[104] A company cannot be terminated like a contract. It needs to be wound up to come to an end. From a theoretical perspective this, once again, shows that company law is designed to facilitate the autonomous operation of organizations.

6.3.3 Rectification

The already rare instances in which contract law permits the rectification of contracts are further limited in relation to the corporate constitution.[105] It is not enough for there to be evidence of the intentions of the shareholders to set up the company.[106] The courts are only prepared to consider circumstances which are public knowledge either because everyone knows or because they can be inferred from the company's annual accounts.[107] It seems that the reason for this is not that the constitution is a publicly registered document. The courts are prepared to imply terms into registered charges over land, which are also public documents.[108]

The reluctance to apply the standard contractual rules can, however, be supported by reasons which chime with the theory advanced in this book. In *Scott v Scott* Luxmore LJ pointed to the role of the constitution as the foundational document of the company which comes into existence on the basis of the registered constitution.[109] Once the

---

[102] *Bratton Seymore Service Co Ltd v Oxborough* [1992] BCC 471 at 475; Robin Hollington, *Hollington on Shareholders' Rights* (9th edn, Sweet & Maxwell 2020) para 3-17.

[103] *Flanagan v Liontrust Investment Partners LLP* [2015] Bus LR 1172 at [241] (note that case concerns a partnership).

[104] See section 4.3.1 in this book.

[105] For an account of these rare instances see Hugh Collins, 'Implied Terms: The Foundation in Good Faith and Fair Dealing' (2014) 67 Current Legal Problems 297 (319).

[106] *Scott v Frank F Scott (London) Ltd* [1940] Ch 794 (CA), 796 and 800.

[107] *Attorney General of Belize v Belize Telecom Ltd* [2009] UKPC 10 [36] (Lord Hoffmann); *Cosmetic Warriors Ltd v Gerrie* [2017] EWCA Civ 324, [2017] 2 BCLC 456 [23]; *Re Euro Accessories Ltd* [2021] EWHC 47 [34] (Snowden J); see also *Eclairs Group Ltd v JKX Oil and Gas plc* [2015] UKSC 71, [2016] BCLC 1, [30] (Lord Sumption). Richards J held in *Re Coroin Ltd* [2011] EWHC 3466 (Ch) [68]–[70] that in exceptional circumstances a shareholder agreement might also provide the basis for the implication of terms.

[108] *Cherry Tree Investments Ltd v Landmain Ltd* [2012] EWCA Civ 736, [2013] Ch 305.

[109] *Scott v Frank F Scott (London) Ltd* [1940] Ch 794 (CA) 802.

company has been registered, the constitution ceases to be a contract. It has statutory force.[110] It can only be amended through the statutory alteration procedures, which cannot impose an extra burden on a member without their consent.[111] A final and perhaps the most persuasive reason undermining the ability of courts to rectify terms is the fact that the members of the company fluctuate.[112] An implication of terms could result in a situation where 'different implications would notionally be possible between the company and different subscribers. . . . The consequence would be prejudicial to third parties, namely, potentially shareholders who are entitled to look to and rely on the articles of association as registered.'[113]

6.3.4 Mutual understanding of quasi-partners

In *Scott v Scott* Luxmore LJ spoke of an hypothetical case where a company was registered with articles that gave preference shareholders a dividend of 70 per cent instead of 7 per cent, 'the "0" having been inserted owing to a clerical error, and the shareholders who controlled more than one-fourth of the voting power opposed the passing of any special resolution to put the mistake right'.[114] He suggested that the 'short answer to such a case is that the proper remedy would be to petition the Court for an order for the compulsory winding up of the company on the ground that it was in the circumstances just and equitable to do so'.[115]

It is worth mentioning here that it is no longer necessary for a winding up to be carried out in such cases. This problem can be solved through the unfair prejudice remedy. Companies Act 2006, section 994 provides a mechanism for shareholders to argue that the formal constitutional wording does not adequately and exhaustively reflect their mutual understanding and that it would be unfairly prejudicial for other shareholders to insist on the wording of the constitution.[116] For such a claim to succeed, however, it is not enough for the company to be a quasi-partnership. It is necessary to demonstrate that the shareholders concerned had reached an agreement, albeit an informal one.[117]

---

[110] *Bratton Seymore Service Co Ltd v Oxborough* [1992] BCC 471, 474.

[111] *Scott v Frank F Scott (London) Ltd* [1940] Ch 794 (CA) 802; *Bratton Seymore Service Co Ltd v Oxborough* [1992] BCC 471, 474; *Evans v Chapman* 86 LT 381; note, however, that an alteration becomes effective once it has been adopted by a special resolution or by unanimous consent under the *Duomatic* principle (*Gunewardene v Conran Holdings* [2016] EWHC 2983 (Ch), [2017] BCC 135).

[112] *Re Coroin Ltd* [2011] EWHC 3466 (Ch) [63] (Richards J).

[113] *Bratton Seymore Service Co Ltd v Oxborough* [1992] BCC 471, 475–76.

[114] *Scott v Frank F Scott (London) Ltd* [1940] Ch 794 (CA) 804.

[115] ibid; see also Lord Hoffmann in *O'Neill v Phillips* who wrote that winding up on just and equitable grounds is analogous to contractual frustration (*O'Neill v Phillips* [1999] 1 WLR 1092, 1101H–1102B).

[116] *Ebrahimi v Westbourne Galleries Ltd* [1972] 2 All ER 492.

[117] No mutual agreement was held to exist in *O'Neill v Phillips* [1999] 1 WLR 1092; and *Re Edwardian Group Ltd* [2018] EWHC 1715 (Ch), [2019] 1 BCLC 171; but see *VB Football Assets v Blackpool Football Club (Properties) Ltd* [2017] EWHC 2767 (Ch), *Strahan v Wilcock* [2006] EWCA Civ 12, [2006] 2 BCLC 555; *Re Compound Photonics Group Ltd* [2021] EWHC 787 (Ch).

From a theoretical perspective we can observe that the unfair prejudice remedy operates as a tool that connects the formal constitutional framework with the reality of what those setting up the company had thought they had agreed.

6.3.5 Enforcement

Membership rights only

The constitution is not enforced like any other contract. It is only possible to enforce 'membership rights'. Membership rights are rights that are organizational in character. Rights that do not serve an organizational purpose will not be enforced by the courts.

The foundational authority establishing that members can only enforce 'membership rights' is *Hickmann v Kent or Romney Marsh Sheep-Breeders' Association*.[118] Astbury J discussed previous conflicting authority and concluded that outsider rights are not enforceable. He stated that 'no right merely purporting to be given by an article to a person, whether a member or not, in a capacity other than that of a member, as for instance, as a solicitor, promoter, director, can be enforced against the company'.[119]

In *Eley v Positive Government Security Life Assurance Co Ltd*, for example, it was held that a provision in the articles appointing Mr Eley, who had advanced money for the purposes of setting up the company, as the company's solicitor was unenforceable. Amphlett B observed that the articles merely regulated the 'internal affairs of the company' and that the signature of the directors was for the purpose of 'binding them to such regulations'.[120] Likewise a member who was employed by a company was unable to enforce a provision in its articles granting 'every . . . officer and servant of the company' an indemnity for 'all damages, fines, costs, losses and expenses' which he may incur.[121] In *London Sack and Bag Co Ltd v Dixon and Lugton Ltd* two members of the United Kingdom Jute Goods Association Ltd had entered into a contract for the sale of cotton flour bags. When a dispute arose between them the sellers applied to have the case stayed on the basis that the articles of the association contained a clause referring 'all disputes arising out of transactions connected with the trade . . . to arbitration'. That application failed because the statutory contract was held not to 'constitute a contract between [members] . . . about rights of action created entirely outside the company relationship such as trading transactions between members'.[122]

---

[118] *Hickman v Kent or Romney Marsh Sheep-Breeders' Association* [1915] 1 Ch 881 applied by the Court of Appeal in *Beattie v Beattie* [1938] Ch 708.

[119] *Hickman v Kent or Romney Marsh Sheep-Breeders' Association* [1915] 1 Ch 881 at 900; see also *Re Tavarone Mining Co, Pritchard's Case* (1873) 8 Ch App 956 (sale of a mine).

[120] *Eley v Positive Government Security Life Assurance Ltd* (1875) 1 ExD 20 at 29; affirmed by the Court of Appeal (1876) 1 ExD 88 (CA).

[121] *In Re Famatina Development Corporation* [1914] 2 Ch 271 (CA).

[122] *In London Sack and Bag Co Ltd v Dixon and Lugton Ltd* [1943] 2 All ER 763 (CA) at 765.

A well-known example of a membership right is the right to receive a dividend in the form set out by the articles once it has been declared. In *Wood v Odessa Waterworks* the plaintiffs obtained an injunction restraining the directors from acting on an ordinary shareholder resolution whereby dividends would be paid in the form of debentures.[123] The Court of Appeal also granted an injunction prohibiting the directors, who held the majority of the shares of the company, from transferring these on terms that were in breach of the articles of association.[124] In *Salmon v Quin & Axtens Ltd* the Court of Appeal granted an injunction preventing the company from acting on an ordinary resolution of the shareholders.[125] That resolution approved two property transactions which, according to the articles, could not go ahead when either of two shareholder directors vetoed them. Mr Salmon was one of the shareholder directors entitled to exercise this right. He vetoed the transactions. The court granted him an injunction enforcing his constitutional veto rights.[126] Shareholders also have statutory rights to inspect certain documents held by the company.[127] In particular they are entitled to inspect the shareholder register.[128] They can inspect the directors' service contract and indemnity provisions.[129] They are entitled to have the shareholder register rectified.[130] They can also request an audit for the accounts and reports of a company for which the statute does not require an audit.[131] Every member and every debenture holder can request a copy of the accounts and the reports.[132]

The limitation of the enforcement of the constitution to membership rights not only applies to claims advanced by members—it also applies to claims brought by the company against its members. In *Bisgood v Henderson's Transvaal Estates Ltd*, for example, it was held that the articles cannot place an obligation on its members other than in their capacity as members.[133] Buckley LJ reasoned that 'The purpose of the memorandum and the articles is to define the position of a shareholder as a shareholder, not to bind him in his capacity as an individual.'[134]

---

[123] *Wood v Odessa Waterworks Company* (1889) 42 Ch D 636.

[124] *Heron International v Lord Grade* [1983] BCLC 244.

[125] *Salmon v Quin & Axtens Ltd* [1901] 1 Ch 311.

[126] The case is sometimes used as authority for the proposition that each member can have all provisions in the articles enforced even if they concern outsider rights (KW Wedderburn, 'Shareholders' Rights and the Rule in *Foss v. Harbottle*' [1957] CLJ 194 at 207–09; see also Paul L Davies and Sarah Worthington, *Gower: Principles of Modern Company Law* (10th edn, Sweet & Maxwell 2016) paras 3–30. The better position is, however, to conclude that the right to participate in the decision-making process of the company is a governance right and as such a membership right (see also Victor Joffe and Giles Richardson, 'Personal Claims' in Victor Joffe et al, *Minority Shareholders* (6th edn OUP 2018) para 3.20).

[127] CA 2006, s 744(1) (register of debenture holders), s 162(5) (register of directors), s 229 (directors' service contract or memorandum), s 238 (copy of qualifying indemnity provisions), s 811 (register of interests disclosed), s 116 (register of members), s 358 (records of resolutions and meetings).

[128] *Houldsworth Village Management Co Ltd v Barton* [2020] EWCA Civ 980.

[129] CA 2006, ss 229 and 237--38.

[130] ibid s 125; *Boston Trust Co Ltd v Szerelmey Ltd* [2020] EWHC 1352 (Ch).

[131] CA 2006, s 476 (no less than 10 per cent of the nominal value of the company's issued share capital).

[132] ibid s 431.

[133] *Bisgood v Henderson's Transvaal Estates Ltd* [1908] 1 Ch 743 (CA).

[134] ibid 759.

While it is possible to set out examples illustrating both outsider rights and member-ship rights, the line between what is a membership right and what is not is difficult to draw and it is not possible to reconcile the cases decided in this area.[135] In addition, the decision in *Hickmann* has been criticized as being unsupportable by previous au-thority and as contradicting the explicit words of the statute.[136] Sarah Worthington has observed that, 'it is really quite remarkable that so shaky a first-instance decision was tacitly accepted . . . and endorsed by the Court of Appeal'.[137]

Restricting the enforcement of the company's constitution to membership rights nev-ertheless has a sound theoretical basis. It is not helpful to approach the questions arising in this area through the lens of contract law. The constitution is a special type of private arrangement that has been recognized by statute for a particular purpose. Its purpose is to provide an organization with a decision-making and governance framework. It is not a contract from which non-corporate rights can arise. This does admittedly not re-solve the problem that the line between outsider and membership rights is difficult to draw. It does, however, explain why such a distinction exists. In addition to limiting the enforcement of the constitution to membership rights the courts also decline to enforce 'mere internal irregularities'.

No 'mere internal irregularities'

The courts do not permit shareholders to enforce the constitution if the matter com-plained of is a 'mere internal irregularity'.[138] The phrase 'mere internal irregularity' is unfortunate because every breach of the procedures governing a meeting is a breach of 'internal' rules. These are the rules applying to the governance of a company through its directors and its members. What is meant, of course, is that the courts distinguish between more and less serious breaches of the internal rules set out in the constitution and the Companies Act.[139]

The proposition that a 'mere internal irregularity' does not give rise to a personal claim by a shareholder can rely on support from the leading authorities on deriv-ative claims. In *Edwards v Halliwell* Jenkins LJ allowed the claim and rejected the submission that the omission to hold a ballot and obtain a two-thirds majority as required by the articles was a 'mere internal irregularity'. The omission could not be dismissed as a matter of form.[140] This confirms, albeit indirectly, that the distinction exists. Likewise in *Prudential v Newman* the Court of Appeal referred to the principle that 'an individual shareholder cannot bring an action in the courts to complain of an

---

[135] Sarah Worthington, *Sealy and Worthington's Texts and Materials on Company Law* (11th edn, OUP 2016) 268–69.

[136] Roger Gregory, 'The Section 20 Contract' (1981) 44 MLR 526.

[137] Sarah Worthington, *Sealy and Worthington's Texts and Materials on Company Law* (11th edn, OUP 2016) 268.

[138] KW Wedderburn, 'Shareholders' Rights and the Rule in *Foss v. Harbottle*' [1957] CLJ 194 at 210; Sarah Worthington, *Sealy and Worthington's Texts and Materials on Company Law* (11th edn, OUP 2016) 262 and 703ff.

[139] It is worth noting that the phrase 'mere internal irregularity' cannot be found in the more recent cases.

[140] *Edwards v Halliwell* [1950] 2 All ER 1064 at 1066; see also Asquith LJ at 1065–66.

irregularity . . . if the irregularity is one which can be cured by a vote of the company in general meeting'.[141]

The Law Commission and Lord Wedderburn in his seminal article on derivative actions also refer to *MacDougall v Gardiner* as authority for the proposition that a mere internal irregularity does not give rise to a personal claim.[142] The case states reasons explaining why the courts are unwilling to give a remedy if the complaint concerns a 'mere internal irregularity'.[143] The Court of Appeal reasoned that 'nothing connected with internal disputes between shareholders is to be made the subject of a bill by some one shareholder, . . . unless there is something illegal, oppressive or fraudulent . . . on the part of the majority of the company, so that they are not fit persons to determine it'.[144] A shareholder cannot complain of 'a question of internal management'.[145] Shareholders have no right 'to have a meeting held in strict form in accordance with the articles'.[146] If the affairs of the company are managed in a way in which they ought not to be managed the company is the proper person to complain.[147]

As with the distinction between outsider and membership rights it is not possible to reconcile all of the cases or to point to a clear line allowing the prediction of the outcome of individual cases.[148] It is nevertheless useful to look at some of the cases distinguishing 'mere' internal irregularities from other breaches.

An example of a case involving a 'mere internal irregularity' can be found in the decision in *The Amalgamated Society of Engineers v Jones* where the society adopted an amendment to its articles that had not be notified in the agenda in the form set out

[141] *Prudential Assurance v Newman Industries* (CA) [1982] 1 Ch 204 at 210 E–F; see also *Smith v Croft (No 2)* [1988] 1 Ch 114 at 167B.

[142] KW Wedderburn, 'Shareholders' Rights and the Rule in Foss v. Harbottle' [1957] CLJ 194 at 209–13; Law Commission, Shareholder Remedies Consultation LC 142 (1996) para 2.23.

[143] While *MacDougall v Gardiner* articulates the underlying principles clearly and in this regard deserves continued attention, in terms of its application of these principles the case is probably no longer good authority. The decision seems unduly harsh to the plaintiff who held the majority of the votes at the shareholder meeting and whose complaint was that the chair had deliberately deprived him of the ability to conduct business at a meeting he had requested (*MacDougall v Gardiner* (1975) 1 ChD 13 at 15–17). It was decided in 1875 applying the procedural rules of the time which made it impossible for the court to grant the declaratory remedies requested by the plaintiff (*MacDougall v Gardiner* (1975) 1 ChD 13 at 24 and 27). It has not been endorsed by subsequent case law. In *Universal Project Management Services v Fort Gilkicker* [2013] EWHC 348 (Ch), [2013] Ch 551 it was referred to in a skeleton argument. In *Choudhury v Bhattar* [2009] EWHC 314 (Ch), [2009] 2 BCLC 108 it was distinguished at first instance. David Donaldson QC pointed out that in the case before him the central dispute was about the composition of the shareholders. The question was if an allotment of shares was effective (para 26). Accordingly, so long as the court has not resolved the questions at the heart of the case, 'a general meeting would merely confirm and reflect the fissure and dispute and resolve nothing' (para 27). But even if there was no dispute as to the shareholdings, the court must have 'jurisdiction to make an appropriate order regulating the conduct of the affairs of the company until such time as a general meeting could be convened and vote' (para 27). This suggests that a modern court might take a different view of the facts in *MacDougall*; The decision in *Choudhary v Bhattar* at first instance was reversed by the Court of Appeal but on the grounds that the court did not have jurisdiction against one of the defendants who resided in India.

[144] *Macdougal v Gardiner* (1975) 1 ChD 13 at 18–19.

[145] ibid 23.

[146] ibid.

[147] ibid.

[148] Victor Joffe and Giles Richardson, 'Personal Claims' in Victor Joffe et al, *Minority Shareholders* (6th edn, OUP 2018) para 3.23; see also KW Wedderburn, 'Shareholders' Rights and the Rule in Foss v. Harbottle' [1957] CLJ 194.

in the articles.[149] Bailhache J held that the court 'would be very slow to interfere with the . . . exercise by a trade union or friendly society of their rights of private government'.[150] The court would not act on 'an informality' and so the plaintiffs failed to obtain relief.[151] Another example can be found in *Cotter v National Union of Seamen* where the meeting had not been properly convened but the resolutions passed were nevertheless considered to be binding on the company.[152] In *Carruth v Imperial Chemical Industries Ltd* the complaint was that the class meeting for the deferred shareholders was held while the ordinary shareholders were present in the room. The House of Lords held that the presence of ordinary shareholders does, in principle, affect the validity of a class meeting of the deferred shareholders. The deferred shareholders, however, did not object at the time and so had waived their rights to challenge the meeting. They raised the point after the resolution had been presented to the court for approval of the proposed reduction. That was too late.[153]

An example of what constitutes an irregularity that gives rise to a remedy can be found in *Musselwhite v Musselwhite*, where the plaintiff was a registered holder of shares but was deliberately not invited to the annual general meeting of the company. He obtained a declaration that the meeting was invalid.[154] In *Pender v Lushington* the court granted an injunction to a shareholder whose votes had not been counted by the chair of a shareholder meeting. It was held that the plaintiff was 'a member of the company' and 'entitled to have his voted recorded—an individual right in respect of he has a right to sue'.[155] In *Macmillan v Le Roi Mining Company* it was held that the chair had used a format for a poll that was in breach of the articles and so the directors were restrained from acting on the decision.[156] In *Edwards v Halliwell* the Court of Appeal concluded that a member of a trade union was entitled to a declaration that a purported alteration of the tables setting out the membership fees payable was invalid. The alteration was adopted in breach of the rules of the union which required that an increase in fees be approved by the members in a ballot with a majority of two-thirds.[157] In *Kaye v Oxford House (Wimbledon) Management Company Limited* the court held that the chair had no residual power to decide that resolutions on the agenda cannot be put to the meeting and so the shareholders were able to consider these resolutions even after the chair had closed the meeting.[158]

In *Byng v London Life Association Ltd* a very strong Court of Appeal declared the decision of the chair to adjourn the meeting invalid.[159] The case concerned a controversial

[149] *Amalgamated Society of Engineers v Jones* (1913) 29 TLR 484.
[150] ibid 484, 485.
[151] ibid.
[152] *Cotter v National Union of Seamen* [1929] 2 Ch 58.
[153] *Carruth v Imperial Chemical Industries Ltd* [1937] AC 707 at 756 (Lord Blanesburgh), at 761 (Lord Russel of Killowen), 767–68 (Lord Maugham).
[154] *Musselwhite v Musselwhite* [1962] 2 Ch 964.
[155] *Pender v Lushington* (1877) 6 Ch D 70 at 81.
[156] *Mcmillan v Le Roi Mining Company Ltd* [1906] 1 Ch 331.
[157] *Edwards v Halliwell* [1950] 2 All ER 1064.
[158] *Kaye v Oxford House (Wimbledon) Management Co* [2019] EWHC 2181 (Ch), [2020] BCC 117.
[159] *Byng v London Life Association Ltd* [1990] Ch 170 (CA) 189B–D.

merger. The venue for the shareholder meeting to approve this merger proved too small. The audio-visual links to overflow rooms did not work and so the chair adjourned the meeting to a larger venue for the afternoon of the same day. The Court of Appeal held that the chair, in principle, did have a power to adjourn the meeting without seeking approval from the members. He acted in good faith and relied on advice from counsel. On the facts, however, he did not exercise this power for a proper purpose. He should have taken into account that there was enough time to convene a new meeting at a later date and that a significant number of shareholders were unable to attend the adjourned meeting and were also unable to issue proxies.[160] The resolutions adopted at the adjourned meeting were declared invalid at the request of one of the members. The Court reasoned that a decision of the chair of a meeting is invalid if on the facts, which he knew or ought to have known, he failed to take into account all the relevant factors, took into account irrelevant factors, or reached a conclusion which no reasonable chair, properly directing himself to his duties, could have reached. These reasons, however, only explain why the chair had breached his duties as a director. They do not explain why an individual shareholder was permitted to sue. There is no explicit discussion in the decision as to why this irregularity was serious enough to justify an intervention by an individual shareholder. It would seem, however, that the fact that the merger was controversial and that a significant number of shareholders were unable to participate in the original meeting or to attend the adjourned meeting are sufficient to justify the conclusion that the adjournment affected the voting rights of a sufficient number of shareholders.

The Courts are prepared to intervene at the instance of an individual shareholder if it can be shown that a decision by the chair of a shareholder meeting was serious enough to affect their right to vote. No bright line can be drawn between cases where courts are prepared to intervene and cases where the courts decline to enforce a membership right.[161] It is nevertheless fair to observe that a minority shareholder who has insufficient shares to prevent the passing of a particular resolution will find it difficult to obtain relief unless he can show serious prejudice to his rights as a member and the possibility that the outcome of the meeting might have been different had his rights been recognized.[162]

Theoretical observations

The courts do not enforce the constitution in the same way they enforce a contract. Enforcement is limited to membership rights and members cannot complain of 'mere' internal irregularities affecting their voting rights. This has been criticized.[163]

---

[160] *Byng v London Life Association Ltd* [1990] 1 Ch 170 (CA) at 189–90 Sir Nicolas Browne-Wilkinson VC), at 194 (Lord Mustil LJ), and at 196 (Lord Woolf LJ).

[161] Victor Joffe and Giles Richardson, 'Personal Claims' in Victor Joffe and others, *Minority Shareholders* (6th edn, OUP 2018) para 3.23.

[162] Leslie Kosmin and Catherine Roberts, *Company Meetings and Resolutions* (3rd edn, OUP 2020) para 7.67.

[163] See eg Paul L Davies and Sarah Worthington, Gower Principles of Modern Company Law (10th edn, Sweet & Maxwell 2016) para 3-27; Leslie Kosmin and Catherine Roberts, *Company Meetings and Resolutions* (3rd

The position adopted at common law can, however, be explained by the fact that the constitution operates on a statutory basis. The Companies Act has delegated to the constitution the task prescribing the regulations of the company.[164] It is in this context that the constitution can be enforced. The rights of the members under that constitution therefore bend to the requirements of the corporate process. Shareholders are not able to insist on the enforcement of the letter of the constitution. They can only enforce membership rights. They also have to put up with having their voting rights subjected to the procedures governing meetings. These rules balance various interests and allow for reasonably swift decision-making. The aim is to provide shareholders with an opportunity to be heard and participate in the decision-making process but the procedures are not sacrosanct. They are not designed to be enforced for their own sake. Shareholders have to tolerate a certain amount of irregularity. The courts distinguish between more and less serious breaches. And while no bright line separating the two can be drawn the aim is to protect the organizational decision-making process which takes priority over the enforcement of the letter of the constitution.

In addition, even if the court concludes that a procedural breach is serious the courts are only willing to grant a declaration that a meeting is not valid or an injunction instructing the directors not to act in a certain way. Damages claims were always unlikely to succeed because of the rule in *Foss v Harbottle*. The reflective loss principle, which has recently evolved out of the rules relating to derivate actions, imposes a further barrier on such claims.

6.3.6   Conclusions

We have seen in this section that CA 2006, section 33 is best interpreted as a provision providing a statutory basis giving the constitution binding legal force. We have also seen that the normal rules of contract law do not apply to the corporate constitution. It is not possible to conclude that the constitution is null and void because this would deprive the organization which operates through a company of the basis on which it functions. Because of this a company can only be ended through a winding up. We have also seen that the rules on the rectification of contracts only apply with modifications reflecting the fact that the members of the company fluctuate and that it is therefore not generally possible to change the wording of the constitution on the basis of an understanding of shareholders who once set up the company and may no longer be members. We have also seen that the unfair prejudice remedy serves as a mechanism permitting

---

edn, OUP 2020) para 9.73 and 9.78–9.85; see also KW Wedderburn, 'Shareholders' Rights and the Rule in Foss v. Harbottle' [1957] CLJ 194, 209.

[164]   CA 2006, s 18(1).

shareholders to insist on informal agreements in circumstances where the company operates as quasi-partnerships.

Finally, we saw that the law only permits shareholders to enforce membership rights. The enforcement of membership rights is further limited to serious breaches. The courts will not enforce 'mere internal irregularities'. Claimants are unlikely to be awarded damages.

In light of all these exceptions it would be better to conclude that the characterization of the constitution as a contract is not helpful.[165] There does not appear to be a single context in which that characterization assists with the understanding of the law as it stands. In all cases analysed above the courts begins the analysis with contract law and then give reasons why contract law does not apply. Perhaps the better way to approach the corporate constitution is to characterize it as the foundational document for the operation of an organization that has more in common with secondary legislation, adopted on a statutory basis through private action, than it has with a normal contract.[166]

The law also sometimes allows the informal corporate reality to override the formal process. We have encountered two examples: the rule in *Duomatic* and CA 2006, section 994, which the courts have used to override the constitution in cases where there exists an informal agreement between quasi-partners to override the constitution.

6.4 Conclusions

We have seen in this chapter that the basis of the corporate organizational framework is statutory. The Companies Act identifies the key decision-makers and assigns specific roles to them. It also sets out a mandatory decision-making process for shareholder decisions. There is no mandatory process in relation to the decisions of the directors but the Corporate Governance Codes nevertheless provide guidance that has the support of the government. The Companies Act frames the ground on which shareholders proceed to adopt the constitution. We have also concluded that the constitution also should not be characterized as a contract. It is best characterized as secondary legislation adopted by private individuals on a statutory basis and setting out procedures facilitating the operation of an organization.

From a theoretical perspective we could stop here to conclude that the company is a concession. But that would be wrong. The law recognizes organizational action outside

---

[165] See also Sarah Worthington, *Sealy and Worthington's Texts and Materials on Company Law* (11th edn, OUP 2016) 269 who observes that the characterization of the constitution as a contract puts the relationship between the members and the company into a 'contractual straitjacket'.

[166] There is not enough room here to explore the point but it is worth investigating whether the rules that have evolved for the interpretation of statutes could serve as a basis for the interpretation of the corporate constitution (on the difference between contractual and statutory interpretation see Andrew Burrows, *Thinking About Statutes, Interpretation, Interaction, Improvement* (CUP 2018) 34–44).

of the formal legal framework. The rule in *Duomatic* serves as a tool for situations where the statutory process was not followed but where it is nevertheless clear that all shareholders intended to take a decision. It connects the law with the reality of organizational decision-making. Along similar lines, the unfair prejudice remedy constitutes a mechanism through which an informal agreement between quasi-partners receives legal recognition.

7

The Role of the Directors

7.1 Introduction

The role of the directors is set out in the Companies Act, which dedicates chapter 2 of part 10 to the general duties of the directors. Additional duties are set out throughout the Act.

The general duties were codified in the Companies Act 2006 (CA 2006). Before that they were developed by the courts at common law and in equity.[1] The common law and equity continue to be relevant.[2] According to CA 2006, section 170(4) regard shall be had in interpreting the general duties of the directors to the corresponding common law rules and equitable principles on which they were based.[3] The general duties are the duty to act within the powers,[4] the duty to promote the success of the company,[5] the duty to exercise independent judgement,[6] the duty to exercise reasonable care, skill, and diligence,[7] the duty to avoid a conflict of interest,[8] the duty not to accept benefits from third parties,[9] and the duty to declare an interest in proposed transactions or arrangements.[10]

In addition to the general duties, now also contained in the statute, the CA 2006 also imposes a substantial number of specific duties on the directors. These require the directors to systematically record financial information,[11] to produce financial as well as narrative reports,[12] to keep the public information on the company up to date,[13] to ensure that shareholder meetings are conducted in accordance with the Companies Act and the constitution,[14] and to abide by the distribution rules.[15]

This chapter has two aims. The first aim of this chapter is to demonstrate that taken together these duties show that the law primarily protects the corporate process rather

---

[1] Companies Act 2006 (CA 2006), ss 171(a) and 174 have their origins in the common law. CA 2006, ss 171(b), 172, 173, and 175–77 originate from equity.
[2] For an analysis on how the contractual origins of UK Company Law have shaped modern corporate fiduciary law see David Kershaw, *The Foundations of Anglo-American Corporate Fiduciary Law* (CUP 2018).
[3] CA 2006, ss 170(3) and (4).
[4] ibid s 171.
[5] ibid s 172.
[6] ibid s 173.
[7] ibid s 174.
[8] ibid s 175.
[9] ibid s 176.
[10] ibid s 177.
[11] ibid s 386.
[12] ibid s 394.
[13] See eg ibid ss 23 and 30.
[14] ibid s 302.
[15] ibid s 830.

Company Law. Eva Micheler, Oxford University Press. © Eva Micheler 2021. DOI: 10.1093/oso/9780198858874.003.0007

than economic interests. CA 2006, section 171 focuses on the constitution rather than on any particular interest group. CA 2006, section 173 requires directors to exercise independent judgement but this has to be done in the context of the board. A director must not directly approach shareholders to seek their support for his views. CA 2006, section 174 defines the standard of skill and care by reference to the role performed by an individual director. It also requires directors to have in place adequate processes ensuring that decisions are taken based on adequate financial information. The law also requires directors to supervise delegated activity and to make sure that the company complies with statutory and regulatory requirements. CA 2006, section 175 requires the approval of transactions which are affected by a conflict of interest even when there is no risk of economic harm to the company. It also does not matter that the company in fact benefitted from the director pursing the opportunity. The duties to maintain accounting records and to produce financial and narrative reports constitute procedural requirements putting directors in a position where they can base their decisions on an adequate level of information and enabling third parties to interact with the company and informed basis.

The second aim of the chapter is to show that shareholders are important albeit indirect beneficiaries of the rules contained in the Companies Act, but that it would be wrong to conclude that the directors are the agents of the shareholders. This is not possible because duties are formally owed to the company rather than the shareholders. It is also not possible because the law does not exclusively focus on the shareholders. The rules governing directors' duties are nuanced and incorporate the interests of other constituencies.

CA 2006, s 172 states that directors need to promote the success of the company for the benefit of the members as a whole but does not require the directors to maximize return. The shareholders take priority but other interests are integrated. The duty is also subjective and so constitutes a weak mechanism guiding the decision-making of directors. Shareholders also occupy a crucial role in overseeing transactions with directors. They approve substantial property transactions.[16] They approve long-term service contracts,[17] and loans,[18] and payments for loss of office.[19] They oversee the remuneration of directors of listed companies. CA 2006, s 174 was introduced with a view to protecting the public interest. The section also serves as an anchor requiring directors to comply with regulation. The Company Directors Disqualification Act 1986 has been influential in shaping the standard of skill and care of the directors. It aims to protect the interests of all participants in the company equally and is also supported by a government-funded enforcement mechanism.

---

[16] ibid ss 190–96.
[17] ibid ss 188–89.
[18] ibid ss 197–214.
[19] ibid ss 215–22.

Directors need to declare any interest they have in transactions that the company enters into. In addition, shareholder approval is required for substantial transactions, long-term service contracts, payments for loss of office, and for payments in relation to the transfer of the whole or part of the company's undertaking. The shareholders of listed companies need to approve the remuneration policy and long-term incentive plans. In this way the shareholders hold the purse strings for the directors, and this means that the directors will work primarily for the (indirect) benefit of the shareholders. This is, however, not sufficient to characterize the shareholders as principals of the directors. We will see in chapter 8 that the law imposes restrictions on the ability of shareholders to authorize payments to themselves, and this undermines the conclusion that they have principal status.

We will also see in this chapter that the idea of designing remuneration in a way that guides the directors to act either for the benefit of the shareholder or for the benefit of the company is flawed, and has served as a motor justifying increasing rewards without bringing about commensurate increases in performance. It will be argued that the problem is not just one of conflicted interests but primarily one of identifying suitable benchmarks predicting future performance. At a normative level it will be argued that an attempt to design remuneration in a way that incentivizes directors to cause companies to pursue environmental or social goals is bound to fail for the same reason.

In addition to the general duties contained in CA 2006, sections 170–81 we will also analyse the duties of the directors to keep accounting records and to produce financial reports. Failure to do so triggers criminal liability. The law contains detailed provisions setting out the formal and content of both the records and the reports. In addition, there are mandatory requirements to produce certain narrative reports. These reports serve the interests of shareholders but also those of other constituencies. Shareholders cannot remove or override them. Directors also need to support the verification of the company's accounts and reports by an independent auditor and to ensure the filing and publication of these accounts and reports. Again, these duties serve primarily the interests of the shareholders but also protect other constituencies. We will also examine the duty of the directors to ensure that companies publish statements in relation to specific social and environmental concerns.

Finally, we will observe that the directors are responsible for determining the amount of profit to be distributed to the shareholders. We will see that they are bound in this decision by statutory distribution rules which prioritize the interests of creditors over those of the shareholders.

We will conclude that the duties of the directors are primarily, albeit indirectly, focused on the interests of the shareholders but they also take into account the interests of creditors and other constituencies. None of the duties can be explained fully by the interests of the shareholders. In addition, the distribution rules prioritize creditor over shareholder interests. Overall, it would be wrong to characterize the directors as agents of the shareholders.

The role of the directors is best conceptualized as serving the company as the legal operator for an organization rather than as requiring the maximization of returns for any particular constituency.

7.2 Duties are owed to the company

Directors owe all their duties to the company. CA 2006, section 170 states explicitly that the 'general duties specified in sections 171–177 are owed by a director of a company to the company'. This was also the position at common law. In *Cook v Deeks*, for example, Lord Buckmaster observed that directors have as 'their first duty to protect' the interests of the company.[20] In *Regal (Hastings) v Gulliver* Lord Porter pointed out that the company and its shareholders are 'separate entities'.[21] Moreover, the courts have explicitly held that the shareholders, special circumstances aside, do not have a direct claim against the directors.[22] From a theoretical perspective this undermines an approach that characterizes directors as agents of the shareholders.

7.3 Duty to act in accordance with the company's constitution and for a proper purpose

The constitution is appointed by statute to prescribe the regulation of the company.[23] Within the limits set by the Companies Act 2006 it determines the powers of the shareholders and the directors. The law connects to the constitution and proceeds to protect the allocation of power established by it. The courts are concerned to prevent directors from usurping powers that are constitutionally allocated to the shareholders.

According to CA 2006, section 171, a director of a company must (a) act in accordance with the company's constitution and (b) only exercise powers for the purposes for which they are conferred. We have concluded above that the constitution is unable to impose limits on the power of the directors to bind the company to contracts with third parties who act in good faith.[24] But the fact that the company is bound to a contract does not relieve the directors from liability when they have failed to abide by the constitution. Directors are only permitted to act within the boundaries set out in the constitution (CA 2006, section 171 (a)) and so are personally liable when they disregard these boundaries.

---

[20] *Cook v Deeks* [1916] 1 AC 554 at 562.
[21] *Regal (Hastings) Ltd v Gulliver* [1967] 2 AC 134 (HL) at 157.
[22] *Percival v Wright* [1902] 2 Ch 421; examples of special circumstances can be found in *Re Chez Nico (Restaurants) Ltd* [1992] BCLC 192; *Peskin v Anderson* [2001] BCC 874 (CA).
[23] CA 2006, s 18.
[24] Section 5.1 in this book.

CA 2006, section 171(b) integrates the proper purpose doctrine into the Act. It sets out two tests. Section 171(a) involves an exercise of construction of the words used in the constitution. The question is: What is the scope of the terms used in the constitution to describe the power of the directors? CA 2006, section 171(b) adds a further criterion. A director must only exercise powers 'for the purposes for which they are conferred'.

We will see in this section that the proper purpose argument is not structured as an argument that characterizes shareholders as 'economical owners' or 'principals' of the company. The courts are not concerned with enhancing the economic status of the shareholders. The argument connects to the constitution of the company as the source for the allocation of decision-making power between the shareholders and the directors. The courts are primarily concerned with preventing the directors from usurping their constitutional powers.

This structure of the proper purpose argument can be found in the cases decided in equity before the Companies Act 2006 came into force.[25] The following dictum by Lord Wilberforce in *Howard Smith v Ampol* provides for an illustration:

> The constitution of a limited company normally provides for directors, with powers of management, and shareholders, with defined voting powers having power to appoint the directors, and to take, in general meeting, by majority vote, decisions on matters not reserved for management. Just as it is established that directors, within their management powers, may take decisions against the wishes of the majority of shareholders, and indeed that the majority of shareholders cannot control them in the exercise of these powers while they remain in office . . . so it must be unconstitutional for directors to use their fiduciary powers over the shares in the company purely for the purpose of destroying an existing majority, or creating a new majority which did not previously exist. To do so is to interfere with that element of the company's constitution which is separate from and set against their powers.[26]

The court here observed that an exercise of directorial power in a way that undermines the competencies of the shareholders or interferes with the ability of shareholders to sell their shares is improper because it is unconstitutional. The argument in later cases follows that structure. In some cases the courts concluded that the directors had overstepped the line and acted for an improper purpose.[27] In other cases the courts reached the conclusion that the directors' purpose was proper.[28]

---

[25] *Hogg v Cramphorn* [1967] Ch 254 (268) stressed that the rights of the majority were 'constitutional'; *Punt v Symons* [1903] 2 Ch 506, 515–16 was decided on the basis of an interpretation of a power contained in the articles of association.

[26] *Howard Smith v Ampol* [1974] AC 831 (PC) 837–38 (Lord Wilberforce).

[27] *Stobart Group Ltd v Tinkler* [2019] EWHC 258 (Comm), [2019] 2 WLUK 235, [438]; *Lee Panavison v Lee Lighting* [1992] BCLC 22, 30; see also 31.

[28] *Mills v Mills* (1938) 60 CLR 150 (High Court of Australia); *CAS Nominees v Nottingham Forest FC* [2002] 1 BCLC 613 [44] and [49]; see also the well-known obiter dictum by Hart J in *Criterion Properties Plc v Stratford UK Properties LLC* [2002] EWHC 496 (Ch), [2003] 1 WLR 2108, which was cited but not endorsed by Carnwath LJ in the Court of Appeal [2002] EWCA Civ 1783 [2003], 1 WLR 2108, [19] and [60].

The case law decided since the Companies Act 2006 came into force also adopts this line of reasoning. Lord Sumption, for example, observed in *Eclairs Group* that the most common use of the proper purpose doctrine is to prevent the 'use of the directors' powers for the purpose of influencing the outcome of the general meeting'.[29] This was not only a use of the power for a collateral purpose. It also 'offends the constitutional distribution of powers between the different organs of the company, because it involves the use of the board's powers to control or influence a decision which the company's constitution assigns to the general body of shareholders'.[30] He also observed that the proper purpose doctrine performs an important role in the governance of companies. It is 'fundamental to the constitutional distinction between the respective domains of the board and the shareholders'.[31]

Where exactly the line between the constitutional powers of the directors and those of the shareholders lie is hard to state in general terms. Lord Wilberforce observed that it is 'impossible' to define in advance 'exact limits' beyond which directors must not pass.[32] The 'variety of situations' facing directors of different types of companies makes it impossible to set out bright-line rules.[33]

The fact that bright-line boundaries are difficult to draw, however, does not undermine the point that the argument connects to the balance of power set up by the constitution of the company rather than to any particular economic characterization of the shareholders. Directors who exercise a power in a way that encroaches on the decision-making power of the shareholders violate the constitution. Equity characterized such an exercise of power as having been carried out for an improper purpose.

From a theoretical perspective we can observe that the argument in equity and under CA 2006, section 171 connects to the constitution of the company. The constitution allocates powers between the directors and the shareholders. The directors must respect this allocation. They must not exercise a power for the purpose of destroying a majority of the shareholders or for the purpose of influencing decision making by the shareholder meeting. The structure of the argument is that it is unconstitutional for the directors to usurp powers that the constitution has allocated to the shareholders.

The law has evolved to give a central role to the constitution which contains the rules for the taking of corporate decisions. The directors are not allowed to decide matters reserved for the shareholders or to interfere with the ability of the shareholders to sell their shares. From a theoretical perspective this fits with the observation that organizations are characterized by their procedures. The constitution establishes such procedures and so enables the company to act autonomously. The law protects these procedures rather than the economic interest of the shareholders.

---

[29] *Eclairs Group Ltd v JKX Oil and Gas plc* [2015] UKSC 71, [2016] BCLC 1, [16].
[30] ibid [16].
[31] ibid [37].
[32] *Hogg v Cramphorn* [1967] Ch 254.
[33] ibid.

7.4 Duty to promote the success of the company

7.4.1 Introduction

CA 2006, section 172 codifies the equitable rule requiring directors to act in good faith 'in the interests of the company'.[34] From the perspective of this book three observations will be made here. CA 2006, section 172 focuses on the company and only indirectly on shareholders and other constituencies. Shareholders take priority over other constituencies but the law does not require directors to maximize their return. The duty is also subjective and so only a weak mechanism guiding the behaviour of directors.

7.4.2 Companies Act 2006, section 172

CA 2006, section 172 requires a director to act in the way he considers, in good faith, would be most likely to promote the success of the company for the benefit of its members as a whole, and in doing so, he must have regard (amongst other matters) to:

a) the likely consequences of any decision in the long term,
b) the interests of the company's employees,
c) the need to foster the company's business relationships with suppliers, customers and others,
d) the impact on the company's operations on the community and the environment,
e) the desirability of the company maintaining a reputation for high standards of business conduct, and
f) the need to act fairly as between members of the company.

Like the equitable duty the statutory duty connects to the company and only indirectly to the shareholders. The directors are required under CA 2006, section 172 to promote the 'success' of the 'company'. Success is not further defined in the Companies Act. In equity the directors were required to act in the 'interests of the company'.[35] Success can be defined as the 'accomplishment of an aim or purpose'.[36] While that includes financial aims it is worth observing that the Act does not explicitly instruct directors to focus on achieving financial goals.

The statutory duty draws a connection between the 'success of company' which is to be promoted for the benefit of the 'shareholders as a whole'. This connection also existed in equity where the 'interests of the company' were considered to be those of 'the shareholders collectively' or 'the shareholders, present and future'.[37] Equity equated the

---

[34] *Re Smith and Fawcett Ltd* [1942] Ch 204 (CA) 306 (Lord Green MR).
[35] ibid.
[36] See 'success', Oxford English Dictionary.
[37] *Miller v Bain* [2002] 1 BCLC 266 [67]; *Gaiman v National Association for Mental Health* [1971] Ch 317 at 330 (Megarry J): 'The association is, of course, an artificial legal entity, and it is not very easy to determine what is in the best interests of the association without paying due regard to the members of the association. The interests of some particular section or sections of the association cannot be equated with those of the association, and I would accept

company's interest with the interest of the shareholders. But it did not conclude that the company and its shareholders were the same thing. The reference to 'present' as well as 'future' shareholders suggests that directors were responsible for defining what is good for shareholders in general terms rather than doing the bidding of the current body of shareholders.

Equity was also alive to the fact that different shareholders have different interests. In cases where a decision of the directors has no implications for the interests of the company but rather affected the relative rights of different classes of shareholders the directors needed to act in what they honestly believed to be fair as between these share-holders. Here too the directors had considerable discretion.[38]

Directors who acted in the interest of a particular group of shareholders have been held to fall foul of the rule.[39] Directors were also prohibited from discriminating between the interests of any majority or minority factions that may exist.[40] An individual director, who sought to 'pick off' particular shareholders in advance of a general meeting by making 'private approaches to them, individually, and then airing his own views upon board management matter' was held to be in a 'real danger' of falling foul of the duty to act for the benefit of the company's members as a whole.[41]

It has been held that:

> in the expression 'bona fide for the benefit of the company as a whole', the phrase 'the company as a whole' does not mean the company as a commercial entity, distinct from the corporators; it means the corporators as a general body (sc as opposed to discriminating between the majority and the minority).[42]

The duty was nevertheless owed to the company and the question was 'as to what the directors thought was in the *company's* interests'.[43] What 'might have been in the *shareholders'* interest' does not 'matter as such'.[44] The job of the directors was thus to consider the shareholders' interest in an abstracted form as opposed to the interests the company's current shareholders might have.

The position seems to be the same under the statutory codification. The directors are instructed to act for the benefit of the 'members as a whole'.[45] This prioritizes the interests

the interests of both present and future members of the association, as a whole, as being a helpful expression of a human equivalent.' See also *Brady v Brady* [1988] BCLC 20, 40 (Nourse J): 'The interests of a company, an artificial person, cannot be distinguished from the interests of the persons who are interested in it. Who are those persons? Where a company is both going and solvent, first and foremost come the shareholders, present and no doubt future as well.'

[38] *Mills v Mills* (1938) 60 CLR 150 (High Court of Australia).
[39] *Scottish Co-operative Wholesale Society Ltd v Meyer* [1959] AC 324.
[40] *Stobart Group Ltd v Tinkler* [2019] EWHC 258 (Comm), [2019] 2 WLUK 235, [394].
[41] ibid [425].
[42] *Lee Panavision v Lee Lighting* [1992] BCLC 22 at 29h (Dillon LJ).
[43] *GHLM Trading Ltd v Maroo* [2012] EWHC 61 [199] (Newey J) (italics in the original).
[44] ibid.
[45] CA 2006, s 172(1).

THE ROLE OF THE DIRECTORS 133

of the shareholders as a group but does not establish a requirement for the directors to maximize their financial return over any particular time frame. The Company Law Review explicitly stressed that the enlightened shareholder view does not require directors to 'have an exclusive focus on the short-term financial bottom line'.[46]

CA 2006, sections 172(1)(a)–(f) sets out stakeholder interests to which directors must have regard. Before the Companies Act 2006 the position originally was that the interest of the company permitted directors to provide the employees of the company with 'cakes and ale'.[47] In *Hutton v West Cork Rly* the Court of Appeal observed that a company 'which always treated its employ[ees] with Draconian severity, and never allowed them a single inch more than the strict letter of the bond, would soon find itself deserted'.[48] While the company was wound up, however, gratuitous payments to employees were no longer in its interest.[49]

The Companies Act 1985 (CA 1985), section 309(1) codified this position stating that the 'matters to which directors are to have regard' included 'the interests of the company's employees in general, *as well as* the interests of its members'.[50] CA 1985, section 309(2) clarified that the duty was, 'in the same way as any other fiduciary duty' 'owed to the company'. This provision seemed to put the interests of employees on the same plane as the interests of the shareholders.[51] This is no longer the case. The codification prioritizes the interests of members over those of other stakeholders.

Like the equitable rule the codified statutory duty is subjective. In equity the courts do normally not consider if 'viewed objectively' an act or omission was 'in the interests of the company'.[52] The courts enquire if the directors acted in what they honestly believed was in the best interest of the company. The courts defer to the judgement of the directors but they do not naively accept the assurances of the directors as to their good faith. Where it is 'clear' that the act or omission under challenge resulted in 'substantial detriment to the company' the directors have a 'harder task' persuading the court that they honestly believed it to be in the company's interest.[53] Also, when the directors' alleged belief was 'unreasonable' that 'may provide evidence that it was not in fact honestly held at the time'.[54] This, however, does not detract from the subjective nature of the test. The issue is as to the directors' 'state of mind'.[55] The courts give the directors a wide range of discretion.

[46] The Company Law Review Steering Group, *Modern Company Law for a Competitive Economy: A Strategic Framework* (1999) [5.1.12].
[47] *Hutton v West Cork Rly* (1883) 23 ChD 654, 673; see also Marc Moore and Martin Petrin, *Corporate Governance, Law and Regulation* (Macmillan Education UK, Palgrave 2017) 150.
[48] *Hutton v West Cork Rly* (1883) 23 ChD 654, 672–73.
[49] ibid 675–77.
[50] Author's italics.
[51] See also *Re Welfab Engineers Ltd* [1990] BCLC 833.
[52] *Regentcrest plc v Cohen* [2001] BCC 494 [120] (Parker J); *GHLM Trading Ltd v Maroo* [2012] EWHC 61 [194] (Newey J).
[53] *Regentcrest plc v Cohen* [2001] BCC 494 [120] (Parker J).
[54] *Extrasure Travel Insurance Ltd v Scattergood* [2003] 1 BCLC 598 [138] (Mr Jonathan Crow); *Stobart Group Ltd v Tinkler* [2019] EWHC 258 (Comm), [2019] 2 WLUK 235, [397].
[55] *Regentcrest plc v Cohen* [2001] BCC 494 [120] (Parker J).

Only if there is evidence that the directors gave no consideration to the interests of the company will the courts determine 'whether an intelligent and honest man in the position of a director of the company concerned could, in the circumstances, have reasonably believed that the transaction was for the benefit of the company.'[56] It is also worth noting that that test is one of whether the directors 'could' have reasonably believed which suggests that the courts are prepared to accept a range of directorial discretion.

In equity the duty was considered to be proscriptive, prohibiting bad faith decisions.[57] The burden of proof was on the company to show that a director had acted in bad faith.[58] The codification transformed the duty to act in good faith into a prescriptive duty explicitly requiring directors to consider what most likely promotes the success of the company.[59]

CA 2006, section 172(3) ensures the continued application of 'any enactment or rule of law requiring directors, in certain circumstances, to consider or act in the interests of creditors of the company'. The provision incorporates the equitable rules and it has been held that there is nothing in the Reports and White Papers preceding the Companies Act 2006 that would suggest an 'intention' to adopt a test that is wider than that articulated previously by the courts.[60]

Directors need to ensure that the company can pay its creditors and that this affects the content of the duties of the directors. Lord Templeman held in *Winkworth v Edward Baron Development Co Ltd* that 'a company owes a duty to its creditors, present and future'. It is required to 'keep its property inviolate and available for the repayment of its debts'.[61] The conscience of the company is 'confided to its directors'. The directors thus owe a duty to the company to ensure that the affairs of the company are 'properly administered' and that its property is not 'dissipated or exploited for the benefit of the directors themselves' to the 'prejudice of the creditors'.[62]

Moreover, where a company is insolvent or likely to become insolvent the interests of creditors are considered to come to the fore.[63] Notwithstanding this change in focus the duties of the directors continue to be owed to the company.[64] As is the case with the

---

[56] *Charterbridge v Lloyds Bank* [1970] Ch 62, 74E–F (Pennycuick J); *Re HLC Environmental Projects Ltd* [2013] EWHC 2876 (Ch) [92] (John Randall QC).

[57] *GHLM Trading Ltd v Maroo* [2012] EWHC 61 [193] (Newey J).

[58] *Re Smith and Fawcett Ltd* [1942] Ch 204 (CA) 309 (Lord Green MR); *Charles Forte Investments v Amanda* [1964] Ch 240 (CA) 260–61.

[59] *GHLM Trading Ltd v Maroo* [2012] EWHC 61 [193] (Newey J); *BTI 2014 LLC v Sequana SA* [2019] EWCA Civ 112, [2019] 1 BCLC 347, [111] (David Richards LJ).

[60] *BTI 2014 LLC v Sequana SA* [2019] EWCA Civ 112, [2019] 1 BCLC 347, [209] (David Richards LJ).

[61] *Winkworth v Edward Baron Development Co Ltd* [1986] 1 WLR 1512 (HL) 1516.

[62] *Winkworth v Edward Baron Development Co Ltd* [1986] 1 WLR 1512 (HL) 1516; see also *Re RJH Stanhope Ltd v Harris* [2020] EWHC 2808 (Ch).

[63] *Kinsela v Russel Kinsela Pty Ltd* (1986) 10 ACLR 395 (New South Wales Court of Appeal) 367–368; *West Mercia Safetywear v Dodd* [1988] BCLC 250, 252–53; *Bilta v Nazir* [2015] UKSC 23, [2016] AC 1, [104]; *BTI 2014 LLC v Sequana SA* [2019] EWCA Civ 112, [2019] 1 BCLC 347 [193]–[221] (David Richards LJ); *Bowe Watts Clargo Ltd (In Liquidation), Re aka Mander v Watts* [2017] EWHC 7879 (Ch).

[64] *Yukong Line Ltd of Korea v Rendsburg Investments Corporation of Liberia (No 2)* [1998] 1 WLR 294; *BTI 2014 LLC v Sequana SA* [2019] EWCA Civ 112, [2019] 1 BCLC 347, [149].

shareholders, directors are required to act in the interests of the 'creditors as a whole'.[65] Also where the directors have not considered the interests of the creditors as a whole the court will determine if an 'intelligent and honest man in the position of a director of the company concerned could, in the circumstances, have reasonably believed that the transaction was for the benefit of the company'.[66]

There is an ongoing debate as to the point in time at which creditor interests come to the fore.[67] At the moment the last word was spoken in the Court of Appeal decision in the *Sequana* case where David Richards LJ pointed out that the 'precise moment' at which a company becomes insolvent is difficult to 'pinpoint'.[68] Insolvency may occur suddenly, but equally, descent into insolvency may be more gradual.[69] He read the case law as suggesting that the duty to consider creditor interests arises where the company is 'likely' to become insolvent. Likely in this context means 'probable'.[70] He justified his conclusions on the policy ground that limited liability was introduced 'in the public interest and for the purpose of advancing the economic well-being of the country'.[71] A creditor-oriented duty that is triggered too early would have a 'chilling effect on entrepreneurial activity, when such activity is the underlying purpose of most registered companies'.[72]

7.4.3 Conclusions

CA 2006, section 172 requires directors to promote the success of the company. That promotion is to be conducted in a way that benefits the members as a whole in the first instance, but regard is to have had to stakeholder interests. Shareholders take priority over the interests of stakeholders. But shareholder interests are defined by the directors' good faith judgement. They only need to do what they honestly believe promotes the success of the company. The law gives a substantial amount of discretion to the directors and so it would be wrong to conclude that CA 2006, section 172 requires directors to maximize return.

7.4.4 Theoretical observations

It is possible to argue that agency theory explains CA 2006, section 172. Indeed, in *Item Software v Fassihi* Lady Arden explicitly used the term 'agency problems' and stressed that it would be economically 'inefficient' not to impose on a director a duty to disclose

---

[65] *Re HLC Environmental Projects Ltd* [2013] EWHC 2876 (Ch).
[66] ibid [92] (John Randall QC).
[67] See most recently Rosemary Teele Langford and Ian Ramsay, 'The Contours and Content of the Creditors' Interests Duty' [2021] CJLS 1.
[68] *BTI 2014 LLC v Sequana SA* [2019] EWCA Civ 112, [2019] 1 BCLC 347, [218] (David Richards LJ).
[69] ibid [218] (David Richards LJ).
[70] ibid [220]–[221] (David Richards LJ).
[71] ibid [151] (David Richards LJ).
[72] ibid [200] (David Richards LJ).

his own misconduct.[73] This statement engages with the academic literature informed by agency theory. But it only goes as far as acknowledging the existence of agency problems and does not further endorse agency theory either at a positive or at a normative level. The learned judge observed that there is a 'constant dilemma in company law as to the manner in which the shareholders can monitor directors'.[74] She also pointed out that an agency problem also existed between 'the board and executive or managing directors'.[75] She nevertheless assumed that the duties of the directors are owed to the company. In particular her concern was to protect 'the company' from making 'erroneous business decisions because it lacks essential information'.[76]

At a positive level agency theory can connect to the fact that the shareholders, under CA 2006 section 172, take priority over the interests of other participants. That fact can be used to support the conclusion that the directors are the 'agents' of the shareholders. We have, however, seen that neither the common law nor CA 2006, section 172 require directors to maximize financial return for the shareholders. Moreover, while the shareholders take priority, CA 2006, section 172 is satisfied with the directors' subjective good faith judgement of what is in the interests of the shareholders. The subjective good faith standard softens the requirement to act for the benefit of the shareholders as a whole. CA 2006, section 172 is thus a weak anchor for an argument that characterizes the shareholders as the principals of the directors.

Such an argument also ignores the fact that the promotion of the company's success is the primary objective of CA 2006, section 172 and that there are other interests to which directors have to have regard. Professor Andrew Keay has rightly observed that rather than advancing either a shareholder or a stakeholder primacy model, CA 2006, section 172 is best conceptualized as promoting an entity maximization and sustainability approach.[77]

At a positive level CA 2006, section 172 is better explained by the real entity theory advanced here.[78] Real entity theory fits well with the fact that the duty is formally owed to the company, that it connects to the 'success' of that company and that there is no explicit focus on financial return. The idea that the company is a real entity also fits better with the subjectivity of the duty. The directors have the constitutional role to determine in their honest judgement what is best for the success of the company. It is only indirectly that the shareholders and other constituencies are considered. This observation applies irrespective of how much weight is put on the interests of the shareholders relative to other constituencies.

---

[73] *Item Software (UK) v Fassihi* [2004] EWCA Civ 1244 [66]; see also Paul Davies, Introduction to Company Law (3rd edn, OUP 2020) 10–11.

[74] *Item Software (UK) v Fassihi* [2004] EWCA Civ 1244 [66].

[75] ibid [66].

[76] ibid [66].

[77] Andrew Keay, 'Ascertaining the Corporate Objective: An Entity Maximisation and Sustainability Model' (2008) 71 MLR 663.

[78] See also Daniel Attenborough, 'Misreading the Directors' Fiduciary Duty of Good Faith' [2020] JCLS 73.

At a normative level, the Financial Crisis of 2008 combined with the Brexit referendum have triggered a shift in the public discourse away from the aim of maximizing shareholder return.[79] In 2017 the British Academy started a high profile project, led by Colin Mayer, on the Future of the Corporation, examining the purpose of business and its role in society.[80] The normative recommendation that maximizing shareholder return is good for society, which was famously articulated by Milton Friedman,[81] no longer chimes with the tenor of the debate. To reflect this change CA 2006, section 172 could be amended in a way that puts shareholders on the same level as other participants. That would attract the attention of company law academics and perhaps even wider society. It is unlikely however to significantly change the position of the directors.

When CA 2006 was drafted it was argued that a rule that puts shareholders at the same level as other constituencies would deprive the courts of the ability to review the decisions of the directors.[82] It would seem that the force of that argument is undermined by the fact that the subjectivity of the duty provides for a low level of judicial oversight no matter whose interests take priority. As long as the standard continues to be subjective, any tweaking of the balance of the interests of the shareholders and other constituencies will not significantly affect the scrutiny that is applied to the decisions of directors. Moreover, even if the standard was modified to an objective standard, the courts would struggle to overcome their traditional reluctance to second-guess business decisions.

7.5 Duty to exercise independent judgement

The duty to exercise independent judgement is the codification of the equitable duty prohibiting directors from fettering their discretion.[83] It requires nominee directors to be loyal to the company rather than to blindly follow the judgement of those who appoint them.[84] Moreover, a director is required to exercise his or her judgement in the context of the collective decision-making process of the board.[85] He or she must not share his opinions with shareholders with a view to soliciting support from them.[86] A director 'really has no voice otherwise than as a member of the board'.[87] A dissenting

[79] See eg in the US <www.businessroundtable.org/business-roundtable-redefines-the-purpose-of-a-corporation-to-promote-an-economy-that-serves-all-americans

[80] https://www.thebritishacademy.ac.uk/programmes/future-of-the-corporation/>.

[81] Milton Friedman, 'The Social Responsibility of Business is to Increase its Profits' New York Times 13 Sep 1970, Sunday Magazine 32.

[82] Committee on Corporate Governance, Final Report (1998) [1.17]; DTI, White Paper, Company Law Reform (Cm 6456, 2005) (20–21); The Company Law Review Steering Group, *Modern Company Law for a Competitive Economy: A Strategic Framework* (1999) chapter 5.1.

[83] *Fullham Football Club Ltd v Cabra Estates plc* [1994] 1 BCLC 363 (CA).

[84] *Scottish Co-operative Wholesale Society Ltd v Meyer* [1959] AC 324; *Kuwait Asia Bank EC v National Mutual Life Nominee Ltd* [1991] 1 AC 187.

[85] *Stobart Group Ltd v Tinkler* [2019] EWHC 258 (Comm), [2019] 2 WLUK 235, [415].

[86] ibid [413].

[87] ibid [416].

director, who feels strongly about his opinions, can request that these are recorded in the minutes.[88] He or she may opt to resign or the board may decide to put the matter to the shareholders in general meeting.[89] This is further evidence for the importance that the courts attach to the corporate process.

7.6 Duty to exercise reasonable skill and care

7.6.1 Introduction

The duty of skill and care of the directors is regulated in CA 2006, section 174 and in the Directors Disqualification Act 1986. The UK Corporate Governance Code 2018 provides additional guidance.

It will be shown in this section that there was a time when the shareholders were free to determine the professional standard to which the directors had to operate. At that time it would have been possible to explain the law through an agency approach conceiving shareholders as the principals of the directors.

Since then a mandatory objective standard has been introduced. This standard is interpreted by reference to the role performed by an individual director. It depends on factors such as the nature and size of the company's business and the specific role undertaken by the director. We will also observe that the courts are forgiving of mistakes, but strict about requiring directors to keep abreast of the company's financial position. They require directors to oversee responsibilities that they have delegated to others. Directors also need to ensure compliance with regulatory requirements. This supports the conclusion that procedure is a central focus also of the duty of skill and care.

The duty of the directors to keep themselves informed about the company's financial position indirectly benefits shareholders but, of course, also creditors, whose claims the directors are required to keep track of. The duty to ensure compliance with regulation helps those whose interests the respective regulations are designed to serve. This supports the conclusion that the duty of skill and care serves the interests of shareholders but also integrates stakeholder concerns.

CA 2006, section 174 is accompanied by the Company Directors Disqualification Act 1986, which has an explicit focus on the interests of creditors and the public. It is also enforced through a publicly funded regime. From a theoretical perspective we can conclude that this demonstrates the importance that the legislature attaches to the protection of the public interest in the context of company law.

---

[88] ibid [419]–[420].
[89] ibid [422]–[424].

7.6.2 The early common law

The common law originally required directors to comply with the 'standard of an ordinary man on his own behalf'.[90] The expectations of what directors need to do was thus relatively modest. They were not required to come equipped with any particular level of financial literacy or any special knowledge or understanding of the trade that the company engaged in.[91]

The shareholders were also able to further limit the standard in the company's articles. In *Re City Equitable Fire Insurance* the directors were protected from liability by a provision in the articles which limited liability to 'wilful neglect or default'.[92] In the *Brazilian Rubber Plantations* case the articles limited the liability of directors to 'dishonesty'.[93]

On an agency approach such a standard can be justified by reference to the fact that the shareholders appoint directors. If shareholders appoint directors they determine the standard of competence that they are comfortable with and then go on to identify individuals who meet this standard. Indeed, in the *Brazilian Rubber Plantations* case Neville J pointed out that the prospectus disclosed all facts and so the directors knew as much as the shareholders did.[94] In *Lagunas Nitrate Company* Collins LJ pointed out that 'the company and every member thereof have agreed to be bound' by the acts of the directors.[95]

Since the Companies Act 1929 there has existed a mandatory rule enabling shareholders to remove directors using a statutory process requiring a simple majority.[96] It is thus also possible to argue that when shareholders find that directors are less competent than they appeared at first or have otherwise changed their mind in relation to which level of competence they require they can use what is now Companies Act 2006, section 168, and remove the directors.

From a theoretical perspective a model that characterizes shareholders as principals and directors as their agents fits well with the early common law approach.

7.6.3 The later common law and statutory intervention

The twentieth century saw a number of changes to the duty of skill and care. In response to *City Equitable* the Companies Act 1929 adopted a new mandatory rule

---

[90] *Lagunas Nitrate Company v Lagunas Syndicate* [1899] 2 Ch 392 (CA) 428; *Re Cardiff Savings Bank* [1892] 2 Ch 100.

[91] *Re Brazilian Rubber Plantations and Estates Ltd* [1911] 1 Ch 425; *Lagunas Nitrate Company v Lagunas Syndicate* [1899] 2 Ch 392 (CA).

[92] *Re City Equitable Fire Insurance* [1925] Ch 407.

[93] *Re Brazilian Rubber Plantations and Estates Ltd* [1911] 1 Ch 425.

[94] ibid 438.

[95] *Lagunas Nitrate Company v Lagunas Syndicate* [1899] 2 Ch 392 (CA) 465–66.

[96] Companies Act 1948, s 184.

prohibiting shareholders to adopt articles that lowered the standard of skill and care.[97] The Company Directors Disqualification Act 1986 (CDDA 1986) and the Insolvency Act 1986 (IA 1986), section 214, which contain an objective standard of skill and care, were adopted. That objective standard was absorbed into the common law by Hoffmann LJ (as he then was). In *Re D'Jan of London* he adopted the standard expressed in IA 1986, section 214(4) as 'accurately stat[ing]' 'the duty of care owed by a director at common law'.[98] The Law Commission referred to this as a 'remarkable example' of the modernization of the law by judges.[99] It also pointed out that determining the standard in the same way irrespective of the company is approaching insolvency was both consistent and coherent.[100] The standard was then adopted by the CA 2006.

CA 2006, section 174 now states that a director must exercises 'reasonable care, skill and diligence'.[101] This means the care, skill, and diligence that would be exercised by a reasonably diligent person with:

(a) the general knowledge, skill and experience that may be reasonably expected of a person carrying out the function carried out by the director in relation to the company, and

(b) the general knowledge, skill and experience that the director has.[102]

Under the modern standard a director needs to take an active interest in the company and he or she must not surrender their obligations to others.[103] At a more granular level directors who did not address their minds to the question of whether certain payments were in the interest of the company have been considered to have breached the duty of skill and care.[104]

The standard is defined by reference to the respective company and the way it is organized.[105] The court adjusts the standard depending on the type of company and its size. The standard for a director of a bank is, for example, more onerous that the standard of a director of a company that operates a small business. The court also takes account of how the company has divided up roles and of which role has been assigned to the director. An executive director will, for example, be expected to devote more time and attention to the company than a non-executive director.[106]

[97] Companies Act 1929 (19 & 20) Geo. 5c 23; Wrenbury Committee 1918, the Green Committee 1925, Rosendorf (1932) at 96.
[98] *Re D'Jan of London* [1994] 1 BCLC 561, 563 (Hoffmann LJ sitting as a chancery judge); *Norman v Theodore Goddard* [1991] BCLC 1028, 1031 (Hoffmann J); see also *Daniels v Anderson* (1995) 16 ACSR 607.
[99] Consultation Paper No 153, 1998, [14.19].
[100] ibid [15.27]–[15.29].
[101] CA 2006, s 174(1).
[102] ibid s 174(2).
[103] *Lexi Holdings Plc v Luqman & Ors* [2009] EWCA Civ 117, [2009] 1 BCLC 1, [45] and [47]–[49]; see also *Weavering Capital (UK) Ltd v Peterson* [2012] EWHC 1480 (affd) [2013] EWCA Civ 71; and *Cohen v Selby* [2001] 1 BCLC 176.
[104] *Madoff Securities International v Raven* [2013] EWHC 3147 (Comm) [264].
[105] *Re City Equitable Fire Insurance Co* [1925] Ch 407.
[106] Simon Witney, 'Corporate Opportunities Law and the Non-executive Director' (2016) 16 Journal of Corporate Law Studies 145.

The courts do not overstretch the requirement for skill and care and give directors room to take risks and make mistakes.[107] A director of a small company will, for example, be excused for not carefully reading sixty pages of 'turgid legal prose'.[108] More generally courts do not interfere with the commercial judgement of the directors. Lord Eldon famously observed in *Carlen v Drury Lord* that, 'This Court is not to be required on every Occasion to take the Management of every Playhouse and Brewhouse in the Kingdom'.[109]

Notwithstanding this reluctance to involve themselves in commercial decisions, the courts readily intervene when directors fail to operate an appropriate process for ensuring compliance with statutory requirements. A director of even a small company thus breaches the duty of skill and care when he or she fails to maintain accounts or fails to ensure that the company registers for taxes.[110] It is arguable that non-executive directors have a duty to seek professional advice on the legality of certain insurance policies.[111] Directors also need to ensure that the company complies with the regulatory requirements applying to the company.[112]

There has been an evolution from a situation where the shareholders were able to adjust the standard to their preferences in the company's articles to a situation where an objective standard is now mandatory. This is a departure from a contractual model of the company.

Shareholders nevertheless continue to be the primary indirect beneficiaries of the duty of skill and care. Evidence for this proposition can be found in *Re D'Jan of London*. In that case Hoffmann LJ (as he then was) observed that 'for the purposes of the law of negligence the company is a separate entity' to which the director owes a duty of care and that that duty does not vary according to the number of shares he owns.[113] He nevertheless concluded that the director who owned 99 per cent of the shares can reasonably be excused for his negligent conduct under what is now CA 2006, section 1157. This was because the company was prosperous at the time and so the only interest which the director was reasonably putting at risk then was his own and that of his wife, who held the remaining 1 per cent.

In addition to protecting shareholders, a mandatory objective standard also protects and is intended to protect the interests of other stakeholders. The Cork Committee,

---

[107] *Re Elgindata Ltd* [1991] BCLC 959.
[108] *Re D'Jan of London* [1994] 1 BCLC 561; for an empirical analysis of the transformation in the standard of skill and care over time see Andrew Keay and others, 'Business Judgment and Director Accountability: A Study of Case-law Over Time' [2020] Journal of Corporate Law Studies 359.
[109] *Carlen v Drury* (1812) 1 Ves and B 149 (58), 35 ER 61 (62).
[110] *Westlowe Storage and Distribution Ltd* [2000] 2 BCLC 590 (system of accounting); *Raithatha v Baig* [2017] EWHC 2059 (Ch) (paying VAT).
[111] *Equitable Life Assurance Society v Bowley* [2003] EWHC 2263, [2004] 1 BCLC 180.
[112] *Brumder v Motornet Service and Repair Ltd* [2013] EWCA Civ 195, [2013] 1 WLR 2783 [47] and [58]–[62]; *Raithatha v Baig* [2017] EWHC 2059 (Ch) [35]–[37]; *Re IT Protect Ltd (In Liquidation)* [2020] EWHC 2473 (Ch), 24 Sep 2020 (unreported); see also *Re Ruscoe Ltd* (2012) ChD (Companies Court) 07 August 2012 (unreported).
[113] *Re D'Jan of London Ltd* [1994] 1 BCLC 561, 564.

which proposed both the introduction of CDDA 1986 and the wrongful trading rules of the IA 1986, stressed that the community itself was interested in matters relating to the liability of directors in connection with insolvent companies.[114] In 1994 Hoffmann LJ (as he then was) observed that in older cases the duty of a director to participate in the management of a company is stated in 'very undemanding terms'. The law may be evolving in response to changes 'in public attitudes to corporate governance, as shown by the enactment of the provisions consolidated in the Company Directors Disqualification Act 1986'.[115] A little later the Company Law Review concluded that the 'community as a whole' suffers if companies are run with less than objective standards of competence and it is appropriate to impose a 'universal mandatory standard'.[116]

From a theoretical perspective we can observe that the courts define the duty of skill and care by reference to the organizational needs of each individual company and by reference to role to which an individual director has been appointed. The courts accept commercial judgement but are unforgiving of directors who fail to ensure that the company has procedures in place to comply with the recording and reporting requirements of the Companies Act as well as with other legal and regulatory requirements. Finally, we have seen that the shareholders are the primary focus of the duty of the objective duty of skill and care but that they are not the exclusive focus. The duty is also designed to protect the interest of the public.

7.6.4 Disqualification

CA 2006, section 174 works in tandem with the Company Directors Disqualification Act 1986. The CDDA 1986 enhances CA 2006 in two ways. It is designed to benefit a broader range of interests. It is also associated with an enforcement mechanism that is publicly funded.

The disqualification rules apply when a director has conducted himself in a manner that 'makes him unfit to be concerned in the management of a company'.[117] Disqualification operates like a quarantine prohibiting unfit individuals from running companies. If a disqualification order is made against a person, they are prohibited from being a director of a company, acting as a receiver of a company's property, and from being concerned or taking part in the promotion, formation, or management of a company.[118]

---

[114] Kenneth Cork, Insolvency Law and Practice, Report of the Review Committee, June 1982, Cmnd 8558, chapter 43 in particular [1734]–[1742]; see also Lord Jenkins, Report of the Company Law Committee (June 1962) Cmnd 1749 [497]–[500].
[115] *Bishopsgate Investment Management Ltd v Maxwell* (No 2) [1994] 1 All ER 261 (264b).
[116] Company Law Review Steering Group, *Modern Company Law for a Competitive Economy: Developing the Framework* (March 2000) URN 00/656 [para 3.68].
[117] Corporate Directors Disqualification Act 1986 (CDDA 1986), ss 6(1)(b) and 8(2).
[118] ibid s 1(1)(a); they may also not act as an insolvency practitioner (ibid s 1(1)(b)).

The aim is to protect all those engaging with companies. Lord Wolf MR said in *Re Blackspur Group plc* that the purpose of the CDDA 1986 is to protect the public, 'by means of remedial action, by anticipated deterrent effect on further misconduct and by encouragement of higher standards of honesty and diligence in corporate management'.[119] In *Sevenoaks Stationers* it was held that the purpose of the disqualification regime is to protect the public and in particular potential creditors of companies from losing money through companies when the directors of those companies are people unfit to be concerned with the management of the company.[120] Henry LJ in *Re Grayan Building Services Ltd* observed that some significant corporate failures will occur despite directors exercising best managerial practice but in many cases there have been breaches of rules that would have prevented or reduced the scale of failure. He pointed out that while reliable figures are hard to come by it seems that 'losses from corporate fraud and mismanagement have never been higher'. 'At the same time the regulatory regime has never been more stringent—on paper even if not in practice'. 'The parliamentary intention to improve managerial safeguards and standards for the long term good of employees, creditors and investors is clear.'[121]

Creditors are an important focus of the CDDA 1986. This is evidenced by the fact that CDDA 1986, section 6 'require[s]' the court to disqualify unfit directors of companies which have 'at any time become insolvent'. By contrast under CDDA 1986, section 8, which applies to solvent companies, the court has discretion to disqualify an unfit director.

The importance of the interests of creditors is also reflected in the case law. A deliberate decision to pay only creditors who press for payment allowing an insolvent company to trade at the expense of those creditors who happen to not be pressing is an example of unfitness.[122] Disqualification can also follow an unsuccessful attempt to remove assets from the reach of the holder of a floating charge.[123]

The interests of customers also receive attention. A director who misleads customers by 'grossing up' insurance premiums can thus be disqualified.[124] The failure to ensure compliance with statutory and regulatory requirements can also lead to disqualification.[125] The CDDA 1986 states explicitly that when assessing whether the conduct of

---

[119] *Re Blackspur Group plc* [1998] 1 WLR 422 (CA) 426.

[120] *Re Sevenoaks Stationers* [1991] Ch 164, 176 (Dillon LJ); see also *Secretary of State for Trade and Industry v Swan* [2005] EWHC 603 (Ch) [84] (Etherton J) where it was held that disqualification is mandatory to protect the parties, raise standards and to act as a deterrent; see also *Re Asegaai Consultants Ltd* [2012] EWHC 1899, [2012] Bus LR 1607.

[121] *Re Grayan Building Services Ltd* [1995] Ch 241 (CA) 257.

[122] *Re Sevenoaks Stationers* [1991] Ch 164, 183 (Dillon LJ); see also recently *Secretary of State for Business Innovation and Skills v Khan* [2017] EWHC 288 (Ch); *Secretary of State for Business, Innovation and Skills v Millar* [2014] CSOH 127, 2014 GWD 28–556.

[123] *Secretary of State for Business, Innovation and Skills v Drummond* [2015] CSOH 45, 2015 GWD 14–241.

[124] *Secretary of State for Trade and Industry v Amiss* [2003] 2 BCLC 206; see also *Re Equity and Provident Ltd* [2002] EWHC 186 (Ch), [2002] 2 BCLC 78 where the company was compulsorily wound up because it sold worthless motor warranty plans.

[125] *Re Brooklands Trustees Ltd* [2020] EWHC 3519 [91] and [95]–[98]; *Baker v Secretary of State for Trade and Industry* [2000] 1 BCLC 523 [57], [62], and [79]; see also *ASIC v Cassimatis* [2016] FCA 1023, 336 ALR 209, [482]; the Competition and Markets Authority has powers to apply for a disqualification order and has actively

a director makes him unfit to be concerned with the management of a company the court must have regard to the extent to which the director was responsible for the causes of any material contravention by the company of 'any applicable legislative or other requirements'.[126] A breach of the rules on financial assistance can also lead to disqualification.[127]

Shareholder interests are, however, also relevant. Even if the company has become insolvent the conduct that is under review includes conduct of the director during a time when the company was solvent.[128] In fact in all but a few cases the misconduct complained of will relate to the 'manner in which a director has conducted the affairs of a company prior to the company having become insolvent'.[129] The fact that the creditors can ultimately be paid to a substantial extent may be a mitigating factor but is no defence to disqualification proceedings.[130] A director, who is honest, but nevertheless treats the company as his own, ignoring shareholders and the Companies Act, can be disqualified irrespective of whether the company is wound up with a surplus.[131] A director who is responsible for artificial share transactions which enable him to obtain a majority of voting rights to defeat attempts of other shareholders to take control of the company can be disqualified.[132]

A director, who displays complete inactivity not only breaches CA 2006, section 174 but also risks being disqualified.[133] Here too we encounter the importance of directors setting up adequate procedures. A director who holds no board meetings and provides no financial information to the board risks disqualification.[134] Along similar lines a failure to maintain and preserve adequate accounting records can lead to disqualification.[135] Disqualification looms for a director who deliberately fails to show in the company's financial statements a claim from a customer for a significant amount of compensation and a settlement that he later negotiated.[136] The director will be disqualified in such a case because he concealed information which he knew should be disclosed to the board, the auditors, the Stock Exchange, and others.[137] A director who

used these powers in recent years (Chijioke Chijioke-Oforji, 'Director Accountability for Breach of Competition Law: Important Practical Lessons from the CMA's Increased Use of Disqualification Powers' [2021] ECLR 24).

[126] CDDA 1986, s 12C and Schedule 1(1).
[127] Secretary of State for Business, Innovation and Skills v *Whyte [2014] CSOH 148, 2014 GWD 32–624.*
[128] CDDA 1986, s 6(1): 'director of a company which has at any time become insolvent (whether while he was a director or subsequently)'.
[129] *Official Receiver v Jupe* [2011] 1 BCLC 191, [21].
[130] ibid [21].
[131] *Re Samuel Sherman Plc* [1991] 1 WLR 1070.
[132] *Re Looe Fish* [1993] BCLC 1160.
[133] *Secretary of State for Business, Innovation and Skills v Reza* [2013] CSOH 86, 2013 GWD 19–380; *Secretary of State for Trade and Industry v Griffiths* [1998] 2 BCLC 646; for an example of the early common law see *Re Cardiff Savings Bank* [1892] 2 Ch 100.
[134] *Secretary of State for Business, Innovation and Skills v Whyte* [2014] CSOH 148, 2014 GWD 32–624.
[135] *In Re Samuel Sherman Plc* [1991] 1 WLR 1070; *Official Receiver v Duckett* [2020] EWHC 3016 (Ch); *Secretary of State for Business, Innovation and Skills v Whyte* [2014] CSOH 148, 2014 GWD 32–624; *Focus 15 Trading Ltd (In Liquidation), Official Receiver v Duckett* [2020] EWHC 3016 (Ch).
[136] *Secretary of State for Trade and Industry v Carr* [2006] EWHC 2110 (Ch), [2007] 2 BCLC 495.
[137] ibid [58], [103].

should have been aware of false and misleading treatment of profits, losses, and costs on the company's financial statements also risks disqualification.[138]

A board must not allow one individual to dominate them and use them.[139] Directors are required to act with independence and courage and must not acquiesce in the suppression of information to the auditors and the board.[140] More generally a director who is dishonest and places his own interests before those of the company is likely to face disqualification.[141]

Directors are required to control and supervise delegated activity.[142] The higher the level or reward the greater the responsibilities which may reasonably be expected.[143] Directors collectively and also individually have a continuing duty to 'maintain a sufficient understanding of the company's business to enable them properly to discharge their duties.'[144]

The CDDA 1986 is enforced through the Insolvency Service located with the Department for Business, Energy and Industrial Strategy. The Secretary of State applies for a disqualification on grounds of unfitness if it is 'expedient in the public interest that a disqualification order should be made.'[145] In addition it is now possible for the Secretary of State to ask that the court to make a compensation order requiring disqualified directors to make compensation payments either to the company or to creditors.[146]

From a theoretical perspective we can observe that the CDDA 1986 encourages directors to put in place procedures that ensure compliance with statutory and regulatory requirements, that give them information about the company's financial position and that allow for the supervision of delegated functions. We can also observe that it operates as a conduit through which the interests of creditors and the wider public are integrated into company law. From a theoretical perspective it is worth observing that the legislature has enhanced rules that protect shareholder and stakeholder interests on an equal footing with a publicly funded enforcement regime. The point that stakeholder-oriented duties are associated with public enforcement will be explored further in chapter 9.

---

[138] *SSTI v Bairstow* [2004] EWHC 1730 (Ch), [2005] 1 BCLC 136.

[139] *Re Westmid Packing Services Ltd, SSTI v Griffiths* [1998] 2 BCLC 646 (653); see also UK Corporate Governance Code, principle G.

[140] *Re Landhurst Leasing plc* [1999] 1 BCLC 286 (Hart J).

[141] *Secretary of State for Business, Innovation and Skills v Whyte* [2014] CSOH 148, 2014 GWD 32–624.

[142] *Re Barings Plc (No 5)* [1999] 1 BCLC 433 <page?> (Jonathan Parker J).

[143] ibid <page?> (Jonathan Parker J).

[144] ibid <page?> (Jonathan Parker J).

[145] CDDA 1986 s 7, s 8(1) and 8(2A); the Competition and Markets Authority also has powers to apply for a disqualification order and has actively used these powers in recent years (Chijioke Chijioke-Oforji, 'Director Accountability for Breach of Competition Law: Important Practical Lessons from the CMA's Increased Use of Disqualification Powers' [2021] ECLR 24).

[146] CDDA 1986 s 15A–15B; *Re Noble Vintners Ltd* [2019] EWHC 2806 (Ch), [2020] BCC 198.

7.6.5 UK Corporate Governance Code 2018

Alongside the Companies Act 2006 and the Company Directors Disqualification Act 1986, the UK Corporate Governance Code 2018 provides guidance for decisions taken by the boards of premium listed companies.

The Code creates a system of checks and balances at the level of the board. It recommends that the board should include an appropriate combination of executive and non-executive (and, in particular, independent non-executive) directors, such that no one individual or small group of individuals dominates the board's decision-making. There should be a clear division of responsibilities between the leadership of the board and the executive leadership of the company's business.[147] The board and its committees should have a combination of skills, experience, and knowledge.[148] The roles of the chair of the board and of the chief executive director should not be exercised by the same individual.[149] The Code also recommends that board sub-committees are set up for topics such as nomination, remuneration, and audit, which are thus removed from the direct influence of executive directors.[150] In addition banks are required to operate risk committees.[151]

The Code has always been designed to operate as a tool to protect the public interest. It was first developed as a reaction to corporate scandals.[152] The idea was one of protecting the public, which at the time was thought to be best achieved by making the directors more responsive to the interests of shareholders.[153] The Cadbury Code 1992 opened its analysis with the statement that '[t]he country's economy depends on the drive and efficiency of its companies'.[154] It also observed that shareholders are electing the board and that it is in their interests to see that the board is properly constituted.[155] The problem that governance needed to solve was identified as being the separation of ownership from control which leads to a lack of oversight of directors from shareholders. The Cadbury Code 1992 defined corporate governance as 'the system by which companies are directed and controlled. Boards of directors are responsible for the governance of their companies. The shareholders' role in governance is to appoint the directors and the auditors and to satisfy themselves that an appropriate governance structure is in place'.[156]

---

[147] UK Corporate Governance Code 2018, Principle G.

[148] ibid Principle K.

[149] ibid Provision 9.

[150] ibid Provision 17 (nomination); provision 24 (audit) [and audit directive]; provision 32 (remuneration); banks now also require a risk committee.

[151] Bank of England, Prudential Regulation Authority, Rulebook, rule 3.1.

[152] Report of the Committee on The Financial Aspects of Corporate Governance (Cadbury Report) (1 December 1992), preface and [2.2].

[153] Report of the Committee on The Financial Aspects of Corporate Governance (Cadbury Report) (1 December 1992) [1.1]–[1.6], [3.14] assumes that governance issues are of public as well as shareholder concern.

[154] ibid [1.1].

[155] ibid [4.2].

[156] ibid [2.5].

Under the impression of the Global Financial Crisis of 2008 as well as the Brexit referendum the Code alongside with other regulatory interventions has adopted a more stakeholder-oriented perspective.[157] The Financial Crisis was perceived as the product of financial markets adopting a short-term perspective. The Kay Review concluded that while ultimate investors had a long-term perspective their financial intermediaries operated to meet continuous short-term targets and so exercised pressure on issuers to produce short-term results.[158] The Brexit referendum can be interpreted as an expression of discontent by ordinary people who have not been able to experience the benefits of a globalized economy.

The most recent versions of the Code have all but abandoned the idea that accountability to shareholders enhances the public interest. The 2016 version of the Code stated that the 'purpose of corporate governance is to facilitate effective, entrepreneurial and prudent management that can deliver long-term success of the company.'[159] The 2018 version observes that:

> Companies do not exist in isolation. Successful and sustainable businesses underpin our economy and society by providing employment and creating prosperity. To succeed in the long-term, directors and the companies they lead need to build and maintain successful relationships with a wide range of stakeholders. These relationships will be successful and enduring if they are based on respect, trust and mutual benefit. Accordingly, a company's culture should promote integrity and openness, value diversity and be responsive to the views of shareholders and wider stakeholders.

It is worth observing that notwithstanding this shift away from a shareholder-centred focus the Code continues to recommend the same procedural measures separating out different the chair from the Chief Executive Officer (CEO) and setting up committees for specific tasks.

The literature on the Corporate Governance Code is extensive. It is impossible to do justice to the contributions made in this area.[160] From the perspective of this book it is worth observing that the government takes an interest and invests in developing standards of good corporate governance with a view to enhancing the public interest.[161] The government does not intend to purely focus on enhancing the position of shareholders for their own sake.

---

[157] See generally Iris H-Y Chiu, 'An Institutional Theory of Corporate Regulation' (2018) 71 Current Legal Problems 279 303–08 and 326–30.

[158] The Kay Review of UK Equity Markets and Long-term Decision Making, Final Report, July 2012.

[159] UK Corporate Governance Code 2016, page 1.

[160] For two impressive attempts to do just that see Jeffrey N Gordon and Wolf-Georg Ringe, *The Oxford Handbook of Corporate Law and Governance* (OUP 2018) and Mike Wright and others (eds), *The Oxford Handbook of Corporate Governance* (OUP 2013).

[161] The connection between the protection of the public interest and the improvement of corporate governance is also visible in the most recent government document, BEIS, Insolvency and Corporate Governance, Government Response (26 August 2018), Foreword and (7).

Moreover, the evolution of the UK Corporate Governance Code from a shareholder-centred to a stakeholder-focused document is evidence of the theory advanced in this book. No matter how one defines the goal of corporate governance regulation, corporate behaviour is best steered through social structure. For the field of company law this means that roles are created for specific tasks so that the respective task is represented in the corporate decision-making process. The Code does just that. It goes to the heart of how organizations act. It shapes the process through which decisions are taken by assigning roles to individual participants inviting them to pay attention to a particular aspect with a view to developing their own perspective and to critically examining the actions of executive board members.[162] This fits well with an approach that conceives organizations as autonomous actors characterized by the habits and procedures that form between the participants. A good way of shaping organizational action is to establish a framework for making decisions.[163]

7.6.6 Conclusions

The duty of skill and care has changed from imposing a modest standard that could be modified by the shareholders to a mandatory combination of an objective and subjective standard. This reflects a shift away from a logic that is based on contract law and focuses exclusively on shareholder preferences. The transformation was caused by a change in the public expectation of the expertise and care required of directors.

The change to the mandatory combination of an objective and subjective standard occurred in the context of insolvency law first and was then absorbed into general company law. It is also fortified by the disqualification regime which operates in the public interest and the enforcement of which is funded by the taxpayer.

The UK Corporate Governance Code adds a further dimension to the standard of skill and care for listed companies. While the Code does not have formal legal force it is nevertheless generally adopted and underpinned by the understanding that the government stands ready to use their legislative powers if necessary.

The standard of skill and care provides the conduit through which the company law integrates the interests of stakeholders. Directors are required to ensure that they have full information on the company's financial position and supervise delegated activity. They need to cause companies to comply with regulatory requirements.

Overall, there is a strong connection between the duty of skill and care and the public interest. While the shareholders are the primary albeit indirect beneficiaries, the main

---

[162] See also Terry McNulty, 'Process Matters: Understanding Board Behavior and Effectiveness' in Mike Wright and others (eds), *The Oxford Handbook of Corporate Governance* (OUP 2013) 163.

[163] In Mike Wright and others (eds), *The Oxford Handbook of Corporate Governance* (OUP 2013) chapter 7 stresses the importance of board processes; chapter 6 advises breaking down the fortress of agency theory.

concern explaining the introduction of an objective standard was to improve the health of companies, leading to a more robust economy.

7.6.7 Theoretical observations

From a theoretical perspective, agency theory can connect to the fact that a more demanding standard increases accountability of the directors. In an agency framework this can be conceived of as reducing the cost associated with the agency conflict between directors and shareholders. This characterization does not, however, allow us to fully appreciate that the increase in the standard had its primary connection with the public interest. An improvement of the financial return of the shareholders was not the immediate aim of the change. In fact, while no obligations are imposed on shareholders, the hope was and is nevertheless that shareholders act as controllers overseeing the governance of companies. The Cadbury Code reminded shareholders that it was in their own interest to monitor directors. In this analysis shareholders are an instrument who are told that involving themselves in corporate governance is good for them (also). The connection between engaging in corporate governance and the well-being of shareholders is, moreover, a theoretical assumption. Shareholders may well be financially better off through a short-term agile buy-and-sell strategy rather than by engaging in corporate governance.

From the perspective of real entity theory it is worth observing that the duty of skill and care is, like all duties, owed to the company. The courts also determine the standard of skill and care by reference to the type and size of the company and take into account how the company has divided up the roles to be performed by its directors. This fits well with the idea that companies are characterized by their social structure.

The courts do not overstretch the requirement for skill and care and give directors room to take risk and make mistakes. They intervene readily, however, when directors do not keep abreast of the company's financial position by keeping records and drawing up accounts or when they do not have in place internal control systems. The failure to comply with regulatory requirements is also a sin that the courts are less inclined to treat with leniency.

The UK Corporate Governance Code attempts to influence how companies are run by putting in place granular procedural rules for board decisions.

At a positive level this fits with a model that conceives organizations as autonomous actors which are characterized by the procedures that shape the decision-making through their participants. At a normative level the recent focus on corporate culture acknowledges that an analysis that is limited to individuals and their incentives does not give enough weight to an important factor shaping human behaviour.[164] While it

---

[164] See also Annie Pye, 'Boards and Governance: 25 years of Qualitative Research with Directors of FTSE Companies' in Mike Wright and others (eds), *The Oxford Handbook of Corporate Governance* (OUP 2013) 135.

is important to be aware of incentives it is also necessary to understand human interactions and how the process holding individuals together can affect organizational
action.

From a normative perspective a note of caution needs to be added. Procedural interventions go to the heart of organizational action. They are, however, no silver bullet
and need to be used with care. The focus on procedure and internal controls has led to
directors increasingly ensuring management systems, processes, and procedures are
adequately developed, documented, and applied, and that their application is assured
by systematic measurement, reporting, and audit processes.[165] There is a risk that procedural interventions either degenerate into box ticking or go into overdrive, causing
directors to focus on all things measurable and auditable while overlooking important
factors that cannot be easily quantified.[166]

7.7 Duty to avoid a conflict of interest

7.7.1 Introduction

We have seen in section 7.3 that the proper purpose doctrine protects the allocation
of power between the shareholders and the directors set out in the constitution of a
company. In section 7.5 we observed that a director who undermines the collective
decision-making by the board cannot justify this by reference to the duty to exercise
independent judgement. We have further seen in section 7.6 that directors who do not
put in place an adequate system of accounting and who do not supervise delegated activity breach the duty of skill and care and also risk being disqualified. The corporate
decision-making process is the essential feature of company law.

Corporate procedures are also of crucial importance in conflict of interest situations.
We will see in this section that the procedures that need to be followed for a director to
be permitted to act in circumstances where he or she has a conflict of interest are protected even where there is no economic interest justifying that protection.

We will see below that economic reasoning is useful for analysing the problems that
arise in relation to conflicts of interests. But it is not possible to explain the rules governing transactions affected by a conflict of interest solely on the basis of economic
considerations. We will further see in chapter 8 that it would be wrong to conclude
that shareholders are the sole focus of the fiduciary duties owed by directors. When
the shareholders approve corporate opportunities or authorize or ratify interested

[165] Sarah Worthington, *Sealy and Worthington's Text, Cases and Materials in Company Law* (11th edn, OUP 2016) 381.
[166] Andrea Mennicken and Mike Power, 'Auditing and Corporate Governance', in Douglas Michael Wright and others (eds), *The Oxford Handbook of Corporate Governance* (OUP 2013) 308, 309.

transactions, they cannot override the interests of creditors or undermine the rights of minorities.

7.7.2 Companies Act 2006, section 175

CA 2006, section 175 applies where a director enters into a transaction with someone other than the company in circumstances that constitutes a conflict of interest. It does not apply to a transaction or arrangement between the company and its director.[167] The latter scenario is governed by CA 2006, section 177 which will be analysed below.[168]

CA 2006, section 175 closely reflects the position in equity when it states that, 'A director of a company must avoid a situation in which he has, or can have, a direct or indirect interest that conflicts, or possibly conflicts, with the interests of the company.' This applies in particular to the exploitation of any property, information, or opportunity (and it is immaterial whether the company could take advantage of the property, information, or opportunity).[169] CA 2006, section 170(2)(a) codifies the common law rules on resignation when it states that a person who ceases to be a director continues to be subject to the duties in CA 2006, section 175 as regards the exploitation of any property, information, or opportunity of which he or she has become aware at a time when he or she was a director.[170]

The duty is deliberately wide in scope. Judges do not allow the introduction of limitations to the principle to be distilled from the cases. Parker LJ in *Bhullar v Bhullar*, for example, endorsed a statement by Lord Upjohn in *Boardman v Phipps* that '[r]ules of equity have to be applied to such great diversity of circumstances that they can be stated only in the most general terms with particular attention to the exact circumstances of each case'.[171] The rule is applicable to

> such a diversity of different cases that the observations of judges . . . even in [the House of Lords] . . . in cases where this great principle is being applied must be regarded as applicable only to the particular facts of the particular case in question and not regarded as new and slightly different formulation of the legal principle so well settled.[172]

The most distinctive feature of the duty to avoid a conflict of interest is that it is unwaveringly strict. Lord Cranworth LC observed in *Aberdeen Railway Co v Blaikie Bros* that no fiduciary 'shall be allowed to enter into engagements in which he has or can have a

---

[167] CA 2006, s 175(3); *Re Coroin Ltd* [2012] EWHC 2343 (Ch) [583].
[168] See section 7.8 in this chapter.
[169] CA 2006, s 175(2).
[170] *Industrial Developments Consultants Ltd v Cooley* [1972] 1 WLR 443; see also *Canadian Aero Services Ltd v O'Malley* (1973) 40 DLR (3d) 371; *CMS Dolphin Ltd v Simonet* [2001] EWHC 415 [2001] 2 BCLC 704; *Shepherds Investments Ltd v Walters* [2006] EWHC 836 [2007] 2 BCLC 202.
[171] *Bhullar v Bhullar* [2003] EWCA Civ 242, [2003] 2 BCLC 241, [28].
[172] ibid [28].

personal interest conflicting or which possibly may conflict with the interests of those whom he is bound to protect.' He continued, 'So strict is this principle adhered to that no question is allowed to be raised as to fairness or unfairness of a contract so entered into.'[173] Along similar lines Lord Herschell observed in *Bray v Ford* that the rule is 'inflexible'.[174] A fiduciary:

> is not allowed to put himself in a position where his interest and duty conflict. It does not appear to me that this rule is . . . founded upon principles of morality. I regard it rather as based on the consideration that, human nature being what it is, there is danger . . . of the person holding a fiduciary position being swayed by interest rather than by duty, and thus prejudicing those whom he was bound to protect.[175]

The source of the liability is the 'mere fact' of a profit having been made.[176] It is no defence that the director has acted in good faith.[177] A director cannot escape liability to account by proving that he was honest or well-intentioned.[178] The rule 'in no way depends on fraud, or absence of bona fides'.[179]

The law does not pay attention to economic considerations. Liability arises irrespective of whether the company suffered any loss.[180] It is also immaterial that the company benefitted from the directors' actions.[181] The fact that the opportunity is outside the line of the business of the company is also irrelevant.[182] It is further immaterial that the directors saw 'no way' of securing the opportunity for the company.[183]

And if this was not enough, it is finally irrelevant that the new shareholders of the company are going to receive a windfall as a result of the directors accounting for their profit. In *Regal (Hastings) Ltd v Gulliver* the directors facilitated the acquisition of certain cinema venues by themselves becoming shareholders in a subsidiary company. The company and its subsidiary were sold at a profit benefitting the parent's existing shareholders. The new shareholders had agreed to pay a price for both companies on the basis of their valuation of their combined businesses. When they later discovered that the parent company had not authorized the taking of shares in the subsidiary by its directors, the parent company sued the directors for breach of fiduciary duties. Lord

---

[173] *Aberdeen Railway v Blaikie Brothers* [1843–1860] All ER Rep 249 at 252.

[174] *Bray v Ford* [1896] AC 44 at 51; for a modern case endorsing this proposition see *Bhullar v Bhullar* [2003] EWCA Civ 242, [2003] 2 BCLC 241, [27].

[175] *Bray v Ford* [1896] AC 44 at 51.

[176] *Regal (Hastings) Ltd v Gulliver* [1967] 2 AC 134 (HL) 145 (Lord Russel).

[177] *ibid* 153 (Lord Macmillan); *Towers v Premier Waste Management* Ltd [2011] EWCA (Civ) 923, [2012] 1 BCLC 67, [7]–[12], *Richmond Pharmacology Ltd v Chester Overseas Ltd* [2014] EWHC 2692, [2014] Bus LR 1110, [71].

[178] *Regal (Hastings) Ltd v Gulliver* [1967] 2 AC 134 (HL) 144 (Lord Russel).

[179] ibid 144 (Lord Russel).

[180] *Regal (Hastings) Ltd v Gulliver* [1967] 2 AC 134 (HL) 144 (Lord Russel); see also *Towers v Premier Waste Management* [2011] EWCA Civ 923, [2012] 1 BCLC 67, [51].

[181] *Regal (Hastings) Ltd v Gulliver* [1967] 2 AC 134 (HL) 144 (Lord Russel).

[182] *Allied Business and Financial Consultants Ltd v Shanahan* [2009] EWCA Civ 751, [2009] 2 BCLC 666.

[183] *Regal (Hastings) Ltd v Gulliver* [1967] 2 AC 134 (HL) 144 and 149 (Lord Russel) and 155 and 158 (Lord Porter) who explicitly endorsed the rule in *Keech v Sandford* as applying to companies; see also *Boardman v Phipps* [1967] 2 AC 46; *Davies v Ford* [2020] EWHC 686 (Ch).

Porter observed that the company and its shareholders are 'separate entities'.[184] As a result of the company's successful claim, the group received 'in one hand part of the sum which has been paid by the other'. Part of the purchase price was 'returned' to the new shareholders through an increase in the value in the shares in the parent company. This was an 'unexpected windfall'. But the principle that a 'person occupying a fiduciary relationship shall not make a profit by reason thereof is of such vital importance' that the possible windfall to the shareholders is 'in law an immaterial consideration'.[185]

The only time when it appears to be certain that the duty is not infringed is if the situation cannot reasonably be regarded as likely to give rise to a conflict of interest (CA 2006, s 175(4)). This was held to be the case, for example, where a director had been entirely excluded from the management of the company more than six months before the events occurred.[186]

7.7.3 Contrast with partnership law

We have seen above that the scope of the company's business does not set a boundary for the scope of the duty. Given the strictness of the rule this is hardly surprising. None of the authorities the number of which has been referred to as 'legion' qualify the liability to account for profit 'by reference to whether the impugned transaction was (in the case of an alleged breach by a director) within or without the scope of the company's business'.[187]

What is notable however is that partnership law has adopted a more relaxed approach in this context. The Partnership Act 1890 (c 39), section 29 states that 'partners account for any benefit derived without the consent from any transaction concerning the partnership, or from any use by him of partnership property, name or business connection'. The courts have taken this to mean that the partnership contract sets the boundaries of the fiduciary rules binding the partners. If the partnership contract circumscribes the nature of the partnership business this also sets the boundaries of the fiduciary rules. A partner is thus not required to account for profit he makes by using partnership information for a purpose that is 'beyond the scope of the business of the partnership'.[188]

In *Aas v Benham* it was held that a partner of a firm of shipbrokers was permitted to use information he obtained when negotiating a contract for the partnership in a personal capacity. He used that information when he assisted with the formation of a joint stock company which was engaging in the building of ships. For his services he received

---

[184] *Regal (Hastings) Ltd v Gulliver* [1967] 2 AC 134 (HL) 157.
[185] ibid 157.
[186] *In Plus Group Ltd v Pyke* [2002] EWCA Civ 370, [2002] 2 BCLC 201; see also *Forster Bryant Surveying Ltd v Bryant* [2007] EWCA Civ 200, [2007] 2 BCLC 239.
[187] *Allied Business and Financial Consultants Ltd v Shanahan* [2009] EWCA Civ 751, [2009] 2 BCLC 666, [55].
[188] *Aas v Benham* [1891] 2 Ch 244; *Allied Business and Financial Consultants Ltd v Shanahan* [2009] EWCA Civ 751, [2009] 2 BCLC 666, [68].

remuneration. He was also appointed a director and received a salary. He was allowed to keep both his remuneration and his salary. A strong and unanimous Court of Appeal overturned a first instance decision by Kekewich J.[189] Lindley LJ observed that it was not part of the business of the partnership to 'promote or reconstruct companies'.[190] He continued, 'It is clear law that every partner must account to the firm for every benefit derived by him without the consent of his co-partners from any transaction concerning the partnership or from any use by him of partnership property, name, or business connection . . . but the facts of this case do not bring it within his principle.'[191]

If legal personality was just a 'formality' and companies could be characterized as vehicles set up and operated exclusively for the benefit of the shareholders the conclusion would be inevitable that they are akin to partnerships. Consequently, fiduciary law would have to apply to companies in the same way as it applies to partnerships. That, however, is not the case. The rule in *Aas v Benham* has been explicitly rejected for companies.[192]

Rimer LJ in *Allied Business and Financial Consultants Ltd v Shanahan* endorsed the following dicta by Viscount Hodson in *Boardman v Phipps*:[193] 'The case of a partnership is special in the sense that a partner is a principal as well as the agent of the other partners and works in a defined area of business, so that it normally can be determined whether the particular transaction is within or without the scope of the partnership.'[194] He also endorsed dicta by Lord Guest referring to the fact that in a partnership 'the scope of the partners' power' to bind the partnership can be closely defined in the partnership deed'.[195] We have seen above that this is not the case for companies where the authority of directors cannot be limited by the constitution.[196]

Rimer LJ then went on to acknowledge that to those 'familiar with the wider obligations of accountability to which trustees and directors are subject, the decision in *Aas v Benham* may at first sight appear to reflect a surprisingly narrow approach'.[197] But the explanation is that a trustee's and director's fiduciary duties are not 'similarly circumscribed by the terms of a contract'.[198] Directors have been held as occupying a 'general trusteeship'. As directors of the company their fiduciary position is 'unlimited'.[199] The director of a company providing financial advice, who used an opportunity to invest in

---

[189] *Aas v Benham* [1891] 2 Ch 244 (Lindley LJ, Bowen LJ, and Kay LJ).

[190] ibid 255.

[191] ibid 255.

[192] *Allied Business and Financial Consultants Ltd v Shanahan* [2009] EWCA Civ 751, [2009] 2 BCLC 666, [61]–[69].

[193] ibid 63.

[194] *Boardman v Phipps* [1966] 3 All ER 721 at 746, [1967] 2 AC 36 at 108; *Allied Business and Financial Consultants Ltd v Shanahan* [2009] EWCA Civ 751, [2009] 2 BCLC 666, [63].

[195] *Boardman v Phipps* [1966] 3 All ER 721 at 752, [1967] 2 AC 36 at 117; *Allied Business and Financial Consultants Ltd v Shanahan* [2009] EWCA Civ 751, [2009] 2 BCLC 666, [64].

[196] CA 2006, s 40; see section 3.3 in this book.

[197] *Allied Business and Financial Consultants Ltd v Shanahan* [2009] EWCA Civ 751, [2009] 2 BCLC 666, [68].

[198] ibid [68].

[199] ibid [69].

real estate that he came across while working for the company, was thus unable to keep the profit he had made from that investment.[200]

Unlike partnerships, companies have a legally recognized status in their own right that is independent of their shareholders. Shareholders are not principals of the directors. They do not own the business of the company. They perform a constitutional role that is established on the basis of statute and limited by statute.

Fiduciary law thus protects the corporate interest rather than the shareholders' interest. This indirectly serves the shareholders and to this extent it would be right to say that the interests of shareholders are protected by the law. It would nevertheless be wrong to conclude that the shareholders' interest is the only interest that the law supports. Creditors and other constituencies interacting with the company also benefit from the fact that directors are bound by robust rules prohibiting them from diverting assets from the company. Brooke LJ pointed out in *In Plus Group Ltd v Pyke* that the fiduciary duty of a director to his company was 'uniform and universal'.[201] He referred to the risk to both shareholders and creditors if directors were permitted to hold directorships in a competing company.[202] He emphasized the 'high standards of probity which equity demands of fiduciaries, and the reliance which shareholders and creditors are entitled to place upon it'.[203]

After all, creditors rely on the company's rather than the shareholders' assets to receive payment on their claims. Creditors also take priority over shareholders, who can receive distributions only after creditor claims have been provided for.[204]

7.7.4 Approval of interested transactions

The Companies Act 2006 sets out a process for the approval of interested transactions. Under the statutory regime we need to distinguish between private and public companies. If the company is a private company and if the constitution does not state otherwise the board can authorize an interested transaction.[205] If the company is a public company the board can only authorize an interested transaction if the constitution includes a provision enabling this.[206] The current Model Articles for public companies contain no such provisions.

When responsible for authorizing an interested transaction, however, the board needs to exclude the interested directors. Their votes must not be counted and they also do not count towards any quorum requirement.[207] If a company only has one director, that

---

[200] *ibid.*
[201] *In Plus Group Ltd v Pyke* [2002] EWCA Civ 370, [2002] 2 BCLC 201, [80].
[202] ibid [80] (author's capital letters).
[203] ibid [80] (author's capital letters).
[204] Section 8.5 in this book.
[205] CA 2006, s 175(5)(a).
[206] ibid s 175(5)(b).
[207] ibid s 175(6).

director is unable to authorize the taking of a corporate opportunity for himself.[208] If the board is not permitted to authorize an interested transaction the responsibility to do so falls on the shareholders.[209]

An interested transaction needs to be formally authorized. An earlier decision by the directors, who held the majority of the shares between them, that causes the opportunity to fall outside the board's strategic preferences is also not good enough to amount to authorization. In *Bhullar v Bhullar* there was evidence that the claimant shareholders themselves had earlier instigated a board decision that the company would not, going forward, invest in property.[210] At the board meeting this was agreed by all the directors in principle. The directors between them held the majority of the shares. This evidence of the shareholder directors' intention did not remove the conflict of interest.[211]

It is also not good enough that the directors could 'have protected themselves by a resolution (either antecedent or subsequent) of the . . . shareholders in general meeting'.[212] In 'default of such approval, the liability must remain'.[213] That appears to apply even where the directors control the voting and where the approval by the shareholders is a 'mere matter of form'.[214]

The authorization of an interested transaction must formally run through the corporate process for the conflict of interest to be removed.[215] The company must not be deprived of the 'ability to consider whether or not it objected to the diversion of an opportunity offered by one of its customers away from itself to the director personally'.[216]

The fact that shareholders act for the company in approving interested transactions could be used to support the conclusion that they occupy the role of the principal to whom the duty to avoid a conflict of interest is 'materially owed'. This, however, would be an overstatement of the role of the shareholders in this context. We will see in chapter 8 that shareholders cannot be said to have full control of conflict of interest situations. They must not approve transfers of assets from the company to themselves. Such transfers can only occur after the interests of creditors have been taken care of.[217]

---

[208] *Goldtrail Travel v Aydin* [2014] EWHC 1587, [2015] 1 BCLC 89, [114]–[119]; the decision was confirmed by the Court of Appeal in *Goldtrail Travel v Aydin* [2016] EWCA Civ 371, [2016] BCLC 635.

[209] CA 2006, s 180(4) and s 281(3)(a).

[210] *Bhullar v Bhullar* [2003] EWCA Civ 424, [2003] 2 BCLC 241.

[211] In *Peso Silver Mines Ltd v Cropper* the Supreme Court of Canada adopted the view that the bona fide rejection by the board of the opportunity ended the conflict permitting a director to explore it with his own funds (*Peso Silver Mines Ltd v Cropper* [1966] SCR 673, (1966) 58 DLR (2d) 1), but this does not appear the position in English law.

[212] *Regal (Hastings) Ltd v Gulliver* [1967] 2 AC 134 (HL) 150.

[213] ibid 150.

[214] ibid notes to the case published in [1942] 1 All ER 378, 379.

[215] An exception appears to apply where the shareholders through a shareholder agreement have a veto right to prevent the company from taking the opportunity (*Wilkinson v West Coast Capital* [2005] EWHC 3009, [2007] BCC 717).

[216] *Towers v Premier Waste Management* [2011] EWCA Civ 923, [2012] 1 BCLC 67, [48].

[217] See section 8.3 in this book.

7.7.5 Theoretical observations

The scope of the duty established by CA 2006, section 175 is wide. It is difficult to conceive of circumstances in which a director, while in office, can be advised to take an opportunity without first securing board approval or, depending on the circumstances, approval by the shareholders. The courts justify this by focusing on the 'vital importance' that a fiduciary must not make a profit.[218] The argument thus connects to the perspective of the director of a company and the inability of human beings to realistically override their own interests when they conflict with those of others.[219]

It has also been argued that a strict rule has a prophylactic or deterrent effect.[220] In *Cook v Deeks* Lord Buckmaster LC justified the strictness of the rule using the following words:

> men who assume the complete control of a company's business must remember that
> they are not at liberty to sacrifice the interests which they are bound to protect, and,
> while ostensibly acting for the company, divert in their own favour business which
> should properly belong to the company they represent.[221]

Knowing that they will not be able to supply reasons for not seeking approval for the taking of corporate opportunities, directors will be incentivized to do the right thing and either refrain from taking an opportunity or seek approval.

Historically it is worth observing that the standard of skill and care was very low until the mid-twentieth century.[222] During this period the rules governing interested transactions were the main filter through which the conduct of directors was reviewed. It is therefore no surprise that the courts have rigorously applied the conflict of interest rules.

The above arguments centre around the incentives and motivation of directors. They thus fit with agency analysis. It would be wrong, however, to stop the analysis here.

From a theoretical perspective the contrast with partnership law where the fiduciary duties of partners are limited by the scope of business of the partnership is worth noting. If a company were nothing more than an aggregate of its shareholders the law would apply the same rules to companies as it does to partnerships. That is, however, not the case. Companies are different from partnerships. Their shareholders are not owners of the business. They are not the principals of the directors. They perform a role that is defined by the statute and on the basis of the statute by the constitution.

---

[218] See for example *Regal (Hastings) Ltd v Gulliver* [1967] 2 AC 134 (HL) 157.
[219] *Bray v Ford* [1896] AC 44, 51.
[220] David Kershaw, *The Foundations of Anglo-American Corporate Fiduciary Law* (CUP 2018) 310–12.
[221] *Cook v Deeks* [1961] 1 AC 554, 563.
[222] See section 7.6.2 in this chapter.

The directors in turn are not agents but occupy a role that is specific to company law. Lord Russel said in *Regal (Hastings) Ltd v Gulliver* that directors of a limited company are 'the creatures of statute and occupy a position peculiar to themselves. In some respects they resemble trustees, in others they do not. In some respect they resemble agents, in others they do not. In some respect they resemble managing partners, on others they do not'.[223] This specific role may explain why the fiduciary rules apply to directors in a way that is different from how they apply to partnerships and also that corporate fiduciary law is difficult to reconcile with basic fiduciary principles.[224]

Fiduciary law manages the risk of directors diverting assets to themselves. It is possible to refer to that risk as an 'agency problem' and then to quantify that risk in terms of 'agency costs'.[225] Used in this way agency theory helps to succinctly identify the issue and provides a focus point for expressing it in monetary terms.

It is, however, important to observe that the risk of directors diverting assets to themselves affects creditors as much as it can affect shareholders. The conflict of interest is between the company and the director. It is not between the shareholders and the director.

Moreover, by not taking into account financial considerations such as the fact that the company has suffered no harm, the law primarily protects the formal process by which the company forms a view on whether to take the opportunity. It ensures that the company is not deprived of the formal opportunity to review a transaction that a director wishes to take for himself. The law assists the financial interests of shareholders and creditors but only indirectly.

The importance of this formal process is further highlighted by the fact that it is irrelevant that the directors could have easily secured formal authorization or ratification. Evidence that the majority shareholder directors had explicitly expressed no interest in the type of opportunity exploited by the director also does not remove the conflict.

In theoretical terms the protection of the corporate process displayed in relation to interested transactions can be rationalized by the theory of this book. The company is a separate entity which is characterized by and operates a process through which various interests are mediated. That process shapes decision-making. The law protects the company's interests by requiring formal adherence to that process from the directors when they take corporate opportunities. Mummery LJ observed in *Towers v Premier Waste Management Ltd* that the no-conflict principle prevents a director from

---

[223] *Regal (Hastings) Ltd v Gulliver* [1967] 2 AC 134 (HL) 147.
[224] For the point that corporate agency law does not align with basic fiduciary law see David Kershaw, 'Corporate Law's Fiduciary Persona' (2020) 136 LQR 454.
[225] See eg *Item Software (UK) v Fassihi* [2004] EWCA Civ 1244 [66] (Lady Arden).

'disloyally depriving the [c]ompany of the ability to consider whether or not it objected to the diversion of an opportunity'.[226]

At a normative level the strictness and the breadth of the common law duty can be criticized as imposing a significant burden on directors. After all, honest directors trying to do nothing but good for the company and succeeding in that can still find themselves on the losing side of an argument in court. In *Cook v Deek* Lord Buckmaster LC acknowledged that it is 'quite right' to point out that it is important to avoid imposing on directors 'burdens so heavy and responsibilities so great that men of good position would hesitate to accept office'.[227]

It is, however, worth observing that compliance with the procedural regime set up by the statute is straightforward. If there is an independent director that person can approve the transaction. This is not difficult to do. If a company only has one director, the route of having the transaction approved by the board is not available. But in that case the company is likely to be small enough for it not to be difficult to arrange for approval by the shareholders.

In circumstances where the shareholders have fallen out with each other approval by the board or by the shareholders will be difficult to obtain. In those circumstances, however, the idea that the duty is owed for the benefit of the shareholders also does not help resolve the issue. The shareholders at this point do not exist as homogenous body. Adopting a theoretical approach that aligns the interests of the company with the interests of the body of the shareholders is a fictional exercise. In such circumstances the problem is not one of protecting the shareholders from breaches of the directors but rather one of resolving a dispute between feuding shareholders. While that dispute is ongoing it is reasonable to ask all parties concerned to stay away from opportunities. If the corporate mechanism cannot be made to work the deadlock between shareholders ultimately needs to be resolved through an unfair prejudice petition or through a winding up.

7.8 Self-dealing

7.8.1 Introduction

The aim of this section is to show that shareholders play an important role in authorizing self-dealing transactions. It is possible, on this basis, to assign them the status of principals of the directors. But this is not where the analysis should stop. We will see in section 8.3.3 that the ability of shareholders to authorize self-dealing transactions is subject to important constraints taking into account the interests of creditors as well as those of minority shareholders.

---

[226] *Towers v Premier Waste Management Ltd* [2011] EWCA Civ 923, [2012] 1 BCLC 67.
[227] *Cook v Deeks* [1961] 1 AC 554, 563.

7.8.2 Duty to declare an interest in proposed transactions or arrangements

CA 2006, section 177 applies when a director or a person connected with him enters into a transaction with the company. If a director is in any way, directly or indirectly, interested in a proposed transaction or arrangement with the company, he must declare the nature and extent of that interest to the other directors.[228] The provision also applies if the director is unaware but reasonably ought to be aware of either their interest or the transaction or arrangement.[229] It does not apply if the interest cannot reasonably be regarded as likely to give rise to a conflict of interest.[230]

The declaration must be made before the company enters into the transaction or arrangement.[231] If the declaration has not been made at that point it needs to be made as soon as reasonably practicable after the transaction has been entered into.[232] Failure to do this constitutes an offence.[233]

If a company should have more than one director, but for some reason only has one, that director is required to record any interest in writing.[234] In addition, if the company has only one shareholder who is also the sole director of that company and if a contract is entered into between that shareholder director outside of the ordinary course of business, the contract must be either in writing or recorded in writing in a memorandum or in the minutes of a meeting of the directors.[235] Failure to do this constitutes an offence.[236] The contract is, however, nevertheless valid.[237]

7.8.3 Approval of self-dealing

The declaration of interest is intended to enable the company to make an informed decision as to the desirability of the transaction from the perspective of the company. In relation to the approval of a self-dealing transaction a distinction needs to be drawn between ordinary and substantial transactions.

An ordinary self-dealing transaction can be approved of by the board.[238] The constitution can impose more onerous requirements.[239] The current version of the Model

---

[228] CA 2006, s 177(1).

[229] ibid s 177(5).

[230] ibid s 177(6)(a).

[231] ibid s 177(4); *Fairford Water Ski Club Ltd v Cohoon* [2021] EWCA Civ 143 (CA).

[232] CA 2006, s 182(4).

[233] ibid s 183.

[234] ibid s 186(1).

[235] ibid s 231.

[236] ibid s 231(3).

[237] *ibid* s 231(6).

[238] ibid s 180(1)(b).

[239] ibid s 180(1) last sentence.

Articles provides, for example, that an interested director is not counted as participating in the decision-making process for quorum and voting purposes.[240]

A substantial property transaction requires approval by the shareholders.[241] A substantial property transaction is defined as a transaction between the company and its director or person connected to the director involving a substantial non-cash asset.[242] The scope of application for this provision is wide. A non-cash asset is 'substantial' if its value exceeds 10 per cent of the company's assets and is more than £5,000 or if it exceeds £100,000.[243] This definition of substantial property transactions is wide and leaves only comparatively small transactions to the approval of the board of directors.

The shareholders approve a substantial transaction through a resolution.[244] According to CA 2006, section 281 these are passed either in a meeting or as written resolutions under CA 2006, section 288. The standard requirement of a simple majority applies.[245] The articles can set a more onerous majority requirement.[246] In addition the *Duomatic* principle applies and so it is possible for a single individual who controls 100 per cent of the shares of the company to approve a substantial property transaction.[247]

The Financial Conduct Authority (FCA) Handbook Listing Rules contain additional requirements requiring shareholder approval for a slightly broader range of transactions and also requiring disinterested voting.[248] There is also a requirement for an expert report supporting the directors' statement that the transaction or arrangement is fair and reasonable from the perspective of the holders of the listed securities.[249]

7.8.4 Limits to shareholder approval

Given that the scope of substantial property transactions is relatively broad shareholders play an important role in authorizing self-dealing transactions. That puts them in a crucial position which may tempt us to characterize them as principals of the directors. It would be wrong, however, to end the analysis with this insight. The shareholders are not free to approve self-dealing transactions. Over time, rules have emerged that scrutinize self-dealing transactions. A director who has misappropriated company funds for private purposes, for example, risks disqualification under the Company Directors' Disqualification Act 1986.[250] Moreover, we will see below that transactions

---

[240] Model Articles (private) para 14(1); Model Articles (public) para 16(1).
[241] CA 2006, s 190; similar requirements apply to loan transactions (CA 2006, s 197, s 212); *AMT Coffee Ltd* [2019] EWHC 46 (Ch), [2020] 2 BCLC 50, 126; *Re BM Electrical Solutions Ltd (In Liquidation)* [2020] EWHC 2749 (Ch), 14 Oct 2020 (unreported).
[242] CA 2006, s 190.
[243] ibid s 191.
[244] ibid s 190(1).
[245] ibid ss 281(3) and 282.
[246] ibid 2006, s 180.
[247] *NBH Lt v Hoare* [2006] EWHC 73 (Ch), [2006] 2 BCLC 649, [41].
[248] FCA Handbook Listing Rule (LR) 11.1.5-6 with exceptions set out in LR 11 Annex 1.
[249] FCA Handbook LR 13.6.1(5).
[250] *Secretary of State for Business, Innovation and Skills v Whyte* [2014] CSOH 148; 2014 GWD 32–624.

between companies and directors, who are also shareholders, have come to attract an additional layer of scrutiny.[251]

7.8.5 Conclusions

The shareholders have important influence over self-dealing transactions but this does not make them principals. We will see in chapter 8 that there are limits on their ability to authorize self-dealing transactions and that these are in place to protect the interests of creditors and minority shareholders.[252]

7.9 Remuneration

7.9.1 Introduction

The contract which regulates the remuneration of the directors is an example of a self-dealing transaction. The remuneration of directors has received a substantial amount of attention in recent years. We will see below that the Companies Act 2006 and the UK Corporate Governance Code 2018 have adopted specific rules governing remuneration decisions.

7.9.2 Equity and the statutory regime

Historically the default position has been that remuneration was only payable if the articles so provided.[253] If the articles provided for remuneration the default rule was that it is for shareholders to approve transactions in which directors have a conflict of interest.[254] Over time the standard articles did not only authorize payments of remuneration but also delegated decision-making for remuneration to the board of directors.[255] This position continues to apply today. The current Model Articles provide that remuneration of the directors is determined by the directors.[256]

This creates a situation where the directors might be tempted to help each other to remuneration as they think fit, depriving the company of resources it needs to both pay its creditors and, in addition, reducing the ability of the company to show the profit necessary to enable it to reward its shareholders.

---

[251] Section 8.3.3 Disguised Returns of Capital.
[252] ibid.
[253] See most recently *Yusuf v Yusuf* [2019] EWHC 90 (Ch) [155].
[254] Paul Davies and Sarah Worthington, *Gower & Davies: Principles of Modern Company Law* (10th edn, OUP 2016) para 14–31.
[255] ibid para 14–31.
[256] Model Articles (private companies) para 19(3); Model Articles (public companies) para 23(3).

The conflict of interest associated with remuneration decisions is evidenced on its face and so a director does not need to declare an interest under CA 2006, section 177 when the board or a board committee considers terms of his service contract.[257] Under the Model Articles the director whose remuneration is determined is not counted as participating in the decision making for quorum and voting purposes.[258]

CA 2006 does not set a limit for how much remuneration can be paid to directors. The Model Articles also do not specify any such limits. They only clarify that remuneration may be paid in any form including the payment of a pension, allowance, or gratuity, or any death, sickness, or disability benefits.[259]

When taking decisions on remuneration the directors are required to act in accordance with their general duties. Excessive remuneration can, for example, amount to a breach of CA 2006, section 172.[260] We have already seen that the courts are reluctant to intervene with the good faith judgement of the directors.[261] This also applies to remuneration decisions.[262]

While the courts stress that they are reluctant to interfere with the judgement of the directors in setting remuneration, they nevertheless insist that that this judgement is formally exercised and that the directors abide by the procedures set out in the articles. They need to deliberately fix the remuneration and in doing this determine if the company can afford the respective amount. A failure of the directors to ensure that salaries are affordable can demonstrate the unfitness of a director to be concerned with the management of a company and thus lead to his or her disqualification.[263] Directors need to put their minds properly to the question of directors' remuneration. They need to determine if the company can afford the directors' salary.[264] While a company is not actually insolvent directors deciding what to pay themselves must strike a 'fair balance' taking into account the 'value of their services to the [c]ompany', the 'position on creditors', and the company's 'overall state and the availability of funds to make the payments'.[265] The court allows for 'reasonable latitude' and only 'exceptional circumstances' would justify directors suspending their own remuneration altogether.[266]

The UK Corporate Governance Code 2018 sets out that remuneration policies and practices should be designed to 'support strategy and promote long-term sustainable

---

[257] CA 2006, s 177(6)(c).

[258] Model Articles (private companies) para 14; Model Articles (public companies) para 23.

[259] Model Articles (private companies) para 19(3); Model Articles (public companies) para 23(3).

[260] Re CF Booth Ltd; Booth v Booth [2017] EWHC 457 (Ch); Interactive Technology Corp Ltd v Ferster [2018] EWCA Civ 1594, [2018] 2 P&CR DG 22.

[261] See section 7.4 in this chapter.

[262] Re Halt Garage [1982] All ER 1016 at 1039 per Oliver J; see also Guinness v Saunders [1990] 2 AC 663 at 689, per Lord Templeman: 'The court is not entitled to usurp the functions conferred on the board by the articles'; and at 701, per Lord Goff expressing concern about 'interference by the court in the administration of a company's affairs when the company is not being wound up'.

[263] Secretary of State for Trade and Industry v Van Hengel [1995] 1 BCLC 545.

[264] ibid.

[265] Bednash v Hearsey [2001] 2 WLUK 426 [50].

[266] ibid.

success'. Executive remuneration should be 'aligned to company purpose and values, and be clearly linked to the successful deliver of the company's long-term strategy'.[267] While the definition of what directors should do has changed from serving the (financial) interests of shareholders to delivering 'purpose' and 'long-term sustainable success', this nevertheless retains the idea that remuneration should be engineered in a way that incentivizes directors to 'do the right thing'. It will be argued below that this tactic is fundamentally flawed.[268]

7.9.3 The role of shareholders

Shareholders are responsible for approving certain elements of the directors' service contracts. Following statutory intervention overriding the practice that delegated remuneration decisions to the board, shareholders today need to approve service contracts which bind the company for more than two years.[269] Such a resolution must not be passed unless a memorandum setting out the proposed contract incorporating the provision under which the term of employment of the director is or may be longer than two years.[270] If the requirement for shareholder approval is not complied with the contract is deemed to have a term entitling the company to terminate it at any time by giving reasonable notice.[271]

Shareholders also need to approve a payment that is made to directors for the loss of their office.[272] This includes payments that are made at the direction of a director to another person or to a person connected with a director.[273] Shareholder approval is also required for payments to directors for loss of office that occur in connection with a transfer of the whole or any part of the undertaking or property of the company or in connection with a transfer of the shares in the company.[274] If no such approval is obtained the recipients hold the payment on trust for the company and any director who authorized the payment is jointly and severally liable to indemnify the company.[275]

In relation to listed companies there is an even greater level of involvement of shareholders. These are required to develop a remuneration policy. That policy needs to be approved by the shareholders.[276] Remuneration payments and payments for loss of

---

[267] UK Corporate Governance Code 2018, principle P (https://www.frc.org.uk/directors/corporate-governance-and-stewardship/uk-corporate-governance-code).
[268] Section 7.9.5 in this chapter.
[269] CA 2006, s 188.
[270] ibid s 188(5).
[271] ibid s 189.
[272] ibid s 217.
[273] ibid s 215.
[274] ibid s 218.
[275] ibid s 222.
[276] ibid s 439A. The Companies Act uses the term 'quoted company' which is wider than the term 'listed companies'. In addition to companies whose equity shares have been included in the official list according to the provisions of Part 6 of the Financial Services and Markets Act 2000 (c 8) it also includes companies which are officially listed in an EEA State, or which have been admitted to the New York Stock Exchange or to Nasdaq (CA 2006, s 385(2) and s 226A(1)).

office need to be consistent with this remuneration policy. Inconsistent payments may only be made if the shareholders specifically approve them.[277] Payments made without the required approval are held on trust by the recipient.[278] Directors who authorized the payment are jointly and severally liable to indemnify the company that made the payment for any loss resulting from it.[279]

In addition, the FCA Handbook Listing Rules set out that shareholders need to approve long-term incentive schemes.[280] This was originally a measure to prevent companies from issuing options on terms that would dilute the interests of existing shareholders, but then developed into a mechanism designed to allow shareholders to oversee the performance criteria associated with incentive plans.[281] A long-term incentive scheme makes the receipt of an asset by a director conditional on service or performance to be satisfied over more than one financial year.[282] Shareholders also need to approve discounted option arrangements.[283] These are options, warrants, or other rights where the price per share payable is less than the market value of the share at the date when the exercise price is determined.[284]

Furthermore, the ability of certain financial institutions to pay variable remuneration has been limited by the regulatory rules that were introduced after the financial crisis.[285] There are also reporting requirements relating to gender pay gaps and in relation to pay ratios between CEOs and employees.[286]

The Corporate Governance Code 2018 recommends that a board committee is involved in remuneration decisions. The remuneration committee needs to be staffed with independent non-executive directors.[287] The influence of the committee has recently increased. It is responsible for determining the policy for executive remuneration and for setting the remuneration for the chair, the executive directors, and senior management. It also reviews workforce remuneration and related policies and the alignment of incentives and rewards with culture.[288] Where a remuneration consultant is appointed this should be the responsibility of the committee.[289] There should be a formal and transparent procedure for developing a policy and for determining the remuneration

---

[277] CA 2006, ss 226B and 226C.
[278] ibid s 226E(2).
[279] ibid s 226E(2).
[280] LR 9.4.1 (as of 1 September 2020).
[281] Paul Davies and Sarah Worthington, *Gower & Davies: Principles of Modern Company Law* (10th edn, OUP 2016) para 14–37.
[282] LR 9.4.1 (as of 1 September 2020).
[283] LR 9.4.4 (as of 1 September 2020).
[284] LR 9.4.4(2) (as of 1 September 2020).
[285] Para 15 of the remuneration section of the rulebook of the Bank of England Prudential Regulation Authority (https://www.prarulebook.co.uk/rulebook/Content/Part/292166/19-02-2021); see also FCA Handbook SYSC 19A–19F (https://www.handbook.fca.org.uk/handbook/SYSC).
[286] Equality Act 2010 (Gender Pay Gap Information) Regulations 2017 (SI 2017/172); https://gender-pay-gap.service.gov.uk; The Companies (Miscellaneous Reporting) Regulations 2018 (SI 2018/860).
[287] UK Corporate Governance Code 2018 (https://www.frc.org.uk/directors/corporate-governance-and-stewardship/uk-corporate-governance-code) provision 32.
[288] ibid provision 33.
[289] ibid provision 35.

of directors and senior managers.[290] Directors should exercise independent judgement and discretion when authorizing remuneration outcomes taking account of company and individual performance, and wider circumstances.[291] No director should be involved in deciding their own remuneration outcome.[292]

7.9.4 Conclusions

The shareholders approve long-term service contracts and payments for loss of office. This fact could be used to support an argument that the shareholders are the principals of the directors. We will see below, however, that this argument is undermined by the fact that the shareholders are not free to determine the directors' remuneration. They need to observe the distribution rules and also the rules prohibiting unfair prejudice, and so cannot be characterized as having the status of principals of the directors.[293]

7.9.5 Theoretical observations

The idea of designing remuneration in a way that aligns the interests of directors with the interests of shareholders fits well with agency theory. Remuneration can be conceived of as a tool helping to align the interests of the directors with those of the shareholders.[294] It can also be argued that in companies where shareholders are dispersed a well-aligned remuneration package is a mechanism providing oversight for the directors.[295] If the return of the directors corresponds with how well the shareholders are doing then there would not be much else the shareholders need to do. The directors by acting in their own self-interest then also enhance the return for the shareholders.

The idea of aligning pay with the interests of the shareholders can be found in the Greenbury Report.[296] The Greenbury Report refers to recent concerns about executive remuneration arising because of large pay increases from share options in recently privatized utility industries.[297] The recommendation was to link pay to performance and

---

[290] ibid principle Q.
[291] *ibid* principle R.
[292] ibid principle Q.
[293] Chapter 8 in this book.
[294] MC Jensen and WH Meckling, 'Theory of the Firm: Managerial Behavior, Agency Costs and Ownership Structure' (1976) 3 Journal of Financial Economics 305 at 308; Brian R Cheffins, *Company Law, Theory, Structure and Operation* (OUP 1997) 564, 687–89; Guido Ferrarini and Maria Christina Ungureanu, 'Executive Remuneration' in Jeffrey N Gordon and Wolf-Georg Ringe (eds), *Corporate Law and Governance* (OUP 2018) 334.
[295] For perhaps the foundational contribution setting out this argument see Frank H Easterbrook, 'Managers' Discretion and Investors' Welfare: Theories and Evidence' (1984) 9 Delaware Journal of Corporate Law 540 at 554 and 559–64; see also more recently Alex Edmans and Xavier Gabaix, 'Executive Compensation: A Modern Primer' (2016) 54 (4) Journal of Economic Literature 1232.
[296] The High Pay Commission, Cheques with Balances: why tackling high pay is in the national interest (November 2010) 41 (available from <http://highpaycentre.org/about/>).
[297] Greenbury Report (Study Group on Directors' Remuneration) (1997) <https://ecgi.global/code/greenbury-report-study-group-directors-remuneration> para 1.6.

to align the interests of the directors and shareholders.[298] The Code stated that, 'The performance-related elements of remuneration should be designed to align the interests of [d]irectors and shareholder and to give [d]irectors keen incentives to perform at the highest level.'[299] Performance conditions should be 'relevant, stretching and designed to enhance business'.[300]

We have seen in the previous paragraph that the argument that remuneration can operate as a tool for guiding the directors can be made when one assumes that the corporate interest is identical with the shareholders' collective interest. The same alignment argument can also be articulated from the perspective of the company as a separate real entity. Accepting that the company is an autonomous entity in its own right with a process that mediates relationships with shareholders, creditors, and other constituencies and that company law protects that process rather than any particular interest, agency theory would recommend that remuneration be designed to align the directors' interests with the interest of the company as a separate autonomous entity.

The UK Corporate Governance Code 2018 recommends that remuneration policies and practices should be designed to 'support strategy and promote long-term sustainable success'. Executive remuneration should be 'aligned to company purpose and values, and be clearly linked to the successful deliver of the company's long-term strategy'.[301] While the definition of what directors should do has changed from serving the (financial) interests of shareholders to delivering 'purpose' and 'long-term sustainable success' this nevertheless retains the idea that remuneration should be engineered in a way that incentivizes directors to 'do the right thing'.

It is doubtful if this attempt to regulate executive pay will succeed. It is possible that the culprit for the spiralling of executive remuneration is not that it is difficult to identify an appropriate decision-maker. The problem may rather lie in the idea that remuneration can be designed in a way that aligns the interest of directors with either the shareholder or the company. It is possible that it is too difficult to design remuneration conditions in a way that predicts what will be good performance in a future environment.[302]

The developments since the early 1980s help to illustrate this point. The exponential growth of executive remuneration that began then was in part driven by the desire

---

[298] ibid para 1.15.
[299] ibid C4.
[300] Ibid C5.
[301] UK Corporate Governance Code 2018 <(https://www.frc.org.uk/directors/corporate-governance-and-stewardship/uk-corporate-governance-code)>, principle P.
[302] The High Pay Commission, Cheques with Balances: why tackling high pay is in the national interest (November 2010) 8 (available from <http://highpaycentre.org/about/>); Brian R Cheffins, *Company Law, Theory, Structure and Operation* (OUP 1997) at 685 acknowledges that 'developing and implementing a managerial remuneration scheme under which executives are rewarded in accordance with the contribution they make to changes in shareholders wealth' is a 'complex exercise'. See also Alex Edmans and Xavier Gabaix, 'Executive Compensation: A Modern Primer' (2016) 54 (4) Journal of Economic Literature 1232 at 1233 who observe that a 'theoretically optimal contract is typically highly non-linear and so never observed'; see also Andreas Kokkinis, 'Exploring the Effects of the "Bonus Cap" Rule: the Impact of Remuneration Structure on Risk-taking by Bank Managers' [2019] JCLS 167.

to link pay to performance.[303] The aspiration was to tie the interests of executives to shareholders and to create 'quasi-entrepreneurs' at the top of businesses.[304] This has not worked.[305] Remuneration has turned out not to be the silver bullet. The High Pay Commission observed in 2011 that 'rewards for failure continue' and 'pay levels appear to be increasingly disconnected from the performance of the company'.[306] In 2019 the House of Commons Business, Energy and Industrial Strategy (BEIS) Committee observes that 'executive greed, fed by heavy reliance on incentive pay, has been baked into the remuneration system'.[307]

This alignment argument, which received substantial endorsement during the heyday of neoliberal thinking, has possibly been responsible for an increase in executive remuneration that is out of kilter with executive performance. Executive pay has spiralled in a way that is not connected to performance. In 1979 the lead executive of BP earned 16.5 times the amount of the average employee. In 2011 the multiple was 63. In Barclays Bank the multiples were 14.5 (1979) and 75 (2011).[308] The interventions of the statute and of the UK Corporate Governance Code have attempted to remedy the problem by moving remuneration decisions away from the executive directors. This has not worked. Between 2009 and 2017 the median single total figure for remuneration has increased by 66 per cent.[309] It is possible that the flaw does not only lie in the way remuneration decisions are taken. Perhaps the idea of performance-related pay is defective too.

The idea that remuneration should provide directors with a direct personal financial reason to meet particular financial indicators counterintuitively seems to have caused remuneration to become disconnected from performance. This may have happened because conceiving remuneration as an alignment measure operates as a justification for high rewards. The justification is that the money is only paid because it serves other interests. That then opens the door to awards that are higher than they otherwise would be. Because alignment is evidently difficult to achieve the risk is high that remuneration will be driven up without any alignment effect.

---

[303] House of Commons, Business, Energy and Industrial Strategy Committee, Executive rewards: paying for success (Eighteenth Report of Session 2017–19) 20 March 2019 (HC 2018) 19 (available from <https://publications.parliament.uk/pa/cm201719/cmselect/cmbeis/2018/2018.pdf>); The High Pay Commission, Cheques with Balances: why tackling high pay is in the national interest (November 2010) 16 and 41–42 (available from <http://highpaycentre.org/about/>).

[304] The High Pay Commission, Cheques with Balances: why tackling high pay is in the national interest (November 2010) (available from <http://highpaycentre.org/about/>) 16, 41–42,

[305] ibid 42–43, 47; see also Betty (HT) Wu, Ian MacNeil, and Katarzyna Chalaczkiewicz-Ladna, 'Say on Pay Regulations and Director Remuneration: Evidence from the UK in the Past Two Decades' [2020] JCLS 541.

[306] The High Pay Commission, Cheques with Balances: why tackling high pay is in the national interest (November 2010) 16 (available from http://highpaycentre.org/about/).

[307] House of Commons, Business, Energy and Industrial Strategy Committee, Executive rewards: paying for success (Eighteenth Report of Session 2017–19) 20 March 2019 (HC 2018) 11 (available from <https://publications.parliament.uk/pa/cm201719/cmselect/cmbeis/2018/2018.pdf>).

[308] The High Pay Commission, Cheques with Balances: why tackling high pay is in the national interest (November 2010) 8 (available from <http://highpaycentre.org/about/>).

[309] House of Commons, Business, Energy and Industrial Strategy Committee, Executive rewards: paying for success (Eighteenth Report of Session 2017–19) 20 March 2019 (HC 2018) 7 (available from <https://publications.parliament.uk/pa/cm201719/cmselect/cmbeis/2018/2018.pdf>).

The difficulty associated with drafting remuneration packages that achieve an alignment of interests has also led to complexity. This has caused incentive plans to become increasingly difficult to review prompting the BEIS Select Committee to recommend the abolition of Long-term Incentive Plans.[310]

High levels of remuneration are not problematic on their own. There are many other occupations in which rewards are high. But the problem with executive remuneration is not simply the amount that directors receive. It is the fact that incentive plans can steer directors in the wrong direction, causing them to pursue returns while neglecting or creating risks that will harm the company in the future. Incentive plans can thus backfire causing companies to be managed in a way that produces results in the term that matches the remuneration plan. Over the long term there is a risk that the company will suffer. By that time the negative consequences of performance-related incentive plans materialize, the directors as well as the shareholders may well have changed. So the tab is picked up by a different group of shareholders or, as the financial crises has demonstrated, by the government, when it feels bound to rescue strategically important businesses.

Executive remuneration is an example of why an analysis focusing on incentives does not only fail to describe the law as it stands. It is also undesirable as a normative proposition.

To be sure, this author has no quarrel with executives or other members of society receiving high levels of pay. The critique articulated here only relates to performance-related pay structures. These legitimize remuneration as a reward to be earned following the delivery of a challenging target for the benefit of someone else. They introduce complexity. The task performed by executive directors is so multifaceted that it has so far not proven possible to identify a straightforward target measuring success. If we cannot identify an appropriate target, performance-related pay is a motor for increasing pay without a legitimate explanation as to the appropriateness of the respective level. In addition, the complexity associated with these plans makes it difficult to create oversight. More generally, executive pay serves as an example that incentive-based interventions, which fit well with agency theory, are difficult to put into practice.

7.10 Duty to record and report

7.10.1 Introduction

The Companies Act 2006 does not at any one point set out a comprehensive list of the duties to be performed by the directors. CA 2006, sections 170–81 contain a statement of the directors' general duties. But that list is not complete. In the following sections

---

[310] Federico Mor and Steve Browning, Corporate Governance Reform, House of Commons Briefing paper 8143, 27 May 2020, 23–24 and 42.

we will analyse specific duties contained in other parts of the Companies Act, that also regulate the behaviour of directors. We will see that these duties are procedural in nature. They contain specific granular instructions requiring directors to formally deliver a sequence of actions.

We have already seen in the context of the duty of skill, care, and diligence that directors are required to maintain accounting records and to produce and publish financial and narrative reports.[311] These duties will be further examined in this section. We will see that the Companies Act and the accounting regulations and principles adopted on the basis of the Act prescribe a formal method which the directors have to use to record and report information.

We have already seen that the requirements to maintain financial records are enforced by the Secretary of State through the Company Directors Disqualification Act 1986.[312] In addition the Companies Act 2006 imposes criminal liability on the directors personally. The Act also gives powers to the Secretary of State, who can apply to have accounts rectified and who also performs a role in relation to the appointment of auditors.

It will be shown in this section that the requirement to record and report serves shareholders but cannot be explained fully by their interests. It also serves creditors and employees. It aims to integrate ecological and social goals such as climate change, human rights, and equality or fair payment terms into the corporate decision-making process.

7.10.2 Duty to keep accounting records

Directors need to make sure that the company keeps accounting records.[313] These need to record the assets the company owns and the liabilities it owes.[314] If the company deals in goods it needs to produce a statement of stock held at the end of each financial year.[315] The directors also need to ensure that the company records 'from day to day' the money it spends and receives. This has to be done in a way that makes it possible 'to disclose with reasonable accuracy, at any time, the financial position of the company at that time and to enable the directors to ensure that any accounts required to be prepared comply with the requirements of the Companies Act'.[316] The format of these records differs depending on the nature and complexity of the company's business.[317]

---

[311] Section 7.6 in this chapter.
[312] Section 7.6.4 in this chapter.
[313] CA 2006, s 386.
[314] ibid s 386(3).
[315] ibid s 386(4).
[316] ibid s 386(2).
[317] Explanatory Notes to the Companies Act 2006, para 639; see also ICAEW, Technical Release: TECH 01/ 11: Guidance for directors on accounting records under the Companies Act 2006 (<https://www.icaew.com/-/media/corporate/files/technical/technical-releases/legal-and-regulatory/tech-01-11-guidance-for-directors-on-accounting-records-under-the-companies-act-2006.ashx?la=en>).

The requirements for record keeping are mandatory for all companies. They are for-tified by criminal liability. Every officer of a company who fails to comply is liable.[318] Liability is strict, but the officer can avoid liability by showing that he 'acted honestly and that in the circumstances in which the company's business was carried on the de-fault was excusable'.[319]

Directors who do not keep adequate accounting records face disqualification under the Company Directors Disqualification Act 1986. There is well-established jurisprudence that the failure to keep accounting records is evidence of 'unfitness'.[320]

In addition, the Finance Act 2009 requires large companies to identify a Senior Accounting Officer. The Senior Accounting Officer occupies a role within a large com-pany, which cannot be assumed by an agent or an adviser.[321] The officer has overall responsibility for the company's financial accounting arrangements.[322] They are re-quired to establish and monitor appropriate tax accounting arrangements.[323] They have to certify to HM Revenue & Customs (HMRC) that the company has appropriate tax accounting arrangements through the financial year.[324] Failure to do this or careless or deliberate inaccuracy renders the officer liable for a fine.[325]

The requirement to keep accounting records is associated with the corporate form. It does not apply to sole traders or individuals with a wealth profile that matches that of large companies. These need to keep records for tax purposes but are not required to maintain records for any other purpose.[326]

The keeping of accounting records by the company benefits shareholders. By keeping accounting records directors are in a position to continuously understand the company's financial situation. This helps them to take better decisions and also facili-tates their accountability to the company. But it would be wrong to explain the require-ment for record keeping solely as tool for enhancing the well-being of shareholders.

Formally, the duty to keep accounting records is owed to the company and not to the shareholders individually. The shareholders are unable to remove or modify the requirement for record keeping. They can also do nothing to prevent directors from incurring liability if they act in breach of the statutory rules. Criminal prosecution and the disqualification of directors is independent of the shareholders' support.

[318] CA 2006, s 387.
[319] ibid s 387(2).
[320] Re Sevenaoks Stationers [1991] Ch 164.
[321] Senior Accounting Officer Guidance 16 March 2016 last updated on 28 January 2020 (<www.gov.uk/hmrc-internal-manuals/senior-accounting-officers-guidance/saog12200>).
[322] Finance Act 2009, (c10) s 1 and schedule 46 para 93.
[323] ibid schedule 46 para 93.
[324] ibid schedule 46 para 2(2).
[325] ibid s 5 schedule 46.
[326] <www.gov.uk/self-employed-records?step-by-step-nav=01ff8dbd-886a-4dbb-872c-d2092b31b2cf> (as of 16 July 2020).

The rules on record keeping thus serve a broader purpose. Requiring directors to remain continuously informed about the company's financial position also helps the creditors of companies. It puts directors in a position where they are aware of the company's liabilities, enabling them to ensure timely payment.

The imposition of criminal liability suggests that there exists a wider public interest in the requirement for record keeping. This conclusion is further supported by the requirement for large companies to appoint a specific individual to the position of a Senior Accounting Officer. It is a governance measure that is not contained in the Companies Act but nevertheless applies to all companies of a certain size. Like the requirement to keep accounting records it cannot be overridden by the shareholders and it does not apply to individuals with an asset profile equivalent to that of large companies.

7.10.3 Duty to prepare annual accounts

Based on the company's accounting records the directors of every company must take stock of the company's financial position at the end of each financial year. They must prepare accounts for the company.[327] These are referred to as the 'company's individual accounts'.[328] They consist of a balance sheet and a profit and loss account.[329] The accounts need to be accompanied by notes which record further information on matter such as related undertakings,[330] off-balance sheet arrangements,[331] employment numbers and costs,[332] and directors' remuneration,[333] as well as advances, credits, and guarantees granted to them.[334]

The balance sheet shows the company's financial position at the end of the financial year. It lists assets and liabilities of a company.[335] Assets are items such as land, buildings, machinery, but also patents and trademarks. Liabilities are bank loans, money owed to trade creditors, or money owed in tax. The balance sheet enables its user to compare the assets and the liabilities of the company at the end of the financial year.

The profit and loss account shows the company's transactions. It displays items such as the company's turnover, the change in stock, and other operating income. It also displays staff costs, depreciation of assets, and other operating expenses.[336] It adds up all

---

[327] CA 2006, s 394.
[328] ibid s 394. There is also a duty to prepare group accounts (ibid ss 399–413). These will not be analysed further here.
[329] ibid s 396(1).
[330] ibid s 409.
[331] ibid s 410A.
[332] ibid s 411.
[333] ibid s 412.
[334] ibid s 413.
[335] The format is set out on the basis of CA 2006, s 396(3) in the Large and Medium-sized Companies and Groups (Accounts and Reports) Regulation 2008/410 Schedule 1, part 1, section b, para 1 and in the Small Companies and Groups (Accounts and Directors' Report) Regulations 2008/409, schedule 1, section b, para 1.
[336] The format is set out on the basis of CA 2006, s 396(3) in the Large and Medium-sized Companies and Groups (Accounts and Reports) Regulation 2008/410 Schedule 1, part 1, section b, para 1 and in the Small Companies and Groups (Accounts and Directors' Report) Regulations 2008/409, schedule 1, section b, para 1.

income and expenses that have occurred during the financial year. Expenses are subtracted from income with the company showing a profit or loss. That profit or loss is then also displayed on the balance sheet.

The exercise of making a list of assets and liabilities and of income and expenses involves arithmetical operations. In addition, a significant amount of judgement is involved. Each asset and each liability needs to be described with a monetary value. This value could, for example, be the price at which the asset was bought. It could be the price at which the asset, having been used by the company for a period of time, would sell in the market now. It could be the price the company would have to pay to acquire such an asset now. For a liability the value could be the amount the company is legally required to pay when the debt falls due. It could also be that there is possibility that the creditor the company owes the money to will agree to accept a lower amount, and so that amount could be associated with the liability.

The approach adopted to valuations matters. If the directors were free to exercise discretion as to valuing assets and liabilities they might be tempted to value assets highly and to understate the extent of liabilities. This would show the company in a favourable light and thus reflect well on their own performance. The law does not permit this. The directors are not free to determine the content and form of the balance sheet and profit and loss account.

Under the Companies Act the Secretary of State makes regulations setting out the format and the content of the profit and loss account.[337] The format for the balance sheet and the profit and loss account is more developed for large and medium-sized companies than for small and micro- companies.[338]

In addition to the format the regulations contain valuation rules. They state, for example, that the amount to be included for a fixed asset in the accounts must be its purchase price or production cost. This value is referred to as historic cost.[339] In addition, if a fixed asset has a limited useful economic life this amount must be reduced systematically over the period of its useful economic life.[340] The directors are thus unable to adopt their own approach to the valuation of assets.

The determination of the 'production cost' of a fixed asset or of its 'useful economic life' require a further exercise of judgement, where again the directors might be tempted to

---

[337] CA 2006, s 396(3).

[338] Compare Large and Medium-sized Companies and Groups (Accounts and Reports) Regulation 2008/410 Schedule 1, part 1, section b, para 1 with the Small Companies and Groups (Accounts and Directors' Report) Regulations 2008/409, schedule 1, section b and c, para 1.

[339] Large and Medium-sized Companies and Groups (Accounts and Reports) Regulation 2008/410, Schedule 1, para 17; Small Companies and Groups (Accounts and Directors' Report) Regulations 2008/409, schedule 1, para 16.

[340] Large and Medium-sized Companies and Groups (Accounts and Reports) Regulation 2008/410 Schedule 1, para 18; Small Companies and Groups (Accounts and Directors' Report) Regulations 2008/409, schedule 1, para 18.

form a view that reflects well on the company's financial position and consequently on them. This further problem is also managed by the law.

The accounts must be prepared either in accordance with the Companies Act or in accordance with International Accounting Standards.[341] International Accounting Standards are adopted by the International Financial Reporting Standards Foundation.[342] The Financial Reporting Council (Audit, Reporting and Governance Authority) publish the UK Generally Accepted Accounting Principles (UK GAAP). We have already seen that UK GAAP have a legal force that elevates them above the level of default rules.[343]

The responsibility for producing the annual accounts and reports lies with the directors. It cannot be delegated to the shareholders. The board of directors must approve the accounts. They must be signed on behalf of the board by a director of the company.[344] The signature and the name of the director who signed must be on the company's balance sheet.[345] There is criminal liability attached to the production of accounts that do not comply with the requirements of the Companies Act. Every director of the company who knew that the accounts did not comply or was reckless as to whether they complied and who failed to take reasonable steps to ensure compliance commits an offence.[346]

Moreover, the Secretary of State can request a revision of the accounts if it appears that there is or may be a question whether the accounts comply with the requirements of the Companies Act.[347] The Secretary of State or any person authorized by him can apply to court for an order instructing the directors to prepare revised accounts.[348] HMRC may disclose information to a person who is authorized to request a revision of the accounts.[349] Such a person can also apply to court to request disclosure of documents, information, and explanations from the company, any officer, employee, or auditor.[350] The government is currently consulting on giving powers to Secretary of State to direct changes to company accounts without having to ask for a court order.[351]

The aim of the rules on annual accounts and reports is to capture the financial position of the company at least once in each financial year. This helps shareholders to exercise their rights in the company. But that is not the only purpose.

---

[341] CA 2006, s 395.

[342] <www.ifrs.org>; recently the principle of prudence has been re-introduced into chapter 2 of the Conceptual Framework for Financial Reporting (<www.iasplus.com/en/news/2018/03/cf>).

[343] See section 6.2.4 in this book.

[344] CA 2006, s 414(1).

[345] ibid s 414(2).

[346] ibid s 414(4 and 5); The Government is planning to require directors to verify the effectiveness of internal control and risk management systems (Department for Business, Energy & Industrial Strategy, Restoring Trust in Audit and Corporate Governance (March 2021)) paras 2.1.16–2.1.27.

[347] ibid s 455.

[348] ibid s 456.

[349] ibid s 458.

[350] ibid s 459.

[351] Department for Business, Energy and Industrial Strategy, Restoring Trust in Audit and Corporate Governance, CP 382, March 2021 [4.2].

If the purpose of the annual accounts was limited to the purpose of providing information to the shareholders, the law would use default rules. It would be possible for the shareholders to override the statutory regime by removing the requirement to produce accounts. This is not possible. Only shareholders of dormant companies and of certain subsidiaries for whom the parent company has given a guarantee can permit the directors not to produce accounts.[352]

Shareholders are also unable to permit directors to deviate from the statutory format or from the true and fair view requirement. They cannot, for example, instruct directors to adopt specific valuations reflecting the shareholders' preferences. They cannot stop the Secretary of State from requesting a revision of the accounts. The law does not trust the shareholders to set accounting standards.

This suggests that the requirement to directors to annually draw together information on the company's financial position serves a purpose that goes beyond allowing the shareholders to monitor directors. It also supports the conclusion that it would be wrong to characterize shareholders as the principals of the directors or of the company. A principal would be able to determine if and how records concerning his or her own affairs are to be kept.

7.10.4 Duty to prepare narrative reports

Introduction
In recent years the requirements for directors to report have substantially increased in volume and broadened in scope. In 2000 the annual report and financial statements for the Marks and Spencer Group were 45 pages long. They consisted mainly of financial information.[353] In 2020 the same document consisted of 200 pages and integrated a much wider range of topics.[354]

In addition to annual accounts company directors now also need to produce narrative reports. The narrative reports required under the Companies Act are: the directors' report, the strategic report, and the directors' remuneration report. The government is currently consulting on imposing a requirement on directors of public interest entities to prepare a resilience statement.[355] Like the financial reporting requirements, the requirements for narrative reporting are more onerous for larger companies than for smaller companies. In addition, the UK Corporate Governance Code requires the production of a nomination report and an audit report.

---

[352] CA 2006, s 394A.
[353] <https://corporate.marksandspencer.com/documents/reports-results-and-publications/annual-reports/annual-report-2000.pdf>.
[354] <https://corporate.marksandspencer.com/investors/reports-results-and-presentations>
[355] Department for Business, Energy and Industrial Strategy, Restoring Trust in Audit and Corporate Governance, CP 382, March 2021 [3.1].

The Modern Slavery Act 2015, the Finance Act 2016, the Equality Act 2010, the EU Transparency Regulation 2007, the Small Business, Enterprise and Employment Act 2015, and the Accounting Directive 2013 require companies of a certain size to report on certain specific matters.

Like the requirement to produce financial information, the requirement for narrative reports is mandatory and, while also serving shareholders, operates as a conduit integrating wider interests into company law.

Directors' report

The directors of all companies, except for micro-companies, need to produce a directors' report.[356] It contains the directors' verbal assessment of the company's business during the financial year that the report relates to. The required content increases with size. The larger the company the greater the amount of reporting on wider interests such as employees, carbon emissions, and equality. The content of the directors' report is set out in regulations adopted by the Secretary of State.[357]

The directors' report, for example, needs to contain the particulars of any important events affecting the company which have occurred since the end of the financial year and an indication of likely future developments in the business of the company.[358] It also needs to contain information on the use of financial instruments,[359] and on its own shares that it has purchased.[360] There is also a requirement to report information on political donations,[361]

A company with over 250 employees needs to report its policies 'for giving full and fair consideration to applications for employment of disabled people'.[362] The report must contain a statement on engagement with employees describing, inter alia, how it provides employees 'systematically with information on matters of concern to them as employees' and how it consults with 'employees or their representatives on a regular basis so that the views of employees can be taken into account'.[363] The report must contain a statement summarizing how the directors have had regard 'to the need to foster

---

[356] CA 2006, s 415.

[357] Large and Medium-sized Companies and Groups (Accounts and Reports) Regulation 2008/410, Schedule 7; Small Companies and Groups (Accounts and Directors' Report) Regulations 2008/409, Schedule 5.

[358] Large and Medium-sized Companies and Groups (Accounts and Reports) Regulation 2008/410, Schedule 7 para 7.

[359] ibid Schedule 7 para 6.

[360] ibid Schedule 7 paras 8 and 9.

[361] ibid Schedule 7 paras 3 and 4; Small Companies and Groups (Accounts and Reports) Regulation 2008/409, Schedule 5 paras 2 and 3.
Political donations and expenditure require shareholder approval (CA 2006, s 366). This requirement was introduced by the Political Parties, Elections and Referendums Act 2000, ss 139–40. If shareholders do not approve the company can recover the donation (Companies (Interest Rate for Unauthorised Political Donations or Expenditure) Regulations 2007/2242).

[362] Large and Medium-sized Companies and Groups (Accounts and Reports) Regulation 2008/410, Schedule 7 para 10; Small Companies and Groups (Accounts and Reports) Regulation 2008/409, Schedule 5, para 5.

[363] Large and Medium-sized Companies and Groups (Accounts and Reports) Regulation 2008/410, Schedule 7 para 11.

business relationships with suppliers, customers and others, and the effect of that regard, including on the principal decisions taken by the company during the financial year'.[364]

For quoted companies, information on the capital structure, transfer restrictions, and voting restrictions needs to be added.[365] For large companies the report must also quantify and provide information about the emission of carbon dioxide that the company is responsible for.[366]

The directors' report needs to be approved by the board and signed on behalf of the board by a director or the secretary of the company.[367] The shareholders play no role in the production or approval of the report. If the report does not comply with the statutory requirements an officer who knew or recklessly did not know and who failed to take reasonable steps to ensure compliance incurs criminal liability.[368]

Strategic report

A Strategic Report must be prepared by the directors of all but small companies.[369] Here too the scope of the report increases with size. Larger companies have to integrate a greater amount of stakeholder related content. All strategic reports need to contain a fair review of the company's business and a description of the principal risks and uncertainties facing the company.[370] The review needs to provide a balanced and comprehensive analysis of the development and performance of the company's business during the financial year and the position of the company at the end of the year.[371] The strategic report of a quoted company must include the main trends and factors likely to effect the future development of the company's business as well as information about environmental matters (including the impact of the company's business on the environment), employees, and social, community, and human rights issues.[372] It must also describe the company's strategy, its business model, and a break-down of the number of persons of each sex who were directors of the company, who were senior managers of the company, and who were employees of the company.[373]

The strategic report of traded companies, banking companies, insurance companies, and companies carrying on insurance market activity with more than 500 employees must contain a non-financial statement.[374] This must include information, to the extent

---

[364] ibid Schedule 7 para 11B.
[365] ibid Schedule 7 para 13.
[366] ibid Schedule 7 para 15.
[367] CA 2006, s 419(1).
[368] ibid s 419(3) and (4).
[369] ibid s 414A and 414B.
[370] ibid s 414C(2).
[371] ibid s 414C(3).
[372] ibid s 414C(7); the term 'quoted company' which is wider than the term 'listed companies'. In addition to companies whose equity shares have been included in the official list according to the provisions of Part 6 of the Financial Services and Markets Act 2000 (c 8) it also includes companies which are officially listed in an EEA State, or which have been admitted to the New York Stock Exchange or to Nasdaq (CA 2006, s 385(2) and s 226A(1)).
[373] CA 2006, s 414C(8).
[374] ibid s 414CA.

necessary for an understanding of the company's development, performance, and position, and the impact of its activity relating to, as a minimum, environmental matters (including the impact of the company's activity on the environment), the company's employees, social matters, respect for human rights, and anti-corruption and bribery matters.[375] The statement must also include a brief description of the company's business model, its policies in relation to the matters set out above, and the effectiveness of these policies, as well as a description of the principal risks relating to the matters. These must include a description of the company's business relationships, products, and services which are likely to cause negative impacts in those areas of risk.[376]

The strategic report needs to be approved by the board and signed on behalf of the board by a director or the company secretary. If the report does not comply with the statutory requirements, each officer who knew or was reckless in not knowing that the company did not comply and who failed to take reasonable steps to secure compliance commits a criminal offence.[377]

CA 2006, section 414C(1) states that the purpose of the strategic report is to inform the members of the company and to help them assess how the directors have performed their duty under CA 2006, section 172.[378] The shareholders, however, play no role in the production or approval of the strategic report. They are also unable to exempt directors from the obligation to produce a strategic report or to modify the requirements for its content. This suggests that the strategic report serves more than just the shareholders' interests.

Separate corporate governance statement
A separate Corporate Governance Statement must be approved by the board and signed on behalf of the board by a director or the company secretary.[379] Under the UK Listing Rules a corporate governance statement must contain a reference to the corporate governance code to which the company is subject, the corporate governance code, which it may have voluntarily decided to apply, and all relevant information about the corporate governance practices applied over and above the requirements of national law.[380]

Remuneration report
Directors of quoted companies need to prepare an annual remuneration report which needs to contain information on the directors' remuneration and the remuneration policy.[381] Directors are required to give notice to the company on any matter on which it is required to report. A failure to do so is an offence resulting in a fine.[382]

---

[375] ibid s 414CB(1).
[376] ibid s 414CB(2)(d).
[377] ibid s 419(3) and (4).
[378] ibid s 414C(1).
[379] ibid s 419A.
[380] Listing rule DTR 7.2.2.
[381] CA 2006, s 420.
[382] ibid s 421(3) and (4).

There are regulations that contain highly detailed rules on what information on the directors remuneration is to be included and how it is to be displayed.[383] There is, for example, a requirement to display a table comparing the CEO's pay with the remunerations of UK employees in the twenty-fifth, fiftieth, and seventieth percentile respectively of the pay and benefits of UK employees.[384] The report must also set out the relationship between the remunerations paid to all employees and the distributions paid to shareholders.[385] There are also highly granular rules setting out the content of the remuneration policy.[386]

The remuneration report must state whether, and if so, how the views expressed by shareholders at the general meeting or otherwise on the formulation of the remuneration policy have been taken into account.[387] It must also set out how the company consulted with employees when drawing up the remuneration policy and on whether, and if so, which comparison measures were used.[388]

The report needs to be approved by the board and signed by a director or the company secretary on behalf of the board.[389] If the approved report does not comply with the statutory requirements, every director who knew this, recklessly did not know this, or failed to take reasonable steps to secure compliance commits a criminal offence.[390]

In relation to remuneration the shareholders have greater involvement than in relation to other reports. The shareholders of a quoted company approve the remuneration report.[391] The shareholders are also responsible for approving the remuneration policy.[392] The shareholders are unable to dispense with or modify the reporting requirement set up by the statute.

Conclusions and theoretical observations

It is possible to argue that narrative reporting helps to manage the agency conflict between shareholders and directors. In relation to the strategic report, CA 2006, section 414C(1) explicitly states that its purpose is to inform the members of the company and to help them assess how the directors have performed their duty under CA 2006, section 172. More generally all narrative reports cover topics that directly or indirectly relate to the financial position of the company. In so far as narrative reports are required to include information on ecological and social factors this also serves shareholders. Risks emanating from these areas can affect the prosperity of the company.

---

[383] Large and Medium-sized Companies and Groups (Accounts and Reports) Regulation 2008/410, Schedule 8, paras 6–18.
[384] ibid Schedule 8, para 19A–19G.
[385] ibid Schedule 8, para 20.
[386] ibid Schedule 8, paras 24—33.
[387] ibid Schedule 8, para 40.
[388] ibid Schedule 8 para 39.
[389] CA 2006, s 422.
[390] ibid s 422 (2) and (3).
[391] ibid s 439.
[392] ibid s 439A; see further above section 7.9.

But the statutory requirements cannot be explained by reference to the shareholders' interests only.

The duty to produce narrative reports is owed by the directors to the company rather than to the shareholders individually. They are liable to compensate the company for false or misleading statements in reports and statements. Liability arises for any untrue or mis- leading statements as well as omissions. A director is liable if he or she knew that the state- ment is untrue or misleading, was reckless as to whether it was untrue or misleading, or knew the omission to be a dishonest concealment of a material fact.[393] Compensation is to be paid to the company.[394]

In addition, shareholders are unable to modify or waive the statutory requirements. They are unable to delegate the responsibility to produce the reports away from the directors, or to exempt directors from the criminal liability that is attached to the failure to comply with the statutory requirements.

As is the case with the annual accounts, the Secretary of State can request a revision of the accounts if it appears that there is or may be a question whether the accounts comply with the requirements of the Companies Act.[395] The Secretary of State or any person author- ized by him can apply to court for an order instructing the directors to prepare revised accounts.[396] HMRC may disclose information to a person who is authorized to request a revision of the accounts.[397] Such a person can also apply to court to request disclosure of documents, information, and explanations, from the company, or any officer, employee, or auditor of the company.[398]

All of this suggests that there is public interest associated with the production of narrative reports that are compliant with the statutory requirements.

7.10.5 Duty to have the accounts and reports verified

The annual accounts and sections of the annual reports of larger companies need to be verified for the compliance with the statutory requirements by independent auditors.[399] There is a public expectation that auditors perform or at the very least should perform a general role in preventing companies from experiencing misconduct by the directors or their employees. While some of what auditors do is designed to guard against wrong- doing by the directors, auditors generally play a more modest role. The primary pur- pose of the audit is for the auditors to certify the compliance of the financial accounts

---

[393] ibid s 463.
[394] Liability for civil or criminal penalty is unaffected (ibid s 463(6)).
[395] ibid s 455.
[396] ibid s 456.
[397] ibid s 458.
[398] ibid s 459.
[399] ibid s 475 and s 495.

and certain sections of the reports with the statutory framework.[400] This, however, is a highly debated area and the government is currently consulting on putting in place more onerous duties for auditors.[401]

If a company is exempt from audit the directors must place a statement to that effect above their signature on the balance sheet. That statement must acknowledge the directors' responsibility for complying with the requirements of the CA 2006 with respect to accounting records and the preparation of accounts.[402]

For companies which are required to have their accounts audited, the directors are obliged to set up and support this verification process. In certain circumstances they are responsible for appointing the company's auditor.[403] Otherwise they recommend an auditor to the company's members, with whom the main responsibility for appointing auditors lies.[404] For public interest companies the statutory appointment process is more elaborate. If a public interest company has an audit committee, that committee needs to administer a tender process and make reasoned recommendations to the board of directors.[405] The board need to share the committee's recommendations with the members and give reasons in case they decide to deviate in their own recommendations from those of the committee.[406]

The appointment of auditors is of sufficient importance to the law to involve the Secretary of State. If no auditor has been appointed within the statutory time window or if the appointment of an auditor has been defective the directors need to give notice to the Secretary of State.[407] The notification enables the Secretary of State to exercise his powers to appoint the required auditor himself.[408] Failure to notify the Secretary of State constitutes an offence and triggers liability of the company and every officer in default for a fine.[409] Directors also have important administrative duties in the process of auditors being removed or ceasing to hold office.[410] These, too, are supported to a significant extent with public liability.[411]

To support the audit process the directors are required to give the auditors access to the company's books, accounts, and vouchers.[412] They need to provide auditors and the

---

[400] ibid s 498.
[401] Department for Business, Energy and Industrial Strategy, Restoring Trust in Audit and Corporate Governance, CP 382, March 2021, Chapter 6.
[402] CA 2006, s 475(2) and (3).
[403] ibid ss 485(3) and 489(3).
[404] ibid ss 485(4) and 489(4).
[405] ibid ss 485A and 489A. The definition of a public interest company is contained in Companies Act 2006, s 519A. If there is no audit committee the tender process is operated by the directors (ibid ss 485B and 489B).
[406] ibid ss 485A and 489B.
[407] ibid ss 486, 486A, 490 and 490A.
[408] ibid ss 486(1), 486A(1) and (2), 490(1), and 490A(1) and (2).
[409] ibid ss 486(3) and (4), 486A(5) and (6), 490(3) and (4) and 490A(5) and (6).
[410] eg: ibid s 520(2) (circulating a statement of auditors ceasing to hold office); ibid s 523 (duty to notify the appropriate audit authority if an auditor ceases to hold office); ibid s 511 (administering the requirements for shareholder resolutions removing auditors from office).
[411] eg: ibid s 520(7) and (8) or s 523(4)–(6).
[412] ibid s 499(1)(a).

auditors of their parent companies with such information or explanations as they think necessary for the performance of their duties as auditors.[413] They also have to take reasonable steps to obtain information from overseas subsidiaries.[414] If they fail to comply with these requirements without delay they commit an offence.[415] If they knowingly or recklessly make a statement to an auditor that is misleading, false, or deceptive in a material particular they commit a criminal offence.[416]

The statute gives shareholders a significant role in the audit process. They appoint auditors and have a power to remove them at any time by ordinary resolution subject to special notice requirements.[417] They fix their remuneration and approve permitted limited liability agreements.[418]

Notwithstanding the involvement of the shareholders in general meeting it would be wrong to say that that the audit process serves only them. The rules on auditors are mandatory and to a significant extent fortified by public liability. The shareholders cannot override these. They are also restricted in their ability to agree terms with auditors.[419] It has already been mentioned that the Secretary of State can appoint auditors.[420] In certain circumstances he or she can also apply to court to have them removed.[421] This suggests that there is a public interest associated with the audit process.

In addition, minority shareholders have specific mandatory rights. They can, for example, request an audit for the accounts and reports of a company for which the statute does not require an audit.[422] Minority shareholders of private companies can veto a re-appointment of an auditor.[423] Minority shareholders of a public interest entity have a right to apply to court to have auditors removed if there are proper grounds to do so.[424] Minority shareholders of quoted companies can require the publication of a statement setting out any matter relating to the audit of the company's account.[425] Failure to do so is an offence on the part of the company and every officer in default.[426]

More generally the audit process protects the company rather than the shareholders. Auditors owe their duties to the company and shareholders do not normally have a claim against negligent auditors. Such a claim can only arise on grounds other than company law. This happens, for example, where the auditors have either contracted

---

[413] ibid s 499(1)(b).
[414] ibid s 500.
[415] ibid s 501(3).
[416] ibid s 501(2).
[417] ibid ss 485(4), 489(4), and 510.
[418] ibid ss 492 and 534.
[419] For restrictions on liability agreements see ibid ss 532–38.
[420] ibid ss 486(1), 486A(1) and (2), 490(1) and 490A(1) and (2).
[421] ibid s 511A.
[422] ibid s 476 (no less than 10 per cent of the nominal value of the company's issued share capital).
[423] ibid s 488 (5 per cent of the voting rights).
[424] ibid s 511A(5) (not less than 5 per cent of the voting rights).
[425] ibid s 527 (5 per cent of the voting rights).
[426] ibid s 530(2).

separately to provide services to particular shareholders or where there are special facts allowing the conclusion that the auditors have assumed a duty of care towards them.[427]

In addition to the role assigned to the Secretary of State there is a professional liability regime governing auditors which has in recent years grown in its robustness. These involve sanctions such as reprimands, fines, and also the withdrawal of the license to practice. These are evidence of the public interest component associated with the role of auditors.

There is a great deal to say about the effectiveness of audit and recent reforms are evidence that there has been and very likely continues to be substantial room for improvement. There is no room here to explore the statutory audit process in further detail. It suffices to say that the battle for making the process more effective does not undermine the main point made here. Company law sets up a framework for the operation of an organization in a way that focuses on the company as a separate entity but with a process that integrates a wide range of interests.

7.10.6 Duty to publicize accounts and reports

The accounts need to be sent to every member of the company, to every holder of debentures, and to every person who is entitled to receive notice of the general meetings.[428] If all shareholders agree small companies may share an abridged rather than a full version of their annual accounts.[429] The Companies Act specifies a time limit within which accounts and reports need to be sent.[430] The company and every officer who do not comply in a timely fashion with the requirement to send out the accounts and reports commit a criminal offence.[431]

Every member and every debenture holder can request a copy of the accounts and the reports.[432] If a demand is made and not complied with within seven days of receipt by the company, the company and every officer are criminally liable.[433]

Public companies need to lay their accounts and reports before the general meeting.[434] If this requirement is not complied with, every person who immediately before the end of the period was a director of the company has committed a criminal offence. Liability is strict but a director will not be charged if he or she can prove that he or she took all reasonable steps for securing compliance with the requirements.[435]

---

[427] *Caparo Industries Plc v Dickman* [1990] 2 AC 605.
[428] CA 2006, s 423(1); see also CA 2006, s 431.
[429] Small Companies and Groups (Accounts and Directors' Report) Regulations 2008/409, Schedule 1, part 1, para 1A to 1C.
[430] CA 2006, s 425.
[431] ibid ss 425 and 431(3).
[432] ibid s 431.
[433] ibid s 431(3) and (4).
[434] ibid s 437.
[435] ibid s 438.

Published accounts need to state the name of the person who signed the accounts on behalf of the board. If a copy is published without the signatory's name the company and every officer of the company who is in default is liable on summary conviction to a fine.[436]

The accounts and reports of limited companies also have to be filed with Companies House, through which they can be accessed by anyone.[437] Directors who fail to comply with this duty commit a criminal offence unless they are able to prove that they took all reasonable steps for securing compliance with the filing requirements.[438] In addition the court, on application of any member or creditor of the company, can order directors to make good the default.[439] Companies House can also impose a civil penalty on the company.[440]

The directors of quoted companies need to make them available on the company's website.[441] Failure to do so also triggers criminal liability.[442]

It is possible to argue that the requirement to produce and publicize accounts and reports is a tool designed to enhance the well-being of shareholders, enabling them to exercise their corporate rights in an informed way. After all, the shareholders have a right to receive a copy of the accounts and reports. While this is true, it does not fully explain the law as it stands.

The duty to publicize accounts and reports is owed by the directors to the company rather than to the shareholders individually. Shareholders have a personal statutory right to receive the accounts and reports but that right is against the company rather than against the directors individually.

Moreover, the right to receive copies of the accounts and reports is not limited to shareholders. Debenture holders are also entitled to receive copies. The shareholders are unable to remove the requirement for the accounts and reports to be made available through Companies House. Criminal liability for the failure to file and publish accounts and reports as required is independent of the shareholders. Furthermore, the law enables, in addition to any member, also any creditor and Companies House to apply to court for an order directing the directors to file the required accounts and reports.[443]

The rules governing the production and publication of accounts do more than serve the shareholders' interests. The law acknowledges a public interest component in the availability of standardized financial and narrative information on limited companies for

---

[436] ibid s 433(4).
[437] ibid s 441.
[438] ibid s 451(1) and (2).
[439] ibid s 452.
[440] ibid s 453.
[441] ibid s 430.
[442] ibid s 430(6) and (7).
[443] ibid s 452.

all. The larger the business operated by the company the greater the recognized public interest and the more information needs to be disclosed.

7.10.7 Reports on specific social and environmental matters

Additional reporting requirements are set out in the Modern Slavery Act, the Accounting Directive, the Equality Act, the Finance Act, the Small Business Enterprise and Employment Act, and the Market Abuse Regulation. These will be analysed in this section.

The Modern Slavery Act 2015, section 54(4) requires certain large companies to publish on their website a statement of the steps they have taken to ensure that slavery and human trafficking is not taking place in any of its supply chains or in any part of its own business, or a statement that it has taken no such steps.

Companies which are active in extractive industries or in industries involving the logging of primary forest and whose securities are admitted to the trading of a regulated market must publish a report on payments made to governments for each financial year on their website.[444] Extractive industries are oil, gas, or mining. The aim of this type of disclosure is to help governments of resource-rich countries to implement the Extractive Industries Transparency Initiative (EITI) principles and criteria and to account to their citizens for payments such governments receive.[445] The EITI is an international organization which develops standards to promote the open and accountable management of extractive resources.[446]

The Equality Act 2010 (Gender Pay Gap Information) Regulations 2017 require private and voluntary sector employers in Great Britain with at least 250 employees to publish information relating to the differences in pay between male and female employees on their website.[447] The information must also be published on a website designated for that purpose by the Secretary of State.[448] This information must be accompanied by a written statement signed by a director confirming that the information is accurate.[449]

The Small Business, Enterprise and Employment Act 2015 contains a requirement for certain large companies to report on the payment terms, practices, policy, and performance on their website.[450] The report must describe the company's standard payment

---

[444] LR DTR 4.3A.

[445] Accounting Directive 2013/34/EU of 26 June 2013, Preamble (44)–(53) and Articles 41–48, OJ L 182/19 of 29 June 2013; EU Transparency Regulation 2004/109/EC of 15 December 2004, Preamble (14), OJ L390/38 of 31 December 2004.

[446] www.eiti.org.

[447] Equality Act 2010 (Gender Pay Gap Information) Regulations 2017/172, regs 2 and 15; see also <https://www.gov.uk/government/collections/gender-pay-gap-reporting>.

[448] Equality Act 2010 (Gender Pay Gap Information) Regulations 2017/172, reg 15(2).

[449] ibid reg 14.

[450] Small Business, Enterprise and Employment Act 2015, s 3.

terms, its payment practices and policies, and its performance, by reference to those practices and policies.[451]

The Finance Act 2016, schedule 19 requires UK groups and certain large companies to publish a group tax strategy on their website. This strategy must set out the group's approach to risk management and governance arrangements in relation to UK taxation, the group's attitude to tax planning as it affects the UK, the level or risk in relation to UK taxation that the group is prepared to accept, and the group's approach to dealing with HMRC. The aim is to discourage groups from organizing their business in a way that takes aggressive advantage of the existing legal framework to shift their income outside of the UK. The government would like to discourage groups from systematically applying the law in a way that forces HMRC into costly litigation to recover a fair share of tax.

7.10.8 Sanctions

There are sanctions for the failure to report. Sanctions vary, reflecting the blameworthiness the legislature intended to express. The requirements to report on slavery and human trafficking can be enforced against the company by injunction and a failure to comply with such an injunction constitutes contempt of court which is punishable by an unlimited fine.[452] The failure to report on payment practices is an offence which triggers liability by the company and every person who was a director. A director can avoid liability if they can prove that they took all reasonable steps for securing compliance.[453] The failure to comply with the requirement to publish a tax strategy results in the head of the group being liable for a penalty of £7,500, which increases for a prolonged failure to comply. There is no specific sanction for the failure to report gender pay gap information but the Equality and Human Rights Commission can enforce a failure to comply under Equality Act 2006, section 20.[454]

The reporting requirements set out in this section are not contained in the Companies Act. They nevertheless apply to companies and do not apply to sole traders or other individuals. They aim to encourage companies to reflect on their practices in relation to certain interests and to report accordingly. It is true that shareholders will be interested in this information but the fact that they cannot override the statutory requirements in terms of content and that publication to all is mandatory suggests that the aim is to enable all to engage with companies on the basis of this information. It would be wrong to explain this requirement for publication solely by reference to an agency conflict between shareholders and directors.

[451] Reporting on Payment Practices and Performance Regulations 2017/395, reg 3.
[452] Modern Slavery Act 2015, s 54(11) and Home Office Guidelines: Transparency in Supply Chains, s 2.6.
[453] Reporting on Payment Practices and Performance Regulations 2017/395, reg 8.
[454] Explanatory Memorandum to the Gender Pay Gap Regulations, para 7.12.

7.10.9 Conclusions and theoretical observations

Statute requires company directors to keep accounting records and to annually produce and publish accounts and reports. The respective requirements are set out to a substantial level of detail. Recording, accounting, and reporting requirements increase with the size of the company. Company size also affects the depth and breadth of narrative reports. The larger the company the more information on matters relating to employees, customers, and environmental and social matters needs to be reported on.

This makes sense. It is not difficult for shareholders and other constituencies to informally interact with smaller companies. The larger a company the more useful a formalized process of recording and reporting will be. Moreover, larger companies have a more significant impact on a wider range of constituencies.

The Companies Act 2006 assigns the responsibility for record keeping, accounting, and reporting to the board directors. In addition, the shareholders of quoted companies are appointed to approve the remuneration report. Shareholders of public companies have the accounts and all reports laid before their general meeting.

Record keeping and reporting are mandatory statutory duties. The company articles cannot delegate this responsibility to either the shareholders, or to managers below the board, or to a third-party advisor. They can also not modify the content of the requirements.

Personal criminal liability attaches to the failure of directors to cause the company to keep records and to produce and share the required accounts and reports. It is worth setting out a summary of the respective rules.

Strict criminal liability attaches to the failure of directors:

- to keep accounting records, but a director can defend himself by proving that he acted honestly and in the circumstances the company's business was carried on, the default was excusable.[455]
- to send out copies of the accounts and reports to members and debenture holders;[456]
- to publish accounts without the name and signature of the person who signed these on behalf of the board.[457]
- to publish accounts without the required audit report.[458]
- to publish non-statutory accounts without the required statement indicating that they do not comply with the statutory requirements.[459]

---

[455] CA 2006, s 387; see also s 389.
[456] ibid ss 425, 431, and 432 (failure to send out accounts and reports).
[457] ibid s 433.
[458] ibid s 434.
[459] ibid s 435.

- (of a quoted company) to make available the accounts and reports on the company's website.[460]
- to file accounts and reports with Companies House but directors can exonerate themselves if they prove that they have taken all reasonable steps to ensure compliance.[461]
- (of a public company) to lay accounts and reports before the general meeting, but directors can exonerate themselves if they prove that they have taken all reasonable steps to ensure compliance.[462]

There is also personal criminal liability attached to the failure to ensure that the published accounts and reports comply with the statutory requirements. In this context liability is not strict. A director is liable only if he knew or recklessly did not know that the accounts or reports were not compliant and also if he did not take reasonable steps to ensure compliance.[463]

We have concluded in this section that the duty to keep records and to produce and publish accounts serves the interests of shareholders, but that it would be wrong to explain the law as it stands by reference only to an agency conflict between directors and shareholders.

Shareholders are unable to modify the statutory requirements or to exonerate directors from the respective criminal liability. There are also investigatory powers, which enable the Secretary of State and parties authorized by him to request a revision of defective accounts and reports.

Record keeping and financial and narrative reporting integrate a number of goals. They serves a governance purpose. They enable directors to have available continuous information about the company. The exercise of writing financial and narrative reports also requires directors to annually take stock of where the business of the company stands. In addition, the availability of annual reports provides shareholders with information that helps them to exercise their rights against the company.

Information on employees and social and environmental issues is useful for shareholders. It makes it possible for the shareholders to assume stewardship responsibilities and to exercise their rights, not only in their own short term financial interest, but also with a view to causing companies to act in a sustainable way and for the benefit of society as a whole.

---

[460] ibid s 430(6) and (7).
[461] ibid s 451.
[462] ibid s 438.
[463] ibid s 414 (4) and (5) (annual accounts); s 414D (2) and (3) (strategic report); s 419 (3) and (4) (directors' report); s 422 (2) and (3) (remuneration report).

Accounts and reports need to be shared with individual debenture holders. They are also all publicly available through Companies House and, for quoted companies, on their website. This enables creditors to obtain standardized and verified information on the companies that owe them money.

The public availability of standardized information on companies is also useful for those who are intending either to become shareholders or to lend money to the company. It can help both potential shareholders and creditors to make better-informed investment decisions. This enhances the quality of equity and debt markets but also the quality of consumer and other marketplaces.

Narrative reporting can also integrate wider interests into corporate decision-making. This is done through a strategy that can be referred to as civil regulation.[464] The law identifies a constituent interest that companies should consider in their decision-making process. The law does not tell companies how to do this or in some cases to do anything at all. It requires companies to produce a statement setting out whether, and if so, how they have integrated a particular interest. That puts the ball into the court of the company. It requires the companies concerned to work out how their business relates to the interest concerned. It is a soft form of governmental intervention but it is well suited to organizational decision-making. The hope is that this triggers a process of self-reflection helping companies to onboard the interest concerned in a way that suits their organizational framework best. The publication of the statement facilitates public scrutiny enabling shareholders, creditors, customers, and the general public to review the company's behaviour in light of its own statement. The aim is not only to inform markets but also to encourage companies to actively integrate the interest concerned. The strategy applies to large companies as defined by the respective rules.

It is possible to take the view that narrative reporting is unlikely to achieve much for the wider interests it is designed to foster. Indeed, the Financial Reporting Council (FRC) observed in its recent review of the UK Corporate Governance Code 2018 that many companies simply concentrated on achieving strict compliance with the provisions of the Code rather than giving insight into their governance practices.[465] The risk with using narrative reporting as mechanism is that companies could ignore the encouragement to integrate the topics concerned into their decision-making and revert to producing boilerplate reports. At their worst these requirements could encourage a bureaucratic exercise fuelling an industry of advisors helping companies to tick the required boxes.

---

[464] John Parkinson, 'Disclosure and Corporate Social and Environmental Performance: Competitiveness and Enterprise in a Broader Social Frame' (2003) 3 Journal of Corporate Law Studies 3.

[465] Page 1 of <www.frc.org.uk/getattachment/53799a2d-824e-4e15-9325-33eb6a30f063/Annual-Review-of-the-UK-Corporate-Governance-Code,-Jan-2020_Final-Corrected.pdf>.

7.11 Duty to abide by the statutory distribution rules

7.11.1 Introduction

The directors play an important role in determining the returns that can be paid to shareholders. They recommend the amount of profit to be distributed to share-holders.[466] They are not free to identify that amount, but are bound by the statutory distribution rules. These are currently connected to rules governing the company's annual accounts. A company 'may only make a distribution out of profits available for that purpose'.[467] The profit of a company consists of its accumulated realized profit less its accumulated realized losses.[468] Whether a profit or a loss is realized is to be determined in accordance with 'the generally accepted' principles when the accounts are prepared.[469]

Under these rules a company needs to determine each year if there is a profit or a loss. The profit is calculated by reference to the profit and loss account. If a loss has occurred in one year that loss is recorded in the balance sheet. It is carried forward to the next year. If there are several years of loss these will accumulate and the entry on the balance sheet relating to losses increases accordingly. If the company turns its fortunes around in one year and achieves a profit in that year the company must not distribute that profit. It will be used to reduce the losses that have been carried over from the previous years. A profit can only be distributed when there are either no accumulated losses or when and as far as the profit exceeds the accumulated loss.

For a public company there is an additional requirement. Profit can only be distributed to the extent that its net assets (assets minus liabilities) are larger than its called-up share capital and its undistributable reserves.[470] These companies therefore need to retain more assets than they currently need to balance their liabilities. This is why the share capital and the undistributable reserves are sometimes referred to as a buffer.

The regime for calculating distributions takes into account creditors in two ways. It connects to the accounting rules which require the company to keep a record of all assets and liabilities. Creditors are protected because the accounting rules require a company to keep track of the liabilities they are owed. The liabilities need to be valued according to the regulations made under the Companies Act and in line with the requirement for the accounts to display a true and fair view. In addition, losses from previous years need to be carried forward. A distributable profit only arises if losses from previous years have been compensated and if assets exceed liabilities. Creditor interests thus take priority when the return to shareholders is calculated. This applies to the distributions of dividend as well as to returns of capital.

---

[466] Model Articles (private) para 30(2) and Model Articles (public) para 70(2).
[467] CA 2006, s 830.
[468] ibid s 830(2).
[469] ibid s 830(4).
[470] ibid s 831.

The rules for calculating profit are mandatory. They bind the directors as well as the shareholders. At present the method for calculating profit connects to company's accounts and takes into account legal capital.[471]

The distribution regime dates from a time that predates modern accounting practices. It has been criticized as ineffective. The debate intensified following the introduction of International Accounting Standards.[472] It has gained new momentum when, in a number of high profile insolvency cases, it emerged that companies had paid dividends shortly before their financial collapse.[473] Most recently a BEIS White Paper has recommended that directors prepare a statement confirming the legality of dividends and also confirming that any proposed dividend will not threaten the company's solvency over the next two years.[474] In addition, the government suggests that public interest entities should be required to publish a resilience statement setting out the company's approach to exploring and mitigation risks and uncertainties over the short term, a statement of resilience in the medium term, and a consideration of the risks to resilience in the long term.[475]

These plans supplement rather than replace the existing rules. But even if the government decided to replace the capital maintenance regime to rely on a solvency test, that test also prioritizes the interests of creditors over the interests of shareholders.

It is also very likely that the regime will continue to be mandatory. There is no mention in the recent reports that the shareholders should be enabled to override the statutory distribution rules. It is a fundamental principle of company law that limited liability can only be available if the claims of creditors take priority over return paid to shareholders. The question is not 'if' creditors take priority. The question is 'how' to do this. The argument is about the mechanism that the law should adopt to ensure that creditor claims are prioritized over shareholder claims.

7.11.2 No shareholder approval

We will see below that shareholders cannot authorize, ratify, or otherwise approve of an unlawful distribution.[476] This was the position also at common law where Jessel MR

---

[471] ibid s 836.

[472] Jonathan Rickford, Report of the Interdisciplinary Group on Capital Maintenance (April 2004) (<www.biicl.org/files/916_capital_maintenance_report_-_final.pdf>).

[473] BEIS, Insolvency and Corporate Governance (20 March 2018) <https://assets.publishing.service.gov.uk/government/uploads/system/uploads/attachment_data/file/691857/Condoc_-_Insolvency_and_Corporate_Governance_FINAL_.pdf> page 28-29.

[474] Department for Business, Energy and Industrial Strategy, Restoring Trust in Audit and Corporate Governance, CP 382, March 2021 [2.2.20]–[2.2.23].

[475] ibid [3.1.6]–[3.1.18]; Sir Donald Brydon, Assess, Assure and Inform, Improving Audit Quality and Effectiveness, Report of the Independent Review into the Quality and Effectiveness of Audit (December 2019) <https://assets.publishing.service.gov.uk/government/uploads/system/uploads/attachment_data/file/852960/brydon-review-final-report.pdf> [2.4.4] and [18.0.1]–[18.1.7].

[476] See chapter 8 in this book.

reasoned in *Flintcroft's case* that shareholder approval would not have 'sanctioned' the payment of unlawful dividends.[477]

7.11.3 Liability of the directors

Directors are personally, and it seems strictly liable, if they pay a dividend in excess of the amount shown as distributable on the accounts of the company.[478] If the directors distribute sums as dividends that are larger than the distributable reserves shown on the face of the company's accounts the directors are personally liable to repay these. It is no defence in such circumstances that the company would have been able to show a profit if the company had caused its subsidiaries, which had distributable reserves, to pay these up.[479] Directors are also liable if they make a distribution relying on accounts for which they have not yet received a full report by the auditors.[480]

If the directors distribute as a dividend an amount that is equal to or smaller than the amount shown as distributable on the accounts and if it later emerges that the accounts were inaccurate, we need to distinguish. Directors are personally, and it seems again, strictly liable if they knew of the inaccuracy of the entries on the accounts.[481] They are also liable if they ought to have known that the accounts were misleading.[482] This is to be judged according to the modern standard for the duty of skill and care.[483]

Directors who prepare accounts with reasonable care and cause them to be audited can therefore rest assured that they do not incur liability if they proceed to pay out as dividends and amount equal to or smaller than the distributable reserves shown on these accounts. In this context being able to show that they have relied on the advice of accounting and legal professionals will assist directors to show that they took reasonable

---

[477] *Re Exchange Banking Co, Flintcroft's Case* (1882) 21 ChD 519, 533 (Jessel MR); see also *Precision Dippings Ltd v Precision Dippings Marketing Ltd* [1986] Ch 447; *Allied Carpets Group Plc v Nethercott* [2001] BCC 81; *In re Burnden Holdings, Hunt v Fielding* [2019] EWHC 1566 (Ch), [2019] Bus LR 2878, [113] (Zacaroli J).

[478] *In Re Marini* [2003] EWHC 334 (Ch), [2004] BCC 172, [36] and [43] where the directors were liable for the amount paid in excess of the amount shown as distributable on the accounts; see also *Re Ruscoe Ltd* (2012) ChD (Companies Court) 07 August 2012.

[479] *Bairstow v Queen's Moat House* [2001] EWCA Civ 712, [2001] BCLC 531 where the directors were liable for the amount paid in excess of the amount shown as distributable on the accounts. See, however, *Auden MacKenzie v Patel* [2019] EWCA Civ 2291, [2020] BCC 316, [58]–[64] where the company had at all times the same two shareholders, who could have caused it to pay a legal dividend. The court concluded in a strike-out application that it was arguable that this could be a defence to a claim against the directors.

[480] *Precision Dippings Ltd v Precision Dippings Marketing Ltd* [1986] Ch 447 where the directors authorized a distribution after they had received an audit report that was not 'unqualified'. It was immaterial that the information they later received about the qualification was not material for the purposes of the dividend.

[481] *Bairstow v Queen's Moat House* [2001] EWCA Civ 712, [2001] BCLC 531 where it was held in relation to the 1991 accounts that the directors knew that they were misleading and could thus not benefit from relief under what is now CA 2006, s 1157; see also *In re Exchange Banking Co, Flintcroft's case* (1882) 21 Ch 519 (CA).

[482] *Dovey v Corey* [1901] AC 477.

[483] *In re Burnden Holdings (UK), Hunt v Fielding* [2019] EWHC 1566 (Ch), [2019] Bus LR 2878, [148] and [157]–[159]; see also *Revenue and Customs Commissioners v Holland* [2010] UKSC 51, [2010] 1 WLR 2793 where it was held *obiter* that Mr Holland, had he been found to have been a de facto director, would have been considered liable for dividends paid after he had received advice from counsel that the tax position adopted by the company was untenable. The court at first instance identified this date as being the 18 August 2004 and allowed for a short grace period of reflection which came to an end on 22 August 2004.

care in the preparation of the accounts.[484] The courts also appreciate that 'reasonable business people and accountants differ over the degree of accuracy and comprehensiveness, and that there may be more than one view of a financial position, any of which could be described as true and fair'.[485]

7.11.4 Liability of the shareholders

A shareholder must return a dividend that he or she has received if, at the time of the distribution, he or she knows or has reasonable grounds for believing that the distribution is unlawful.[486] A dividend has most recently been characterized as a transaction that can be set aside under the Insolvency Act 1986, section 423.[487]

7.12 Theoretical observations

The Companies Act 2006 installs the constitution of the company as the source of the power of the directors. That constitution is adopted by the shareholders. But they are not free to determine its content. The Companies Act has put in place restrictions limiting the shareholders' freedom to set the terms upon which companies operate. This is supplemented by Listing Rules for listed companies. It is also supplemented by the Takeover Code. Through these statutory interventions the interests of creditors and the public market are woven into the foundational document of the company.

The courts derive their analysis from an interpretation of the constitution. This involves an interpretation of the scope of the power. It also involves an analysis of what the purpose of the respective power is in light of the constitutional setup of the company.

The directors owe all of their duties to the company rather than to the shareholders. They need to abide by the constitution of the company. They are required to promote the success of the company. They need to put in place adequate procedures keeping abreast with financial information about the company, supervising delegated responsibility and ensuring compliance with regulatory requirements. They also need to follow the procedures associated with managing their own conflicts of interest in both

---

[484] *In re Burnden Holdings (UK), Hunt v Fielding* [2019] EWHC 1566 (Ch), [2019] Bus LR 2878, [139] and [158]; *Dovey v Corey* [1901] AC 477.

[485] *In re Burnden Holdings (UK), Hunt v Fielding* [2019] EWHC 1566 (Ch), [2019] Bus LR 2878, [201]–[202] endorsing the 'almost iconic' opinions written by Leonard Hoffmann QC and Mary Arden (as they then were) and later updated by Martin Moore QC on the True and Fair Concept (available from <www.frc.org.uk/accountants/accounting-and-reporting-policy/true-and-fair-concept>); see also *BTI 2014 LLC v Squana SA* [2019] EWCA Civ 112, [2019] 1 BCLC 347 where the court concluded that the directors had acted reasonably in valuing a long-term liability.

[486] CA 2006, s 847; *It's a Wrap (UK) Ltd v Gula* [2006] EWCA Civ 544, [2006] 2 BCLC 634 and *Precision Dippings Marketing Ltd* [1986] Ch 477; for a critique of this see Jennifer Payne, 'Unjust Enrichment, Trusts and Recipient Liability for Unlawful Dividends' (2003) 119 Law Quarterly Review 583.

[487] *BTI 2014 LLC v Sequana SA* [2019] EWCA Civ 112, [2019] BCC 631.

transactions they enter into with the third parties and in transactions they enter into with the company. Directors need to maintain accounting records and produce annual financial and narrative reports. They are required to apply mandatory rules to determine if the company has a profit that can be distributed to the shareholders.

From a theoretical perspective we have observed that the courts primarily protect the corporate process rather than any particular economic interest. The interests of the shareholders, creditors, and other participants are only indirectly protected. We have also seen that the shareholders are the primary indirect beneficiaries of the rules governing directors' duties. They are, however, not the exclusive beneficiaries. The law integrates creditor interests and also wider societal interests into the duties imposed on directors. Notably, creditor interests take priority when it comes to distribution decisions.

Agency theory has a place in explaining the effects of conflicts of interest on directorial decisions.[488] But the courts have explicitly stated that the directors are not agents of the company or of the shareholders. Characterizing shareholders as agents in an economic sense would, moreover, neglect the nuances contained in the statutory regime and in the case law.

Overall, the law as it stands is best understood as setting out a decision-making process for autonomous organizational action. The directors play a leading role in that process but are bound by considerations relating predominantly to the shareholders but also to a significant extent to creditors and also wider society.

---

[488] See also Paul Davies, *Introduction to Company Law* (3rd edn, OUP 2020) 10–11.

8

The Role of the Shareholders

8.1 Introduction

Shareholders have substantial influence over the company. It is therefore right to conclude that UK company law operates a shareholder-centred model of the company. It will be argued in this chapter that the law nevertheless does not support the conclusion that the shareholders are principals of the company. The law is better understood as serving the operation of an organization and shareholders are best conceptualized as performing a role in the decision-making process of an autonomous organization.

We will see in section 8.2.1 that shareholders set up companies by private action and they can also decide to bring them to an end but that they have to follow the statutory process on formation and winding up. Both processes serve the interests of third parties interacting with the company and are therefore best understood through the theory advanced in this book.

The theory advanced in this book also explains why the shareholders cannot cause the company to opt out of the possibility to amend its articles and why the courts are generally reluctant to restrict the ability of the majority of the shareholders to pass such amendments. The rules allowing for the amendment of the constitution create flexibility and this helps organizations to adapt to changing circumstances (section 8.2.2).

Historically, deed of settlement companies were established without legislative involvement. The governance of these companies was thus determined by those setting them up. The modern law still shows traces of that model. Those setting up companies have some freedom to determine who takes which decisions. But the law no longer leaves the determination of the procedures for corporate decision-making entirely to private acting. We have seen above that there are a substantial number of mandatory rules that limit the freedom of those setting up companies to create their own constitutional model.[1] The Companies Acts have, over the years, created an increasing list of powers that are reserved for shareholders and cannot be delegated to the directors or anyone else. The Companies Act also contains a substantial number of mandatory rules that integrate constituencies other than shareholders into the analysis and that shareholders cannot override. Public companies have experienced a greater level of statutory intervention than private companies.

The source for the allocation of the power between shareholders and directors is the statute in the first instance followed by the constitution as a secondary source appointed

---

[1] Section 6.2 of this book.

Company Law. Eva Micheler, Oxford University Press. © Eva Micheler 2021. DOI: 10.1093/oso/9780198858874.003.0008

by statute to supplement its regime. The statute together with the constitution govern the corporate decision-making process. They assign roles to the different participants. The role of the directors has been examined in chapter 7.

In this chapter we will analyse the role of the shareholders. We will see that shareholders normally appoint the directors and that they have a mandatory power to remove them (section 8.2.3). They also appoint and remove the auditors (section 8.2.5). This serves as evidence that the UK is shareholder-centred (section 8.2.3). We will, however, see that the courts have explicitly rejected the proposition that the directors are the agents of the shareholders (section 8.2.4).

The shareholders are responsible for approving certain transactions (section 8.3). These are: share issues,[2] takeover defences,[3] political donations, provisions made for employees on the cessation of business, and (under the Listing Rules) certain large transactions.[4] They approve transactions between the company and its directors such as certain interested transaction, long-term service contracts, the remuneration policy of a listed company, substantial property transactions, and payments for loss of office.[5] Shareholders can ratify a breach of duty of the directors.[6]

Taken together these powers give the shareholders significant influence over the management of the company. The rights of shareholders are, however, also subject to constraints. These constraints operate for the benefit of minority shareholders and creditors.

Minority shareholders are protected through the pre-emption rights and valuation rules, which operate when the company issues shares.[7] They are protected by the unfair prejudice remedy through which the courts review transactions between the company and its majority shareholders.[8] Companies Act 2006 (CA 2006), section 239 assists minority shareholders by preventing shareholders, who are also directors, from ratifying their own wrongdoing.

The interests of creditors are integrated into the decisions of shareholders by the rule prohibiting disguised returns of capital. This rule operates when a company enters into a transaction with a shareholder. It prevents such transactions from operating as vehicles to pay returns to shareholders in circumstances where there is no distributable profit.[9] Creditors are also protected through the mandatory requirements that the law has established for corporate reporting. The shareholders cannot modify the rules governing the valuation of assets and liabilities.[10] They can also not override the rules

---

[2] Section 8.3.1 of this chapter.
[3] Section 8.3.2 of this chapter.
[4] Section 8.3.3 in this chapter.
[5] ibid.
[6] Section 8.3.4 in this chapter.
[7] Section 8.3.1 in this chapter.
[8] Section 8.3.3, Unfair prejudice, in this chapter.
[9] Section 8.3.3, Disguised returns of capital, in this chapter.
[10] Section 8.4 in this chapter.

determining how the directors are to calculate profit.[11] While shareholders have considerable influence in relation to the governance of the company, they are unable to manipulate its ability to pay returns to them.

We will further examine the UK Stewardship Code, through which the government attempts to exercise pressure on institutional shareholders to refrain from requesting short-term return.[12] Finally we will analyse the reflective-loss principle, which restricts shareholders in pursuing damages claims against third parties in circumstances where the company has a competing claim.[13]

This chapter reaches the conclusion that UK company law is shareholder-centred but that it would be wrong to conclude that shareholders are the principals of the directors or of the company. Company law is not designed around a binary conflict between shareholders and directors. It sets up a process that enables an organization to act autonomously of its participants.

We will also observe that at a normative level a good way of integrating interests other than shareholders would be to appoint an individual representing their interests in the corporate decision-making process. This has recently happened in the UK Corporate Governance Code 2018 for workforce interests.

8.2 Constitutional matters

8.2.1 Forming and ending the company

Shareholders decide to begin and end companies. But both the process of forming and ending companies is subject to statutory restrictions. Decisions to form and wind up a company can only be executed through a statutory process that integrates the interests of third parties interacting with the company.

We have seen in earlier chapters that formation is associated with certain formalities designed to facilitate the interaction of the company with third parties.[14] We have also seen that a registered company is not considered void notwithstanding the fact that its formation is affected by fraud or other vitiating defects.[15] It needs to be wound up to be brought to an end.

Along similar lines the shareholders cannot validly agree to informally wind up the company.[16] A company can be ended by a special resolution of the shareholders but that also triggers a process of winding up.[17] It is also not possible for an individual

---

[11] Section 8.5 in this chapter.
[12] Section 8.6 in this chapter.
[13] Section 8.7 in this chapter.
[14] Section 2.5 in this book.
[15] See section 2.5 and section 6.3.2 in this book.
[16] *MacPherson v European Strategic Bureau Ltd* [2000] 2 BCLC 683.
[17] Insolvency Act 1986 (IA 1986), s 122(1)(a).

shareholder to give notice to a company. This contrasts with the position under partnership law where any partner can terminate a partnership entered into for an undefined period of time by 'giving notice to the other or others of his intention to dissolve the partnership'.[18] An individual member of a company can only cause a company to be wound up if he or she can show just and equitable grounds.[19]

8.2.2 Power to amend the constitution

Every company has a constitution.[20] We have concluded in section 6.3 that the constitution cannot be characterized as a contract and that it can be amended according to CA 2006, section 21 by the shareholders through a special resolution. We will see in this section that the power to amend the constitution can be explained by the fact that company law facilitates the operation of an organization.

The statutory provisions permitting the amendment of the constitution are mandatory. Shareholders can agree in a shareholder agreement to exercise their voting rights in a certain way.[21] But it is not possible for a company to agree not to amend its constitution.[22] It is also not possible for the constitution to altogether remove or restrict the company's ability to alter that constitution.[23]

This mandatory regime enabling the company to modify its constitution can be justified from the theoretical perspective adopted in this book. Companies are designed to run organizations. These have to adapt to the environment in which they operate. This context helps to explain why the law does not allow companies to contract out of the ability to modify the constitution. The rules allowing shareholders to amend the constitution are an essential mechanism through which the formal legal procedural framework of the company can be adapted to changes in their environment.

In addition to giving the company the ability to have the constitution amended through the procedures governing special resolutions, the courts have made available a further vent for flexibility. The *Duomatic* principle, which dispenses with the formalities associated with shareholder resolutions in circumstances where shareholders act unanimously,[24] also applies to shareholder decisions intending to amend the constitution. In *Cane v Jones* it was held that principle applied to an agreement amending the articles

---

[18] Partnership Act 1890, s 32(c).

[19] IA 1986, s 122(2)(f).

[20] Companies Act 2006 (CA 2006), s 18; if the first shareholder(s) do (does) not adopt or register a bespoke constitution the Model Articles apply (CA 2006, s 19 and 20) (The Companies (Model Articles) Regulations 2008, SI 2008/3229, Sch 1 (Model Articles for Private Companies Limited by Shares) and Sch 3 (Model Articles for Public Companies)).

[21] *Russel v Northern Bank Development Corporation Ltd* [1992] 1 WLR 588.

[22] *Punt v Symons & Co Ltd* [1903] 2 Ch 506.

[23] *Walker v London Tramways Co* (1879) 12 Ch D 705; see also *Russel v Northern Bank Development Corporation Ltd* [1992] 1 WLR 588.

[24] Section 6.2.6 (above).

notwithstanding the absence of a formal resolution at general meeting.[25] The *Duomatic* principle was also held to apply when the company conducted business in accordance with an amended version of the articles without objection from either shareholder.[26] While formalities can be dispensed with, the shareholders nevertheless need to intend to amend the constitution.[27] In *The Sherlock Holmes International Society* Mark Anderson QC held that evidence was required that there was an intention to amend the articles. It is not enough for there to be a shareholder resolution even if unanimous to conclude that an amendment of the constitution has occurred. A decision that is inconsistent with the articles, even if adopted by unanimous consent, thus does not without more amend these articles.[28]

This requirement for organizational flexibility also goes some way towards explaining why the courts have largely refused to allow minority shareholders to challenge decisions by the majority to alter the articles. At common law a constitutional amendment can be challenged only if the majority has not acted for the benefit of the company as a whole.[29] The barrier established by that test is high. Amendments only fail the test if there is evidence that the intention of the majority approving the amendment was not to promote the interests of the company. If there is no evidence of bad faith the amendment will stand.[30]

On one occasion a first instance judge held that the question was whether an alteration was 'in fact . . . genuinely for the benefit of the company' and concluded that the expropriation of a shareholder 'at the will and pleasure' of the majority cannot be said to be 'for the benefit of the company as a whole'.[31] There is also Australian authority supporting a test that is more accommodating of the interests of minority shareholders.[32]

In the UK, however, this approach has been rejected by the Company Law Review on the grounds that the alteration in the well-known *Gambotto* case was in the interest of the company observing also that the minority shareholder received full compensation.[33]

The judges too have declined to follow *Gambotto* and the most recent decisions have reaffirmed the position stated in *Shuttleworth v Cox*. In *Citco v Pusser* the Privy Council explicitly rejected *Gambotto* as not supported by English authority.[34] Lord Hoffmann

---

[25] *Cane v Jones* [1981] 1 All ER 533 see also *Re Sherlock Holmes International Society Ltd* [2016] EWHC 1076 (Ch), [2017] 2 BCLC 14, para 61—but there was no express agreement in *Sherlock*.

[26] *Re Home Treat Ltd* [1991] BCLC 705 cited in *Re Sherlock Holmes International Society Ltd* [2016] EWHC 1076 (Ch), [2017] 2 BCLC 14, para 63.

[27] See also *Dixon v Blindley Health Investments Ltd* [2015] EWCA Civ 1023, [2016] 4 All ER 490 (108) where doubt was expressed if the *Duomatic* principle can apply when some shareholders are represented by proxies held by other shareholders.

[28] *Re The Sherlock Holmes International Society Ltd* [2016] EWHC 1076 (Ch), [2017] 2 BCLC 14.

[29] *Allen v Gold Reefs of West Africa Ltd* [1900] 1 Ch 656.

[30] ibid; *Shuttleworth v Cox Brothers and Co (Maidenhead) Ltd* [1927] 2 KB 9.

[31] *Dafen Tinplate Co Ltd v Llanelly Steel Co* (1907) Ltd [1920] 2 Ch 124, 141-42.

[32] *Peters' American Delicacy Co Ltd v Heath* (1939) 61 CLR 457 (High Court of Australia); *Gambotto v WPC Ltd* (1995) 182 CLR 432 (High Court of Australia).

[33] Sarah Worthington, *Sealy and Worthington's Texts and Materials on Company Law* (11th edn, OUP 2016) 241; CA 2006, s 979, which provides that a majority shareholder of 90 per cent has a right to buy out the minority, makes the decision in *Gambotto* obsolete.

[34] *Citco Banking Corporation NV v Pusser's Ltd* [2007] UKPC 13 [19]–[20] (Lord Hoffmann).

went on to assert the rule that the court is only justified to interfere in light of evidence impugning the honesty of shareholders or where the proposed amendment was so unreasonable that no reasonable shareholder could consider it beneficial to the company.[35] In *Charterhouse Capital Ltd* the Court of Appeal held that an amendment will stand unless there is 'evidence of bad faith or improper motive' and that it was sufficient that 'a reasonable person would have thought' that an amendment was 'in the company's interest'.[36]

From the perspective of this book it is worth observing that the ability of the company to amend its constitution provides it with the flexibility it needs to serve as the legal anchor for the operation of an organization. This can also help to explain why the shareholders cannot cause the company to contract out of the rules allowing for the amendment of the constitution.

8.2.3 Power to appoint and remove directors

The Companies Act 2006 does not regulate how directors are appointed. The Act only states that a public company needs to have two directors and a company secretary and that a private company only requires one director.[37]

It is therefore for the shareholders to determine in the constitution how directors are to be appointed. The Companies (Model Articles) Regulations 2008 state that the directors are appointed either by an ordinary resolution of the shareholders or by a decision of the directors.[38] The general meeting of a public company can only appoint two or more directors through a single resolution after a resolution that such a single resolution can be passed has been adopted by the meeting.[39] In addition the UK Corporate Governance Code 2018 recommends that listed companies engage with the workforce by one or a combination of the following methods: a director appointed from the workforce, a formal workforce advisory panel, or a designated non-executive director.[40] This constitutes a method for integrating employee interests into corporate decision-making. Employee interests are personified through the creation of a particular role representing these interests on the board. It would, of course, be possible to integrate the interests of other stakeholders in the same way.[41]

---

[35] ibid [16] (Lord Hoffmann).
[36] *Re Charterhouse Capital Ltd* [2015] EWCA Civ 536, [2015] BCC 574, [65] and [90]; see also *Staray Capital Ltd v Yang (aka Stanley)* [2017] UKPC 43 [34].
[37] CA 2006, s 154.
[38] Companies (Model Articles) Regulations 2008, No 3229, Model Articles (private) reg 17; Model Articles (public) reg 20.
[39] CA 2006, s 160.
[40] UK Corporate Governance Code 2018, provision 5.
[41] Irene-Marie Esser and Iain MacNeil, 'Disclosure and Engagement: Stakeholder Participation Mechanisms' (2019) 30 European Business L Rev 201; Benedict Sheehy, 'Sustainability, Justice and Corporate Law: Redistributing Corporate Rights and Duties to Meet the Challenge of Sustainability' [2021] EBOR, forthcoming, available at SSRN: https://ssrn.com/abstract=3829319.

According to the Model Articles, directors of a public company must retire at the first annual general meeting of the company. At every subsequent annual general meeting any directors who have been appointed by the directors since the last AGM or who were not appointed or reappointed at one of the two preceding AGMs must retire from office.[42] The UK Corporate Governance Code 2018 recommends annual re-election of all directors.[43]

The articles can provide additional rules governing the retirement of directors. An illustration of this can be found in *Stobart Group v Tinkler*.[44] In that case the articles contained a provision enabling a director to be removed from office at the unanimous request of his co-directors.

Following a recommendation by the Cohen Committee in 1945 the Companies Act contains a mandatory rule permitting the shareholders to remove a director by ordinary resolution at any point in time.[45] This rule can now be found in CA 2006, section 168. A company may by ordinary resolution at a meeting remove a director before the expiration of his period of office. This right is not limited to particular reasons, but special procedures apply giving the director concerned a right to be heard on the resolution at the meeting. There is also a requirement for special notice for this meeting and the director concerned is entitled to receive a copy of the notice of the meeting.[46] This power to remove a director is mandatory. Neither the articles nor a contract between the company and the director can override it.[47] The power can also not be delegated to other directors or any other committee that may exist within the company.[48] The articles can contain additional powers for removing directors but may not modify the power of members to remove a director by way of ordinary resolution.[49]

The ability of shareholders to remove directors at any point is a factor supporting the conclusion that the UK operates a shareholder-centred model of the company. Removal rights constitute a powerful mechanism ensuring accountability to a particular constituency. In the context of constitutional law, for example, Sir Karl Popper has argued that the right to remove is more important than the right to appoint a holder of power.[50]

8.2.4 Directors are not agents of the shareholders

Because the shareholders are responsible for adopting and amending the constitution, historically one salient question has been whether the shareholders can revoke the

---

[42] Model Articles (public) reg 21.
[43] UK Corporate Governance Code, provision 18.
[44] *Stobart Group v Tinkler* [2019] EWHC 258 (Com).
[45] Report of the Committee on Company Law Amendment (Cohen Report 1945) (Cmd 6659) [130].
[46] CA 2006, s 169.
[47] ibid s 168(1).
[48] ibid s 168(1) requires the power to be exercised 'at a meeting'.
[49] Simon Mortimore, *Company Directors* (3rd edn, OUP 2017) para 1.05 and 1.41.
[50] Sir Karl Popper, 'The Open Society and its Enemies Revisited' The Economist 23 April 1988, 25.

power of the directors to manage the company at their discretion and whether they are able to do this by way of the default simple majority requirement. In an agency model the answer to that is straightforward. The principal instructing an agent can at any time remove authority from his agent. It is possible to modify this by contract. Estate agents, for example, sometimes use terms binding vendors for a certain period of time. If no such clause is contained in the contract, however, the power of an agent can be revoked at the discretion of the principal.

Company law operates on a different approach. The constitution sets out the procedures that govern decision-making. The courts do not conceive shareholders as principals or directors as agents. They do not focus on any one interest group but construe the words of the constitution to determine the powers and rights of the respective parties in front of them.[51] As we have discussed the constitution is adopted and amended by the shareholders.[52] But this does not give them any special status beyond what is contained in the constitution that they have adopted from time to time.

An early landmark case in this context is *Ilse of White Railway Company v Tahourdin*.[53] The case concerned a statutory company.[54] The company's constitution was supplemented by the Companies Clauses Consolidation Act 1845.[55] Section 90 of the 1845 Act qualified the power of the directors through the following words: 'the exercise of all such powers shall be subject also to the control and regulation of any general meeting specially convened for the purpose'. This justified the conclusion that the directors were subject to instructions issued by decisions taken in such a shareholder meeting.[56] The case shows that there was a time when the default position was that shareholders had a power to give instructions to directors by way of simple majority in matters of general management of the company.[57]

The position in relation to registered companies developed from the decision in *Automatic Self Cleansing v Cuninghame*.[58] In that case there was no provision in the articles enabling the majority of the shareholders to instruct the directors.[59] Nevertheless a simple majority of the shareholders issued an instruction to the directors to sell the assets to another company incorporated for that purpose.

Confirming the decision at first instance, the Court of Appeal held that this was a matter to be decided by way of interpreting the articles. These contained a rule that the powers of the directors to manage the company were 'subject . . . to the provisions of the statutes and of these presents, and to such regulations, not being inconsistent with these

---

[51] Section 7.3 in this book.
[52] Section 8.2.2 in this chapter.
[53] *Ilse of White Railway Company v Tahourdin* (1884) LR 25 ChD 320.
[54] ibid 335 (Fry LJ).
[55] ibid 326 (Kay J).
[56] ibid 331–32; see also 335 (Fry LJ).
[57] Alan Dignam and John Lowry, *Company Law* (9th edn, OUP 2016) para 13.4.
[58] *Automatic Self Cleansing v Cuninghame* [1906] 2 Ch 24.
[59] ibid 46 (Cozens-Hardy LJ). Another important qualification is that the case only decided that no injunction was to be granted preventing the shareholders from calling the meeting.

presents, as may from time to time be made by extraordinary resolution'.[60] There was also a clause providing for the removal of the directors by special resolution.[61]

Counsel for the majority shareholders advanced the argument that the directors were subject to the general rule that agents must obey the directions of their principal. The company 'does not part with its powers by delegating them to its directors'.[62] His point was that the company was the principal and so can revoke the delegation contained in the articles at any time and in the normal way through an ordinary shareholder resolution. This argument assumes that standard agency principles apply to the delegation contained in the articles. It also assumes that the shareholders either 'are' the company or alternatively that they represent the company and either way that they do so by way of ordinary resolution.

The court did not follow this argument. Collins MR reasoned that there was

> no doubt [that] for some purposes directors are agents. For whom are they agents? You have, no doubt, in theory and law, one entity, the company, which might be a principal, but you have to go behind that when you look to the particular position of directors. . . . If the mandate of the directors is to be altered, it can only be under the machinery of the memorandum and articles themselves.[63]

Cozens-Hardy LJ held that this was not a case where 'you have a master on the one side and a mere servant on the other'.[64] 'You are dealing here . . . with parties having individual rights as to which there are mutual stipulations for their common benefit'.[65]

In *Salmon v Quin Axtens* the Court of Appeal and the House of Lords confirmed the decision in *Automatic Self Cleansing*. The substantive judgments are delivered at the level of the Court of Appeal. These demonstrate that the judges' primary objective is the enforcement of the constitution. They show that the shareholders are bound by the constitution as much as the directors are and that they are not to be considered to be the principals of the company.

In the Court of Appeal Farewell LJ wrote:

> The directors are not servants to obey the directions given by the shareholders as individuals; they are not agents appointed by and bound to serve the shareholders as their principals. They are persons who may by the regulations be entrusted with the control of the business, and if so entrusted they can be dispossessed from that control only by the statutory majority which can alter the articles. Directors are not, I think, bound to comply with the directions even of all the corporators acting as individuals.[66]

---

[60] ibid 35.
[61] ibid 35.
[62] ibid 37.
[63] ibid 42–43.
[64] ibid 45.
[65] ibid 45.
[66] *Salmon v Quin & Axtens* [1908] 1 Ch 311 at 319.

In *Shaw v Shaw* we find dicta that explain that the constitution is strictly enforced by law because it serves as a framework for autonomous organizational action. Greer LJ wrote:

> A company is an entity distinct alike from its shareholders and its directors. Some of its powers may, according to its articles, be exercised by directors and certain other powers may be reserved for shareholders in general meeting . . . The only way in which the general body of shareholder can control the exercise of the powers vested by the articles in the directors is by altering the articles, or, if opportunity arises under the articles, by refusing to re-elect the directors of whose actions they disapprove. They cannot themselves usurp the powers which by the articles are vested in the directors any more than the directors and usurp the powers vested by the articles in the general body of the shareholders.[67]

Along similar lines Slesser LJ mentioned: 'If the . . . directors had power under the articles to bring [an] . . . action, I do not see how the shareholders could interfere with that power, otherwise than by altering the articles which they have not proposed to do.'[68] The proper procedure is for the shareholders to amend the articles first and then to proceed to give instructions on the basis of the amended version.

Automatic Self Cleansing v Cuninghame over time came to stand for the proposition that 'directors, within their management powers, may take decisions against the wishes of the majority of shareholders, and indeed that the majority of shareholders cannot control them in the exercise of these powers while they remain in office'.[69]

The modern position is that the Model Articles contain a provision whereby the shareholders by way of special resolution can give directions to the directors. The position continues to be that no residual power rests with the shareholders.[70] The position is different when the board is unable to act, is deadlocked, or has ceased to exist.[71]

From a theoretical perspective the analysis in this subsection supports a real entity rather than an agency model of the company. The first shareholder(s) adopt(s) the articles by private action, but then the articles become the constitution of the company. That constitution determines the organizational structure of the company. It allocates decision-making power between the different organs and receives protection of the law in that capacity. The constitution is a document with rules that reflect a balance of various interests and considerations. Its rules work together to create procedures which govern how decisions are made. That procedural framework characterizes how the company operates and is thus protected by the law.

---

[67] *Shaw v Shaw* [1935] 2 KB 113 at 134 (Greer LJ).
[68] ibid 143.
[69] *Howard Smith v Ampol* [1974] AC 821 at 837 E (Lord Wilberforce); most recently *AS (Nominees) Ltd v Nottingham Forest FC Plc* 5 April 2001 para 39.
[70] Brenda Hannigan, *Company Law* (5th edn, OUP 2018) para 9–5.
[71] ibid para 9–5.

From a theoretical perspective we can observe that the courts have explicitly held that the shareholders are not principals of the directors and the directors are not agents of the shareholders.

8.2.5 Power to appoint and remove auditors

We have seen above that the directors are responsible for keeping records, producing reports, and ensuring that these are audited.[72] Shareholders are responsible for the appointment and removal of auditors.[73] They also approve permitted limited liability agreements.[74] This influence of the shareholders in the statutory reporting process constitutes further evidence that the UK operates a shareholder-centred model of the company.

8.3 Managing the company

In this section we will analyse the influence of shareholders over the management of the company. We will see that the shareholders have significant influence over a number of management decisions but that they are also subject to constraints. These constraints operate for the benefit of minority shareholders and creditors. This supports the conclusion that it would be wrong to characterize the shareholders as the principals of the directors or of the company. Their interests bend to minority interests and creditor rights.

8.3.1 Issuing shares

Introduction
The allocation of the power to issue shares was once a matter for the articles and shareholders were free to determine how new shares were going to be issued. They could, for example, give an unfettered power to issue new shares to the directors. The early landmark cases establishing the proper purpose doctrine were decided during that time.[75]

This is no longer the case. The Companies Act has intervened to restrict the ability of the constitution to determine how decisions to issue shares are taken. The model on which the proper purpose doctrine developed has only been adopted for private companies with only one class of shares. Their directors are permitted to issue further shares of that class. The shareholders can remove this power in the articles.[76]

---

[72] Section 7.10 in this book.
[73] CA 2006, ss 485, 489, and 510.
[74] ibid ss 534–36.
[75] See section 7.3 in this book.
[76] CA 2006, s 550(b).

For all other companies the articles or a shareholder resolution can only give limited power to the directors to issue shares. The date at which the authorization expires must not be more than five years from the date of incorporation or from the date on which the resolution which contains the authorization is passed.[77] The authorization can be renewed but only for a period not exceeding five years.[78] It can also be revoked or varied at any time by ordinary rather than by special resolution.[79] The shareholders must state a maximum amount of shares that may be allotted under a power enabling the directors to issue shares.[80] Compared to the rules in equity the statute insists on a more granular level of shareholder oversight of the power to issue shares.

In addition, the Companies Act 2006 also contains rules designed to protect minority shareholders. These will be examined in the next sections.

Pre-emption rights

There are now statutory rules on pre-emption rights.[81] These allow minority shareholders to participate in share issues with a view to preserving their relative influence in the company. They were introduced in the Companies Act 1980.[82] Pre-emption rights arise when ordinary shares are issued, when rights are issued that can be converted into ordinary shares, and when the company sells treasury shares.[83] The shareholders must not authorize the directors to allot such securities to anyone unless the company has made an offer to each existing ordinary shareholder 'on the same or more favourable terms' and in 'proportion to those securities that is as nearly as practicable equal to the proportion in nominal value' of the ordinary share capital of the company held by that shareholder.[84] The shareholder concerned can transfer the right to receive these shares to someone else.[85] This enables shareholders who are not interested in taking up a pre-emption offer to realize the monetary value associated with that offer. There are also mandatory requirements instructing the company to make pre-emption offers either in hard copy or in electronic form.[86] The rules do not apply to bonus shares, to issues where the consideration is paid wholly or partly otherwise than in cash, and when the allotment occurs pursuant to an employee share scheme.[87]

Pre-emption rights are mandatory for public companies.[88] The shareholders of such companies can only modify the pre-emption provisions if they have issued more than

---

[77] ibid s 551(3)(b).
[78] ibid s 551(4)(a).
[79] ibid s 551(4)(b).
[80] ibid s 551(3)(a).
[81] ibid s 561.
[82] Companies Act 1980 (c 22).
[83] CA 2006, s 560.
[84] ibid s 561(1); treasury shares held by the company are disregarded for the purpose of calculating entitlements in relation to pre-emption rights (ibid s 561(4)).
[85] ibid s 561(2).
[86] ibid s 562(2).
[87] ibid ss 564–66.
[88] ibid s 567.

one class of shares. In that case their articles may provide that pre-emption rights are granted on a per class basis.[89]

Shareholders of private companies may exclude pre-emption rights either in the articles or generally in relation to an allotment of a particular description.[90] The Model Articles for Private Companies currently do not exclude pre-emption rights. Shareholders wishing to exclude pre-emption rights must follow the statutory rules for amending the articles.

There are also special statutory rules permitting the disapplication of pre-emption rights. For most companies, pre-emption rights can only be disapplied or modified by a special resolution by the shareholders. Moreover, this special resolution may only be granted in relation to a specific allotment.[91] The resolution may only be passed if it is recommended by the directors. Before the resolution is passed the directors must make a written statement setting out their reasons for making the recommendation, the amount to be paid in respect of the shares being allotted and their justification for that amount.[92] This statement must be circulated together with the notice to the meeting.[93] If the resolution is a written resolution the statement must be sent to the member at or before the time at which the resolution is sent.[94]

The content of the statement is protected by CA 2006, section 572. A person who 'knowingly or recklessly' authorizes or permits the inclusion of any matter that is 'misleading, false or deceptive in a material particular' in the statement commits an offence and is liable to imprisonment or a fine, or both.[95]

Less onerous rules apply to private companies with only one class of shares. If the articles of such a company or a special resolution by the shareholders authorize its directors to issue shares, the directors may also be given the power to issue these shares without granting pre-emption rights. This authorization can only be awarded for a period of five years. It can be renewed but not for more than five years at any one point in time.[96]

The directors and majority shareholders of private companies also need to be aware of the rules prohibiting unfair prejudice. It is possible for a share issue to amount to unfair prejudice.[97] The shareholders are unable to isolate themselves or the company from unfair prejudice claims, and so the rules governing unfair prejudice form a barrier that the shareholders are unable to override.

---

[89] ibid s 568.
[90] ibid s 567.
[91] ibid s 571(1).
[92] ibid s 571(6).
[93] ibid s 571(7)(b).
[94] ibid s 571(7)(a).
[95] ibid s 572(2).
[96] ibid ss 570(3) and 551(3)(b).
[97] *Re A Company (No 007683 of 1984)* [1986] BCLC 362 (367); *Sunrise Radio* [2010] 1 BCLC 367 [113]; see also *Clemens v Clemens* [1976] 2 All ER 268 (ChD); It is possible that the unfair prejudice remedy, which did not exist at the time, would have assisted Mr Greenhalgh in his claim against Arderne Cinemas Ltd (*Greenhalgh v Arderne Cinemas* [1951] Ch 286 (CA).

Valuations of contributions in kind

There are also rules governing the valuation of contributions in kind. These are designed to prevent the rights of existing shareholders from being diluted when shares are issued in return for a non-cash asset. Dilution happens when the asset received by the company is worth substantially less than the shares issued in return.[98]

If a public company allots shares for a non-cash asset, the consideration that the company receives for the shares must be valued independently according to CA 2006, section 593.[99] The contract must be approved by an ordinary resolution of the company.[100] A copy of the valuer's report must be sent to the members entitled to notice of the meeting and also to the other party to the proposed transaction.[101] A copy of the resolution must be delivered to the registrar.[102] These rules have been criticized as having little effect while also being administratively burdensome.[103] Post-Brexit the UK is able to remove or relax these requirements. But even if they are deleted from the statute book shareholders will be bound by the case law, which has developed rules in relation to contributions in kind which are also mandatory.

The rules developed in equity currently apply to private companies. A contribution in kind needs to be valued by the company. Under the standard constitutional framework the directors are responsible for a valuation of a contribution in kind. The valuation standard is, however, not onerous.[104] The courts apply what is now CA 2006, section 172 and assume that all is in order, and are reluctant to second-guess the decision of the directors to ascribe a particular value to an asset.[105] The directors need to honestly regard the consideration given as fairly representing the nominal value of the shares in cash.[106] The courts will, however, intervene in a situation where it is clear on the facts that no valuation has taken place.[107] Along similar lines a company cannot for a fixed present consideration validly contract that a certain percentage of shares issued from time to time by the company shall be allotted as fully paid to the contributor of that asset.[108] The court will also intervene if the valuation is colourable or dishonest.[109] Another example is a situation where the company accepts, as payment for shares, debt instruments in circumstances where their value was wholly speculative and that

---

[98] *Pilmer v Duke Group Ltd* [2001] HCA 31, (2001) 207 CLR 165.

[99] *Zavarco UK Plc v Sidhu* [2021] EWHC 1526 (Ch).

[100] CA 2006, s 601.

[101] ibid s 601(1).

[102] ibid s 602.

[103] Eilis Ferran, 'Revisiting Legal Capital' (2019) EBOR 521; John Armour, 'Legal Capital: an Outdated Concept?' (2006) EBOR 5.

[104] It has been pointed out that the low standard associated with the valuation requirement can induce companies that are in want of money and whose shares are unsaleable, except at a discount, to pay extravagant prices for goods or work to persons who are willing to take payment in shares (*Tintin Exploration Syndicate v Sandys* [1947] 177 LT 412 (after the citation of *Ooregum Gold Mining v Roper* [1892] AC 125)).

[105] For an analysis of CA 2006, s 172 see section 7.4 in this book.

[106] *Tintin Exploration Syndicate v Sandys* [1947] 177 LT 412 (after the citation of *Ooregum Gold Mining v Roper* [1892] AC 125).

[107] ibid.

[108] *Hong Kong and China Gas Company v Glen* [1914] 1 Ch 527.

[109] *Re Wragg* [1897] 1 Ch 796.

fact was well known to the directors of the company.[110] The valuation requirement, although not onerous, is nevertheless a mandatory requirement that neither the directors nor the shareholders can override.

The case law relating to the valuation of contributions in kind dates from the late nineteenth/early twentieth century. The current regime for directors' duties is more onerous than it was at the time. In particular, the duty of skill and care now requires directors to operate to an objective standard.[111] It is arguable that in the modern context more than evidence of good faith would be required.

Issues at a discount

There are also rules governing the issue of shares that are intended to benefit creditors. There is a long-established common law rule prohibiting shares to be issued at a discount.[112] An issue at a discount occurs when the company issues shares for less than their nominal value. The nominal values of all the shares issued by the company constitute the company's capital. Issues at a discount are prohibited because the common law assumes that third parties rely on the figure disclosed by the company as capital. The common law further assumed that third parties, when they see that the company has a certain amount of capital, conclude that that it has either received that amount from shareholders already or is entitled to receive it in the future. An issue at a discount would be misleading because the company would signal that it had received more money that it actually had, or is entitled to receive more money than it actually is.

This reasoning has not withstood the test of time and so several proposals have been made to abolish this rule and allow non par value shares,[113] but none of these have been implemented. Most recently the discussion has been revived by the Rickford Report.[114] The Second Company Law Directive (CLR), however, prevented any reform of this rule for public companies and the CLR did not go ahead with reform in relation to private companies. It remains to be seen if the government will make non par value shares possible post-Brexit.[115] It is worth pointing out that while other rules relating to legal capital have significant impact the problem that the share price drops below par can be managed by the use of low par values.

Conclusions

We have seen in this section that the shareholders have certain powers to issue shares and so can exercise influence over the ability of the company to raise finance. These powers are, however, restricted by rules that are designed to protect the interests of

---

[110] *Re White Star Line Ltd* [1938] Ch 458, 478.
[111] See section 7.6 in this book.
[112] CA 2006, s 580; *Ooregum Gold Mining v Roper* [1892] AC 125.
[113] Gedge Committee (Cmnd 9112, 1954), Jenkins Committee (Cmnd 1979, 1962 paras 32–34) and the Wilson Committee (Cmnd 7937, 1980).
[114] Jonathan Rickford, *Report of the Interdisciplinary Group on Capital Maintenance* (April 2004) (<www.biicl.org/files/916_capital_maintenance_report_-_final.pdf>).
[115] Eilis Ferran, 'Revisiting Legal Capital' (2019) EBOR 521.

minority shareholders and also creditors. Of these rules the rules on pre-emption rights and unfair prejudice have more practical significance than the valuation requirements and the no-discount rule. It is nevertheless worth observing, as a matter of principle, that in this area, as elsewhere in company law, the interests of minority shareholders and of creditors are woven into the statute and into the case law.

8.3.2   Takeovers

Another area where we can observe that UK law has a strong focus on the interests of the shareholders is takeovers. The City Code on Takeovers and Mergers ('Takeover Code') requires shareholders to approve actions taken by the directors in defence of a takeover bid.[116] The Takeover Code applies to companies that are registered in the UK and which have any of their securities admitted to trading on a regulated market or multilateral trading facility in the UK. It also applies to companies which are registered in the UK, which have their centre of administration in the UK, and which have had any of their securities traded on a regulated market or multilateral trading facility in the UK during the last ten years.[117]

The Takeover Code sets out rules for both companies that make takeover offers and companies whose shareholders are presented with a takeover offer. The Code is designed to ensure that the shareholders of the target company of the same class receive equal treatment and that they have sufficient time and information to enable them to reach a properly informed decision the bid.[118] The directors of the target company must act in the interests of that company as a whole and must not deny the holders of securities the opportunity to decide on the merits of the bid.[119]

Central to the investigation of this book, we need to discuss the non-frustration rule.[120] During the course of an offer and if the board of the offeree company has reason to believe that a bona fide offer might be imminent that board must not, without the approval of the shareholders in general meeting, take any action which may result in any offer or bona fide possible offer being frustrated or in shareholders being denied the opportunity to decide on its merits.[121] In particular the board of the offeree company must not issue any shares or sell treasury shares, issue or grant options, issue securities convertible into shares, sell, dispose of, or acquire assets of a material amount, or enter into contracts otherwise than in the ordinary course of business unless they have received shareholder approval. These requirements are independent of what the constitution of

---

[116] City Code on Takeovers and Mergers, rule 21 <www.thetakeoverpanel.org.uk/wp-content/uploads/2021/01/25227_008_The_Take_Over_Bookmarked_31.12.20.pdf?v=7Nov2019>; The Takeover Code is underpinned by CA 2006, ss 942–91.
[117] Takeover Code, para 3.
[118] ibid principles 1 and 2.
[119] ibid principle 3.
[120] ibid rule 21.1(a).
[121] ibid rule 21.1(a).

the company provides for and allows or any subjective intentions the directors may have or do not have to interfere with the shareholders' decision on the merits of the bid.

The non-frustration rule applies notwithstanding the fact that the directors have good commercial reasons which support the conclusion that it is in the company's interest to issue securities or purchase or dispose of an asset.[122] It applies irrespective of any rules contained in the constitution of the company concerned.[123] The shareholders cannot insert provisions in the article that undermine this process. They cannot waive these rights in the constitution.[124] The process requires shareholder approval at the time the bid is imminent and not at any point before.

The Takeover Code has a number of aims. One aim is to provide oversight for directors. This aim is highlighted by the proponents of agency theory. They advance the well-known argument that the take-over rules support a 'market for corporate control'. The argument runs as follows. In a takeover situation the directors are exposed to the risk that existing shareholders sell their shares and that the new shareholders remove these directors and appoint their own set of new directors. Anticipating the possibility of their removal the directors of a company have an incentive to promote the interests of the shareholders.[125]

The market for corporate control has been referred to as a tool for disciplining management and reducing the agency costs of dispersed shareholders.[126] It has been characterized as a much more powerful mechanism for the promotion of the interests of shareholders than the law of directors' duties.[127] At a normative level it has been argued that the threat of a takeover makes directors too responsive to shareholders and causes them to act with a view to enhancing shareholder value in the short term. This can have negative consequences for the shareholders in the long term but also for other stakeholders in the company.[128] This book will not engage in the debate on the market for control.[129] We only need to observe here that the theory advanced in this book

---

[122] David Kershaw, *Principles of Takeover Regulation* (OUP 2016) para 11.05.

[123] David Kershaw and Edmund Schuster, 'The Purposive Transformation of Company Law' The American Journal of Comparative Law (forthcoming).

[124] Takeover Code, rule 21.1.

[125] This book will not engage in the debate about the advantages and disadvantages of the board neutrality rule, but see David Kershaw, *Principles of Takeover Regulation* (OUP 2016) paras 11.32–11.38.

[126] Paul Davies and Sarah Worthington, *Gower & Davies: Principles of Modern Company Law* (10th edn, OUP 2016) para 28-1 (with a footnote referring to the fact that the market for corporate control argument is contested.)

[127] ibid para 28-19.

[128] ibid para 28-19.

[129] For this debate see, for example, David Kershaw, 'The Illusion of Importance: Reconsidering the UK Takeover Defence Prohibition' (2007) 56 International and Comparative Law Quarterly 267; Richard Noland, 'The Proper Purpose Doctrine and Company Directors' in BAK Rider (ed), *The Realm of Company Law—A Collection of Papers in Honour of Professor L Sealy* (Kluwer 1998) at 7–13; Paul L Davies and Sarah Worthington, *Gower: Principles of Modern Company Law* (10th edn, Sweet & Maxwell 2016) para 16–46; Andrew Keay, *Directors' Duties* (2nd edn, Jordan 2014) 5.11; US: FH Easterbrook and DR Fischel, 'The Proper Role of a Target's Management in Responding to a Tender Offer' (1981) 94 Harvard L Rev 1161, for board neutrality, directors should remain passive; L Bebchuk, 'The Case for Facilitatng Competing Tender Offers' (1982) 95 Harvard L Rev 1028 proposes a rule that would allow directors to solicit a competing takeover bid as long as that would not thwart the existing bid.

also applies if we assume that such a market exists and that it steers directors towards favouring the interests of the shareholders.

It is further worth noting that the Takeover Code does not stop at requiring shareholder oversight for measures defending a takeover. There are also rules that ensure equal treatment of shareholders. These aim to protect minority shareholders who may not have the bargaining power to look after their own interests.[130]

The Takeover Code also addresses the problem that a takeover offer is disruptive of the normal running of the business of the target company. To minimize this disruption the Code sets a firm timetable. Bidders need to either 'put up or shut up' within a relatively short period of time. The aim is to make a takeover a relatively quick and self-contained event that is not capable of infinite repetition.[131] From a theoretical perspective it is worth observing that this serves the company in priority to its shareholders. Individual shareholders might well be better off with a prolonged battle giving them the chance to receive increasingly higher offers as time progresses.

Takeover law also serves the public interest in the operation of a market in shares. The ability of the directors to prevent the shareholders from selling their shares would interfere with the operation of such a market.[132] The proper operation of such a market has been held to be not only in the interest of individual shareholders but also in the interest of the public. Lord Sumption pointed out that, 'there is not only a private but a significant public interest' in 'the proper operation of the market in . . . shares'.[133]

From a theoretical perspective we can conclude that we have assumed here that the board neutrality rule contained in the current takeover rules is a tool orienting the focus of the directors of publicly traded companies towards the interests of shareholders. It is worth observing nevertheless that the Takeover Code also protects the company as the operator of an organization from disruption, and serves the public interest in supporting an orderly securities market.

8.3.3 Approving transactions

The shareholder focus of UK law is also demonstrated by the fact that shareholders play an important role in approving certain transactions.

---

[130] Paul Davies and Sarah Worthington, *Gower & Davies: Principles of Modern Company Law* (10th edn, OUP 2016) para 28-1.

[131] ibid para 28-2.

[132] This point was articulated from the inception of takeover law in the UK. The Queensberry Rules, which preceded the current Takeover Code, stated that there should be no interference with the free market in shares and securities of companies (Notes on Amalgamation of British Businesses (1959) https://webb-site.com/codocs/UKcode1959.pdf).

[133] *Eclairs Group Ltd v JKX Oil and Gas plc* [2015] UKSC 71, [2016] 1 BCLC 1, [36] (with all other judges concurring).

The Companies Act appoints shareholders to decide on all political donations.[134] They also approve provisions that are made for employees on cessation of the company's business.[135] In relation to listed companies the shareholders need to approve significant transactions that the company enters into with third parties. These are transactions that have passed both certain quantitative thresholds and are outside of the company's ordinary course of business.[136]

Shareholders play a pivotal role in approving transactions between the company and its directors. They are responsible for approving an interested transaction in circumstances where the entire board is affected by that conflict of interest.[137] They approve long-term service contracts,[138] the remuneration policy,[139] substantial property transactions,[140] loans,[141] and payments for loss of office.[142]

The influence of the shareholders in this context supports the conclusion that UK company law is shareholder-focused. It would be wrong, however, to end the analysis with this insight. The shareholders are not free to approve self-dealing transactions. There are rules in place that limit the ability of shareholders to approve such transactions. These apply in circumstances where the directors of the company are also its shareholders and serve the interests of minority shareholders and the interests of creditors. They also apply to corporate groups when members of the group enter into contracts with each other.

Unfair prejudice

Transactions between a company and a director who is also a shareholder frequently occur in private companies. For these the rules prohibiting unfair prejudice are relevant.[143] The courts have paid particular attention to remuneration paid to directors who are also shareholders. The courts stress here too that remuneration is a commercial decision, with which the court will not generally interfere.[144] They nevertheless point out that remuneration decisions by the directors are 'subject to the proper needs of the company to ensure that it is not trading in a risky manner and that there are adequate reserves for commercial purposes'.[145]

In addition, directors must follow the procedures set out in the constitution when determining their remuneration. If they draw remuneration without actually fixing it in

---

[134] CA 2006, s 336.
[135] ibid s 247.
[136] Financial Conduct Authority Listing Rules 10, Significant transactions.
[137] CA 2006, ss 180(4) and 281(3)(a).
[138] ibid s 188.
[139] ibid ss 226B and 226C.
[140] ibid s 190.
[141] ibid ss 197, 198, 201, and 203.
[142] ibid ss 217, 218, and 219.
[143] CA 2006, s 994; Re Blue Arrow plc [1997] BCLC 585.
[144] AMT Coffee Ltd [2019] EWHC 46 (Ch), [2020] 2 BCLC 50, [120].
[145] ibid [141] relying on Re a Company, Ex p Gossop [1988] BCLC 570, [576]–[577] and pointing out that under the Companies Act 2006 unfair prejudice includes conduct that applies to members generally.

accordance with the articles, they need to justify, by reference to 'objective commercial criteria', that the company's dividend policy was reasonable and that the remuneration of the directors was 'within the bracket that executives carrying the sort of responsibility and discharging the sort of duties that they were carrying and discharging would expect to receive'.[146]

A failure to declare dividends in circumstances where the company has sufficient reserves to do so while paying out 'large sums' by way of bonuses to shareholder directors constitutes unfair prejudice.[147] Likewise unfair prejudice occurs when the board substantially increases the remuneration of the company's chief executive who is one of the principal shareholders for 'personal reasons' rather than to 'remunerate him properly'.[148] It is also possible for loans to shareholders to constitute unfair prejudice.[149] This constitutes an improper distribution of profit and prejudices the other shareholders.[150]

Unfair prejudice also occurs if the shareholder directors simply take their own remuneration, only take into account liabilities, and do not direct their mind properly or at all to the company's interest, and if they draw remuneration 'in excess of a fair commercial level of remuneration' (10 per cent of the company's turnover).[151] It can also constitute unfair prejudice if shareholder directors simply 'pile up profit in the company without benefitting themselves' without considering 'how much can properly distributed to members'.[152]

The constitution cannot override CA 2006, section 994. Unfair prejudicial conduct that damages the company can also not be validated through the *Duomatic* principle.[153] The rules developed in this context constrain the ability of the shareholders to approve transactions between the company and its directors. They serve the interests of minority shareholders.

Disguised returns of capital

In this section we will analyse rules that protect creditors and also limit the ability of shareholders to approve transactions of the company. These concern circumstances where a transaction is entered into between the company and a shareholder director or between the company and a shareholder, who is not a director. Historically such payments have been analysed through the lens of the *ultra vires* doctrine, which has always eyed gratuitous transactions with suspicion.[154] In the context of the *ultra vires* analysis,

---

[146] *AMT Coffee Ltd* [2019] EWHC 46 (Ch), [2020] 2 BCLC 50, [121] endorsing *Irvine v Irvine* [2006] EWHC 206 (Ch), [2007] 1 BCLC 349, [267]–[268].

[147] *AMT Coffee Ltd* [2019] EWHC 46, (Ch) [2020] 2 BCLC 50, [144].

[148] *Re Edwardian Group Ltd* [2018] EWHC 1715 (Ch), [2019] 1 BCLC 171, [537]–[542].

[149] *AMT Coffee Ltd* [2019] EWHC 46 (Ch), [2020] 2 BCLC 50, [126].

[150] *Re Edwardian Group Ltd* [2018] EWHC 1715 (Ch), [2019] 1 BCLC 171, [562]–[565].

[151] *Re Blue Index Ltd* [2014] EWHC 2680 [47] and [53].

[152] *AMT Coffee Ltd* [2019] EWHC 46, (Ch) [2020] 2 BCLC 50, [141] relying on *Re a Company, Ex p Glossop* [1988] BCLC 570, 576–77 and pointing out that under the Companies Act 2006 unfair prejudice includes conduct that applies to members generally.

[153] *AMT Coffee Ltd* [2019] EWHC 46, (Ch) [2020] 2 BCLC 50, [180] and [181].

[154] Eva Micheler, 'Disguised Returns of Capital—An Arm's Length Approach' [2010] CLJ 151.

transactions with shareholders have had to meet a more rigorous test than transactions with other individuals.[155] The *ultra vires* doctrine has since been transformed from a doctrine that limits the capacity of the company to a doctrine that shapes the internal powers of the directors.[156] The question arises of how transactions between the company and its shareholders are to be analysed following this development.

One approach is to observe that the *ultra vires* doctrine has always applied to more than just to the now abolished rule that the capacity of the company was limited by its objects. It was also used to invalidate transactions that the company was prohibited from entering into by the Companies Act. Such transactions, too, are 'outside of the powers' of the company and thus can be characterized as *ultra vires*.[157] The reason for the inability of the company to enter into such transactions is, however, not the object clause but the Act itself. In this analysis a transaction where the shareholders receive value from the company without some form of consideration is characterized as a distribution. It offends the principle of company law that return can only be paid to shareholders after creditors have been provided for.[158]

For a company that is a going concern this means that the distribution rules must be complied with. CA 2006, section 830 states that such distributions may only be made out of 'distributable profits'. These are determined by reference to the company's account which need to be adopted formally by the directors.[159] If this is not done a transfer of value to a shareholder amounts to a disguised return of capital. It is illegal because it is not permitted by the Companies Act.[160] Because it is illegal shareholders are unable to ratify it even by unanimous consent.

This approach was adopted by the Supreme Court in *Progress Property v Moore*. Lord Walker stated that a company not in liquidation cannot lawfully return capital to its shareholders except by way of a reduction of capital.[161] 'Profits may be distributed to shareholders but only out of distributable profits computed in accordance with the complicated provisions of the Companies Act.'[162] He also pointed out that this rule now enshrined in statute has a common law basis. 'The common law rule devised for the protection of the creditors of a company is well settled: a distribution of a company's assets to a shareholder, except in accordance with specific statutory procedures, such as a winding up of the company, is a return of capital, which is unlawful and ultra vires of the company.'[163] The rule is essentially 'judge-made', 'almost as old as company law itself, derived from the fundamental principles embodied in the statutes by which Parliament

---

[155] ibid.
[156] See section 3.3 in this book.
[157] See eg *Progress Property v Moore* [2010] UKSC 55, [2011] 1 WLR 1, [15] (Lord Walker) referring to *Rolled Steel v British Steel* [1986] Ch 246, 276–78.
[158] Eva Micheler, 'Disguised Returns of Capital—An Arm's Length Approach' [2010] CLJ 151.
[159] See section 7.11 in this book.
[160] Eva Micheler, 'Disguised Returns of Capital—An Arm's Length Approach' [2010] CLJ 151.
[161] *Progress Property v Moore* [2010] UKSC 55, [2011] 1 WLR 1, [15].
[162] ibid [1].
[163] ibid [15].

has permitted companies to be incorporated with limited liability.' [164] The approach
was also applied by the Court of Appeal in Clearwell *International Ltd v MSL Group
Holdings Ltd*, where the claim failed because it could not be said that the amounts allocated to the directors by agreement were 'clearly disproportionate to the services'.[165]

Most recently, the approach was applied in *Toone v Ross*. [166] The case concerned a
company, which had set up a tax avoidance scheme that HMRC rejected. The scheme
was designed to avoid PAYE and National Insurance Contributions. The case came
before the court at a time when the company was insolvent. Its only liability was the
tax resulting from the re-characterization of the scheme. The claim was brought by
the liquidator. Briggs J applied *Progress Property* to conclude that the payments to the
shareholder directors constituted an unlawful distribution.[167] He examined the parties'
subjective intentions but also considered objective criteria.[168] He also observed that
the payments were distributions that were not supported by 'board minutes identifying
"relevant accounts" or recording a consideration of such accounts'.[169] 'There was an absence of any relevant resolutions'.[170]

It is necessary to devise a test identifying transactions which are characterized as a disguised return of capital. The courts have not articulated a particular test but stress that
they leave a 'wide margin of appreciation' and that they do interfere only because a
bargain turned out, in hindsight, to have been bad for the company.[171] Whether a transaction is characterized as a distribution to shareholders does not depend on what the
parties chose to call it. 'The court looks at the substance rather than the outward appear-
ance.'[172] They also take into consideration the good faith of the directors concerned,
for which an arm's length commercial transaction is referred to as an example.[173] If a
company sells at a low value an asset which is difficult to value precisely but which is
potentially very valuable, the transaction may call for close scrutiny, and the company's
financial position and the actual motives and intentions of the directors will be highly
relevant.[174] Questions may be asked as to whether the company was under financial
pressure compelling it to sell at an inopportune time, what advice was taken, how the
market was tested, and how the terms of the deal were negotiated.[175] While this means
that arm's length transactions will stand, it does not mean that transactions have to

---

[164] ibid [15].
[165] *Clearwell International Ltd v MSL Group Holdings Ltd* [2012] EWCA Civ 1440 [40]–[47] and [51]. The quote
is taken from [47] which quotes from [42] of the decision at first instance.
[166] *Toone v Ross* [2019] EWHC 2855 (Ch).
[167] ibid [7], [73]–[80].
[168] ibid [76] arg: 'was intended to' and 'did act as a conduit through which the shareholders, who were also directors and/or employees of the [c]ompany, were given a tax free sum taken out of the [c]ompany's capital'; see also
[78]–[80].
[169] *Toone v Ross* [2019] EWHC 2855 (Ch) [96].
[170] ibid [96].
[171] *Progress Property v Moore* [2010] UKSC 55, [2001] WLR 1, [24] and [29].
[172] *Aveling Barford Ltd v Perion Ltd* [1989] BCLC 626 (631) (Hoffmann J) endorsed by the Supreme Court in
Progress Property v Moore [2010] UKSC 55, [2001] WLR 1, [1].
[173] *Progress Property v Moore* [2010] UKSC 55, [2001] WLR 1, [29].
[174] ibid [29].
[175] ibid.

meet an arm's length test to be lawful. The courts are not prepared to go as far as to accept that the directors' (proper) subjective motives will always heal the transaction because there may come a point at which, looking at all the relevant factors, an agreement cannot be regarded as involving in substance anything other than a return or distribution of capital.[176]

The payment of interest which was 'grotesquely out of proportion to the principal amounts secured' was thus (*obiter*) considered to be gratuitous (and so unlawful) disposition of the company's money.[177] In *Aveling Barford v Perion* a property was valued at least £650,000. It was sold by Aveling Barford Ltd to Perion Ltd for £350,000. Both companies were indirectly owned by the same person. Perion later sold the property for £1.5 million. Hoffmann J (as he then was) observed that the rule that capital may not be returned is a rule for the protection of creditors, which operates even when a company is not insolvent, and concluded that the transfer was illegal.[178]

Statute has since intervened and CA 2006, section 845 regulates such distributions in kind. These occur when a company sells, transfers, or otherwise disposes of an asset for the benefit of a shareholder. If the company has distributable profits at the time, the amount of the distribution is taken to be the book value of the asset. If the shareholder gives consideration for the asset, the amount of the distribution is calculated by subtracting the consideration from the asset's book value.[179] The effect of this is that a company, which has distributable profits, can sell an asset to a shareholder at book value without having to consider whether it falls foul of the rules prohibiting disguised contributions. Companies which do not have distributable profits do not benefit from the provision.

The boundary between an unlawful distribution and a lawful bad bargain cannot be drawn with precision. There is nevertheless a boundary which operates for the benefit of creditors and which shareholders cannot overrule.

Another method of scrutinizing remuneration paid by the company to shareholder directors would be to apply CA 2006, sections 171 and 172.[180] The argument then is to say that when shareholder directors decide to pay themselves an unreasonable amount of remuneration they have acted outside of their powers. In addition, the fact that the remuneration is unreasonable can serve as evidence that they were not giving consideration to the company's interest and thus have acted in breach of CA 2006, section 172.

This appears to be the approach adopted in *Chalcot Training Ltd v Ralph*. The case concerned a tax structure which was designed to enable the company to avoid corporation tax and PAYE and also to assist the shareholder directors in avoiding income tax.

---

[176] ibid [42].

[177] ibid [17].

[178] *Aveling Barford Ltd v Perion Ltd* [1989] BCLC 626 at 633 (Hoffmann J) endorsed by the Supreme Court in *Progress Property v Moore* [2010] UKSC 55, [2001] WLR 1, [21].

[179] CA 2006, s 845(2)(b).

[180] See also David Kershaw, *The Foundations of Anglo-American Corporate Fiduciary Law* (CUP 2018) 48.

HMRC unsurprisingly challenged this.[181] It proceeded on the basis that the payments to the shareholder directors were 'remuneration'. In response the shareholder directors, who had previously adopted the structure, turned around to unwind the transactions on the basis that they were an illegal return of capital. Against this background Michael Green QC, sitting as a first instance judge, noted that Lord Mance observed that 'the courts will not second-guess companies with regards to the appropriateness or wisdom of the terms of any transaction'.[182] Michael Green QC then observed that the case in front of him was not a sale at an undervalue and so he went back to the cases decided before *Progress Property*.[183] He went on to frame his analysis in terms of breach of duty rather than illegality.[184] He pointed out that in *Re Halt Garage* the company was insolvent.[185] In the case in front of him the company was not insolvent and that it was thus 'open to the directors to reward themselves by way of remuneration rather than dividends and that is what the decided to do because of the huge tax savings they thought they would achieve by doing so'.[186] He also detected that in *Re Halt Garage* Oliver J took into account a 'strong element of subjective intention' of the directors. He identified the question as being whether the 'exercise of the power to award remuneration was done genuinely and in good faith'.[187] On appeal, the decision at first instance was upheld. Lewison LC quoted a paragraph from the first instance decision, where the judge observed that the company did not 'argue that the remuneration was excessive in the sense that a smaller figure would have been acceptable'.[188] It is further worth pointing out that Michael Green QC left room for illegality. He held obiter that there may 'come a point, even in a solvent company, where the remuneration that the directors award themselves is so outlandish that it should more properly be described as a disguised return of capital'.[189] In addition, *Chalcot Training* was an unusual case with shareholder directors insisting on re-characterizing transactions when faced with a challenge by HMRC.

An approach that is based on the duties of the directors also needs to adopt a test that identifies remuneration decisions that constitute a breach of duty. Here too the test has objective and subjective elements. The objective element arises from CA 2006, section 171, which requires a determination as to what the limits of the powers of the directors are. The subjective element arises from CA 2006, section 172 where the question arises of whether the director acted in good faith in what they honestly believed to be in the best interest of the company. Here too it is impossible to identify a bright line. In that sense there is not much of a difference between the two approaches.

---

[181] *Chalcot Training Ltd v Ralph* [2020] EWHC Ch [1].
[182] ibid [139].
[183] ibid [138] and [140].
[184] ibid [150].
[185] ibid [149].
[186] ibid [223].
[187] ibid [156].
[188] *Chalcot Training Ltd v Ralph* [2021] EWCA Civ 795 [32].
[189] *Chalcot Training Ltd v Ralph* [2020] EWHC Ch [132].

A difference emerges, however, when it comes to the ability of the shareholders to sanction remuneration decisions that have not met the required test. While shareholders are unable to ratify illegal transactions, they are in principle able to ratify a breach of duty by the directors. We will see below that CA 2006, section 239 prevents the votes of the shareholder directors who have breached the duty from being counted at the shareholder meeting.[190] If remuneration has been paid to all directors and they are all shareholders the breach cannot be ratified. Under this route it would be possible for ratification to occur, however, if the company has one or more shareholders who have received no remuneration and agree to ratify the remuneration paid to others.

It is submitted here that the distribution rules apply irrespective of whether a company is insolvent.[191] Under the Companies Act 2006 a going-concern company is allowed to reward shareholders only out of a distributable profit and not otherwise. That profit is currently determined by reference to the relevant accounts. This method has come under criticism but still applies. If it is replaced by a solvency test the analysis would remain the same. Creditors are paid first. Shareholders can only be rewarded out of a profit, however that is to be determined. The distribution rules serve creditors and limit the ability of shareholders to approve transactions causing return to be paid to shareholders.

8.3.4 Ratification of breaches of duty by the directors

In addition to approving certain transactions shareholders are able to authorize and ratify breaches of duty by the directors.[192] The views of the majority of the shareholders are also taken into account when courts decide on whether to authorize a derivative action.[193] This demonstrates further that UK law has a shareholder focus.

Here too, however, the picture is nuanced. The Companies Act permits shareholders to ratify breaches and makes it difficult for derivate actions to be brought against the wishes of majority shareholders, but at the same time also restricts the ability of shareholders to design a liability regime to govern directors. The shareholders are unable to adopt provisions in the constitution that protect directors from liability.[194]

---

[190] Section 8.3.4 in this chapter.

[191] See also *Re TXU Europe Group Plc* [2011] EWHC 2072 (Ch), [2012] BCC 363: Newey J did not sanction a scheme because it involved a return of capital to shareholders. This was notwithstanding the fact that creditor interests would not have been prejudiced.

[192] CA 2006, s 239; *Re D'Jan of London* [1994] 1 BCLC 561. In *Multinational Gas & Petrochemical Co v Multinational Gas & Petrochemical Services Ltd* ([1983] Ch 258) it was held that an act authorized by all the shareholders is an act of the company. In *Multinational Gas* the allegedly negligent act was specifically mandated by the shareholders. In *Re D'Jan* neither of the shareholders gave any thought to director's conduct. In my view the *Multinational* principle requires that the shareholders should have, whether formally or informally, mandated or ratified the act in question. It is not enough that they probably would have ratified it if they had known or thought about it before the liquidation removed their power to do so. See *Rolfe v Rolfe* [2010] EWHC 244 (Ch) on the application of the *Duomatic* principle when there is only one shareholder.

[193] CA 2006, s 263(3)(e).

[194] ibid s 232.

There are limits to the extent to which shareholders can authorize an indemnity for directors.[195]

Moreover, shareholders are unable to ratify or authorize their own breaches of duty as directors. CA 2006, section 239 states that a decision by a company to ratify a breach of duty or breach of trust by a director must be made by a resolution of the members of the company. If, however, the director concerned is also a shareholder he and any member connected with him must not take part in the decision-making. He and any member connected with him are also not eligible to participate in a written resolution.[196] He may attend the meeting, but a resolution is only passed if the necessary majority is obtained disregarding votes in favour of the resolution by the director or any member connected with him.[197]

Shareholders are also unable to ratify or approve transactions that are illegal. The sole shareholder and director of an insolvent company or a company that is of doubtful solvency or on the verge of insolvency can thus not authorize his own breach of duty. This is because once the company becomes insolvent the interests of its creditors come to the fore.[198] 'While the company is solvent its interests are normally identified with those of its members. The interests of creditors become relevant if a company has financial difficulties.'[199]

But also, while the company is not near insolvency, creditor interests matter. The rules prohibiting disguised returns of capital also apply here. It was held in *Bilta v Nazir* that 'The only means of a shareholder to extract assets from the company is by a distribution . . . carried out in accordance with s 830 of the Companies Act 2006.'[200] This also applied to a one-person company where a single individual owned all shares and also acted as the sole director. The 'property of such a company also belongs to the company' and not to either its director or its shareholder.[201] The sole shareholder/director is therefore unable to 'use his control of the company to ratify his fraudulent acts against the company particularly where the interests of creditors would be prejudiced'.[202]

The inability of a sole shareholder to ratify his own wrongdoing in general meeting is also not alleviated by the *Duomatic* principle.[203] Even a director who owns 100 per cent

---

[195] ibid s 234; there are also limits on the ability of shareholders to approve limited liability agreements with auditors (ibid s 531).
[196] ibid s 239(3).
[197] ibid s 4.
[198] *Goldtrail Travel v Aydin* [2014] EWHC 1587, [2015] 1 BCLC 89, [114].
[199] ibid quoting from Newy J in *Vivendi SA v Richards* [2013] EWHC 3006 (Ch).
[200] *Bilta v Nazir* [2013] EWCA Civ 968, [2014] 1 BCLC 302, [20] applied by Rose J in *Goldtrail Travel v Aydin* [2014] EWHC 1587, [2015] 1 BCLC 89, [116].
[201] *Bilta v Nazir* [2013] EWCA Civ 968, [2014] 1 BCLC 302, [20], applied by Rose J in *Goldtrail Travel v Aydin* [2014] EWHC 1587, [2015] 1 BCLC 89, [116].
[202] *Bilta v Nazir* [2013] EWCA Civ 968, [2014] 1 BCLC 302, [20], applied by Rose J in *Goldtrail Travel v Aydin* [2014] EWHC 1587, [2015] 1 BCLC 89, [116].
[203] *Goldtrail Travel v Aydin* [2014] EWHC 1587, [2015] 1 BCLC 89, [117].

of a company cannot 'simply take the assets of the company for himself'. [S]uch conduct could not be considered a bona fide distribution of profits and would be a reduction of capital and *ultra vires* of the company without the sanction from the court.'[204]

The interests of creditors are thus integrated into the rules permitting shareholders to authorize breaches of duty by the directors and show that shareholders have significant powers, but rather than acting as principals perform a particular role in company law.

8.4 Accounting records and annual accounts

It has been mentioned that shareholders appoint auditors and fix their remuneration.[205] That gives them influence over who verifies the accounts. Otherwise, however, shareholders have minimal involvement in the production of the company's annual accounts and reports.[206] The format and content of the annual accounts and reports needs to comply with either International Account Standards or UK Generally Accepted Accounting Principles.[207] Shareholders are unable to override or modify these requirements. They are unable to determine how accounting records are kept and how the annual accounts are drawn up. They are largely unable to override the rules governing audit.[208]

The shareholders of public companies will have the accounts and reports laid before the general meeting.[209] All shareholders are entitled to receive a copy of the company's annual accounts and reports.[210] It has been held that the purpose of the accounts is to inform the shareholders about the company's financial position, enabling them to exercise their membership rights.[211]

Notwithstanding the involvement of the shareholders in the general meeting it would be wrong to say that that the audit process serves only them. The rules on auditors are mandatory and to a significant extent fortified by public liability. The shareholders cannot override these. They are also restricted in their ability to agree terms with auditors.[212] We have seen already that the Secretary of State can appoint auditors.[213] In

---

[204] *Ultraframe v Fielding* [2004] RPC 479 [40], applied by Rose J in *Goldtrail Travel v Aydin* [2014] EWHC 1587, [2015] 1 BCLC 89, [117].
[205] Section 7.10.5 in this book.
[206] Section 7.10 in this book.
[207] Section 7.10.3 in this book.
[208] Section 7.10.5 in this book.
[209] CA 2006, s 431.
[210] ibid s 423.
[211] *Caparo Industries Ltd v Dickman* [1990] 2 AC 605.
[212] For restrictions on liability agreements see CA 2006, ss 532–38; section 7.10.5 in this book.
[213] CA 2006, ss 486(1), 486A(1) and (2), 490(1), and 490A(1) and (2).

certain circumstances he can also apply to court to have them removed.[214] This suggests that there is a public interest associated with the audit process.

In addition, minority shareholders have specific mandatory rights. They can, for example, request an audit for the accounts and reports of a company for which the statute
does not require an audit.[215] Minority shareholders of private companies can veto a
re-appointment of an auditor.[216] Minority shareholders of a public interest entity have a
right to apply to court to have auditors removed if there are proper grounds to do so.[217]
Minority shareholders of quoted companies can require the publication of a statement
setting out any matter relating to the audit of the company's account.[218] Failure to do so
is an offence on the part of the company and every officer in default.[219]

More generally the audit process protects the company rather than the shareholders.
Auditors owe their duties to the company and shareholders do not normally have a
claim against negligent auditors. Such a claim can only arise on grounds other than
company law. This happens, for example, where the auditors have either contracted
separately to provide services to a particular shareholder or where there are special facts
allowing the conclusion that the auditors have assumed a duty of care towards them.[220]

In addition to the role assigned to the Secretary of State there is a professional liability
regime governing auditors, which has in recent years grown in its robustness.[221] These
involve sanctions such as reprimands, fines, and also the withdrawal of the license to
practice. These are evidence of the public interest component associated with the role
of auditors.

There is a great deal to say about the effectiveness of audits, and recent reform proposals
are evidence that there has been and very likely continues to be substantial room for
improvement. There is no room here to explore the statutory audit process in further
detail.[222] It suffices to say that the battle for making the process more efficient does not
undermine the point made here. Company law sets up a framework for the autonomous operation of an organization in a way that gives that organization separate legal
statues with a process that emphasizes the interests of the shareholders but that also integrates the interests of minority shareholders, creditors, and the public.

---

[214] ibid s 511A.
[215] ibid s 476 (no less than 10 per cent of the nominal value of the company's issued share capital).
[216] ibid s 488 (5 per cent of the voting rights).
[217] ibid s 511A(5) (not less than 5 per cent of the voting rights).
[218] ibid s 527 (5 per cent of the voting rights).
[219] ibid s 530(2).
[220] *Caparo Industries Ltd v Dickman* [1990] 2 AC 605.
[221] Financial Reporting Council (FRC), Recent Enforcement Sanctions Imposed Against Audit Firms and
Audit Partners (22 May 2019) < www.frc.org.uk/getattachment/b83a8000-f065-4d32-9678-523947f21be8/
Enforcement-sanctions-imposed-against-Audit-firms-and-Audit-(August–2019).pdf>.
[222] For the most recent attempt to reform the area see Department for Business, Energy and Industrial Strategy,
'Restoring Trust in Audit and Corporate Governance', CP 382, March 2021.

8.5 Distributions

Shareholders have limited influence over the decision of whether returns are paid to them. The decision of whether a distribution is made is taken by the directors. Under the current Model Articles dividends can only be declared if the directors have made a recommendation as to its amount.[223] The shareholders then approve an annual dividend through an ordinary resolution.[224] For interim dividends no shareholder approval is required. This has recently been criticized.[225]

Moreover, we have already seen that dividends can only be paid if and to the extent that the accounts of the company show distributable profit.[226] Likewise, interim dividends can only be declared if it appears that there are profits available for distribution.[227] In this way the interests of creditors are integrated into decisions about return for shareholders. They are integrated in two ways. Both International Financial Reporting Standards (IFRS) and UK Generally Accepted Accounting Practice (GAAP) require directors to keep track of all assets and liabilities of the company and irrespective of whether the shareholders are happy to hear about any of these or agree with the valuations carried out under the statutory regime.

At the moment the accounts are the basis on which distributable profit is determined. Like the requirement to keep accounting records and produce annual accounts the method for calculating profit is enshrined in mandatory law and also binds the shareholders.

We have discussed earlier that the current distribution rules have been criticized as ineffective. It has been proposed that the current balance sheet test be replaced with a solvency-focused test. The government has proposed to retain the balance sheet test and to supplement it with a solvency statement.[228] Whatever the outcome of this discussion we need to observe that the aim of a solvency-based regime is also to put creditor interests before shareholder interests. Directors and shareholders will be bound by a new regime to the same extent than they are bound by the current rules.

Reductions follow a similar logic. They are proposed by the directors and require approval from the shareholders.[229] Moreover, they are only possible either following an approval by the courts or, in relation to private companies, on the basis of a solvency certification conducted by the directors.[230] During the approval process the court

---

[223] Model Articles, para 30 (private) and para 70 (public).
[224] ibid.
[225] The Investment Association, Shareholder Votes on Dividend Distributions in UK Listed Companies (May 2019) available from <http://cdn.roxhillmedia.com/production/email/attachment/740001_750000/Shareholder%20votes%20on%20dividend%20distributions%20in%20UK%20listed%20companies.pdf>.
[226] Section 7.11 in this book.
[227] Model Articles, para 30(6) (private) and para 70(6) (public); Zacaroli J in *Burnden Holdings (UK) Ltd v Fielding* [2019] EWHC 1566 (Ch), [2019] Bus LR 2878.
[228] Section 7.11 in this book.
[229] CA 2006, s 641(1).
[230] ibid s 641(1).

reviews the proposed reduction from the perspective of the company's creditors and imposes conditions protecting their interests. The court needs to settle a list of all creditors who have a right to object to a reduction.[231] Creditors on this list have a right to object to a reduction if they can show that there is a real likelihood that the reduction would result in the company being unable to discharge their debt or claim when it falls due.[232]

The importance of the interests of creditors in this context is also highlighted by the fact that an officer of the company who intentionally or recklessly conceals the name of a creditor who is entitled to object or misrepresents the amount of their debt or claim commits a criminal offence.[233]

Individual shareholders thus have limited means to extract return from the company.[234] They can require the directors to call a meeting where a special resolution of the shareholders can give instructions to the directors. But this resolution cannot override the distribution rules. It can only replace the directors' judgement as to the desirability of a distribution.

A persistent failure of the directors to distribute profits can amount to unfairly prejudicial conduct. But for this, the failure to pay returns has to continue over a long period of time.[235]

From a theoretical perspective this suggests that shareholders, who enjoy substantial governance rights, do not have a status that should be described as principals of either the directors or the company. Such a status cannot be ascribed to a group of people who have so little control over the returns produced by the company.

8.6 Stewardship

So far we have concluded that shareholders play an important role in the governance of the company. They are responsible for taking a significant number of management decisions. These are taken by the shareholders through majority votes. In taking these decisions shareholders are not as free as principals would be in their own affairs. They are restricted by rules that protect minority shareholders and creditors. The conclusion has been that shareholders are best characterized as performing a role in an organization which acts autonomously of the shareholders.

---

[231] ibid s 641(2).
[232] ibid s 641(1)(b).
[233] ibid s 647.
[234] Once a dividend has been declared, individual shareholders are able to use a personal action to enforce the payment of this dividend in the way that is set out in the constitution (*Wood v Odessa Waterworks Co* (1889) 42 ChD 636).
[235] CA 2006, s 994; *Re Saul D Harrison & Sons Plc* [1994] BCC 475; *Re CF Booth Ltd; Booth v Booth* [2017] EWHC 457 (Ch).

Notwithstanding this we need to observe that shareholders, unlike directors, do not owe fiduciary duties to the company.[236] Lord Sumption said in *Eclairs Group Ltd v JKX Oils & Gas Plc* that 'Directors owe a duty of loyalty to the company, but shareholders owe no loyalty either to the company or its board. . . . [T]hey are entitled to exercise their rights in their own interest as they see it and to challenge the existing management for good reasons or bad'.[237]

We will see in this section that there are nevertheless certain expectations of how share-holders should exercise their rights. These expectations apply to institutional share-holders of listed companies.

This development began with the Cadbury Code and has intensified after the Financial Crisis of 2008. It has received a further boost most recently with the Stewardship Code of 2020. The government has worked intensively to encourage investors to act as stew-ards of the companies they invest in. Stewardship used to be defined as an activity that would enhance the financial return for investors. The government now has broadened its scope. Stewardship now is defined as 'the responsible allocation, management and oversight of capital to create long-term value for clients and beneficiaries leading to sustainable benefits for the economy, the environment and society'.[238]

The Stewardship Code 2020 has no legal force. It applies to those who choose to adopt it. There is nevertheless significant governmental muscle behind the Code. The Financial Reporting Counsel/Audit Reporting and Governance Authority, the Financial Conduct Authority, the Competition and Markets Authority, HM Treasury, the Department for Business, Energy & Industrial Strategy, the Department for Work and Pensions, and The Pensions Regulator all have workstreams designed to encourage investors to en-gage in stewardship.[239]

In addition, the government has substantial financial power that can help to persuade the providers of investment products to adopt and comply with the recommendations set out in the Stewardship Code. In the 1960s asset managers and the industry sup-porting them did not exist.[240] Individual shareholders relied on brokers, who charged high fees. The growth of the investment services industry coincided with an important change in the provision of pensions. Rather than providing pensions through a state-run mechanism the government now contributes tax revenue to pension schemes set

[236] *Northern Counties Securities Ltd v Jackson & Steeple Ltd* [1974] 1 WLR 1133.

[237] *Eclairs Group Ltd v JKX Oils & Gas Plc* [2015] UKSC 71 [40]; see also *Greenhalgh v Arderne Cinemas* [1951] Ch 286; but see *Lehtimaki v Cooper* [2020] UKSC 33, [2020] 3 WLR 461 (in relation to a charitable company).

[238] UK Stewardship Code 2020 page 4, available from <https://www.frc.org.uk/getattachment/5aae591d-d9d3-4cf4-814a-d14e156a1d87/Stewardship-Code_Final2.pdf>.

[239] Dionysia Katlouzou and Eva Micheler, 'The Market for Stewardship and the Role of the Government' in Dionysia Katelouzou and Dan W Puchniak (eds), *Global Shareholder Stewardship: Complexities, Challenges and Possibilities* (CUP forthcoming); Anna Tilba and Arad Reisberg, 'Fiduciary Duty under the Microscope: Stewardship and the Spectrum of Pension Fund Management' (2019) 82 MLR 456.

[240] John Kay, 'The Kay Review of UK Equity Markets and Long-Term Decision Making' (July 2012) available at https://assets.publishing.service.gov.uk/government/uploads/system/uploads/attachment_data/file/253454/bis-12-917-kay-review-of-equity-markets-final-report.pdf.

up by private providers. The Competition and Markets Authority found in 2018 that 90 per cent of the revenue of investment consultants and fiduciary managers derives from pensions. The Office for National Statistics reports that the cost of pension tax relief in 2017–18 was £37.8 billion. From the perspective of asset managers and other financial intermediaries the government is an important if indirect customer. While the government currently does not formally connect pension credit and other tax benefits to a requirement for active stewardship, the robust request sent out by every single government department with a connection to the topic is bound to have some effect on the industry. It remains to be seen whether this leads to cosmetic changes or causes a more fundamental shift of attitudes in the financial services community.[241]

It is possible that the Stewardship Code 2020 will be as ineffective as its predecessors were. But this does not undermine the observations made here. From the perspective of this book we can note that shareholders are now to a large extent institutions which, rather than acting in their own interest, serve pension and other savers. This setup serves a social policy aim; the government has instigated this development and financially contributes to this effort. The providers of the associated financial services are not only publicly visible and but also receive public scrutiny. The government has legitimacy to involve itself because of the social policy background, but also because of its own financial contribution.[242] It has acted by developing a framework within which today's shareholders exercise their rights. The current method of intervention is open to criticism but this does not deflect from the shift that has occurred in relation to shareholders of public companies. They are now conceived of as stewards. There is an expectation discouraging them from maximizing short-term monetary return.[243]

8.7 Reflective loss

8.7.1 Introduction

The reflective loss principle is an example of a legal intervention that imposes restrictions on shareholders by virtue of their role within the company. Unlike the Stewardship Code the principle is set in law. It constitutes a recent addition to company law. Thirty years ago reflective loss was a minor point discussed in the context of

[241] For a recommendation that the government should connect tax credit to stewardship see Dionysia Katelouzou and Eva Micheler, 'The Market for Stewardship and the Role of the Government' in Dionysia Katelouzou and Dan W. Puchniak (eds), *Global Shareholder Stewardship: Complexities, Challenges and Possibilities* (CUP forthcoming), available at SSRN: https://ssrn.com/abstract=3704258 or http://dx.doi.org/10.2139/ssrn.3704258.
[242] ibid.
[243] For an argument in favour of a reasonableness review of shareholder decisions see John Lowry and Ernest Lim, 'Reconsidering the Rule on Shareholders' Exercise of Voting Powers' [2020] Journal of Business Law 345; see also Dionysia Katelouzou, 'Reflections on the Nature of the Public Corporation in an Era of Shareholder Activism and Stewardship' in Barnali Choudhury and Martin Petrin (eds), *Understanding the Company* (CUP 2017) 117 and Tom Giles Kelly, 'Institutional Investors as Environmental Activists' [2021] JCLS forthcoming; see further Ernest Lim, *A Case for Shareholders' Fiduciary Duties in Common Law Asia* (CUP 2019).

derivative actions.[244] Now the reflective loss principle has its own place in the field of company law.[245] It is connected with the rule in *Foss v Harbottle* and descendants and also with the rule that shareholders can only enforce 'membership rights' against the company.[246] It has attracted a substantial amount of judicial and academic attention.

The reflective loss principle applies when the company and a shareholder have a claim against a third party. In those circumstances the claim of the company stands in the way of the claim of the shareholder. Until recently the principle was held to also apply to claims of creditors.[247] This was, however, rejected by the Supreme Court in *Marex Financial Ltd v Sevilleja*.[248] The reflective loss principle therefore no longer applies when a company and one of its creditors have a cause of action against a third party.[249]

It is important to stress from the outset that the principle does not affect the cause of action of the shareholder. It rather removes the ability of a shareholder of the company to claim for certain losses from the wrongdoer.[250] They cannot claim for loss that would disappear if the company pursued its claim against the wrongdoer. The company's potential claim irrespective of whether it pursues or is capable of pursuing the claim or not bars its shareholder from claiming against the third party.[251] The principle does not apply, however, if a shareholder has sold his holding and suffered a loss as a result. This is because compensation paid to the company would not remove the loss suffered by a claimant who is no longer a shareholder.[252]

Examples of reflective loss that a shareholder cannot claim can be found in *Prudential v Newman* and in *Johnson v Gore Wood*. In *Prudential v Newman* the directors caused the shareholders to approve an agreement whereby the company substantially overpaid for an asset it acquired. The shareholders were induced to give their approval through fraudulent statements by the directors. The Court of Appeal held that the shareholders had a claim against the directors. On the facts the directors owed the shareholders a duty to advise them 'in good faith and not fraudulently'.[253] The shareholders were,

---

[244] Andrew Tettenborn, 'Creditors and Reflective Loss—A Bar Too Far?' (2019) 135 LQR 182, 183; *Marex Financial Ltd v Sevilleja* [2020] UKSC 31, [2021] AC 29, [25] (Lord Reed).

[245] *Marex Financial Ltd v Sevilleja* [2020] UKSC 31, [2021] AC 39.

[246] Section 9.2 in this book.

[247] *Sevilleja v Marex Financial Ltd* [2018] EWCA Civ 1468, [2019] QB 173, [35]–[36] (Flaux J).

[248] *Marex Financial Ltd v Sevilleja* [2020] UKSC 31, [2021] AC 29; *Naibu Global International Co Plc v Daniel Stewart and Co Plc* [2020] EWHC 2719 (Ch), [2021] PNLR 4; it also does not apply to individuals who hold shares indirectly through a chain of custodians, but whose names are not entered into the shareholder register (*Broadcasting Investment Group Ltd v Smith* [2020] EWHC 2501 (C)).

[249] *Naibu Global International Co Plc v Daniel Stewart and Co Plc* [2020] EWHC 2719 (Ch), [2021] PNLR 4; *Broadcasting Investment Group Ltd v Smith* [2020] EWHC 2501 (Ch).

[250] *Gardener v Parker* [2004] 2 BCLC 554, [49] (Neuberger LJ); *Marex Financial Ltd v Sevilleja* [2020] UKSC 31, [2021] AC 29, [47] (Lord Reed); see also *Bank Mellat v HM Treasury* [2016] EWCA Civ 452, [2017] QB 67 where it was held that the shareholder did not have a separate cause of action. There is an arguable case that the principle does not apply to an action for specific performance of an obligation to pay money to the company under a shareholder agreement (*Latin American Investments Ltd v Maroil Tranding Inc* [2017] EWHC 1254 (Comm), [2017] 2 CLC 45); but see *Marex Financial Ltd v Sevilleja* [2020] UKSC 31, [2021] AC 29, [52]–[55] and *Broadcasting Investment Group Ltd v Smith* [2020] EWHC 2501 (Ch).

[251] *Marex Financial Ltd v Sevilleja* [2020] UKSC 31, [2021] AC 29, [69]–[71] and [74] rejecting the decision in *Giles v Rhind* [2002] EWCA Civ 1428, [2003] Ch 618.

[252] *UCP Plc v Nectrus Ltd Damages* [2019] EWHC 3274, [2020] PNLR 9, [26].

[253] *Prudential Assurance v Newman Industries* [1982] 1 Ch 204 (CA) 222.

however, unable to claim for the reduction in the value of the shares they suffered as a result. They were also unable to claim for a reduction in dividends. These losses are 'merely a reflection of the loss suffered by the company'.[254] In *Johnson v Gore Wood* a firm of solicitors negligently advised both a company and its principal shareholder in relation to property transactions. The company settled the claim with the firm. That settlement expressly did not extend to the potential claim of the shareholder. The shareholder was held to have a cause of action in his own right. But the reflective loss principle prevented him from claiming for the reduction in the value of shareholding and of the loss of contributions to his pensions which the company was, as a result of the negligent advice of its solicitors, unable to make.[255] These losses were reflective.

Four reasons are advanced in support of the reflective loss principle: the prohibition of double recovery, causation, ease of settling claims, and the need to preserve the autonomy of the company. These will be examined in turn below. It will be shown that only the third and the fourth argument fully explain the rule barring claims for reflective loss. It will also be argued that the argument advanced under the third and the fourth heading squarely fits with the theory advanced in this book.

8.7.2 Double recovery

Double recovery is prohibited under English law. This prohibition protects the wrongdoer. He or she must compensate for the loss they caused. But that is all. They do not have to do more.

Admittedly the reflective loss principle does prevent double recovery. It identifies one victim (the company) as the primary and exclusive claimant. This protects the wrongdoer from having to pay more than the loss he caused.

The reflective loss principle nevertheless goes beyond the prevention of a double recovery. A shareholder of the company is permanently excluded from claiming for a loss that is reflective of the loss of the company.[256] The exclusion persists even when the company has given up the claim.[257] At that point the concern for the wrongdoer disappears because he is no longer at risk of being sued by the company.[258]

More generally, the reflective loss principle is a mechanism biased in favour of the company.[259] Allowing only one victim to sue for a loss that is shared by two or more victims

---

[254] ibid 223.

[255] *Johnson v Gore Wood* [2000] UKHL 65, [2002] 2 AC 1, 36–37 (Lord Bingham), 41–42 (Lord Goff).

[256] The principle does not affect individuals who have sold their shares *UCP Plc v Nectrus Ltd Damages* [2019] EWHC 3274, [2020] PNLR 9.

[257] In *Johnson v Gore Wood* [2000] UKHL 65, [2002] 2 AC 1 the company had settled the claim with the wrongdoer; *Marex Financial Ltd v Sevilleja* [2020] UKSC 31, [2021] AC 29, [10] (Lord Reed).

[258] *Marex Financial Ltd v Sevilleja* [2020] UKSC 31, [2021] AC 29, [10] (Lord Reed).

[259] ibid [193] (Lord Sales).

is generally perceived to be unfair. There are other, fairer, ways of preventing double recovery.[260]

The standard English method designed to prevent a double recovery is to permit any victim to sue and to recover the loss. Payment to one of the victims extinguishes the wrongdoer's liability. This prevents double recovery. Any further victims have an unjust enrichment claim against the victim who recovered from the wrongdoer.[261] It would also be possible to insist that all victims join proceedings and avoid the double recovery problem by sorting out all claims at the same time.[262] Both methods protect the wrongdoer. They are also more sensitive to the interests of shareholders and creditors of companies who have an independent cause of action against the wrongdoer.

The prohibition of double recovery therefore does not fully explain the reflective loss principle.[263]

8.7.3 Causation

The reflective loss principle has been justified by arguments relating to lack of causation. Two points are made here. The first point is expressed in *Prudential v Newman*. Vinelott J at first instance held that the shareholders of the company had been induced by the fraud of the company's directors to approve an agreement under which it paid about £450,000 more than the value of the assets acquired. There were two causes of action. The company had a claim against the directors for breach of duty. The shareholders also had a claim against the directors. Their claim was a claim in tort. They were the victims of a fraud procured by the directors.

Vinelott J at first instance concluded that the shareholders were entitled to claim personally against the directors. The Court of Appeal held that this personal claim was 'misconceived'.[264] It was, of course, correct that the directors in advising the shareholders owed them a duty to give such advice in good faith and not fraudulently. It was also correct that if the directors convene a meeting on the basis of a fraudulent circular, a shareholder will have a right to recover any loss which he has personally suffered in consequence of the fraudulent circular. This might include the expense of attending the meeting. But what he cannot do is to recover damages merely because the company in which he is interested has suffered a loss. He cannot recover a sum equal to the diminution in the market value of his shares, or equal to the likely diminution in dividend because such a 'loss' is merely a reflection of the loss suffered by the company.

---

[260] Charles Mitchell, 'Shareholders' Claims for Reflective Loss' (2004) 120 LQR 457 at 462–64; see also *Marex Financial Ltd v Sevilleja* [2020] UKSC 31, [2021] AC 29, [4]–[7] (Lord Reed).
[261] Charles Mitchell, 'Shareholders' Claims for Reflective Loss' (2004) 120 LQR 457 at 462–64.
[262] ibid at 463–64.
[263] *Marex Financial Ltd v Sevilleja* [2020] UKSC 31, [2021] AC 29, [33]–[34] and [51] (Lord Reed) but see [117] (Lord Sales).
[264] *Prudential Assurance v Newman Industries* [1982] 1 Ch 204 (CA) at 222.

The shareholder does not suffer a personal loss. The shares are merely a right of participation in the company on the terms of the articles of association. The shares are not affected. The plaintiff still holds all the shares as his absolutely unencumbered property. The deceit practiced upon the plaintiff does not affect the shares.[265]

This argument has been rightly criticized as adopting an indefensibly narrow view of the value of shares.[266] It assumes that the value of shares only consists in the rights to participate in the governance of the company.[267] This is at odds with the approach generally adopted in private law. Establishing a causal link between an event and the price of shares is admittedly not straightforward.[268] But that does not normally prevent a claim where such causal link can be established. Lack of causation is therefore not a basis on which the reflective loss principle can be explained.[269] Lord Reed held in *Marex Financial Ltd v Sevilleja* that the principle was not premised on 'any necessary relationship between a company's assets and the value of its shares (or its distributions)'.[270]

The second articulation of the causation argument applies in circumstances where the company has settled or otherwise given up the claim. It runs as follows: If the company decides not to claim against the wrongdoer the loss of the shareholder is caused by that decision and not the wrongdoing. The argument characterizes the company's decision not to pursue a claim as an event that interrupts the chain of causation between the wrongdoer and the shareholder. A closer look at this argument reveals that the loss of the shareholder in fact only arises because of the bar imposed by the reflective loss principle.[271] If there was no such principle normal procedural rules would apply. The shareholder would have a claim. The company would have a claim. A payment either to the company or to the shareholder would relieve the wrongdoer from liability. If the company does not claim, the shareholder's claim remains unaffected. It seems that this version of the causation argument also does not explain the reflective loss principle.

8.7.4 Ease of settling claims

The third argument is that the reflective loss principle makes it easier for the company to settle claims with wrongdoers. Lord Hutton articulated the argument as follows:

---

[265] ibid 222–23.

[266] Charles Mitchell, 'Shareholders' Claims for Reflective Loss' (2004) 120 LQR 457 at 459; *Marex Financial Ltd v Sevilleja* [2020] UKSC 31, [2021] AC 29, [147] (Lord Sales).

[267] Charles Mitchell, 'Shareholders' Claims for Reflective Loss' (2004) 120 LQR 457 at 459.

[268] *Prudential Assurance v Newman Industries* [1982] 1 Ch 204 (CA), 223; *Marex Financial Ltd v Sevilleja* [2020] UKSC 31, [2021] AC 29, [32]–[33] and [38] (Lord Reed).

[269] Charles Mitchell, 'Shareholders' Claims for Reflective Loss' (2004) 120 LQR 457, 459–60; *Marex Financial Ltd v Sevilleja* [2020] UKSC 31, [2021] AC 29, [42], [32]–[38], and [57] (Lord Reed)

[270] *Marex Financial Ltd v Sevilleja* [2020] UKSC 31, [2021] AC 29, [49] (Lord Reed).

[271] Charles Mitchell, 'Shareholders' Claims for Reflective Loss' (2004) 120 LQR 457, 469–70; *Marex Financial Ltd v Sevilleja* [2020] UKSC 31, [2021] AC 29, [152]–[153] (Lord Sales).

I further consider that the (reflective loss) principle has the advantage that, rather than leaving the protection of creditors and other shareholders of the company to be given by the trial judge in the complexities of a trial to determine the validity of claim made by the plaintiff [shareholder] against the defendant [solicitors], where conflicts of interest may arise between directors and some shareholders, or between the liquidator and some shareholders, the principle ensures at the outset of proceedings that where the loss suffered by the plaintiff [shareholder] is sustained because of loss to the coffers to the company, there will be no double recovery at the expense of the defendant [solicitors] nor loss to the creditors of the company and other shareholders.[272]

The concern is thus one of 'conflict of interest between directors and some shareholders' or 'between the liquidator and some shareholders'. Admittedly a conflict of interest can arise when the person who negotiates the settlement on behalf of the company with a third party also has a personal claim against the same third party.

But that does not mean that we need a rule on reflective loss that permanently blocks the claims of shareholders and directors. Company law has developed mechanisms to deal with conflict of interests. The normal method for dealing with conflict of interest problems is set out in CA 2005, section 175.[273] In addition, *Item Software v Fassihi* was a case where a director caused the company to adopt an aggressive negotiating strategy that ultimately caused it to lose the contract, thus helping the director to secure the contract for himself.[274] The Court of Appeal held that the director had a duty to disclose to the company the negotiations that had been going on with the third party. The case can operate as starting point for a situation where a director is involved in settlement negotiations on behalf of the company the outcome of which affects his ability to claim from a third party.

The reflective loss principle has the effect of removing the conflict of interest, but again goes beyond this. It bars the claim of a shareholder even in circumstances where the shareholder concerned is not a director. It also applies if the conflict has been declared to the board. So why is it that, in addition to normal fiduciary rules, the law imposes a block on the ability of those shareholders, who have no involvement in negotiating the arrangement between the company and the third party, to enforce claims against third party wrongdoers?

The idea seems to be that it is better to leave the sorting out of reflective loss to the company rather than engage in a *post facto* investigation of how the rules on directors' duties and distributions affect the situation where both a shareholder and a company have a claim against a third party. The courts prefer the corporate process to operate for the loss suffered by the company rather than untangling a web of individual interests *ex*

---

[272] *Johnson v Gore Wood* [2000] UKHL 65, [2002] 2 AC 1 at 55 (Lord Hutton).
[273] See section 7.7 in this book.
[274] *Item Software (UK) Ltd v Fassihi* [2004] EWCA Civ 1244, [2005] 2 BCLC 994.

post facto.[275] These considerations lead on to the final argument that has been accepted as a justification for the reflective loss principle.

8.7.5 Protecting the autonomy of the company

The argument about the autonomy of the company is underpinned by idea is that no harm is done by giving the company's claim priority over the claim of its shareholder. On this view the reflective loss principle does not cause unfairness to the shareholders whose claims it affects.[276] It treats them in accordance with the terms that they agreed to when they lent money to or took equity in a limited company.

When a shareholder has a claim that competes with a claim of the company a recovery by the company will flow to that shareholder, not directly but indirectly in accordance with the procedures of company law. This may or may not result in a distribution. It may or may not increase the value of his shareholding. But whatever happens will be in line with the terms that shareholders are taken to have accepted.[277]

Lord Reed observed in *Marex Financial Ltd v Sevilleja* that a shareholder has 'entrusted the management of the company's right of action to its decision-making organs'.[278] If such a decision is taken 'otherwise than in the proper exercise of the relevant powers, then the law provides the shareholders with a number of remedies, including a derivative action, and equitable relief from unfairly prejudicial conduct'.[279] Otherwise, however, the company is bound by the corporate decision-making process.

There was disagreement between the majority and the minority in *Marex Financial Ltd v Sevilleja* over the ability of the courts to sort out issues of causation and double recovery through a trial. Lord Sales wrote that the price paid by a shareholder for a simple and speedy resolution of disputes' was 'far too high'.[280] He also concluded that questions of causation and double recover were capable of being worked out 'in a practical way' achieving 'overall justice for all ... parties'.[281]

The majority of the Supreme Court, however, accepted the decision by Lord Reed who reasoned that the 'protection of creditors and other shareholders of the company should not be left to the judge in the complexities of a trial'.[282] He observed further that these 'complexities should not be underestimated'.[283] This chimes with the point that

---

[275] *Marex Financial Ltd v Sevilleja* [2020] UKSC 31, [2021] AC 29, [38], [47], and [51] (Lord Hodge), but see [126], [128], [162]–[165], [197] (Lord Sales).
[276] But see ibid [191]–[193] (Lord Sales).
[277] ibid [31] and [51] (Lord Reed).
[278] ibid [81] (Lord Reed).
[279] ibid [81] (Lord Reed); Lord Sales gave the dissenting judgment. He reasoned that the reflective loss principle has the effect of imposing an obligation on a shareholder to give up a personal asset (ibid [127] and [150]).
[280] ibid [192] (Lord Sales).
[281] ibid [126].
[282] ibid [38] (Lord Reed).
[283] ibid [38] (Lord Reed).

the judges prefer to refrain from involving themselves in deciding substantive matters for companies, which is as much of a long established principle of company law as the principle that shareholders are liable to the extent limited by the constitution. It seems that in the context of reflective loss the concern that a shareholder might draw the company into litigation is greater than the concern that a shareholder might be deprived of proving a personal loss in court.

Along similar lines the reflective loss principle can also be justified by a desire to protect the autonomy of the company through the case law. Lord Reed endorsed a dictum by Lord Bingham that it is important to 'respect the principle of company autonomy'. The courts should 'ensure that the company's creditors are not prejudiced by the action of individual shareholders'.[284] Lord Millet reasoned that allowing a shareholder to claim for reflective loss would either be a double recovery at the expense of the wrongdoer or a recovery by the shareholder 'at the expense of the company and its creditors and other shareholders. Neither course can be permitted.' Justice to the wrongdoer requires the exclusion of one claim to the other. '[P]rotection of the interests of the company's creditors requires that it is the company which is allowed to recover to the exclusion of the shareholder'.[285]

> It is . . . obvious that the . . . defendant cannot be made liable for more than £100,000 in total. It is equally obvious, however, that if the damages were recoverable by the shareholder instead of by the company this would achieve the same extraction of the company's capital to the prejudice of the creditors of the company as the defendant's misappropriation had done.[286]

Lord Cooke also observed that 'the interests of creditors may require consideration'.[287]

8.7.6 Theoretical observations

Company law supports autonomous organizational action by making available a mechanism for taking decisions through a process incorporating participants performing different roles. The law defines the rights and obligations of individual participants and sequences these rights and obligations into a process.[288] Shareholders are bound by this process. This justifies the conclusion that they can only recover reflective loss indirectly through the company.

---

[284] *Johnson v Gore Wood* [2000] UKHL 65, [2002] 2 AC 1, 36; *Marex Financial Ltd v Sevilleja* [2020] UKSC 31, [2021] AC 29, [48], but see [197] (Lord Sales).
[285] *Johnson v Gore Wood* [2000] UKHL 65, [2002] 2 AC 1, [62].
[286] ibid [62] (Lord Millet).
[287] ibid see also [55] (Lord Hutton).
[288] See also Giora Shapira, 'Shareholder Personal Action in Respect of a Loss Suffered by the Company and "Reflective Loss" in English Company Law' (2003) 37 International Lawyer (ABA) 137.

8.8 Conclusions

The shareholders set up companies and are able to decide to wind them up. In doing so they are bound by a process protecting third parties. They take constitutional decisions but cannot deprive the company of the organizational flexibility associated with constitutional amendments. While shareholders normally appoint directors and can remove them under CA 2006, section 168 the courts have explicitly held that they are not the principals of the directors.

The shareholders are involved in a number of management decisions. They have mandatory powers to oversee share issues but are constrained by the rules on pre-emption rights, which can only be disabled following a special process, and also by the prohibition of unfair prejudice. There are also requirements for the validation of contributions in kind, and the issue of shares at a discount is prohibited. Shareholders are required to oversee takeover defences.

Shareholders also approve certain transactions. In particular, they are involved in overseeing transactions between the company and its directors. In taking these decisions shareholders of private companies are constrained by the rules prohibiting unfair prejudice, which protect minority shareholders. Shareholders of all companies are prohibited from authorizing transactions that transfer value to them in circumstances where there is no distributable profit. Shareholders can ratify breaches of duty by the directors, but they are not able to ratify their own misconduct.

It is possible to argue that the constraints affecting shareholders are not onerous. The requirements for the valuation of contributions in kind that apply to private companies only insist that the directors carry out a valuation in good faith. For public companies a valuation report is required but this could change post-Brexit. The no-discount rule hardly matters in practice because companies use small nominal values. Unfair prejudice prohibits majority shareholders from syphoning off remuneration to themselves while neglecting the financial interests of the minority shareholders. But the courts are not prepared to interfere with commercial judgement. Transactions between a company and a shareholder are illegal as disguised returns of capital but the test the courts use to identify such transactions leaves considerable freedom to the directors and the shareholders. Illegality only affects transactions where there is a gross mismatch in value between what the company gives up and what it receives from a shareholder in return. Moreover, the Companies Act has explicitly authorized transactions at book value between solvent companies and their shareholders.

As a matter of principle, it is nevertheless worth observing that such restrictions exist. Moreover, we have seen that there are further and more onerous restrictions on the influence of shareholders. They are unable to override the rules for the valuation of assets and for the production of financial information. They are unable to modify the rules governing the calculation of profit. All of these take into account the interest of creditors and directly affect the ability of shareholders to receive return.

We have also seen that the government is exercising pressure on institutional share-holders of public companies to act as stewards rather than with a view to maximizing short-term return. Finally, the reflective loss principle requires shareholders to set aside and let the company decide on whether or not to claim for losses from third parties.

Overall, the law gives more influence to shareholders than to any other constituency but it stops short of giving shareholders a role that would justify the conclusion that they are principals of the directors or of the company.

We have also seen that the UK Corporate Governance Code 2018 has identified a way of integrating the interests of stakeholders into the corporate decision-making process. The recommendations that listed companies identify an individual or advisory panel with responsibility to represent the concerns of the workforce to the board fits well with the way in which organizations operate. If there was a desire to integrate the interests of other stakeholders the Code could serve as a role model.

The assertion that the shareholders are the principals of the directors is the brainchild of a theoretical model that, like all models, simplifies the object of its analysis. Agency theory identifies participants in the company on a binary basis. It asks whose well-being depends on whose decisions. In this analysis the directors are the agents of shareholders because the well-being of the shareholders depends on the decisions of the directors. The profitability of the company and thus the return that flows to shareholders is deter-mined by the decisions made by the directors. This statement is, of course, correct but it is incomplete. Company law does more than ensure that shareholders receive returns. Moreover, it is unhelpful. It would equally be right to say that the well-being of the dir-ectors depends on the decisions of the shareholders. Under the statutory framework the shareholders can remove the directors at any point in time using a simple majority resolution. The shareholders of listed companies determine the remuneration policy of the directors. The shareholders of all companies approve long-term service contracts.

Agency theory makes it possible for company law scholarship to engage with and ben-efit from scholarship from other disciplines. The theory emphasizes that shareholders interact with the company differently than other participants. This statement is accu-rate at the highest level of abstraction. It is also useful at a micro level for the analysis of provisions of the Companies Act which focus on the interests of shareholders. Agency theory nevertheless has serious shortcomings. It shifts the focus of analysis to the shareholder-centred elements of the law and so prevents scholars from understanding how the provisions of the Act work together to create a framework that underpins the operation of an organization.

Some of the statutory restrictions on the ability of the constitution to set the boundaries for the directors have required the mandatory involvement of the shareholders and so can be characterized as enhancing the shareholder interest. The shareholder interest on its own, however, does not explain why the law is mandatory. The rules making share-holder decisions mandatory for certain decisions are usually proposed with a view to addressing a concern that has a public-interest element attached to it. The concern that companies are badly run is a public macro-economic concern as well as a private investor concern. Investors can vote with their feet and stay away from share markets altogether. That would have undesirable consequences for the economy. It would deprive business of an important source of finance which might inhibit growth in the economy.

An increase in shareholder oversight is the standard go-to response to corporate governance scandals. It is not a perfect solution because dispersed shareholders lack the incentives to exercise these governance rights. Increasing shareholder influence against this background only creates a theoretical possibility for shareholders to involve themselves. There is no guarantee that shareholders will take advantage of that opportunity. There is also no guarantee that if shareholders use these mandatory rights they will exercise them in a way that chimes with the public preference for long-term sustainable growth. The present strategy takes advantage of the fact that shareholders are mostly institutional investors rather than individuals, and encourages these investors through a Stewardship Code to embrace the government's preference for sustainability. We will see going forward if this produces the desired effect.

Increasing shareholder influence may not be a silver bullet and can also have counterproductive effects. There are, however, no obvious alternatives and so it seems that shareholder influence is the best tool that the government has been able to come up with to protect a public interest in well-run companies.

9

Enforcement

9.1 Introduction

This chapter analyses the rules governing the enforcement of the duties imposed on directors. We will distinguish between private and public enforcement.

Directors owe their duties to the company and so the company is responsible for enforcing these duties. We will see in section 9.2 that law prefers such litigation decisions to be taken by the company through its normal process. The courts only interfere if that process cannot be made to work independently of the wrongdoers. It is unlikely for a derivative claim to succeed against the wishes of an independent majority and so it is right to observe that the shareholders are the main focus of the law. But here too the law is more nuanced and integrates the interests of minority shareholders and creditors.

We will observe in the section that the duties of the directors are also enforced through the means of public law. We will see in section 9.3 that public law sanctions particularly attach in relation to duties that enhance the interest of third parties interacting with the company. This leads to the conclusion that these interests are at least formally better protected than those of the shareholders.

9.2 Private enforcement

9.2.1 Introduction

Derivative actions are an area of company law that squarely supports the theoretical position advanced in this book. The law conceives companies as entities with organizational autonomy. The rule in *Foss v Harbottle* asserts that the company is the proper plaintiff to bring a remedy for the breach of duty by the directors. This is because the company is a separate legal person. The directors act for the company and owe their duties to the company. If they breach these duties the wrong is done to the company. Because the company is not a natural person there exists a corporate decision-making process. The decision to enforce a claim against directors is taken through that process. That process operates on the basis of the Companies Act and the constitution of the company but is not limited to it.

The courts have over time developed rules that identify circumstances in which that corporate process cannot be trusted with the decision to enforce a claim for breach of duty against a director. The corporate decision-making process has achieved an

Company Law. Eva Micheler, Oxford University Press. © Eva Micheler 2021. DOI: 10.1093/oso/9780198858874.003.0009

independent legal status that is protected through judicial decision-making. The courts only interfere when that corporate decision-making process cannot operate independently of the wrongdoer.

9.2.2 The supremacy of the corporate decision-making process—*Foss v Harbottle*

Evidence of the courts' deference to the corporate decision-making process can be found in the foundational case establishing the doctrine. *Foss v Harbottle* does more than articulate the proper-plaintiff principle and the majority rule.[1] After establishing that the company was the proper plaintiff,[2] Sir James Wigram, VC went on to explore, on the facts in front of him, if the corporation was capable of taking the litigation decision. He examined the corporation's decision-making process extensively. He concluded that while there were problems with operating the process in practice it was possible for that process to operate and to address the question as to whether the corporation should sue the directors. The extent and the depth at which this analysis is carried out highlights the importance of the decision-making process as a whole. The fact that the majority of the shareholders can sanction a breach was part of this analysis but the scope of the analysis was much broader.

The court at first examined the statute by which the corporation was created to conclude that under that statute the 'proprietors' were the 'supreme governing body' of the corporation. While that body remained functioning there was no power for a minority shareholder to bring a claim on behalf of the company.[3] The court then indicated that an action by an individual shareholder will be entertained when it can be shown that 'all means to set in motion the procedures of the corporation has been resorted to and found ineffectual'.[4] For example, the statute required that a request to call a meeting be addressed to the clerk or secretary of the company. No one was appointed to that role. The court nevertheless concluded that the procedure for a shareholder to call a meeting was capable of functioning. The mode of service set out in the Act was merely 'directional'. It was possible for a request to be served to the place where the directors carried out the business of the company.[5] There was 'no insurmountable impediment to the exercise of the powers of the proprietors assembled in general meeting to control the affairs of the company . . . and such general meetings were actually held'.[6] Like the shareholder meeting the board of directors did not fully comply with the requirements set out in the Act of Incorporation but was nevertheless capable of operating.[7] Mr Foss was therefore unable to claim derivatively.

[1] *Foss v Harbottle* (1843) 2 Hare 461, 67 ER 189.
[2] ibid 2 Hare 461, 491; 67 ER 189, 202.
[3] ibid 2 Hare 461, 494; 67 ER 189, 204.
[4] ibid 2 Hare 461, 496; 67 ER 189, 204.
[5] ibid 2 Hare 461, 496; 67 ER 189, 204.
[6] ibid 2 Hare 461, 502–03; 67 ER 189, 207.
[7] ibid 2 Hare 461, 496; 67 ER 189, 204.

The overriding question was not: Can the majority sanction the breach? But rather: Is the company able to operate a decision-making process that is independent of the wrong-doers?[8] This form of enquiry continued to operate at common law. Over time the cases developed a set of instances identifying cases where the corporate decision-making process could not be trusted and in which therefore a derivative action could succeed.

9.2.3 Fraud and wrongdoer control

Foss v Harbottle itself pointed towards the fact that exceptions exist to the proper-plaintiff rule.[9] The best known of these is the fraud on the minority exception. Fraud in this context is broadly defined and includes situations where the majority directly or in-directly appropriates to themselves money, property, or an advantage which belonged to the company or in which the shareholders as a whole were entitled to participate.[10] No derivative action can be brought at common law by a minority shareholder when wrongdoing directors do not benefit themselves. Mere negligence by the directors does not entitle a minority shareholder to bring an action.[11]

In addition to showing the presence of a fraud a derivative claimant also needs to show that the wrongdoers are 'in control'. It is at this point that the courts examine the inde-pendence of the corporate decision-making process. The leading modern authority on the requirement for majority control at common law is *Prudential v Newman*.[12]

The Court of Appeal rejected the proposition that a derivative action was available 'whenever the interests of justice so require'.[13] The learned judges then offered extensive reasoning on the availability of derivative claims. These show that the court aimed to determine if somehow between the shareholders and the directors it was possible for the litigation decision to be taken by the company through an independent process.

The learned judges pointed out that a board, of which all the directors save one were disinterested and which was acting on the basis of independent advice, had reached the conclusion before the start of the action that the proceedings were likely to do more harm than good. They held that the board's decision 'might prove a sound or unsound assessment, but it was a commercial assessment of an apparently independent board'.[14] The 'board clearly doubted whether there were sufficient reasons for supposing that the company would at the end of the day be in a position to count its blessings; and clearly feared that it might be killed by kindness'.[15] Neither the Companies Act nor the articles

---

[8] ibid 2 Hare 461, 492; 67 ER 189, 203–07.

[9] ibid 2 Hare 461, 494; 67 ER 189, 204.

[10] *Estmanco v Greater London Council* [1982] 1 WLR 2, 12.

[11] *Pavlides v Jensen* [1956] Ch 565; recently *Harris v Microfusion 2003–2 LLP* [2016] EWCA Civ 1212, [2017] 1 BCLC 305.

[12] *Prudential Assurance v Newman Industries* (CA) [1982] 1 Ch 204.

[13] ibid 212[H].

[14] ibid 221[D].

[15] ibid 221 [D]–[E].

of association explicitly referred the litigation decision to an independent board. The court nevertheless concluded that such a board could be entrusted with bringing about an independent evaluation of the litigation decision by the company itself.[16]

The court also remarked that 'it may well be right for [a] . . . judge trying the preliminary issue to grant a sufficient adjournment to enable a meeting of shareholders to be convened by the board so that he can reach a conclusion in light of the conduct of, and the proceedings at, that meeting'.[17] Here, the court did not simply determine if the majority of the shareholder has approved or rejected the litigation. What was suggested is an investigation of the 'conduct of, and the proceedings at, [the] . . . meeting'.

Finally, throughout the judgment the Court of Appeal used the term 'control' by the wrongdoers in quotation marks. For example, the learned judges reasoned that '[i]t is commonly said that an exception to the rule in *Foss v Harbottle* arises if the company is "controlled" by persons implicated in the fraud complained of, who will not permit the name of the company to be used as plaintiffs in the suit'.[18] They went on to explain that 'control':

> embraces a broad spectrum extending from an overall absolute majority of votes at one end, to a majority of votes at the other end made up of those likely to be cast by the delinquent himself plus those voting with him as a result of influence or apathy.[19]

In *Smith v Croft (No 2)* the majority of the shareholders were controlled by the wrongdoers. The minority shareholder, who brought the derivative claim, argued that there was no reported authority where the court had gone 'beyond seeing whether the wrongdoers are in control and count[ed] heads to see what the other shareholders, i.e. those other than the plaintiffs and the wrongdoers think should be done'.[20] Knox J accepted this submission but went on to point out that the fact that no such investigation was previously not conducted did not mean that it could not be conducted. He then accepted submissions on behalf of the company that there was authority where the courts had subjected the 'propriety of the shareholders' voting activities' to 'careful scrutiny'.[21] He relied on *Prudential v Newman (No 2)* to conclude that voting control by the defendants 'was not necessarily the sole subject of the investigation'.[22] In the words of Knox, J, the question which has to be answered in order to determine whether the rule in *Foss v Harbottle* applied to prevent a minority shareholder seeking relief as plaintiff for the benefit of the company is: 'Is the plaintiff being improperly prevented from bringing these proceedings on behalf of the company?'[23] 'If it is an expression of the corporate will of the company by an appropriate independent organ that is preventing

---

[16] See also *Bhullar v Bhullar* [2015] EWHC 1943 (Ch), [2016] 1 BCLC 106.
[17] *Prudential Assurance v Newman Industries* (CA) [1982] 1 Ch 204, 222[A]–[B].
[18] ibid 219[D].
[19] ibid 219[E].
[20] *Smith v Croft (No 2)* [1988] Ch 114, 184[D].
[21] ibid 184[F].
[22] *Prudential Assurance v Newman Industries* [1982] Ch 204, 219.
[23] *Smith v Croft (No 2)* [1988] Ch 114, 185[B].

the plaintiff from prosecuting the action he is not improperly but properly prevented and so the answer to the question is "No." '[24]

He then went on to say more about the concept of an 'an appropriate independent organ'. 'The appropriate independent organ will vary according to the constitution of the company concerned and the identity of the defendants who will in most cases be disqualified from participating by voting in expressing the corporate will.'[25] He then pointed out that he remained 'unconvinced that a just result is achieved by a single minority shareholder having the right to involve a company in an action for recovery of compensation for the company if all the other minority shareholders are for disinterested reasons satisfied that the proceedings will be productive of more harm than good.' He supported these conclusions by pointing out that a derivative action was 'originally introduced on the ground of necessity alone in order to prevent a wrong going without redress'.[26]

The question was not: Do the wrongdoers control the majority of the votes of the shareholders? It was rather: Is the company able to operate a process allowing for the formation of a corporate will in a way that is independent of the wrongdoers?

9.2.4 *Ultra vires* and illegality

Another instance where the courts have allowed derivative claims are *ultra vires* or illegal acts. Majority shareholders are, of course, unable to authorize or ratify *ultra vires* or illegal acts.[27] These are, for example, distributions in circumstances where there is no profit or reductions of capital that have not been either authorized by the court or made following a solvency statement. The majority of the shareholders are also unable to authorize other statutory breaches. They cannot authorize the company, for example, to act in violation of regulatory requirements. It is at this point that the interests of constituencies other than the shareholders are taken into account.

In *Smith v Croft (No 2)* the directors had authorized certain payments in breach of the rules prohibiting financial assistance.[28] Knox J rejected the proposition that minority shareholders can always bring a derivative action to claim for damages arising out of an *ultra vires* or illegal act conducted by the directors. He pointed out that there may be in practice good financial reasons supporting the conclusion not to pursue such a claim.[29]

Knox J distinguished claims restraining directors from acting illegally or *ultra vires* from claims recovering on behalf of the company money or property which the

---

[24] ibid 185[B].
[25] ibid 185[B]–[C].
[26] *Smith v Croft (No 2)* [1988] Ch 114, 185 [C]–[D].
[27] *Edwards v Halliwell* [1950] 2 All ER 1064, 1066–67.
[28] *Smith v Croft (No 2)* [1988] Ch 114, 165[F].
[29] ibid 166[G].

company is entitled to claim as a result of the *ultra vires* or illegal transaction.[30] A claim to restrain the company can be brought by an individual shareholder. A compensation claim, on the other hand, is a claim of the company and can only be brought by an individual shareholder derivatively.

For the compensation claim there is a further distinction between authorization/ratification and the decision to sue the directors for breach of duty. While the company cannot authorize or ratify an *ultra vires* or illegal act, it can take a decision not to sue a director who has caused the company to act *ultra vires* or illegally.[31] The shareholders, for example, do not have the power to ratify a transaction involving financial assistance but they can nevertheless take the decision that it is not in the corporate interest to litigate against the director who brought about such an assistance.[32] The litigation decision is subject to the normal corporate procedures. Minority shareholders are unable to bring a derivative action unless they can show that the company cannot operate an independent decision-making process in relation to the litigation decision. The courts are in search of a proper organ that has the power and the ability to take decision on behalf of the company.

This allows the independent shareholders or directors to take a litigation decision in the interest of the company without disposing of the claim altogether. A different board or the company's liquidator can at a later stage decide to enforce the claim. The law leaves the litigation decision to the normal corporate decision-making process while preventing the company from permanently disposing of the claim.

9.2.5 Special resolutions

A similar approach applies in relation to decisions that can only be taken by a special resolution of the shareholders.[33] Shareholders can bring actions to prevent the company from carrying out actions for which a special majority of the shareholders is required. The company, for example, must not increase the membership fee other than by way of special resolution and a member will be able to obtain an injunction instructing the company to comply with its constitution.[34]

This, however, does not mean that an action on behalf of the company against a director for breach of duty can automatically be brought by an individual shareholder.[35] The distinction between authorization and ratification and the taking of the litigation decision

---

[30] *Smith v Croft (No 2)*, [1988] Ch 114, 168[H], 170[B], and [F]–[G].
[31] ibid 172[H]–173[A]; see also Sarah Worthington, 'Corporate Attribution and Agency: Back to Basics' (2017) 133 LQR 118.
[32] *Smith v Croft (No 2)*, [1988] Ch 114, 172[G]–173[C].
[33] *Cotter v National Union of Seamen* [1929] 2 Ch 58 [69]–[70] (Romer J); *Edwards v Halliwell* [1950] 1 All ER 1064, 1067.
[34] *Edwards v Halliwell* [1950] 1 All ER 1064.
[35] Law Commission, Shareholder Remedies Consultation LC 142 (1996) [4.34].

also applies here. The decision to sue the directors for damages is subject to the ordinary corporate decision-making process. A minority shareholder can only sue when this process cannot operate independently.[36]

9.2.6 The statutory regime

Like the common law, the statutory regime defers to the corporate decision-making process. Individual members can bring derivative actions in relation to claims 'in respect of a cause of action arising from an actual or proposed act or omission involving negligence, default, breach of duty or breach of trust by a director of the company'.[37] Claims can be brought against directors, former directors, and shadow directors.[38] They can also be brought against another person, for example a third party who has dishonestly assisted a breach of fiduciary duty or who has knowingly received trust property.[39] Claims against third parties that are not 'in respect of a cause of action arising from' a directorial act or omission cannot be brought derivatively.[40] They are not for a shareholder to bring. Companies Act 2006 (CA 2006), section 260(3) states explicitly, that 'A derivative claim . . . may be brought *only* . . .',[41] compared to the common law that slightly narrows the instances in which a shareholder to sue derivatively.

9.2.7 Stage one

The statutory derivative action is staged.[42] In the first stage a shareholder who wants to sue derivatively needs to make a *prima facie* case to the court. At this stage the company is not involved. The stage also does not involve a hearing.[43] The court receives a claim form and any written evidence that the shareholder relies on to support his claim. The company is normally notified of the application but not required or expected to make submissions. If it volunteers to involve itself it cannot claim for cost. CA 2006, section 261 constitutes an attempt to avoid a situation where the company has to engage in a lengthy trial to determine if there should be another lengthy trial on the substance of the claim.[44] Unless the company volunteers to involve itself a shareholder cannot draw

---

[36] *Smith v Croft (No 2)* [1988] Ch 114, 182[E]–[F] and 183[C].
[37] Companies Act 2006 (CA 2006), s 260(3).
[38] ibid s 260(5)(a) and (b).
[39] *Iesini v Westrip Holdings Ltd* [2011] 1 BCLC 498 [75].
[40] ibid [103]–[104].
[41] Author's emphasis.
[42] These stages have to be observed by the court and are not a procedural 'nicety' (*CJC Media Ltd v Clark* [2020] SAC (Civ) 110).
[43] A hearing is only held when the shareholder has had his application refused and has requested an oral hearing. That request needs to be made within seven days from the notification of the decision that the application has been refused. (Civil Procedure Rules 19.9A(10)).
[44] In *Prudential Assurance v Newman Industries* (CA) [1982] 1 Ch 204, 221[B] the learned judges held that, 'it . . . [was] not right to . . . subject the company to a 30-day action . . . in order to enable [the judge at first instance] . . . to decide whether the plaintiffs were entitled in law to subject the company to a 30-day action'.

the company into a trial on the *prima facie* question. By setting up a first hurdle that a shareholder has to overcome to sue derivatively the law protects the autonomy of the corporate decision-making process to a greater extent than the common law.

Based on the papers submitted the court considers if there is a *prima facie* case for allowing the shareholder to bring a derivative action. The court determines whether, prima facie, the company has a good cause of action arising out of an act or omission of a director. Stage one involves 'precisely the decision that the Court of Appeal required in *Prudential v Newman*'.[45]

9.2.8 Stage two—permission must be refused

Stage two consists of two sub-stages. There are knock-out criteria which require the court to refuse permission.[46] If none of these criteria applies the court can move on to evaluate the factors set out in CA 2006, section 263(3). Both the knock-out criteria and the criteria for evaluation reflect the principle that the litigation decision should be left to the company's internal process. The court will only intervene if this corporate process is incapable of working independently. The criteria also integrate the interests of the company's creditors.

Authorization or ratification by the company

Permission to pursue a derivative claim must be refused if the act or omission complained of has been either authorized or ratified by the company.[47] The shareholders are responsible for ratifying a breach of duty by the directors.[48] It is worth noting that the application is blocked only if authorization or ratification has already occurred. At common law ratifiability was enough to stop a derivative claim.

The courts do more than verify if there has been a formal authorization or ratification. They review the decision-making process. For example, a validly passed shareholder resolution ratifying a transaction does not automatically block a derivative action. It is possible for such a ratification to be ineffective where the wrongdoers contrived a sequence of events amounting to an abuse of the minority shareholders.[49] Moreover, a purported ratification only blocks a derivative action if the shareholders have received 'fair and candid' information.[50]

Wrongs that are not ratifiable by the shareholders are also considered here. Examples are distributions in breach of the capital maintenance rules or reductions carried out

---

[45] *Iesini v Westrip Holdings Ltd* [2011] 1 BCLC 498 [78].
[46] CA 2006, s 263(2).
[47] ibid s 263(2)(b) and (c); for an example see *Brannigan v Style* [2016] EWHC 512 (Ch) (unreported).
[48] CA 2006, s 239.
[49] *Hook v Sumner* [2015] EWHC 3820, [2016] BCC 220, [86] and [92]–[96].
[50] *Stainer v Lee* [2010] EWHC 1539, [2011] BCC 134, [43] and [45]–[46]; see also *Cullen v Brown* [2015] EWHC 473, [2016] 1 BCLC 491, [38]–[47].

without the approval of the court or, in relation to private companies, without the required solvency statement. Shareholders can also not sanction breaches of a duty owed to creditors under CA 2006, section 172(3).[51] This integrates the interests of creditors and of other stakeholders into the analysis. A purported ratification of transactions in breach of these rules does not block a derivative claim.

Brenda Hannigan includes claims for the misappropriation to the majority of money, property, or other advantages which belong to the company in the category of wrongs that are unratifiable by the shareholders.[52] This means that such claims will automatically proceed to be evaluated by reference to what a person acting in accordance with CA 2006, section 172 would do.

At common law it was possible for the wrongdoing shareholder directors to ratify their own breaches of duty in their capacity as shareholders. That is no longer possible. Now CA 2006, section 239 states that the votes of the wrongdoer director or any person connected with him are disregarded. A breach can now only be ratified by shareholders who are not connected to the breach. This enhances the requirement for an independent decision-making process.

Person acting in accordance with section 172

The statutory derivative action places significant weight on how 'a person acting in accordance with section 172 (duty to promote the success of the company)' would evaluate the claim.[53] The test appears twice in the statutory regime. It appears as a knock-out factor and also as a discretion factor. The court must refuse permission if it is satisfied that a section 172 person 'would not seek to continue the claim'.[54] At the discretion stage the court must integrate 'the importance' that a section 172 person 'would attach to continuing the [claim]' into the analysis.[55]

The test requires the court to assess the desirability of the claim from the perspective of the company. In *McCaskill v Fulton*[56] Norris J held that the question is 'whether the case advanced is the sort of case which a properly advised and governed company would lay out money on in pursuit of its own interests'. If a judge concludes that some directors, acting in accordance with section 172, would think it worthwhile to continue a claim at least for the time being, while others, also acting in accordance with section 172, would reach the opposite conclusion s/he is not bound to refuse permission and can proceed to exercise discretion.[57]

---

[51] Brenda Hannigan, Company Law (5th edn, OUP 2018) paras 20–49.
[52] ibid paras 20–49; *Franbar Holdings Ltd v Patel* [2008] EWHC 1534 (Ch), [2009] 1 BCLC 1 [45].
[53] CA 2006, s 263(2)(a) and s 263(3)(b).
[54] ibid s 263(2)(a).
[55] ibid s 263(3)(b).
[56] *McCaskill v Fulton*, 31 October 2014 cited with approval in *Montgold Capital LLP v Ilska* [2018] EWHC 2982 (Ch), [2019] BCC 309, [21].
[57] *Iesini v Westrip Holdings Ltd* [2009] EWHC 2526 (Ch), [2011] 1 BCLC 498, [85]–[86]; *Hook v Sumner* [2015] EWHC 3820, [2016] BCC 220, [96]: *Cullen v Brown* [2015] EWHC 473, [2016] 1 BCLC 491, [29].

Lewison J set out eight criteria that a person, acting in accordance with section 172, would consider in this context.[58] These criteria have become well-accepted with recent cases using them as a starting point to evaluate the position of a section 172 person in relation to the claim.[59] The eight criteria are: the size of the claim, the strength of the claim, the cost of proceedings, the company's ability to fund proceedings, the ability of the potential defendants to satisfy a judgment, the impact on the company if it lost the claim and had to pay not only its own costs but the defendant's as well, any disruption of the company's activities while the claim is pursued,[60] and whether the prosecution of the claim would damage the company in other ways (eg by losing the services of a valuable employee or alienating a key supplier or customer).[61]

Judges carry out a cost-benefit analysis.[62] In *Goodwin v Cook*, for example, the company had no assets and was overdrawn by approximately £7000. It had ceased trading. One of the defendants also had no assets and the other had a claim against the company.[63] The case was not a strong one and the costs were likely to be high.[64] The court therefore refused permission to continue the claim.[65] In *Zavahir v Shankleman* the company found itself with few assets and no future prospects. The downsides and costs of losing far outweighed the benefits of winning even if a significantly greater chance of winning than losing was factored in. Permission was refused.[66]

In *Stainer v Lee* Roth J held that 'if the case is very strong it may be appropriate to continue it even if the likely level of recovery is not so large since such a claim stands a good chance of provoking an early settlement or may indeed qualify for summary judgement'.[67] On the other hand 'it may be in the interest of the company to continue even a less strong case if the amount of potential recovery is very large.'[68] In *Hook v Sumner* it was held that, while the cost of the litigation was going to be high, the damages, if the claim was successful, were potentially substantial and so the claim was permitted.[69]

In *Cullen v Brown* the company was no longer trading and the claimant shareholder did not apply for an indemnity for costs. Mark Anderson QC therefore held that a

---

[58] *Iesini v Westrip Holdings Ltd* [2009] EWHC 2526 (Ch), [2011] 1 BCLC 498 [85].
[59] *Montgold Capital LLP v Ilska* [2018] EWHC 2982 (Ch), [2019] BCC 309 [22]–[34]; *Bridge v Daley* [2015] EWHC 2121 (HC), 2015 WL 4744908 [17]; see also *Bhullar v Bhullar* [2015] EWHC 1943, [2016] 1 BCLC 106.
[60] In *Hook v Sumner* the distraction caused by the litigation was not a factor in favour of refusing permission because the relationship between the individuals was already bad and the realistic risk of loss of all possibility of future income was remote (*Hook v Sumner* [2015] EWHC 3820, [2016] BCC 220 [115]–[117].
[61] *Iesini v Westrip Holdings Ltd* [2011] 1 BCLC 498 [85]; *Franbar Holdings Ltd v Patel* [2009] EWHC 2526 (Ch) [2009] 1 BCLC 1; *Airey v Cordell* [2006] EWHC 2728 (Ch) [2007] BCC 785, 800.
[62] See eg *Brannigan v Style* [2016] EWHC 512 (Ch) (unreported) where it was held that a section 172 director would conclude that the claim was weak. Quantum might not be insubstantial so the court did not refuse permission at the knock-out stage. At the discretion stage, however, permission was refused because a section 172 person would have concluded that, while quantum was not insubstantial, pursuing the claim to a positive outcome would be very difficult and not cost effective.
[63] *Goodwin v Cook*, Chancery Division 21 June 2018 HC-2017-000742 [11] and [64].
[64] ibid [49], [67].
[65] ibid [85], [87].
[66] *Zavahir v Shankleman* [2016] EWHC 2772, [2017] BCC 500, [39].
[67] *Stainer v Lee* [2010] EWHC 1539, [2011] BCC 134, [29].
[68] ibid [29].
[69] *Hook v Sumner* [2015] EWHC 3820, [2016] BCC 220, [119]–[120].

hypothetical director would ask to what extent the funds of the company available for distribution to its members are likely to be enhanced or diminished by continuing the litigation. Since the litigation was entirely funded by the shareholder it was difficult to see any reason why a hypothetical director would not want to continue the claim.[70]

9.2.9 Stage two—discretion of the court

Once the court has determined that there are no grounds that require the refusal of permission for the derivative action it proceeds to the discretion stage. CA 2006, section 263(3) lists factors for the court to take into account at this stage. We have already seen that the court needs to consider the importance that a person acting in according with CA 2006, section 172 would attach to bringing the claim as a factor at discretion stage. In addition CA 2006, section 263(3) lists five other factors. The list is not exhaustive. The court is free to consider other factors in addition to those listed in CA 2006, section 263(3). The court's discretion is wide. Here too the law defers to the corporate process. The additional factors to consider at discretion stage will be examined below.

Whether the member is acting in good faith in seeking to continue the claim
This is designed to eliminate claims that are advanced for ulterior motives. The courts accept a 'considerable amount of vitriolic criticism' between the individuals involved as long as the claimant does not bring the claim in order to aggravate the dispute or to obtain an ulterior advantage.[71] It is possible for a claimant to act in good faith but to be nevertheless not an appropriate person to be allowed to front the litigation. In *Bridge and Daley* the claimant was a litigant in person who was described as being 'a highly opinionated individual' who was 'incapable of any objective analysis of evidence placed before him'. He asserted that there was considerable corruption in the company and that the directors had breached every single section of the Companies Act in one way or another.[72] The court also found that the claimant would not act 'responsibly in accordance with such appropriate professional advice as he might receive, and his continued conduct of the litigation would be 'a recipe for disaster'.[73] The court concluded that any reasonable director would 'not allow him to have the conduct of a derivative claim'.[74]

Likelihood of authorization/ratification
We have already seen that authorization and ratification blocks a derivative claim. At common law derivative actions were also barred for wrongs that were ratifiable regardless of whether ratification had occurred. The statutory procedure takes a more nuanced approach. The fact that the wrong is ratifiable continues to be relevant but only as

---

[70] *Cullen v Brown* [2015] EWHC 473, [2016] 1 BCLC 491, [55].
[71] *Hook v Sumner* [2015] EWHC 3820, [2016] BCC 220, [124]–[126].
[72] *Bridge v Daley* [2015] EWHC 2121 (HC), 2015 WL 4744908, [84], [85].
[73] ibid [86].
[74] ibid [84].

a factor to be taken into account at the discretion stage. This has opened up the possibility for a derivative action to succeed in relation to a ratifiable wrong.

For wrongs that are not ratifiable the statutory rules prohibiting creditor or other statutory breaches ratification is not only 'unlikely', it is impossible. The fact that a breach cannot be ratified by the majority of the shareholders is thus a factor in favour of the availability of a derivative claim.

Decision of the company to not to pursue the claim

The courts are keen to find a way for the company to take the litigation decision. They, for example, do not allow the continuation of a claim in circumstances where the vast majority of disinterested shareholders were against the continuation of the claim and where the independent directors have decided not to continue the claim.[75]

The courts also use their discretionary powers to refer the decision back to the company. For example, in *Iesini v Westrip* Lewison J concluded that the company had a strong case to assert a trust claim over assets held by another company. The board of directors had originally decided not to pursue the claim, but that was on the basis of legal analysis that relied on facts supplied to the lawyers by individuals who had a conflict of interest. Lewison J therefore used CA 2006, section 261(4)(c) to adjourn the hearing and gave directions that the board reconsider the company's position in relation to the trust claim.[76]

The position of creditors is also integrated into this analysis. In relation to a company that is insolvent the court has examined the views of creditors.[77] A canvassing of their views revealed that they were opposed to the proceedings and that there was frustration about the delay in payment. HH Judge Simon Barker QC then analysed if the derivative claim would materially extend the time for the creditors to be paid. He concluded that this was not the case and granted permission for the claim to be continued.[78]

Cause of action of the member in his own right

From the point of view of the company a petition under CA 2006, section 994 is 'far preferable, principally because it will only be a nominal party and will not incur any legal costs'.[79] If the complaint is better resolved through an unfair prejudice petition the courts will generally not give permission to continue a derivative claim. *Godwin v Cook*, for example, concerned three friends who became business partners carrying out a loss-making development through a company. All three of them had potential claims against the other two. A derivative action was not the obvious legal vehicle to resolve the real disputes between them and so the claim was not allowed to continue.[80]

---

[75] *Bridge v Daley* [2015] EWHC 2121 (HC), 2015 WL 4744908, [74].
[76] *Iesini v Westrip Holdings Ltd* [2011] 1 BCLC 498, [108].
[77] *Montgold Capital LLP v Ilska* [2018] EWHC 2982 (Ch), [2019] BCC 309, [45].
[78] ibid [45]–[46].
[79] *Iesini v Westrip Holdings Ltd* [2011] 1 BCLC 498 [124].
[80] *Godwin v Cook*, Chancery Division 21 June 2018 HC-2017-000742 [79]; see also *Mission Capital plc v Sinclair* [2008] EWHC 1339 (C), [2010] 1 BCLC 304.

The availability of an unfair prejudice claim under CA 2006, section 994 is, however, not an absolute bar.[81] Even if a shareholder has, in the course of the dispute, requested to be bought out that does not prevent him from later seeking a financial remedy for misconduct and an order for restitution against certain directors. Neither of these remedies can be obtained on an unfair prejudice petition.[82] If the claimant wishes to keep his interest in the future value and the exploitation of the main asset held by the company (the back music catalogue of the band 'New Order') that also justifies a derivative action.[83] The fact that a personal claim under a joint venture agreement might be affected by the reflective loss principle is a factor that has been considered in favour of a derivative action.[84]

Views of members without a personal interest

The court 'shall have particular regards to any evidence before it as to the views of members of the company who have no personal interest, direct or indirect, in the matter'.[85] This echoes the decision in *Smith v Croft (No 2)*. If the overwhelming majority of the disinterested shareholders is against the continuation of the claim the court will not give permission.[86]

In *Stainer v Lee* the claimant was a minority shareholder. He held 0.08 per cent of the share capital and had secured letters of support and financial contributions from thirty-five other small shareholders. There had been significant developments since the other shareholders had given their initial support. It was therefore inappropriate to give weight to those expressions under section 263(4), but the court nevertheless considered the applicant's conduct in seeking and obtaining support as 'strong evidence' that he was acting in good faith.[87]

9.2.10 Stage two—no prescribed standard of proof

CA 2006, sections 263 (2) and (3) do not set out a specific standard of proof for stage two. This follows a recommendation from the Law Commission that there should be no such test partly to avoid the risk of a detailed investigation into the merits of the case taking place at leave stage, and partly to avoid the drawing of fine distinctions based on the language of a particular rule.[88]

The court decides on the basis of the particulars of claim, skeleton arguments, and the written evidence submitted by the parties. The evidence available at this stage includes

[81] *Mumbray v Lapper* [2005] EWHC 1152, [2005] BCC 990 citing *Barrett v Duckett* [1995] BCC 362, 367.
[82] *Stainer v Lee* [2010] EWHC 1539, [2011] BCC 134, [49]–[52].
[83] *Hook v Sumner* [2015] EWHC 3820, [2016] BCC 220, [132].
[84] *Cullen v Brown* [2015] EWHC 473, [2016] 1 BCLC 491, [60].
[85] CA 2006, s 263(4).
[86] *Bridge v Daley* [2015] EWHC 2121 (HC), 2015 WL 4744908, [73]–[74].
[87] *Stainer v Lee* [2010] EWHC 1539, [2011] BCC 134, [49].
[88] *Kleanthous v Paphitis* [2011] EWHC 2287, [2012] BCC 676, [41] and [42].

witness statements, printed out emails, information downloaded from a website, newspaper articles, copies of written agreements, credit card statements, or the company's accounts.[89] Parties have also supplied written expert reports.[90] There has not yet been a full disclosure exercise.[91] No witnesses are heard or cross-examined.

The courts have held that the claimant has to establish 'something more' than a *prima facie* case but not necessarily a 'strong case'.[92] This is because the *prima facie* case has already been established in stage one. The case does not necessarily need to be 'strong' because it would be 'quite wrong . . . to embark on anything like a mini-trial of the action'. The court has to

> form a view on the strength of the claim in order properly to consider the requirements of s 263(2)(a) and 263(2)(b) . . . Of course any view can only be provisional where the action has yet to be tried: but the court must, I think, do the best it can on the material before it.[93]

The court can 'potentially grant permission for a derivative action to be continued without being satisfied that there is a strong case'.[94]

In *Hook v Sumner* the action was permitted to continue on the basis that there was 'at least a reasonable prospect' that the claimant would establish at trial that the directors had breached their duty by causing the company to enter into a trademark agreement.[95] There was also 'at least a good arguable case' that the resolutions by the allegedly wrongdoing directors in their capacity as shareholders were not valid to ratify the directors' actions.[96]

In *Montgold Capital LLP v Ilska* the claimant alleged a conspiracy which involved the directors of the company conspiring with an accountant, an insolvency practitioner, and an Alternative Investment Market (AIM) listed company to sell the company at an undervalue in a pre-pack insolvency arrangement. Simon Barker QC held that it was a fair starting point that these allegations were 'inherently improbable', but that the claimant's evidence and submissions by the claimant's counsel which drew attention to the events over time and the nondisclosure by some of the defendants 'point[ed] to a realistic case in unlawful means of conspiracy'.[97] He concluded that there were 'good reasons for working on the premise that [the company] . . . was not insolvent' when it was put into administration by the directors.[98] There was also 'credible evidence' that

---

[89] See eg *Saatchi v Gajjar* [2019] EWHC 2472 (Ch) (unreported) [9]–[23], [64], and [73].
[90] *Montgold Capital LLP v Ilska* [2018] EWHC 2982 (Ch), [2019] BCC 309, [4] and *Hook v Sumner* [2015] EWHC 3820, [2016] BCC 220 [4].
[91] *Cullen v Brown* [2015] EWHC 473, [2016] 1 BCLC 491, [36].
[92] *Iesini v Westrip Holdings Ltd* [2011] 1 BCLC 498 [79]; *Saatchi v Gajjar* [2019] EWHC 2472 (Ch) (unreported) [29].
[93] *Iesini v Westrip Holdings Ltd* [2011] 1 BCLC 498 [79].
[94] *Kleanthous v Paphitis* [2011] EWHC 2287 [40] (Newey J).
[95] *Hook v Sumner* [2015] EWHC 3820, [2016] BCC 220, [66].
[96] ibid [92]–[93].
[97] *Montgold Capital LLP v Ilska* [2018] EWHC 2982 (Ch), [2019] BCC 309, [25].
[98] ibid [29].

a number of independent restaurateurs had offered to buy the company's business at a much higher price.[99]

9.2.11 Limited permission to continue

Courts tread carefully and exercise restraint in permitting derivative actions. They are reluctant to grant permission outright even in cases that appear strong and tend to limit permission to certain limited procedural steps. In *Stainer v Lee*, for example, the court allowed the claim to proceed to disclosure stage and capped the cost indemnity to £40,000.[100]

9.2.12 Indemnity for cost

In *Iesini v Westrip Holdings Ltd* it was held that if the court finds that a claim is being properly pursued for the benefit of the company, it should ordinarily order that the company should pay the cost of doing so.[101] That dictum was, however, later qualified. The fact that the claimant does not seek an indemnity for cost can be a factor weighing in favour of granting permission to continue the claim.[102] In *Hook v Sumner* it was held that in a dispute between shareholders 'the court can be properly concerned that . . . an indemnity given by the company to one side or the other gives an unfair advantage to that side'.[103] Moreover, the fact that it was a relatively close decision as to whether a derivative claim or a shareholders' petition was the better course to pursue persuaded the court not to exercise discretion in favour of an indemnity.[104]

9.2.13 Theoretical observations

Derivative claims are a good example supporting the theory put forward in this book. The law acknowledges that organizations are autonomous actors characterized by their procedural framework. Company law integrates this insight and prescribes procedures with a strong focus on the interests of the shareholders while also integrating other interests. The aim of the rule in *Foss v Harbottle* and the statutory derivative action is to protect the decision-making process of the company.

This principle is sometimes referred to as the 'majority rule'.[105] It is true that derivative actions do not succeed at common law and are still unlikely to succeed under the

---

[99] ibid [23].
[100] *Stainer v Lee* [2010] EWHC 1539, [2011] BCC 134, [55]–[56].
[101] *Iesini v Westrip Holdings Ltd* [2011] 1 BCLC 498, [125]–[126].
[102] *Cullen v Brown* [2015] EWHC 473, [2016] 1 BCLC 491, [55].
[103] *Hook v Sumner* [2015] EWHC 3820, [2016] BCC 220, [139].
[104] ibid [138]–[141].
[105] Sarah Worthington, *Sealy and Worthington's Texts and Materials on Company Law* (11th edn, OUP 2016) 667.

statutory regime in circumstances where the majority of the shareholders has ratified or can ratify a breach of duty by the directors. The 'majority rule' label does capture such cases. But it does not fully describe the scope of the investigation that is carried out both at common law and under the statute.

Rather than just determining whether an arithmetical majority of the shareholders have taken or could have taken the litigation decision the courts determine if there was an independent organ capable of taking that decision. They examine if a process can operate that is independent and appropriate to form the 'corporate will'.[106] This acknowledges the existence of a 'corporate will' that is independent of the will of any of the participants.

At common law this point is well expressed in following the dictum by Knox J in *Smith v Croft (No 2)*: The courts aim to secure that a 'realistic assessment of the practical desirability of the action going forward should be made and should be made by the organ that has the power and ability to take decisions on behalf of the company'.[107]

> If it is an expression of the corporate will of the company by an appropriate independent organ that is preventing the plaintiff from prosecuting the action he is not improperly but properly prevented . . . The appropriate independent organ will very according to the constitution of the company concerned and the identity of the defendants who will in most cases be disqualified from participating by voting in expressing the corporate will.[108]

In their analysis the courts do more than apply the procedures set out in the Companies Act or in the constitution. If the majority of the shareholder is associated with the wrongdoers the courts defer to a decision by those shareholders or those members of the board who are independent of the wrongdoers. Both of these possibilities were established at common law without any backing from the Companies Act or company's constitution. They have now been integrated as discretionary factors into the statutory derivative action.

The courts acknowledge that a self-interest can exist that disqualifies the wrongdoing shareholders from ratifying a breach. But they do not analyse the problems arising in this area in terms of a binary conflict between majority and minority shareholders. They do not refer to the interests of any particular group of participants. They refer to the interests of the company. They determine if the company is able to operate an independent decision-making process. By doing that they integrate the interests of shareholders and shareholder sub-groups as well as the interests of creditors into the analysis.

---

[106] *Smith v Croft (No 2)* [1988] 1 Ch 114, 184[F] and 185[A]–185[C]; see also John Armour, 'Derivative Actions: A Framework for Decision' [2019] 135 LQR 412.

[107] *Smith v Croft No 2* [1988] 1 Ch 114, 184[A].

[108] ibid 185[B].

The statutory derivative action rests on the same principles as the common law. CA 2006 made a number of changes to the common law. For example, shareholder directors can no longer ratify their own breaches of duty.[109] But it left the logic of the common law intact.[110] The company is the proper plaintiff. As far as the corporate decision-making process is concerned the statutory process was put in place because the common law had become too complicated and unwieldy.[111] The idea nevertheless continues to be that the courts will only interfere when the no decision-making process can be found that operates independently of the wrongdoers.

Like the common law the statutory derivative action adheres to the principle that the decision to bring a claim for a wrong is a matter 'to be decided by the company internally; that is to say by its board of directors, or by a majority of its shareholders if dissatisfied by the boards' decision.'[112] The court does 'not second guess a decision made by the company in accordance with its own constitution.'[113] The exception to these principles are 'necessitated where the company's own constitution could not properly be operated.'[114]

The statutory criteria for testing if such a situation has arisen have taken inspiration from the considerations that underpinned the common law. These considerations have, however, been removed from the encrusted structure that had formed around them. Courts now have more flexibility in assessing the ability of the corporate process to take a decision to litigate.[115]

Sometimes the courts justify their deference to the corporate decision-making process by reference to their own limited commercial aptitude. When Lewison J, for example, articulated his eight criteria for determining what a person acting in accordance with CA 2006, s 172 would do, he observed that, 'weighing of all these considerations is essentially a commercial decision, which the court is ill-equipped to take, except in clear cases'.[116] It is suggested that Lewison J was not commenting on the court's limited commercial ability in this dictum. UK judges are well qualified to assess the benefits of bringing legal proceedings. Prior to their judicial appointment they have spent many

---

[109] CA 2006, s 239(2).

[110] David Kershaw argues that the majority rule is a necessary component of the proper plaintiff rule. He suggests that it is not possible to adopt the proper plaintiff rule without also having to accept the majority rule. I agree that there is a connection. But that connection operates between the proper plaintiff rule and the requirement for the law then to review the process whereby the corporate decision is taken. The litigation decision can be allocated to the majority of the shareholders. It can also be allocated to a majority of 5 per cent of the shareholders. We could also adopt a rule whereby one shareholder irrespective of how large their holding has the right to bring a derivative claim. Either way, the company is the proper plaintiff.

[111] Law Commission, Shareholder Remedies Report (Law Com No 246) [6.4].

[112] *Iesini v Westrip Holdings Ltd* [2009] EWHC 2526 (Ch), [2011] 1 BCLC 498, [73].

[113] ibid.

[114] ibid.

[115] The expectation that this would lead to an increase in shareholder litigation has, however, not materialized (David Gibbs-Kneller and Chidiebere Ogonnaya, 'Empirical Analysis of the Statutory Derivative Claim: De Facto Application and the Sine Quibus Non' [2019] JCLS 303).

[116] *Iesini v Westrip Holdings Ltd* [2009] EWHC 2526 (Ch), [2011] 1 BCLC 498 [85], [107].

years observing and assisting clients in analysing and weighing the factors surrounding litigation decisions. The decision whether or not to litigate is admittedly a commercial decision, but it is one that judges are qualified to engage with. The observation that the court is 'ill-equipped' is better understood as an expression of the court's preference not to involve itself (regardless of how commercially minded the judges are). It echoes the analysis at common law showing a preference of the judges for the corporate process to run its course wherever possible.

Iesini, in particular, was a case where the directors had taken certain legal steps after having received legal advice from counsel.[117] Lewison J did not hold back on giving his opinion on the legal questions that were in front of the board of directors and on the legal advice prepared by counsel.[118] He, for example, expressed the view that the 'trust case' was a strong one and found it surprising that certain documents had not been given any weight by Australian counsel.[119] He nevertheless concluded that the best course of action for him was to exercise the power under CA section 261(4)(c) to direct the board to reconsider the company's position.[120]

In *Carlen v Drury* Lord Lord Eldon made his well-known comment that 'This Court is not to be required on every Occasion to take the Management of every Playhouse and Brewhouse in the Kingdom.'[121] That comment is then qualified with the dictum that the Court will interfere if 'the Case justifies' such an interference. For that 'there must be a positive Necessity . . . arising from the Refusal or Neglect of the Committee [responsible for the decision] to act.'[122]

The point that the reluctance of the courts to interfere through derivative actions is explained by a deliberate decision to defer to the corporate decision-making process is also supported by the fact the courts have been comfortable with intervening through the unfair prejudice remedy. Judging from their attitude in relation to derivative actions this was unexpected.[123] In relation to unfair prejudice an intervention is usually carried out through a purchase order and this allows the courts to resolve problems without having to interfere with autonomous decision-making by the company.

At the moment the unfair prejudice remedy does not appear to be easily available to listed or other companies that cannot be characterized as quasi-partnerships.[124] At a normative level it would be possible to build on the insight that the courts are less

---

[117] ibid [87].
[118] ibid [91]–[98].
[119] ibid [107], see also [106].
[120] ibid [109]–[110].
[121] *Carlen v Drury* (1812) 1 Ves and B 149, 158; 35 ER 61, 62.
[122] ibid 63.
[123] Paul Davies and Sarah Worthington, *Gower & Davies: Principles of Modern Company Law* (10th edn, OUP 2016) para 20-3.
[124] *Re Blue Arrow plc* [1997] BCLC 585; *Re Leeds United Holdings plc* [1997] BCC 131; *Re Astec* (BSR) *plc* [1998] 2 BCLC 556.

hesitant to intervene when they are given a tool that allows them to respect the corporate decision-making process. This book is agnostic as to whether more, and if so, how much more directorial accountability is needed.[125] If more accountability was desired it would be possible to design a remedy that permits significant shareholders of companies, whose directors have breached their duties, to request that the wrong-doing directors purchase their shares on terms that the court thinks fit.

In addition, even in cases where the company has no business of its own and is an entity to organize the distribution of income to its shareholders the court operates on the assumption that there is a corporate interest. In *Hook v Sumner* the court was presented with the point that the company did not have a business of its own. It was a shell. It collected income derived from the music catalogue created by the band 'New Order' and distributed that income to the shareholders. The court held that this was not a relevant consideration in whether to permit a derivative claim. It was 'irrelevant' what the company does with the income it receives. 'A company's interest in carrying on its business encompasses making the revenue that it does from its activities, whether it uses that revenue for its own corporate purpose, for instance in paying its creditors and liabilities, or in distribution to its shareholders.'[126] 'In the present case, the distribution is made by way of payments under service agreements, but whether that is characterized as a payment of creditors or a distribution to shareholders, it seems to me that it makes no difference at all. The company nevertheless has an interest in maximizing the amount of revenue it receives and deals with.'[127]

Any award will be paid to the company and dealt with there in accordance with the duties owed by the directors. It becomes part of the company's revenue. That revenue is then for the directors to use for the benefit of the company and in accordance with their duties. Shareholders will benefit indirectly from an increase in the value of the business of the company. They may also benefit directly through a distribution. The distribution rules build creditor interests into the company's procedural framework. Either way the shareholders' return is mediated through the company.

Creditor interests are woven into both the common law and the statutory remedy. Creditor-oriented and other statutory wrongs are not ratifiable by the shareholders. At common law a derivative action is therefore generally unavailable. Under the statutory regime any purported authorization or ratification of such wrongs does not block a statutory derivative action. At discretion stage the fact that a wrong cannot be ratified is a relevant factor in allowing the derivative action.

---

[125] For an argument in favour of making derivative claims more widely available see eg Andrew Keay, 'Assessing and Rethinking the Statutory Scheme for Derivative Actions under the Companies Act 2006' [2016] Journal of Corporate Law Studies 16; see also Arad Reisberg, 'Derivative Claims Under the Companies Act 2006: Much Ado About Nothing?' in John Armour and Jennifer Payne (eds), *Rationality in Company Law: Essays in Honour of Dan Prentice* (2009 Hart Publishing) 17.
[126] *Hook v Sumner* [2015] EWHC 3820, [2016] BCC 220, [112].
[127] ibid [113].

The law not only protects the company from claimants who are acting in bad faith. We have seen that the courts are also reluctant to allow claimants to proceed when their conduct of the litigation would be 'a recipe for disaster'.[128] This is because any reasonable director would not allow such an individual to conduct legal proceedings on behalf of the company.[129]

The rules governing derivative actions protect the 'corporate interest' by mediating between the interests of the different participants. It is possible at the most granular level to isolate two participants and discuss how the law mediates a conflict between them. It is also possible at the highest level of abstraction to observe that ultimately a decision of the shareholders will go a long way towards barring a claim. But for everything in between a binary analysis does not reflect the law at a positive level. Creditor interests are integrated into the distribution rules which determine the extent to which shareholders will benefit from any money recovered in a derivative claim. Shareholders cannot override these. They can also not sanction breaches of these rules and so the rule in *Foss v Harbottle* does not obstruct derivative claims. Minority shareholder interests are integrated into the procedure for calling meetings. They are also integrated in terms of special majority requirements, breaches of which again cannot be ratified by the majority, and there is no ban for derivative claims. Analysing derivative claims solely from the perspective of agency theory misses how the rules interact with each other creating a web of procedure which balances the interests of the participants involved.

9.3 Public enforcement

We have throughout this book encountered examples of instances in which directors encounter publicly enforceable liability for the failure of directors to comply with certain requirements of the Companies Act. We have seen, for example, that such liability arises in connection with the duty of the directors to keep the information maintained by Companies House up to date.[130] Criminal liability also attaches to the failure to comply with requirements such as in the keeping accounting records and to the production, authorization, verification, and publication of accounts.[131] There is also personal criminal liability attached to the failure to ensure that the published accounts and reports comply with the statutory requirements. A director is however liable only if he

---

[128] *Bridge v Daley* [2015] EWHC 2121 (HC) 2015 WL 4744908, [86]. Similar consideration were expressed at common law albeit in a milder form. In *Prudential Assurance v Newman Industries* (CA) [1982] 1 Ch 204 at 224 it was observed that the plaintiffs overwhelmed the court with thirty or more accusations of fraud but in the end fell back on six claims. Of the six the second was abandoned. Large sums of money were spent on the litigation. This was unfair on those shareholders who were not involved in the fraud but were also not involved in pursuing the claim.

[129] *Bridge v Daley* [2015] EWHC 2121 (HC), 2015 WL 4744908, [84].

[130] Section 6.2.4 in this book.

[131] Section 7.10.9 in this book.

knew or recklessly did not know that the accounts or reports were not compliant and also if he did not take reasonable steps to ensure compliance.[132] The sanctions for the failure to produce reports on specific social and environmental matters have also been discussed above.[133]

From a theoretical perspective we can observe that the duties of directors, which are designed to protect the interests of third parties, have a publicly funded enforcement mechanism attached to them. The government has, however, conceded that prosecutions particularly in relation to solvent companies have been rare and is currently consulting on implementing a more robust liability regime for directors.[134] The point that stakeholder-oriented duties are associated with public enforcement nevertheless stands.

We have also seen above that the Company Director Disqualification Act 1986 sets up a statutory regime through which directors of both insolvent and solvent companies can be disqualified. The court can also order a director to indemnify the company against any loss it has suffered.[135] We have seen that the disqualification regime operates if a director has shown him- or herself to be unfit to be concerned with the management of a company. We have also seen that in relation to disqualification creditor interests are a main focus.[136] The disqualification rules operate when a director has committed a criminal offence in relation to companies. He may be disqualified if he has been convicted of an indictable offence in connection with the promotion, formation, management, liquidation, or striking off of a company, has persistently breached companies legislation, has been guilty of fraud or fraudulent trading or has been in breach of any provision in the companies legislation requiring a return, account, or other document to be filed or notice to be given to the registrar of companies.[137]

At a positive level we can observe that the legislature attaches publicly enforceable sanctions to breaches of the directors that can be considered to serve the interests of third parties. At a normative level it is worth taking note here of a debate that is ongoing more generally in relation to personal regulatory sanctions imposed on individual decision-makers.[138] Such sanctions are designed to provide an incentive for such decision-makers to comply with regulatory requirements. This has most recently been criticized as falling short of addressing an important factor shaping the ability of organizations to comply with regulation. It overlooks

[132] CA 2006, s 414 (4) and (5) (annual accounts); CA 2006, s 414D (2) and (3) (strategic report); CA 2006, s 419 (3) and (4) (directors' report); CA 2006, s 422 (2) and (3) (remuneration report).
[133] Section 7.10.8 in this book.
[134] Department for Business, Energy and Industrial Strategy, *Restoring Trust in Audit and Corporate Governance*, CP 382, March 2021 [5.1].
[135] Section 7.6.4 in this book.
[136] Section 7.6.4 in this book.
[137] Company Director Disqualification Act 1986, s 2–5.
[138] See eg the discussion provided in Law Commission, Criminal Liability in Regulatory Contexts, Consultation Paper No 195 (August 2010).

the importance of corporate culture for ensuring that organizations comply with regulatory requirements.[139] Corporate culture can be a factor undermining the compliance.[140] It is not enough to focus on individual actors and their incentives. Sometimes the processes operated by organizations create a toxic culture and this problem cannot be explained or solved solely through the analysis and alignment of incentives.

[139] See Nien-he Hsieh, Benjamin Lange, David Rodin, and Mira LA Wolf-Bauwens, 'Getting Clear on Corporate Culture: Conceptualisation, Measurement, and `Operationalisation' (2018) 6 Journal of the British Academy 155; Christopher Hodge, 'Science-Based Regulation in Financial Services: From Deterrence to Culture' Oxford Legal Studies Research Paper 19/2020, available from https://papers.ssrn.com/sol3/papers.cfm?abstract_id=3590176; see also Amir N Licht, 'Culture and Law in Corporate Governance' in Jeffrey N Gordon and Wolf-Georg Ringe (eds), The Oxford Handbook of Corporate Law and Governance (OUP 2018), 129.
[140] For an illustrative example of this phenomenon see Kweku Adoboli, 'How to Stop Finance Companies from Succumbing to Cultural Failure' Financial Times 13 March 2017 available from https://www.ft.com/content/5a4019d8-f842-11e6-bd4e-68d53499ed71.

10

Stakeholders

The observation made in this book is that we should not limit ourselves in the analysis of company by dissecting the law at a positive level into binary conflicts between two particular participants. It has been shown in this book that the law gives shareholders more influence than creditors, employees, or other constituencies but that the interests of these stakeholders are integrated into company law.

We have seen that creditor interests are woven through the fabric of company law. The process of setting up companies and the requirement to update these records ensures that third parties dealing with companies have information enabling them to enter into contractual arrangements with the company. Corporate personality exists from registration until a company has been wound up. No third party dealing with a registered company has to reckon with the fact that its foundational process might be affected by vitiating factors.[1] The *ultra vires* doctrine was abolished because it made it difficult for companies to interact in a commercial environment.[2]

Veil piercing at common law is rare. But limited liability (rather than separate legal personality) is removed for directors and shadow directors who trade wrongfully, operate phoenix companies, or have proven unfit to be concerned with the management of a company. Tort law provides a mechanism for imposing liability on parent companies which rather than behaving as shareholders involve themselves operationally in the business of their subsidiary.[3] Statutes increasingly accommodate the phenomenon that corporate groups operate as organizations that stretch beyond the formal legal boundaries of the corporate form.[4]

Companies are recognized as autonomous actors both in tort and criminal law, ensuring that third parties can reach the assets owned by companies but also providing an incentive for corporate decision-makers to operate a process that prevents blameworthy organizational behaviour.

Companies Act 2006, section 172 requires directors to have regard to stakeholder interests.[5] The duty of skill and care requires directors to ensure that companies comply with the legal requirements imposed on companies through regulation. It operates as a conduit through which stakeholder interests protected by law are channelled into company law.[6]

---

[1] Sections 2.5, 2.6, 6.2.4, and 6.3 in this book.
[2] Chapter 3 in this book.
[3] Chapter 4 in this book.
[4] Section 4.4 in this book.
[5] Section 7.4.2 in this book.
[6] Section 7.6 in this book.

Company Law. Eva Micheler, Oxford University Press. © Eva Micheler 2021. DOI: 10.1093/oso/9780198858874.003.0010

The rules regulating conflicts of interest have explicitly been described by the courts as also serving creditor interests.

The extensive recording and reporting requirements established in the Companies Act are designed to ensure that directors have a realistic and up-to-date understanding of the assets and liabilities owed by their companies. There are narrative reporting requirements that encourage directors to clarify and report on the company's position in relation to wider societal interests.[7]

Shareholders have powers to take certain corporate decisions but in taking these decisions they are bound by rules protecting minority shareholders and also cannot override rules that protect creditors.[8]

Both directors and shareholders are bound by mandatory distribution rules that are designed to ensure that shareholders receive returns only after creditor interests have been taken into account.[9]

The level of stakeholder involvement has changed over time. The combination of financial crises of 2008 and the 2016 Brexit Referendum has prompted reform shifting away from the shareholder-focused debate of the earlier corporate governance debate. The UK Corporate Governance Code 2018 now recommends that companies focus on purpose rather than simply on turning a profit.[10] The legislature has introduced a number of stakeholder-focused reporting requirements encouraging companies to consider and address their impact on certain interests in anticipation of the reports they are required to publish. This technique has been referred to as civil regulation.[11]

The theory adopted in this book explains company law at a positive level from the insight that organizations are real social actors that are characterized by habits, routines, process, and procedures that form naturally when human beings interact. The law builds on this phenomenon and formalizes it in the way described in this book. This perspective is neutral as to how much shareholder versus stakeholder influence there should be.

Three normative conclusions nevertheless flow from the theoretical perspective advanced in this book. The first one is that we should give up on the idea that financial incentives can serve interests other than those of the directors. In light of the difficulties experienced with designing remuneration such that it aligns with shareholder interests, this author believes that any attempt to align remuneration with long-term goals as suggested in the UK Corporate Governance Code 2018 or with ecological or social aims is doomed to fail.[12]

---

[7] Section 7.10 in this book.
[8] Section 8.3 in this book.
[9] Sections 7.11 and 8.5 in this book.
[10] Section 3.4 in this book.
[11] Sections 7.10.7 and 7.10.9 in this book.
[12] UK Corporate Governance Code 2018, principle P states: 'Remuneration policies and practices . . . be designed to support strategy and promote long-term sustainable success.' Executive remuneration should be aligned to company purpose and values, and be clearly linked to the successful delivery of the company's long-term strategy.

The problem associated with performance-related remuneration is the difficulty associated with identifying performance indicators that lead to outcomes that serve particular goals combined with the ability of directors to game any performance criteria imposed on them rather than one of identifying an appropriate decision-maker.

The second normative observation is that programmatic statements encouraging companies to have a purpose or encouraging directors to consider stakeholder interests in the same way as shareholder interests are unlikely to have much effect.[13] This is because they do not reach into the social structure of the company.

Thirdly, if there is a desire to further integrate non-shareholder interests into company law, this is, from the perspective of this book, best achieved through an integration of their interests into the decision-making process of the company.[14] Non-shareholder interests can be incorporated through the creation of roles that represent these interests. The technique of personifying certain responsibilities in the structure of organizations is currently applied in the context of financial services where roles have been created that ensure compliance with financial regulation.[15] Under the Senior Managers Certification Regime certain senior management roles must be either pre-approved by the regulator or certified in house.[16] The Financial Conduct Authority authorized firms must also have a management responsibility map.[17] Along similar lines certain large companies need to appoint a senior accounting officer to ensure that they are able to comply with their tax-accounting responsibilities.[18]

More generally the UK Corporate Governance Code recommends the integration of workforce-related concerns through a director appointed from the workforce, a formal workforce advisory panel, or a designated non-executive director. Other societal interests could be integrated in the same way. It would be possible for companies to be encouraged to identify specific board members or committees as representing ecological or social goals on the board. It has already been mentioned that there is a risk that the designation of certain roles is no silver bullet. It is possible for the culture of an

[13] See sections 3.4 and 7.4.4 in this book.
[14] For a recent and high-profile academic statement in favour of a greater integration of stakeholder concerns into company law see Andrew Johnston and others, 'Corporate Governance for Sustainability' (11 December 2020) <https://papers.ssrn.com/sol3/papers.cfm?abstract_id=3502101>; see also Abraham A Singer, *The Form of the Firm* (OUP 2019).
[15] I am grateful to Deborah Sabalot Deane for helping me identify the sources on the Senior Management Certification Regime.
[16] For an overview see: Deloitte, Senior Managers Regime, Individual Accountability and Reasonable Steps (2016) <www2.deloitte.com/content/dam/Deloitte/uk/Documents/financial-services/deloitte-uk-senior-manager-regime.pdf>; Bank of England, Prudential Regulation Authority and Financial Conduct Authority, Senior Managers Regime: Statement of Responsibilities <www.bankofengland.co.uk/-/media/boe/files/prudential-regulation/authorisations/senior-managers-and-senior-insurance-managers-regimes-approvals/smr-statement-of-responsibilities-september-2019.pdf>; Financial Conduct Authority, The Senior Managers and Certification Regime, Guide for FCA solo-regulated firms (July 2019) <www.fca.org.uk/publication/policy/guide-for-fca-solo-regulated-firms.pdf>; Bank of England, Strengthening Accountability <www.bankofengland.co.uk/prudential-regulation/key-initiatives/strengthening-accountability>.
[17] Financial Conduct Authority, Finalised Guidance 19/2 Senior Managers and Certification Regime: Guidance on Statements of Responsibilities and Responsibilities Maps for FCA Firms <www.fca.org.uk/publications/finalised-guidance/fg19-2-smcr-guidance-statements-responsibilities-and-responsibilities-maps>
[18] Section 7.10.2 in this book.

organization to undermine the interests represented in that role and the designation of a particular role can degenerate into a license for other members of the organization to disengage with these interests.[19] But overall, the technique of creating a role representing an interest in the corporate decision-making process is closer to the way organizations act than the setting of individual financial incentives.

---

[19] Section 3.4 in this book.

11

Conclusions

In this book company law has been explained through a real entity theory. In the theory advanced by this book the law does not create organizations but finds them as a real social phenomenon.

When human beings interact, habits, routines, processes, and procedures form. These affect the way participants of an organization act and so are real in their consequences. Organizations are characterized by this social structure. There also exists individual agency, which enables participants to deviate from the social structure and over time also to modify it.

At a positive level company law can be explained as making it easier for organizations to act autonomously and also as supplying a decision-making process that assigns roles to directors, shareholders, auditors, and a company secretary.

Not all organizations are companies and not every company operates as an organization. But we have seen in this book that company law is nevertheless designed with a view to facilitating autonomous organizational action.

Organizations are real in their consequences but have no permanent physical manifestation. Separate legal personality overcomes this problem by giving an organization operated through a company autonomous legal status.

The capacity of a company used to be limited by its memorandum. This can be justified on a concession argument and also on a contract-based analysis. But it proved unsuitable for the operation of commercial organizations and so the ultra vires doctrine has been abolished. Because organizations act autonomously, they need flexibility and so a legal rule that tied companies to objects identified by their first shareholders invariably disappeared from the law.

Unlike normal contracts companies are not considered void because of vitiating factors that affect their constitution. They need to be wound up to come to an end. A contract can disappear with one stroke of the law, an organization cannot be dissolved in this way.

The rules permitting veil piercing on the limited basis available at common law do not affect the separate legal personality of the company but rather remove the principle of limited liability in particular circumstances. There are a number of statutory provisions that address abuses of the corporate form such as fraudulent trading, wrongful trading, and directors' disqualification. The law of negligence can operate to allow tort victims

Company Law. Eva Micheler, Oxford University Press. © Eva Micheler 2021. DOI: 10.1093/oso/9780198858874.003.0011

to 'pierce the corporate veil'. In all of these instances, however, the legal personality of the company stands. Veil piercing only affects limited liability.

To facilitate interaction with third parties the Companies Act also prohibits the shareholders of non-charitable companies from limiting the authority of the directors through the constitution. Companies are also liable in tort and crime, which demonstrates that the law recognizes them as autonomous actors. Criminal law has recently also developed a technique for defining organizational fault.

The Companies Act sets out a basis for the allocation of decision-making power within the company. It defines four roles: shareholders, directors, auditors, and a company secretary. The Act also identifies responsibilities for each of these. The shareholders are bound by this allocation but are able to further specify the corporate decision-making process. The constitution is not a contract but rather an instrument adopted on a statutory basis through private action.

Directors owe their duties to the company. The law primarily requires directors to abide by their constitutional powers and follow the procedures set out in the Act and in the constitution. It is not designed to directly enhance economic interests. Directors are also not required to maximize return. Shareholders are indirect beneficiaries of the directors' efforts. Their interests are reflected in the law to a greater extent that those of the creditors or wider society. But it would be wrong overall to characterize the shareholders as agents of the directors or the shareholders as principals of the directors or of the company. The law integrates the interests of creditors and also of wider society through the Act and also through the case law. Directors need to pay attention to these interests and shareholders are also restricted by these interests. There exists publicly funded enforcement for breaches of duty that can be characterized as mainly protecting third party interests.

Agency theory performs an important role in relation to the analysis of conflicts of interests affecting the decisions of directors. It helps to illuminate the problem the law is trying to address. But the rules managing such conflicts cannot be solely explained by economic reasoning. They fit better with the real entity theory advanced in this book.

The book does not express a preference as to how much influence shareholders should have as opposed to other constituencies. It also expresses no view as to whether directors are adequately overseen by either the shareholders or through external oversight. It rather acknowledges that there is no single factor explanation for the allocation of power at a positive level. This author believes that economic factors are an important explanatory factor, but that political, historical, and cultural factors also play a role. At a normative level these factors will and should also inform development of the law in the future. The real entity model advanced in this book does not tell us 'if' the law should intervene. It does, however, tell us 'how' the law should intervene.

The normative recommendation flowing from this book is that organizational action should not be compartmentalized into binary conflicts focusing on relationships between two participants at any one time. This author believes that the best way of guiding organizational action is through process-oriented intervention. Interventions that modify the decision-making process of the company go to the heart of organizational action. We can observe this in the failure-to-prevent model which holds companies to account when they do not have effective risk management procedures in place. We can also observe this throughout the Companies Act and in the UK Corporate Governance Code, which create roles and distribute decision-making between these. This is likely to be more effective than the manipulation of individual incentives.

Interventions that are designed to manipulate economic incentives of individual participants have proven too difficult to implement. Performance-related pay has so far failed to ensure that directors are rewarded for success while receiving less when they fail. This may be difficult to achieve but this author believes that shareholders should abandon the idea that performance-related remuneration can be made to work in their favour. We should also give up on the aspiration that pay packages can be designed with a view to serving stakeholder interests.

If there is a desire to strengthen the accountability of the board of directors this is best achieved through a modification of the rules governing enforcement rather than through rules modifying the content of the duties of the directors. The courts are reluctant to interfere with organizational decision-making and this reluctance is not only deeply ingrained but also justified from the perspective of the theory advanced in this book. The courts nevertheless have demonstrated in the context of the unfair prejudice claims that they are prepared to review the conduct of directors provided that they are given access to a remedy that does not involve the taking over of the corporate decision-making process. If there was an interest in strengthening directorial accountability a model could be designed for the enforcement of directors' duties that gives substantial individual shareholders the right to request that the directors who have breached their duties buy them out at a price that reverses the effect of the directors' misconduct. It would be possible to use the standard 5 per cent threshold to identify shareholders that have a significant investment in the company and so are permitted to claim. It would also be possible to permit the courts to order a remedy as they think fit. In this way the courts could overcome their current reluctance to substantively review litigation decisions while at the same time providing increased oversight for the directors.

If there is a desire to further integrate non-shareholder interests into company law this is, from the perspective of this book, best achieved through an integration of their interests into the decision-making process of the company.

Procedural interventions are not a panacea and can degenerate into box-ticking exercises but they nevertheless have the advantage of working with the social structure characterizing organizational action.

Index

For the benefit of digital users, indexed terms that span two pages (e.g., 52–53) may, on occasion, appear on only one of those pages.

Introductory Note
References such as '178–9' indicate (not necessarily continuous) discussion of a topic across a range of pages. Wherever possible in the case of topics with many references, these have either been divided into sub-topics or only the most significant discussions of the topic are listed. Because the entire work is about 'company law', the use of this term (and certain others which occur constantly throughout the book) as entry points has been restricted. Information will be found under the corresponding detailed topics.

abuses 33, 56, 58–59, 69, 244, 263–64
accountability 10–11, 15–16, 35–36, 147, 149, 154–55, 171, 201
    directorial 254–55, 265
accountants 95, 192–93, 250–51
accounting 150, 187, 192–93
    false 97
    International Accounting Standards 107–8, 174, 191
    records 125–26, 127, 170, 171, 172
        adequate 144–45, 171
        duty to keep 170–72
        and shareholders 221–22
    regulations 34–35, 170
    senior accounting officers 71, 171, 172, 261
accounts 107–8, 174, 175, 181, 183, 184, 192–93, 256–58
    annual 172–75, 180–81, 221, 223
    and reports 172–73, 176–77, 183, 184, 188
    required 184, 187
    revised 174, 180
    statutory 187
accuracy 170, 192–93
actors 9, 29, 69, 102
    autonomous 1, 6, 23, 29, 31, 33, 100
    external 79
    human 24, 26–27, 62, 77, 96, 97–98, 100
    individual 3, 26, 82, 102, 257–58
    rational 3, 4–5, 6, 11–12
    real social 29, 260
ad hoc basis 13, 56, 58
adequate accounting records 144–45, 171
adequate financial information 34, 125–26
adequate procedures 72, 94–95, 96, 144–45, 193–94
advisory panels 200, 235, 261–62

agency 39–40, 78, 79–80, 82, 90, 242–43
    approach 78, 138, 139
        standard 78, 79
    conflicts 4–5, 9, 179–80, 188
        between directors and shareholders 149
        between shareholders and directors 186
    costs 4–5, 158, 211–12
    frameworks 46, 77, 149
    human 24, 26, 29, 31
    individual 24–25, 31, 263
    model 10–11, 201–2, 204
    problems 11, 135–36, 158
    relationships 3–4, 5, 23, 42–43
    theory 1–12, 31, 135–36, 235
        evaluation 6–12
agents 3–5, 77, 78–80, 81, 201–2, 203
    of shareholders 4, 235
aggregation 3, 28, 29, 54, 101, 102
alignment, argument 167, 168
allocation of power 5, 128, 150, 264
allotments 206, 207
amendments 104, 110, 112, 119–20, 195, 198–200
    constitutional 106–7, 199, 234
annual accounts 172–75, 180–81, 221, 223
annual general meetings 108, 120, 201
annual reports 103–4, 175, 180–81, 188
anthropomorphic metaphors 82, 83–84, 86, 87, 99
anthropomorphism 15, 29, 82, 99–100
appellants 85
appropriate independent organs 240–41, 252
approval 119–21, 155, 156, 157, 159, 160, 161
    of interested transactions 155–56
    of self-dealing transactions 160–61
    shareholder 105–6, 127, 161–62, 164, 191–92, 210–11

arm's length test 216–17
articles of association 49–50, 85, 86–87, 103,
        112, 113, 114–15, 117
artificial existence 14, 40
artificial individuals 2
assets 61–62, 172–73, 190, 208–9, 210–11, 215–
        17, 246
    fixed 173–74
    and liabilities 172, 173, 190, 223, 260
    non-cash 161, 208
    valuation 173, 196–97, 234
attribution 14–15, 17–18, 77, 82, 84, 87, 90, 98
    rules 33, 81
audit 107–8, 117, 180–81, 182, 183, 221, 222
    committees 181
    processes 150, 181–83, 221–22
    reports 175, 187
auditors 33–34, 103–4, 111, 144–45, 180–83,
        205, 221–22
    appointment 170, 181
    independent 127, 180–81
    negligent 182–83, 222
    role 183, 222
Australia 96, 132, 199
authority of directors 79, 154
autonomous actors 1, 6, 23, 29, 31, 33, 100
autonomous organizational action 1, 35, 63,
        194, 204, 233, 263
autonomous real entities 1, 36
autonomy 102, 232, 233, 243–44
    protecting autonomy of company 232–33

bad faith 134, 199–200, 256
balance sheets 107, 172–73, 174, 181, 190, 223
banks 18, 22–23, 42, 44, 65, 89–90, 140
beginning and ending of companies 44–46
behaviour 1, 8, 21, 22–23, 26–27, 28
    corporate 76, 84, 90
    of directors 131, 169–70
    human 21, 22–23, 26, 28, 149–50
    organizational 1, 23, 27, 76, 84, 259
beneficiaries, indirect see indirect beneficiaries
best interests 131–32, 133, 218
bids 105–6, 210–11, 212
bilateral relationships 4, 29, 54
binary conflicts 8, 9, 197, 252, 259, 264–65
binding effects 113–14
binding force 112–13
blameworthy conduct 101, 102
board committees 111, 163, 165–66
board neutrality rule 211–12
boards 79–80, 110, 137–38, 144–45, 146, 155–
        56, 210–11, 239–40
    members 48, 148, 261–62

bonds 43, 133
book value 217, 234
boundaries 41, 46, 47, 66–67, 153, 217
    legal 37, 43, 68, 73, 74, 75
    organizational 32, 37, 41, 43, 46, 75
box ticking 110, 150, 265
breach of duty 17–18, 218–19, 220, 237–
        38, 242–43
breach of trust 220, 243
Brexit Referendum 53, 137, 147, 260
bribery 71, 72, 94–95, 102, 177–78
brute facts 21, 22–23, 32, 63
bubble companies 39
business conduct 92, 94–95, 131

capacity 48–55
    collapse of ultra vires doctrine 51–53
    contract as explanation for ultra vires
        doctrine 48–51
    and corporate purpose 53–54
    limited 32, 48–49, 52, 54
    theoretical observations 54–55
    unlimited 32, 48, 49, 52, 54, 79
capital 106, 108, 190, 209, 214–19,
        220–21
    legal 191, 209
    maintenance 191, 244–45
    reductions 106, 111, 215–16, 220–21, 241
    structure 177
care 138, 139–40, 141, 142, 148–49
    duty of 18, 42, 94, 139–40, 141, 182–83, 222
    reasonable 125, 140, 192–93
    skill and 125–26, 138, 139–40, 141,
        142, 148–49
        duty of 138, 140, 141, 142, 148–49
cargo 84–85
causation 65, 94–95, 228, 232
    and reflective loss 229–30
CEOs (Chief Executive Officers) 147, 165, 179
certificates of incorporation 38, 44–45
chair of the board 110, 146
charitable companies 32, 225, 264
charitable purposes 37, 54
Chief Executive Officers (CEOs) 147, 165, 179
City Code on Takeovers and Mergers 105–
        7, 210–11
civil penalties 73, 184
civil regulation 189, 260
claimant shareholders 156, 246–47
claimants 123, 247, 249, 250–51, 256
claims 227–28, 229–30, 231–32, 241–42, 245–
        47, 248
    creditor 8, 155, 191, 227
    damages 122, 197

derivate 239, 241, 248, 252, 256
derivative 243, 244–45, 247–48, 255, 256
potential 227–28, 248
unfair prejudice 30, 207, 249, 265
clients 68, 95, 225, 253–54
climate change 169–70
codes, corporate governance 111, 123, 147,
164–66, 178
codification 131, 132–33, 134, 137–38, 151
Cohen Committee 108, 201
commercial decisions 141, 213, 253–54
commercial judgement 141, 142, 234
commercial organizations 30, 32, 72–73, 263
committees 104–5, 110, 140, 147, 165–66, 167–
68, 181, 201
common law 8–9, 98, 102, 139–40, 239, 243,
251–52, 253
crimes 83, 88
early 139
rules 125, 151, 209, 215–16
commons 19–20
Companies House 44–45, 106–7, 184, 188,
189, 256–58
company directors see directors
Company Law Review 132–33, 141–42, 199
Steering Group 133, 142
company secretaries 33–34, 103–4, 106–7, 178,
179, 263, 264
company's business 105, 107, 145, 146, 153,
170–71, 176, 177
compensation 67, 144–45, 180, 199, 227, 241
claims 241–42
competence 139, 141–42
competencies 111, 129
Competition and Markets Authority 143–
44, 225–26
compliance 34, 107–8, 138, 180–81,
188, 256–58
securing 183, 184, 186
systems 90–91, 96
concealment 58–59, 61–62, 74, 180
concession theory 12–13, 15–17, 20, 50, 98
academic contributions 15–17
case law 14–15
evaluation 17–18
modern 13–18
concessions 1, 19, 123–24, 263
concession-style arguments 15–16, 32, 48
conduct 40, 64–65, 94–95, 96, 143–44, 240,
247, 256
blameworthy 101, 102
corporate 90, 93, 97, 98, 101
criminal see criminal conduct
of directors 157, 265

fraudulent 17–18, 41–42, 63, 220
prejudicial 214, 224, 232
conflicts 4, 31, 151, 156, 157, 231, 264
agency see agency: conflicts
binary 8, 9, 197, 252, 259, 264–65
of interest 31, 125–26, 162, 163, 193–94, 231
duty to avoid 150–59
consent 114–15, 153–54
unanimous 198–99, 215
conspiracy 250–51
to defraud 86, 88, 97
constituencies 8–9, 20, 127–28, 131, 136, 137
constitutional amendments 106–7, 199, 234
constitutional documents 51, 112
constitutional matters 33–34, 104, 111
shareholder role 197–205
constitutional powers 102, 129, 130, 264
constitutional roles 136, 155
constitutions 34, 78–79, 128–29, 130, 193–94,
198–99, 201–2, 264
enforcement 116–23
mutual understanding of
quasi-partners 115–16
power to amend 198–200
rectification 114–15
role and nature 112–23
constraints 9, 16, 54, 159, 196, 205, 234
constructive trustees 59, 61–62
consumers 72–73, 189
contract(s) 51, 62, 64, 77–80, 112–13, 114–15
as explanation for ultra vires
doctrine 48–51
freedom of 2, 50
law 48, 51, 60, 112–14, 123
nexus of see nexus of contract
rectification 114, 122–23
service 109, 117, 163, 164
long-term 106, 126–27, 166, 196, 213, 235
statutory 113, 116
contractual analysis 48, 51
contractual arrangements 48, 112–13, 259
contributions 1, 2, 3, 27–28, 29, 208, 209
financial 226, 249
in kind 208–9, 234
validation 234
valuation 208–9, 234
national insurance 71, 216
contributors 7, 26, 27, 102, 208–9
contributory negligence 68
control 61–62, 70–71, 87–88, 92, 129, 130,
203, 240
systems 93, 149
wrongdoer 239–41
controllers 42–43, 59, 61, 62, 66, 74

corporate actions 77–102
    common law crimes 88
    contract 77–80
    crime 83–86
    deferred prosecution agreements and
        rehabilitation 97
    organizational failure to prevent crime 93–96
    statutory offences 86–88, 90, 93, 97
    strict liability offences with due diligence
        defences 91–93
    theoretical observations 97–102
    tort 80–83
    vicarious liability 80–83, 86–87, 90–91
corporate capacity see capacity
corporate constitutions see constitutions
corporate criminal liability 83, 90–91, 94–95,
        98, 102
corporate culture 25–26, 90–91, 96, 102, 147,
        149–50, 257–58
corporate decisions 19, 54, 237–38, 239, 253–54
corporate directors see directors
corporate forms 30, 37, 39, 41, 42, 47, 65, 74
corporate governance see governance
Corporate Governance Code 2018 146–48
corporate groups 33, 37, 42–44, 213, 259
    and limited liability 69, 75
    recognition for reporting purposes 75–76
    regulation in specific contexts 71, 75
corporate life 51, 96
corporate manslaughter 89–90, 91, 94–95, 102
corporate personality 15–16, 19, 37–47, 259
corporate procedures see procedures
corporate process 122, 125–26, 137–38, 156,
        158–59, 194, 231–32, 237–38
corporate purpose 48, 53–54, 55, 255
    statement 53–54
corporate rights 8, 118, 184
corporate veil see veil
corporations see Introductory Note
costs 3, 4–5, 24, 116, 144–45, 149, 172, 246
    agency 4–5, 158, 211–12
    indemnity for 246–47, 251
    production 173–74
    transaction 3
court orders 108, 174
covenants 112–13
creditor claims 8, 155, 191, 227
creditor-oriented duties 9, 135
creditors 4, 134–35, 143, 155, 191, 220, 223–
        24, 233
    interests of 9, 34–35, 134–35, 194, 220, 221,
        223, 255
    protection 71, 217, 231, 232–33
crimes 19, 70, 80, 83–84, 95, 97, 101

common law 83, 88
    identification doctrine 84–86
    organizational failure to prevent 93–96
    statutory offences 86–88, 89, 90, 93, 97
criminal conduct 83–84, 97–98, 102
    corporate 91, 93, 94–95
criminal law 82, 83–84, 91, 92, 97, 101–2
criminal liability 9, 65, 94–95, 170, 171, 172, 184
    corporate 83, 90–91, 94–95, 98, 102
    personal 187, 188, 256–58
criminal offences 86, 92, 95–96, 178, 179, 181–
        82, 183, 184
cultures 1, 22–23, 24, 25–26, 29, 31
    corporate 25–26, 90–91, 96, 102, 147, 149–
        50, 257–58
    organizational 21, 26, 102

damages 84, 116, 214, 233, 241, 242–43, 246
    claims 122, 197
death 89, 90, 94, 163
debenture holders 117, 183, 184, 187, 189
debt 2, 33, 56–57, 66–67, 70, 223–24
deceit 17, 41, 64, 229–30
decision-makers 76, 101, 123, 167, 257–
        58, 260–61
decision-making powers 36, 129, 130, 204, 264
decision-making processes 35, 122, 194, 238,
        243, 254, 261–62
decisions
    commercial 141, 213, 253–54
    corporate 19, 54, 237–38, 239, 253–54
    deliberate 143, 254
    litigation 237, 238, 239–40, 242–43, 244,
        252, 253–54
    management 33–34, 111, 205, 224, 234
    organizational 8, 35–36, 109, 122, 123–24,
        189, 265
    policy 16–17, 102
    remuneration 162, 163, 165–66, 168,
        213, 218–19
    shareholder 30, 108, 123, 198–99, 235–36
deed of settlement companies 2, 13, 37–38,
        49–50, 195
deeds of settlement 37–38, 49–50, 112
defects 10, 32–33, 85, 197
defendants 61, 70–71, 80, 231, 240–41, 246,
        250–51, 252
deference 238, 253–54
deferred prosecution agreements (DPAs) 97
delegated activity 34, 125–26, 145, 148, 150
deliberate decisions 143, 254
deliberate inaccuracy 171
derivate actions 122, 219–20, 239, 241, 247–48, 255
    statutory 243–44, 253

derivate claims 239, 241, 248, 252, 256
derivative actions 241, 242, 243, 244, 248–49,
    254, 255, 256
  statutory 251, 252, 253, 255
derivative claims 243, 244–45, 247–48, 255, 256
deterrent effect 143, 157
dicta 58, 154, 203, 204, 251, 252, 253–54
diligence 93, 125, 140, 143, 170
  due 73, 91–93, 95
"ding an sich" 15, 99
direct liability 69, 81
directing mind and will 84, 85–87, 88, 89–90,
    93, 98–99
  test 82, 88, 99, 102
directorial accountability 254–55, 265
directors
  not agents of shareholders 201–5
  authority 79, 154
  conduct 157, 265
  disqualification see disqualification
  diverting assets 158
  duties
    to abide by statutory distribution
      rules 190–93
    to act in accordance with constitution and
      for a proper purpose 128–30
    to exercise independent judgement 125,
      137–38, 150
    to exercise reasonable skill and
      care 138–50
    to have accounts and reports
      verified 180–83
    to keep accounting records 170–72
    owed to company 128
    to prepare annual accounts 172–75
    to promote success of company 131–37
    to publicize accounts and reports 183–85
    to record and report 169–89
    theoretical observations 193–94
  executive see executive directors
  independent 159, 248
  individual 34, 70–71, 106–7, 125–26,
    138, 142
  insolvent 163
  liability 139, 141–42
  managing 64, 85, 86, 88, 135–36
  nominee 137–38
  power to issue shares 105, 206, 207
  procedures for decisions by 109–11
  of quoted companies 178, 184
  ratification of breaches of duty by 219–21
  reasonable 247, 256
  remuneration 34–35, 162–69, 179
    equity and statutory regime 162–64

  role of shareholders 164–66
    theoretical observations 166–69
  reports 172–73, 176–77
  role 103–4, 111–12, 125–94
  and self-dealing transactions 159–62, 213
  shadow 33, 42–43, 66–67, 243, 259
  shareholder see shareholder directors
  sole 68, 160, 220
  wrongdoing 35–36, 254–55
discounts 209, 234
discretion 35–36, 132, 133, 135, 137–38, 201–2,
    245, 247
  stage 245, 247–48, 255
disguised returns of capital 196–97, 214–
    19, 234
disinterested shareholders 248, 249
disputes 6, 116, 159, 232, 247, 249, 251
disqualification 9, 67–68, 142–45, 171
  orders 67, 142, 143–44, 145
  rules 69, 142, 257
distributable profits 8–9, 190, 196–97, 215–16,
    217, 219, 223
distributable reserves 192–93
distributions 192, 193, 215–17, 223, 231–
    32, 255
  rules 5, 34–35, 125, 219, 223, 224, 255, 256
    statutory 127, 190–93
  and shareholders 216–17, 223–24, 255
  unlawful 109, 191–92, 216, 217
diversion of opportunities 156, 158–59
dividend policies 44, 213–14
dividends 8, 117, 190, 191, 192–93, 223, 224
  interim 109, 223
documents 32, 44–45, 49–50, 52–53, 67, 70–71,
    174, 175
  constitutional 51, 112
donations, political 105, 176, 196, 213
dormant companies 175
double recovery 233
  prohibition 228, 229
  and shareholders 228–29
DPAs see deferred prosecution agreements
due diligence 73, 91–93, 95
dummies 39–40
Duomatic principle 30, 33–34, 81, 109, 111,
    123–24, 198–99
duress 114
duties 125–26, 134–35, 137–50, 169–70, 218–
    19, 237–38
  to abide by statutory distribution
    rules 190–93
    absence of shareholder approval 191–92
    director liability 192–93
    shareholder liability 193

duties (*cont.*)
  to act in accordance with constitution and for
      a proper purpose 128–30
  to avoid conflicts of interest 150–59
    approval of interested transactions 155–56
    Companies Act 2006, s 175 151–53
    and partnership law 153–55
    theoretical observations 157–59
  breach of duty 17–18, 218–19, 220, 237–
      38, 242–43
  of care 18, 42, 94, 139–40, 141, 182–83, 222,
      see also duties: to exercise reasonable
      skill and care
  Companies Act 2006, s 172 131–37
  creditor-oriented 9, 135
  to declare interest in proposed transactions or
      arrangements 160
  directors 128
  equitable 131, 137–38
  to exercise independent judgement 125,
      137–38, 150
  to exercise reasonable skill and care 138–50
    and Corporate Governance Code
        2018 146–48
    and disqualification 142–45
    early common law 139
    later common law and statute 139–42
    theoretical observations 149–50
  fiduciary 61–62, 133, 150–51, 152–53, 155,
      157, 225, 243
  general 42–43, 125, 127, 128, 163, 169–70
  to have accounts and reports verified 180–83
  to keep accounting records 170–72
  to prepare annual accounts 172–75
  to prepare narrative reports 175–80
  to promote success of company 131–37
  to publicize accounts and reports 183–85
  to record and report 169–89
  of skill and care 138, 140, 141, 142, 148–49
  statutory 131–32, 133

ecological goals 170, 179–80, 260–62
economic interests 34–35, 125–26, 130, 150,
    194, 264
economic reasoning 69, 150–51, 264
economic units 43–44, 72
  single 42–43, 47
economics 7, 11–12, 15–16, 23, 26–28
  neoclassical 7, 24, 27–28
economy theory 15
effectiveness 177–78, 183, 222
ego 83–84, 85–86
empirical evidence/proof 20, 22, 25
employees 4, 5–6, 81, 90–91, 133, 176–78, 179

employers 59, 81, 82, 89–90
employment 75, 90, 147, 164, 176–77
enforcement 34, 35, 117, 118, 121–22, 123,
    237–58, 265
  mechanisms 35, 126, 142, 257
  membership rights only 116–18
  and mere internal irregularities 118–21
  private *see* private enforcement
  public 145, 237, 256–57
  publicly funded 264
  theoretical observations 121–22
entity models 36, 264
entity theory 18, 19, 20, 101
  fictional 101
  real 1, 20, 36, 84, 98, 100, 101, 136
environment 24–25, 88, 131, 167, 177–78,
    198, 225
equality 170, 176
equitable duties 131, 137–38
equitable relief 232
equitable rules 61, 62, 131, 133, 134
equity 39–40, 44, 125, 130, 131–32, 133,
    134, 151
evasion 33, 58–61, 62, 74
evolutionary theory 27
exceptional circumstances 57, 163
executive directors 54, 110, 140, 141, 146, 165–
    66, 168, 169
  direct influence 110, 146
executive leadership 110, 146
executives 167–68, 169, 213–14
  remuneration 11, 29–30, 163–64, 165–
    68, 169
existence 32, 38, 40, 44–45, 46, 50, 60–61
  artificial 14, 40
  legal 32–33, 45, 61, 100
  physical 45
expectations, public 148, 180–81
expenses 60, 67, 116, 143, 172–73, 229–30,
    231, 233
expert reports 161, 249–50
external actors 79
extraordinary resolutions 202–3
extreme structural model 29, 82

façades 58–59, 61
facts
  brute 21, 22–23, 32, 63
  social 21, 32, 54
fairness 22–23, 151–52
fault 84–85, 90–91, 92, 93, 98–99
  corporate 91, 102
  presumption of 92, 93
FCA *see* Financial Conduct Authority

fees 3, 120, 225–26
  membership 120, 242
fictional entity theory 101
fictions 2, 10, 29
fiduciary duties 61–62, 133, 150–51, 152–53,
    155, 157, 225, 243
fiduciary law 154, 155, 157–59
fiduciary rules 153, 158, 231
financial assistance 143–44, 241, 242
Financial Conduct Authority (FCA) 105, 143–
    44, 161, 225, 261–62
financial contributions 226, 249
financial incentives 260–62
financial information 34–35, 125, 144–45, 175,
    176, 193–94, 234
  adequate 34, 125–26
financial interests 158, 234
financial intermediaries 147, 225–26
financial position 107–8, 138, 148, 172, 173–
    74, 175
financial records 33–34, 170
financial reports 33–34, 127
financial returns 48, 132–33, 136, 149, 225
financial year 107, 109, 170, 171, 172–73,
    174, 176–77
fines 116, 183, 222
fixed assets 173–74
flexibility 195
  organizational 199, 234
foreign subsidiaries 44, 181–82
formal legal boundaries 73, 74, 75
formal legal force 103, 148
formal processes 33–34, 123, 158
formal workforce advisory panel 54,
    200, 261–62
formalities 39–40, 109, 111, 154, 197, 198–99
  legal 18, 42
  procedural 111
formation 39–40, 45, 46, 67, 111, 142, 153–
    54, 197
Foss v Harbottle 122, 226–27, 237, 238–39,
    251, 256
frameworks 2, 8–9, 11–12, 17, 18, 26–27, 33–34
  agency 46, 77, 149
  deed of settlement 49–50
  organizational 33–34, 103, 113–14, 122–
    24, 189
  procedural 63, 204, 251, 255
  statutory 180–81, 235
fraud 17, 39–40, 41, 229, 239, 240, 256–58
  and personal liability 63–65
  and wrongdoer control 239–41
fraudulent conduct 17–18, 41–42, 63, 220
fraudulent instructions 18, 42

fraudulent misrepresentation 64
fraudulent purposes 63, 64–65
fraudulent trading 65, 257, 263–64
freedom 193, 195, 234
  of contract 2, 50
funds 13, 43, 56–57, 109, 156, 163, 246–47
  misappropriated 62, 161–62

general duties 42–43, 125, 127, 128, 163, 169–70
general knowledge 66, 140
general meetings 85, 109, 129, 130, 183, 221–
    22, 238
  annual 108, 120, 201
  shareholders in 83–84, 85, 137–38, 182,
    204, 210–11
good faith 52, 131–35, 216–17, 218, 247
  judgement 135, 136, 163
  subjective 136
  valuation in 234
goods 3, 84, 170
governance 15–16, 30, 44, 146, 147, 149,
    195, 196–97
  arrangements 111, 186
  corporate governance codes 111, 123, 147,
    164–66, 178
  rights 8, 35, 224, 236
  separate corporate governance statement 178
governments 44, 73, 110, 111, 185, 191, 225–26
granular analysis 8–9, 31, 140, 206, 256
granular rules 111, 149, 179
groups 1, 4, 43, 44, 47, 172–73, 176–77, 186
  application of statutes to 71–73
  corporate *see* corporate groups
  of individuals 101, 110, 146
  interest 5–6, 16–17, 20, 125–26, 202
  multinational 69, 75

habits 1, 21, 22, 28, 29, 101, 102, 260
Her Majesty's Revenue and Customs *see* HMRC
hierarchies 87–88, 90, 101
HMRC (Her Majesty's Revenue and
    Customs) 96, 171, 174, 180, 186, 218–20
honesty 136, 143, 159, 199–200
human action 11–12, 23, 24–25, 26–27, 28, 29
human actors 24, 26–27, 62, 77, 96, 97–98, 100
human agency 24, 26, 29, 31
human behaviour 21, 22–23, 26, 28, 149–50
human bodies 82, 83–84, 86, 98–99, 100, 101
human rights 19, 73, 170, 177–78
human trafficking 71, 72–73, 185, 186

identification doctrine 83–86, 88, 89, 90, 91,
    93, 99–100
  critique 89–90

illegal activity/acts 46, 63, 64–65, 96, 241, 242
illegal companies 56, 63
illegal transactions 219, 241–42
illegality 32, 56, 218, 234, 241–42
imprisonment 65, 207
improper purposes 129, 130
inaccuracy, deliberate 171
incentive plans 127, 165, 169
incentives 4, 8, 31, 149–50, 167–68, 169, 257–58, 259
    financial 260–62
    individual 26–27, 29, 261–62, 264–65
income 172–73, 255
incorporation 13, 15–16, 17, 39, 49, 50
    certificates of 38, 44–45
    date of 44–45, 206
indemnity 116–17, 219–20, 251
    for costs 246–47, 251
independence 20, 29, 145
independent auditors 127, 180–81
independent directors 159, 248
independent judgement 125–26, 137–38, 150, 165–66
    duty to exercise 125, 137–38, 150
independent organs 79–80, 252
    appropriate 240–41, 252
independent subjects of the law 17, 41
indictable offences 67, 257
indirect beneficiaries 126, 148–49, 264
    primary 34, 141, 194
individual incentives 26–27, 29, 261–62, 264–65
individual shareholders 35–36, 120–21, 212, 224, 225–26, 241–43
influence
    shareholders 20, 236
    significant 196, 205
    stakeholders 36, 260
    undue 114
informal agreements 122–24
information 106–7, 174, 176–79, 180, 185, 186
injunctions 59, 70, 117, 120, 122, 186, 242
insolvency 135, 139–40, 220
    law 10, 46, 142, 148
    practitioners 142, 250–51
insolvent companies 66–67, 141–42, 143, 220
insolvent directors 163
insolvent liquidation 66–67
institutional shareholders 197, 235
institutional theory 23–26
    in economics 26–28
instructions 51, 59, 66, 81, 90–91, 109–10, 202, 204
    fraudulent 18, 42
    granular 169–70

intent to deceive 86, 88
intentional torts 82–83
intentions 12, 21, 27, 61, 62, 88, 197–99
    collective 21
    subjective 210–11, 218
interest groups 5–6, 16–17, 20, 125–26, 202
interested transactions, approval 155–56
interests 8–9, 125–27, 131–32, 133, 160, 166–67, 261–62
    collective 167
    company/corporate 131–32, 133, 155, 158–59, 199–200, 211, 255, 256
    of creditors 9, 34–35, 134–35, 194, 220, 221, 255
    economic 34–35, 125–26, 130, 150, 194, 264
    financial 158, 234
    of minority shareholders 162, 199, 209–10, 213, 222, 256
    personal 151–52, 249
    public see public interest
    shareholders 135, 144, 223, 235–36, 260–61
    stakeholders 133, 135, 145, 148, 235, 259–60, 261, 265
    of third parties 46, 195, 197, 237, 257–58
interim dividends 109, 223
intermediaries 101
    financial 147, 225–26
interpretation 21, 99, 193
interpretists 21–22
interventions 30, 31, 35, 74, 75–76, 120–21, 168, 264–65
    normative 35, 76
    statutory 8–9, 139–42, 164, 193, 195
investment 56–57, 154–55, 265
investors 2, 37–38, 39, 43, 56–57, 72–73, 225, 235–36
    institutional 236
irregularities 118–19, 120–21, 122
    mere internal 118–21
issue of shares 105, 205–10, 234

Jenkins Committee 52, 53
joint stock companies 4–5, 13, 85, 153–54
judgement 22–23, 133, 137–38, 163, 173–74, 224, 246
    commercial 141, 142, 234
    independent 125–26, 137–38, 150, 165–66
jurisdiction clauses 64
jurisdictions 8, 30, 44–45, 64, 79–80

knowledge 17–18, 21, 24, 27–28, 72, 96, 110, 146
    constructive 77
    general 66, 140

large and medium-sized companies 172–73, 176–77
large companies 31, 71, 89, 96, 171, 172, 185–86
large private companies 103–4, 111–12
leadership 110, 146
legal boundaries 37, 43, 68, 73, 74, 75
    formal 73, 74, 75
legal capital 191, 209
legal existence 32–33, 45, 61, 100
legal force 30, 107–8, 122–23, 174, 225
    formal 103, 148
legal personality 4–5, 32, 33, 37–38, 46
    for all lawful purposes 39–40
    separate 32, 37–38, 42, 44, 56–58, 63
legal persons 29, 44–45, 237
legal positivism 13–14, 15–16, 17, 21, 40, 98
legal purposes 37, 40, 63
legislation 30, 53, 73–74, 75–76, 98, 110–11
    secondary 34, 103, 123
legislatures 10, 14, 19, 40, 75–76, 98
legitimacy 15–16, 25, 226
lenders 56–57
    sole 41
liability 56, 80–81, 90–91, 97, 170–71, 172, 173, 190
    direct 69, 81
    of directors 139, 141–42, *see also* personal liability
    escaping 64, 152
    limited *see* limited liability
    personal *see* personal liability
    public 181, 182, 221–22
    in tort 68–69, 80–81, 82, 98–99
    vicarious 80–83, 86–87, 90–91
limited capacity 32, 48–49, 52, 54
limited companies 15, 50, 54, 108, 129, 158, 184–85
limited liability 14, 15, 33, 37, 39, 40, 56–76, 263–64
    applying statutes to companies 70–74
    for controllers of companies 42
    personal liability for shareholders and directors *see* personal liability
    principle 58, 263–64
    for shareholders 58
    theoretical observations 74–76
    and veil piercing *see* veil: piercing
liquidation 66–67, 215–16, 257
    insolvent 66–67
liquidators 231, 242
litigation 38, 68, 232–33, 240, 246–47, 256
    decisions 237, 238, 239–40, 242–43, 244, 252, 253–54
living organisms 18, 21

loans 106, 126, 172, 213, 214
long-term service contracts 106, 126–27, 166, 196, 213, 235
long-term strategies 163–64, 167
long-term sustainable success 163–64, 167
losses 164–65, 190, 227–30, 231
    personal 229–30, 232–33
    reflective 122, 197, 226–33, 235, 249

majority rule 238, 251–52, 253
majority shareholders 4, 158, 196, 203, 207, 219–20, 234, 241
majority votes 129, 224
management 66–69, 85, 129, 142–43, 225
    decisions 33–34, 111, 205, 224, 234
    functions 87–88
    powers 129, 204
    senior 94, 165–66, 261
managers 3, 4–5, 6, 65, 85, 87–88, 89, 98–99
    senior 65, 94, 165–66, 177, 261
managing directors 64, 85, 86, 88, 135–36
managing partners 158
mandatory combination of objective and subjective standard 148
mandatory law 4–5, 10, 103, 104, 223
mandatory powers 111, 196, 234
mandatory rules 10, 79, 105, 108, 111, 139, 193–94, 195
manslaughter, corporate 89–90, 91, 94–95, 102
markets 3, 4–5, 7, 10, 21, 173, 211–12
    regulated 185, 210
material amounts 105–6, 210–11
meetings 104–5, 108, 119–21, 122, 201, 229–30, 238, 240
    annual general 108, 120, 201
    general *see* general meetings
    shareholder 33–34, 104, 107, 108, 111, 120–21, 238, 240
membership fees 120, 242
membership rights 107, 116, 117, 118, 119, 121–22, 123, 221
    enforcement 116–18
memorandum 14, 32, 38, 40, 49–50, 52, 86–87, 112
mental element 83–84, 86–87, 89, 91, 92, 93, 94–95
mental state 84, 88, 90, 101
mere internal irregularities 118–21
mergers 105–7, 120–21, 210–11
metaphors 29, 33, 56, 62, 82, 84, 99, 101
    anthropomorphic 82, 83–84, 86, 87, 99
micro-companies 173, 176
minorities 4, 132, 150–51

minority shareholders 4, 182, 196, 199, 209–10,
        222, 239, 240–41
    of private companies 182, 222
    of quoted companies 182, 222
misappropriated funds 62, 161–62
misconduct 135–36, 143, 144, 180–81, 234, 249, 265
misrepresentation 114, 224
    fraudulent 64
    negligent 64
mitigating factors 90–91, 144
Model Articles 78, 112, 155, 162, 163–64, 200–
        1, 204
modern slavery 71, 72–73, 75–76, 176, 185
morality 13–14, 152
motives 40, 80, 216–17
    improper 199–200
    subjective 216–17
    ulterior 247
multinational groups 69, 75
multinational organizations 69
mutual understanding 34, 115–16

names 12–13, 38, 39, 44–45, 66–67, 99,
        107, 153–54
narrative reports 34–35, 125–26, 127, 175–80
national insurance, contributions 71, 216
natural persons 15, 16, 42–43, 49, 52, 61,
        85, 86–87
negligence 33, 68, 69, 75, 141, 239, 263–64
    contributory 68
negligent auditors 182–83, 222
negligent misrepresentation 64
negligent misstatement 68
neoclassical economics 7, 24, 27–28
nexus of contract 2, 3–4, 5, 7, 10–12, 20, 46
    and agency theory 2–36
    model 6, 7, 8, 11–12, 29, 97–98
    theory 2, 3–4, 5, 20, 50
        evaluation 6–12
no-discount rule 234
nominal value 206, 208–9, 234
nominee directors 137–38
non-cash assets 161, 208
non-frustration rule 210–11
normative interventions 35, 76
normative level 5, 20, 31, 135–36, 137, 254–
        55, 257–58
    reforms 102
normative recommendations 1, 7, 16–17, 77,
        137, 264–65

object clauses 51–52, 215
    all-encompassing 51
    wide-form 52

obligations 2, 56, 57, 59, 60, 62, 233
offences 86–88, 92, 93, 96, 97, 181–82
    criminal 86, 92, 95–96, 178, 179, 181–82,
        183, 184
    indictable 67, 257
    statutory 86–88, 89, 90, 93, 97
office, payments for loss of 106, 126–27, 164,
        166, 196, 213
officers 71, 106–7, 171, 177, 178, 183, 184, see
        also directors
omissions 97, 118–19, 133, 180, 243, 244
one-person businesses 37, 42
one-person companies 17, 41–42, 45, 47, 57,
        58, 220
onerous requirements/rules 160–61, 207, 234
one-ship companies 43, 57
orders
    court 108, 174
    disqualification 67, 142, 143–44, 145
ordinary resolutions 104–5, 117, 182, 200, 201,
        203, 208, 223
ordinary shareholders 119–20, 206
ordinary shares 206
organisms, living 18, 21
organizational action 23, 24, 30, 31, 32, 47,
        76, 149–50
    autonomous 1, 35, 63, 194, 204, 233, 263
organizational behaviour 1, 23, 27, 76, 84, 259
organizational boundaries 32, 37, 43, 46, 75
organizational cultures 21, 26, 102
organizational decisions 8, 35–36, 109, 122,
        123–24, 189, 265
organizational failure to prevent crime 93–96
organizational flexibility 199, 234
organizational frameworks 33–34, 103–24, 189
    constitution
        enforcement 116–23
        misrepresentation, duress, and undue
            influence 114
        mutual understanding of
            quasi-partners 115–16
        rectification 114–15
        role and nature 112–23
    role of statute 103–12
        constitutional matters 104–5
        Duomatic case 109
        managing company 105–6
        procedures for director decisions 109–11
        procedures for shareholder decisions 108
        record-keeping and reporting 106–8
organizational purposes 47, 116
organizational reality 33–34, 69, 73–74
organizational structures 24, 111–12, 204
outsider rights 116, 118, 119

owners 4, 5, 8, 20, 47, 84, 85, 157
  economic 5
  ship 84, 86

panels, advisory 200, 235, 261–62
parent companies 42–44, 68–69, 70–71, 72–73,
    75, 152–53
Parliament 12–13, 15, 37–38, 39, 49, 50–51,
    88, 215–16
participants 1, 3–4, 5, 7–8, 36, 54, 256
  individual 148, 233, 265
partners 4–5, 38, 153–54, 157, 197–98
  managing 158
partnerships 37–38, 39, 114–15, 153–54, 155,
    157–58, 197–98
  law 3, 153–55, 157, 197–98
  property 153–54
  quasi-partnerships 34, 115, 122–23
payments 109, 127, 163, 164–65, 185, 216, 255
  gratuitous 133
  for loss of office 106, 126–27, 164, 166,
      196, 213
penalties, civil 73, 184, see also sanctions
pensions 71, 163, 225–26, 227–28
Pensions Regulator 71, 75–76, 225
performance 59, 127, 166–68, 169, 177–
    78, 265
  criteria 165, 260–61
permissions 244, 245, 246, 248, 249, 251
perpetuity 38, 56–57
personal criminal liability 187, 188, 256–58
personal interests 151–52, 249
personal liability 33, 56, 63–69, 82, 105
  for controllers of companies 65, 66
  disqualification of directors 67–68
  fraud 63–65
  fraudulent trading 65
  phoenix companies 66–67
  theoretical observations 69
  in tort 68–69
  wrongful trading 65–66
personal loss 229–30, 232–33
personal responsibility 64, 68
personality 10, 26, 33, 85–86
  corporate 15–16, 19, 37–47, 259
  legal 4–5, 32, 33, 37–38, 39–40, 46
  separate 15, 44, 45, 56, 62
petitions 115, 248, 251
  unfair prejudice 159, 248–49
phoenix companies 66–67, 69, 75, 259
piercing of corporate veil see veil: piercing
plaintiffs 117, 119–20, 229–30, 231, 240,
    252, 256–58
  proper 237, 238, 239, 253

policy decisions 16–17, 102
policy objectives 15, 92
political donations 105, 176, 196, 213
positive level 5, 8, 10, 98, 256, 257–59, 260
positivism see legal positivism
possession, physical 70–71
power(s)
  allocation of 5, 128, 150, 264
  to appoint and remove auditors 205
  to appoint and remove directors 200–1
  constitutional 102, 129, 130, 264
  decision-making 36, 129, 130, 204, 264
  to issue shares 105, 205, 206, 209–10
  management 129, 204
  mandatory 111, 196, 234
  residual 120, 204
precautions 93
  reasonable 92, 93
pre-emption rights 196, 206–7, 234
preference shareholders 115
prejudice, unfair see unfair prejudice
prejudicial conduct 214, 224, 232
pressures 73, 147, 235
  external 24, 79
  financial 216–17
presumptions 72, 92, 93
  of fault 92, 93
prevention procedures 72–73, 95–96
prices 8, 10–11, 27–28, 152–53, 165, 173,
    209, 230
  purchase 152–53, 173
primary indirect beneficiaries 34, 141, 194
principal shareholders 68, 214, 227–28
principals 161–62, 203, 224, 235
  status of 127, 159, 166
private action 34, 44–45, 103, 112, 113–14,
    123, 195
private companies 103–4, 205, 207, 208–9, 234
  large 103–4, 111–12
  minority shareholders of 182, 222
private enforcement 237–56
  and authorization or ratification by
      company 244–45
  cause of action of member in own
      right 248–49
  company decision not to pursue claim 248
  fraud and wrongdoer control 239–41
  indemnity for cost 246–47, 251
  and likelihood of authorization/
      ratification 247–48
  and limited permission to continue 251
  and persons acting in accordance with s
      172 245–47
  special resolutions 242–43

private enforcement (*cont.*)
  and standard of proof 249–51
  and statutory regime 243
  supremacy of corporate decision-making
    process 238–39
  theoretical observations 251–56
  ultra vires and illegality 241–42
  views of members without personal
    interest 249
privity 84–85
procedural frameworks 63, 204, 251, 255
procedural requirements 104, 109, 125–26
procedures 9, 29, 97, 102, 122, 150, 163, 202
  adequate 72, 94–95, 96, 144–45, 193–94
  for director decisions 109–11
  prevention 72–73, 95–96
  for shareholder decisions 108
  statutory 215–16, 247–48
production costs 173–74
profits 109, 152–53, 172–73, 190, 214, 219
  calculating 191, 223
  distributable 8–9, 190, 196–97, 215–16, 217,
    219, 223
proof 45, 88, 94–95, 134, 249
  empirical 22
proper plaintiff rule 237, 238, 239, 253
proper purpose doctrine 129, 130, 150, 205
property 10, 15, 50, 60, 61–62, 151, 217
  partnership 153–54
property transactions 106, 117, 126, 161–62,
    196, 227–28
prosecution 93, 96, 171, 246
  malicious 80
protection 15, 35, 50, 52, 72, 138, 150, 158–59
  of creditors 217, 231, 232–33
  of third parties 35, 234
public availability of information 46, 189
public companies 103–4, 155, 200–1, 208, 209,
    234, 235
  shareholders of 187, 221, 226
public enforcement 145, 237, 256–58
public expectations 148, 180–81
public interest 15, 34, 46, 146, 147, 148–49, 212
  entities 175, 182, 191, 222
public liability 181, 182, 221–22
public scrutiny 189, 226
purchase prices 152–53, 173
purposes
  charitable 37, 54
  fraudulent 63, 64–65
  legal 37, 40, 63
  organizational 47, 116
  proper *see* proper purpose doctrine
    120–21, 128–30,
  sham 32–33

quarantine 68, 75, 142
quasi-loans 106
quasi-partnerships 34, 115, 122–23
  mutual understanding 115–16
quorum 77–78, 155–56, 160–61, 163
quoted companies 177, 178, 179, 182, 187,
    188, 189
  minority shareholders of 182, 222

ratification 158, 219–21, 242–43, 244, 247–
    48, 255
  of breaches of duty by directors 219–21
  purported 244–45
rational action 6, 22
rational actors 3, 4–5, 6, 11–12
real entities 1, 20, 28, 100, 102
  autonomous 1, 36
real entity theory/approach 1, 18–23, 36, 84, 98,
    100, 101, 136, *see also Introductory Note*
  about facts 20–21
  application to company law 29–31
  foundations 20–29
  natural, group, and organizational
    action 21–23
  shareholders v stakeholders 19–20
real social actors 29, 260
reality, social 10, 30, 37–38, 46
reasonable care 125, 140, 192–93
reasonable directors 247, 256
reasonable precautions 92, 93
reasonable steps 174, 177, 178, 179, 181–82,
    183, 184, 188
recklessness 69, 96, 174, 178, 180, 207
recommendations 5, 17, 31, 104–5, 108, 110,
    166–67, 181
  normative 1, 7, 16–17, 77, 137, 264–65
record keeping
  and reporting 106–8
  requirements for 107, 171, 172
records 34–35, 107, 170–72, 187
  false 88
  financial 33–34, 170
recovery 176–77, 186, 229–30, 232, 233, 241
  double *see* double recovery
reductions of capital 106, 111, 215–16, 220–
    21, 241
reflective loss 122, 197, 226–33, 235, 249
  and causation 229–30
  ease of settling claims 230–32
reforms 20, 52–53, 54, 183, 209, 260
registered companies 32–33, 45, 49, 70, 135,
    197, 202, 259
registered offices 44–45
registers 45, 46, 63, 74, 106–7
registrar of companies 45, 67, 208, 257

registration 13, 37, 38, 45, 46, 104, 113
regulation, civil 189, 260
regulatory requirements 25–26, 141, 142, 143–
     44, 145, 148, 149, 257–58
rehabilitation 97
Reisberg, Arad 101
relationships 3–4, 5, 9, 97, 123, 147, 167
   agency 3–4, 5, 23, 42–43
   bilateral 4, 29, 54
relief 119–20, 121, 240
   equitable 232
   interim 59–60
remuneration 162–64, 165–69, 178–79, 213–14,
     217, 219
   decisions 162, 163, 165–66, 168, 213, 218–19
   design 127, 166, 260–61
   directors 34–35, 162–69, 179
   equity and statutory regime 162–64
   executives 11, 29–30, 163–64, 165–68, 169
   policy 106, 127, 163–65, 167, 178–79, 196
   reports 175, 178–79, 187
   role of shareholders 164–66
   theoretical observations 166–69
reporting requirements 44, 142, 165, 185, 186,
     187, 260
reports 127, 176–77, 179–80, 183, 184, 186,
     188, 221
   and accounts 172–73, 176–77, 183, 184, 188
   annual 103–4, 175, 180–81, 188
   expert 161, 249–50
   financial 33–34, 127
   narrative 34–35, 125–26, 127, 175–80
   remuneration 175, 178, 179, 187
   on specific social and environmental
        matters 185–86
   strategic 175, 177–78, 179–80
repudiatory breach 114
reserves, distributable 192–93
residual claimant argument 5–6, 8, 20, 36
residual powers 120, 204
resilience statements 175, 191
resolutions 77–78, 81, 109, 119–21, 161,
     207, 220
   extraordinary 202–3
   ordinary 104–5, 117, 182, 200, 201, 203,
        208, 223
   special 115, 197–99, 206, 207, 242
resources 6, 19–20, 27–28, 162, 185
responsibilities 34–35, 106–7, 145, 146, 181, 187
   exclusive 34–35, 106
   personal 64, 68
   statutory 111
returns
   of capital, disguised 196–97, 214–19, 234
   financial 48, 132–33, 136, 149, 225

maximizing 34, 126, 135, 226, 264
   short-term 197, 226, 235
revenue 225–26, 255
rewards 145, 162, 165–66, 168, 169, 217
rights 8–9, 116, 119–20, 121, 188, 225, 233
   corporate 8, 118, 184
   governance 8, 35, 224, 236
   human 19, 73, 170, 177–78
   mandatory 182, 222, 236
   membership 107, 116, 117, 118, 119, 121–22,
        123, 221
   outsider 118, 119
   pre-emption 196, 206–7, 234
   voting 120–22, 144, 198
risks 54, 57, 81–82, 141, 158, 168, 169
robustness 74, 183, 222
roles
   constitutional 136, 155
   directors 103–4, 111–12, 125–94
   separation of 111
   shareholders 8–9, 164–66, 194, 195–236
Royal Charters 12–13, 37–38, 39

salaries 109, 153–54, 163, *see also* remuneration
sanctions 14, 40, 83, 186, 220–21, 222, 256–58
   for failure to report 186
   personal regulatory 257–58
   public law 237
scrutiny 137, 161–62, 216–17, 240
   public 189, 226
secondary legislation 34, 103, 123
securities 63, 185, 206, 210, 212, *see also* shares
   issuing 105–6, 210–11
self-dealing transactions 159–62, 213
   approval 160–61
   duty to declare interest in proposed
        transactions or arrangements 160
   limits to shareholder approval 161–62
senior accounting officers 71, 171, 172, 261
senior management 94, 165–66, 261
senior managers 65, 94, 165–66, 177, 261
separate corporate governance statement 178
separate legal entities 6, 43, 44, 47, 62
separate legal personality 32, 37–38, 42, 44,
        56–58, 63
   and limited liability 37
   theoretical observations 46–47
separation of roles 111
service contracts 109, 117, 163, 164
   long-term 106, 126–27, 166, 196, 213, 235
services 3, 72, 89–90, 153–54, 163, 165, 177–
        78, 182–83
settlement 8–9, 37–38, 77–78, 144–45, 227–28, 231
   deeds of 37–38, 49–50, 112
   early 246

shadow directors 33, 42–43, 66–67, 243, 259
sham 33, 43, 58–61, 62
  companies 62
  mere cloak or 59
  purposes 32–33
shareholder directors 17, 41, 70, 117, 214–15,
    217, 219
  sole 18, 42
shareholders 8–9, 103–6, 126–27, 193–97, 203–
    5, 209–22, 226–28, 232–33
  and accounting records and annual
    accounts 221–22
  agents of 4, 235
  approval 105–6, 127, 161–62, 164, 191–
    92, 210–11
  approving transactions 212–19
  claimant 156, 246–47
  decisions 30, 123, 198–99, 235–36
    procedures for 108
  directors not agents 201–5
  and disguised returns of capital 196–97,
    214–19, 234
  disinterested 248, 249
  and distributions 216–17, 223–24, 255
  and double recovery 228–29
  in general meeting 83–84, 85, 137–38, 182,
    204, 210–11
  individual 35–36, 120–21, 212, 224, 225–
    26, 241–43
  influence 20, 236
  institutional 197, 225, 235
  interests 135, 144, 223, 235–36, 260–61
  issues at a discount 209
  issuing shares 205–21
  majority 4, 158, 196, 203, 207, 219–20,
    234, 241
  and management of company 205–21
  meetings 33–34, 104, 107, 108, 111, 120–21,
    238, 240
  minority 4, 182, 196, 199, 209–10, 222,
    239, 240–41
  ordinary 119–20, 206
  ordinary resolutions 104–5, 117, 182, 200,
    201, 203, 208, 223
  power to amend constitution 198–200
  power to appoint and remove auditors 205
  power to appoint and remove directors 200–1
  pre-emption rights 206–7
  preference 115
  principal 68, 214, 227–28
  protecting autonomy of company 232–33
  of public companies 187, 221, 226
  ratification of breaches of duty by
    directors 219–21

  and reflective loss 226–33
  role 8–9, 164–66, 194, 195–236
    amending constitution 198–200
    appointment and removal of
      directors 200–1
    constitutional matters 197–205
    forming and ending company 197–98
    sole 17, 41, 220–21
    and stewardship 224–26
    and takeovers 210–12
    theoretical observations 233
    and unfair prejudice 213–14
    v stakeholders 5–6, 19–20, 36
    valuation of contributions in kind 208–9
  shares 104, 206–7, 208–9, 210–11,
    212, 229–30
    bonus 206
    issue of 105, 205–10, 234
    maximum amount of 105, 206
    ordinary 206
    power to issue 105, 205, 206, 209–10
    treasury 105–6, 206, 210–11
  shell companies 47
  ship owners 84, 86
  ships 84–85, 153–54
  short-term returns 197, 226, 235
  signatures 107, 116, 174, 181, 187
  simplicity 8, 10
  single economic units 42–43, 47
  skill 27–28, 66, 125, 140, 144–45, 170,
    192, 209
    and care, duty of 138, 140, 141, 142, 148–49
  slavery, modern 71, 72–73, 75–76, 176, 185
  small and micro-companies 173
  social facts 21, 32, 54
  social goals 127, 170, 261–62
  social interactions 21, 26, 28, 29
  social phenomena 1, 21, 26, 29–30, 46
  social reality 10, 30, 37–38, 46
  social structure 28–29, 31, 148, 149, 261, 263
  sole directors 68, 160, 220
  sole shareholder directors 18, 42
  sole shareholders 17, 41, 220–21
  solicitors 116, 227–28, 231
  solvency 191, 223
    statements 223, 241, 244–45
    test 191, 219
  solvent companies 104, 143, 234, 257
  special notice requirements 104–5, 182, 201
  special purpose vehicles 30, 43, 45, 47
  special resolutions 115, 197–99, 202–3, 206, 207
    and private enforcement 242–43
  stakeholders 1, 19, 35, 36, 147, 235, 259–62
    influence 36, 260

interests 133, 135, 145, 148, 235, 259–60,
    261, 265
  v shareholders 5–6, 19–20, 36
standard of proof 249
standards 24, 107–8, 143, 185
statements 72–73, 176–77, 181, 185, 189,
    207, 235
  corporate governance 178
  resilience 175, 191
  solvency 223, 241, 244–45
status of principals 127, 159, 166
statutes, application to companies 70–74
  generally 70–71
  groups 71–73
  theoretical observations 73–74
statutory accounts 187
statutory contracts 113, 116
statutory derivative actions 251, 252, 253, 255
statutory distribution rules 127
  duty to abide by 190–93
statutory duties 131–32, 133
statutory interventions 8–9, 139–42, 164,
    193, 195
statutory offences 86–88, 89, 90, 93, 97
statutory processes 123–24, 139, 195,
    197, 253
statutory regimes 44–45, 155, 162–64, 175, 194,
    223, 255, 257
statutory responsibilities 111
stewardship 44, 224–26
Stewardship Code 197, 225–27, 236
strategic reports 175, 177–78
strategies 25, 149, 186, 189
  long-term 163–64, 167
strict liability offences 88, 92, 93
  with due diligence defences 91–93
structural model, extreme 29, 82
structuralism 24–25
structures 24, 54, 72–73, 102, 103–4, 129, 130
  organizational 24, 111–12, 204
  social 28–29, 31, 148, 149, 261, 263
subjective intentions 210–11, 216–18
subjects of the law, independent 17, 41
subscribers 38, 114–15
subsidiaries 42–43, 68–69, 70–71, 72–73,
    75, 152–53
  foreign 44, 181–82
sub-units 43–44
success 125, 126, 131–37
  long-term sustainable 163–64, 167
supervision 34, 125–26, 145, 148, 150
supply chains 69, 72–73, 74, 75–76, 185
surplus 8, 144
sustainable success, long-term 163–64, 167

tacit knowledge 27–28, 29
takeover bids see bids
Takeover Code 105–7, 193, 210, 211–12
takeover law 212
takeovers 105–7, 210–12
tax 12–13, 44, 95, 109, 141, 172, 186, 216
termination 46, 74, 114
tests 82, 86, 87, 91, 133–34, 199, 218, 245
  arm's length 216–17
  directing mind and will 86–87, 99
  solvency 191, 219
third parties 46, 52–53, 77–79, 227, 231–32, 259
  interests 46, 195, 197, 237, 257–58
third party wrongdoers 231
tools 15–16, 81, 83–84, 98–99, 166, 167, 211–12
tort 33, 68–69, 80–83, 97, 98–99, 101
  intentional 82–83
  law 69, 81–83, 90, 91, 259
  liability in 68–69, 80–81, 82, 98–99
  victims 68, 69, 75, 91, 263–64
tortfeasors 69, 75, 82
trade 12–13, 50, 66, 116, 139, 143–44, 259
trade unions 119–20
traded companies 108, 177–78, 212
traders 70, 186
  sole 171
trading 14, 40, 65, 66, 69, 70, 75, 185
  fraudulent 65, 257, 263–64
  wrongful 67, 141–42
trafficking, human 71, 72–73, 185, 186
transaction costs 3
transactions 106, 155–56, 160, 196, 212–13,
    214–15, 216, 218, 234
  illegal 219, 241–42
  interested 155–56
  property 106, 117, 126, 161–62, 196, 227–28
  self-dealing 159, 161–62, 213
  substantial 127, 160, 161
transfers 37–38, 56–57, 113, 127, 156, 164,
    215, 217
transparency 44
treasury shares 105–6, 206, 210–11
trust, breach of 220, 243
trust law 2, 13, 48, 61, 74
trustees 2, 37–38, 39–40, 61, 62, 154–55
  constructive 59, 61–62
trusts 2, 37–38, 39–40, 48, 61–62, 147, 164–
    65, 175

ultra vires 32, 48, 49–50, 51, 53, 214–16
  collapse of doctrine 51–53
  contract(s) as explanation for 48–51
  and private enforcement 241–42
unanimous consent 198–99, 215

uncertainties 56–57, 89, 177, 191
undue influence 114
unfair prejudice 70, 166, 207, 209–10, 213, 214,
    234, 254
  claims 30, 207, 249, 265
  petitions 159, 248–49
  remedy 34, 35–36, 115–16, 122–24,
    196, 254–55
unfairness 52, 151–52, 232
unfitness 67, 143, 145, 163, 171
unlawful distributions 109, 191–92, 217
unlimited capacity 32, 48, 49, 52, 54, 79

validation of contributions in kind 234
validity 52, 61, 100, 119–20, 231
valuation 152–53, 175, 208–9, 234
  of assets 173, 196–97, 234
  of contributions in kind 208–9, 234
  rules 173, 196
values
  book 217, 234
  monetary 173, 206
  nominal 206, 208–9, 234
veil 58, 62
  corporate 58, 62
  piercing 32–33, 57–61, 62, 263–64
    and concealment 61–62

and evasion 59–61
  sham and facade 58–59
  theoretical observations 62–63
verification 127, 181, 256–58
veto 117, 182, 222
vicarious liability 80–83, 86–87, 90–91
victims 17, 39, 41, 64, 91, 228–29
  tort 68, 69, 75, 91, 263–64
vitiating factors 32, 259, 263
voting 156, 240–41, 252
  powers 115, 129
  purposes 160–61, 163
  rights 120–22, 144, 198

websites 45, 184, 185–86, 188, 189, 249–50
welfare 3–4, 8
  social 7
workforce 54, 200, 235, 261–62
  interests 197
  remuneration 165–66
wrongdoers 68, 227, 228, 229, 230, 233, 240, 252
  control 239–41
  third party 231
wrongdoing directors 35–36, 254–55
wrongful trading 65–66, 69, 75, 141–
    42, 263–64
  rules 67, 141–42